THE COMPLETE STEP-BY-STEP FAMILY COOKBOOK

Notes on the recipes:

Please note that the measurements provided in this book are presented as 'metric/imperial/US cups', with practical equivalents; certain foods and cooking items that are termed differently in the UK and in North America are presented as 'UK term/US term'; and eggs are medium (UK)/large (US) and large (UK)/extra-large (US).

Each recipe has been given a handy **Health Rating**, from 1 to 5 points; the higher the score, the 'healthier' the recipe. This is a basic at-a-glance way to check whether a recipe may be particularly healthy or unhealthy in terms of its overall fat, sugar or salt content versus its vegetable or nutrition content. It is important to remember that balance and variety are key to a healthy diet, so mix up your choice of recipes, saving those with few points for occasional treats. This rating is in no way intended to constitute a comprehensive guide to a healthy diet.

Publisher and Creative Director: Nick Wells
Project Editor: Cat Emslie
Art Director: Mike Spender
Layout Design: Dave Jones
Digital Design and Production: Chris Herbert
Proofreader: Dawn Laker

Special thanks to Megan Mizanty, Victoria Lyle, Mark Ahrens and Polly Prior

09 11 13 12 10

1 3 5 7 9 10 8 6 4 2

This edition first published 2009 by
FLAME TREE PUBLISHING
Crabtree Hall, Crabtree Lane
Fulham, London SW6 6TY
United Kingdom

www.flametreepublishing.com

Flame Tree Publishing is part of The Foundry Creative Media Co. Ltd

All pictures courtesy of **Foundry Arts**, except the following:
Chris Clark: 12 t © Business AM Survival Guide
Cephas Picture Library/www.cephas.com: 39 t © Eising; 23 © Skip, Dean; 24 © Jackson, James; 25 © Boyer, Jean-Paul; 28 © Holsten/Koops.
Fotolia: 26 © Monkey Business
Shutterstock: 10 © Roman Sigaev; 11 © Mike Flippo.
Topham Picturepoint: 8, 15 t, 37r, 14 l & r, 17; 15 b & 16 © Rachel Epstein/The Image Works; 9 & 19 © Nancy Richmond/The Images Works; 6 & 42 © Larry Kolvoord/The Images Works; 12 b © Bob Daemmrich/The Image Works.

ISBN 978-1-84786-550-2

A CIP Record for this book is available from the British Library upon request

Printed in China

THE COMPLETE STEP-BY-STEP FAMILY COOKBOOK

General editor: GINA STEER

FLAME TREE PUBLISHING

Contents

This chapter will make cooking delicious, healthy meals for the whole family simple. It includes some helpful guidelines, such as appropriate food for different age groups, good cooking rules and store cupboard essentials. Explaining the different varieties of rice and pasta and cuts of meat and including some invaluable recipes for basic sauces and stocks, this chapter is one you will refer to again and again.

Fuel your family with these nutritious, hearty soups. From classics, such as Tomato & Basil, to something new, like Coconut Chicken, there is something to suit every taste. The starter recipes can be served as healthy snacks, light lunches or appetizers – recipes such as Sweetcorn Fritters and Mixed Satay Sticks are so delicious you will look for any opportunity to make them.

Whether stewed, steamed, roasted or grilled, fish and shellfish are easy and quick to cook. So, if you need to get a meal on the table in a hurry, one of these recipes may be the answer. Including family favourites, such as Battered Cod & Chunky Chips and Red Prawn Curry with Jasmine-scented Rice, even the fussiest eater will love these creations.

Meat offers an excellent source of protein, B vitamins and iron. Choose from this delicious selection of pork, lamb and beef recipes; for example, the Sausage & Apple Pot, Roast Leg of Lamb & Boulangere Potatoes or Chilli Beef. All provide a filling family feast for you all to tuck into.

This chapter includes numerous delicious chicken and turkey dishes, including Lemon Chicken with Potatoes, Rosemary & Olives and Turkey & Tomato Tagine. You do not need to be adventurous to try some of the easy-to-follow game recipes; why not give cooking pheasant, guinea fowl or rabbit a go?

Get your family to eat their greens by whipping up some of these fantastic vegetable dishes; they will all enjoy the Marinated Vegetable Kebabs or the Winter Coleslaw. Vegetables add colour, texture and important nutrients to your diet and these recipes can be served either as a whole meal or as an accompaniment to other dishes, so why not experiment with one today?

From risotto to rice cakes to rice-filled peppers, rice is a versatile and popular ingredient. This chapter offers a whole range of rice recipes including Paella and Spring Vegetable & Herb Risotto. Including tasty, easy-to-cook dishes from around the world, make rice part of your family's meal.

Pasta is one of the simplest, fastest and most convenient ingredients available – these dishes are delicious too! It will take no time to cook recipes such as Spaghetti alla Puttanesca or Singapore Noodles. For more substantial meals, this chapter also includes dishes such as Spaghetti Bolognese and Traditional Lasagne – classics that the whole family will enjoy.

Everyone loves dessert! Treat yourself and your family to something sweet. Ranging from the relatively healthy Fruit Salad to the purely indulgent Mocha Pie, this chapter provides recipes that are the perfect way to finish off a great meal. All are easy to make and will disappear in no time!

Including cakes, cookies and quiches, this chapter makes baking easy and fun. Who can resist the smell of freshly baked bread or the taste of a homemade cake? Get the whole family involved by helping children bake Chocolate Chip Cookies or Shortbread Thumbs. With both sweet and savoury recipes, there is something for everyone.

Family Cooking

This chapter will make cooking delicious, healthy meals for the whole family simple. It includes some helpful guidelines, such as appropriate food for different age groups, good cooking rules and store cupboard essentials. Explaining the different varieties of rice and pasta and cuts of meat and including some invaluable recipes for basic sauces and stocks, this chapter is one you will refer to again and again.

Guidelines for Different Age Groups

Good food plays such an important role in everyone's life. From infancy through to adulthood, a healthy diet provides the body's foundation and building blocks and teaches children healthy eating habits. Studies have shown that these eating habits stay with us into later life, helping us to maintain a healthier lifestyle as adults. This reduces the risk of illness, disease and certain medical problems.

Striking a healthy balance is important, and at certain stages in life this balance may need to be adjusted to help our bodies cope. As babies and children, during pregnancy and in later life, our diet assists us in achieving optimal health. How do we go about achieving this?

We know that foods such as oily fish, for example, are advantageous to everyone, as they are rich in Omega-3 fatty acids, which have been linked with more efficient brain functioning and better memory. They can also help lower the risk of cancer and heart disease. But are there any other steps we can take to maximize health benefits through our diet?

Babies and Young Children

Babies should not be given solids until they are at least six months old, then new tastes and textures can be introduced to their diets. Probably the easiest and cheapest way is to adapt the food that the rest of the family eat. Babies under the age of one should be given breast milk or formula milk. From the age of one to two, whole milk should be given and from two to five semi-skimmed /low-fat milk can be given. From then on, skimmed milk can be introduced if desired.

The first foods for babies under six months should be of a purée-like consistency, which is smooth and fairly liquid, therefore making it easy to swallow. This can be done using an electric blender, a hand blender or just by pushing foods through a sieve/strainer to remove any lumps. Remember, however, that babies still need high levels of milk.

Babies over six months old should still be having puréed food, but the consistency of their diet can be made progressively lumpier. Around the 10-month mark, most babies are able to manage food cut up into small pieces.

So, which food groups do babies and small children need? Like adults, a high proportion of their diet should contain grains such as cereal, pasta, bread and rice. Be careful, however, as babies and small children cannot cope with too much high-fibre food in their diet.

Fresh fruits and vegetables should be introduced, as well as a balance of dairy and meat proteins and only a small proportion of fats and sweets. Research points out that delaying the introduction of foods that could cause allergies during the first year (such as cow's milk, wheat, eggs, cheese, yogurt and nuts) can significantly reduce the risk of certain food allergies later on in life. Peanuts should never be given to children under five years old.

Seek a doctor or health visitor's advice regarding babies and toddlers. Limit refined sugar in young children's diets, as sugar provides only empty calories. Use less-processed sugars (muscovado golden brown sugar is very sweet, so amounts can be reduced) or incorporate less-refined alternatives, such as dried fruits, dates, rice syrup or honey, although honey should not be given to infants under one year of age.

As in a low-fat diet, it is best to eliminate fried foods and avoid adding salt – especially for under one-year-olds and young infants. Instead, introduce herbs and gentle spices to make food appetizing. The more varied the tastes that children experience in their formative years, the wider the range of foods they will accept later in life.

Pregnancy

During pregnancy, women are advised to take extra vitamin and mineral supplements. Pregnant women benefit from a healthy, balanced diet, rich in fresh fruit and vegetables, and full of essential vitamins and minerals. Occasionally eating oily fish, such as salmon, not only gives the body essential fats but also provides high levels of bio-available (absorbable) calcium.

Certain food groups, however, hold risks during pregnancy. This section gives advice on everyday foods and those that should be avoided.

Cheese

Pregnant women should avoid all soft, mould-ripened cheese such as Brie. They should also not eat cheese such as Parmesan or blue-veined cheese like Stilton, as they carry the risk of listeria. It is fine for pregnant women to carry on eating hard cheese such as Cheddar, as well as cottage cheese.

Eggs

There is a slight chance that some eggs will carry salmonella. Cooking the eggs until both the yolk and white are firm will eliminate this risk. However, particular attention should be paid to dishes and products that incorporate lightly cooked or raw eggs, such as homemade mayonnaise or similar sauces, mousses, soufflés, meringues, ice cream and sorbets. Commercially produced products, such as mayonnaise, which are made with pasteurized eggs, may be eaten safely. If in doubt, play safe and avoid it.

Ready-made Meals and Ready-to-eat Items

Previously cooked, then chilled, meals are now widely available, but those from the chilled counter can contain bacteria. Avoid prepacked salads in dressings and other foods that are sold loose from chilled cabinets. Also do not eat raw or partly cooked meats, pâté, unpasteurized milk and soil-dirty fruits and vegetables, as they can cause toxoplasmosis.

Meat and Fish

Certain meats and poultry carry the potential risk of salmonella and should be cooked thoroughly until the juices run clear and there is no pinkness left.

Pay particular attention when buying and cooking fish (especially shellfish). Buy only the freshest fish, which should smell salty but not strong or fishy.

Look for bright eyes and reject any with sunken eyes. The bodies should look fresh, plump and shiny. Avoid any fish with dry, shrivelled or damp bodies.

It is also best to avoid any shellfish while pregnant unless it is definitely fresh and thoroughly cooked. Shellfish also contains harmful bacteria and viruses.

Later Life

So what about later on in life? As the body gets older, we can help stave off infection and illness through our diet. There is evidence to show that the immune system becomes weaker as we get older, which can increase the risk of suffering from cancer and other illnesses. Maintaining a diet rich in antioxidants, fresh fruits and vegetables, plant oils and oily fish is especially beneficial in order to either prevent these illnesses or minimize their effects. As with all age groups, the body benefits from government eating plans encouraging the consumption of fruit and vegetables. Leafy green vegetables, in particular, are rich in antioxidants. Cabbage, broccoli, Brussels sprouts, cauliflower and kale contain particularly high levels of antioxidants, which lower the risk of developing cancer.

Foods that are green in colour tend to provide nutrients essential for healthy nerves, muscles and hormones. Foods that are red in colour protect against cardiovascular disease. Other foods that can also assist in preventing cardiovascular disease and ensuring a healthy heart include vitamins E and C, oily fish and essential fats (such as extra virgin olive oil) and garlic. They help lower blood cholesterol levels and clear arteries. A diet high in fresh fruits and vegetables and low in salt and saturated fats can considerably reduce heart disease.

Other foods have recognized properties. Certain types of mushrooms are known to boost the immune system, while garlic not only boosts the immune system but also protects the body against cancer. Live yogurt, too, has healthy properties as it contains gut-friendly bacteria, which help digestion.

Some foods can help to balance the body's hormone levels during the menopause. For example, soya/soy regulates hormone levels. Studies have shown that a regular intake of soya can help to protect the body against breast and prostate cancer.

A balanced, healthy diet, rich in fresh fruits and vegetables, carbohydrates, proteins and essential fats and low in saturates, can help the body protect itself throughout your life. It really is worth spending a little extra time and effort when shopping or even just thinking about what to cook.

Good Cooking Rules

When handling and cooking foods, there are a few rules and guidelines that should be observed so that food remains fit to eat and uncontaminated with the bacteria and bugs that can result in food poisoning.

Good Hygiene Rules

- Personal hygiene is imperative when handling food. Before commencing any preparation, wash hands thoroughly with soap, taking particular care with nails. Always wash hands after going to the bathroom. Wash again after handling raw foods, cooked meats or vegetables. Do not touch any part of the body or handle pets, rubbish or dirty laundry during food preparation.
- Cuts should be covered with a waterproof plaster/bandage, preferably blue so it can be easily seen if lost.
- Do not smoke in the kitchen.
- Keep pets off all work surfaces and out of the kitchen, if possible. Clean surfaces with an anti-bacterial solution. Wash pet eating bowls separately.
- Ensure that hair is off the face and does not trail into food or machinery.
- Use a dishwasher wherever possible and wash utensils and equipment in very hot, soapy water.
- Use clean cloths and dishtowels, replacing regularly. Boil to kill any bacteria, and use absorbent paper towels where possible to wipe hands and equipment.
- Chopping boards and cooking implements must be clean. Boards should either be washed in a dishwasher or scrubbed after each use. Keep separate boards for meat, fish and vegetables and wash knives before using on different types of food. Do not use the same board for raw and cooked food: wash in between or, better still, use a different board.
- Use dustbin liners/garbage bags for rubbish and empty regularly, cleaning your bin with disinfectant. Dustbins should be outside.

Guidelines for Using a Refrigerator

- Ensure that the refrigerator is situated away from any equipment that gives off heat, such as the cooker, washing machine or tumble drier, to ensure the greatest efficiency. Ensure that the vents are not obstructed.
- If not frost-free, defrost regularly, wiping down with a mild solution of bicarbonate of soda/baking soda dissolved in warm water and a clean cloth.
- Close the door as quickly as possible so that the motor does not have to work overtime to keep it at the correct temperature.
- Ensure that the temperature is 5°C/40°F. A thermometer is a good investment.
- Avoid overloading – this just makes the motor work harder.
- Cool food before placing in the refrigerator, and always cover to avoid any smells or transference of taste to other foods.

Stacking Your Refrigerator

- Remove supermarket packaging from raw meat, poultry and fish, place on a plate or dish, cover loosely and store at the base of the refrigerator to ensure that the juices do not drip on other foods.
- Store cheese in a box or container, wrapped to prevent the cheese drying out.
- Remove food to be eaten raw 30 minutes before use so it can return to room temperature.
- Cooked meats, bacon and all cooked dishes should be stored at the top – this is the coldest part.
- Store eggs in the egg compartment and remove 30 minutes before cooking in order to return them to room temperature.
- Butter and all fats can be stored in the door, as can milk, cold drinks, sauces, mayonnaise and preserves with low sugar content.
- Cream and other dairy products, as well as pastries such as chocolate éclairs, should be stored on the middle shelf.
- Vegetables, salad and fruit should be stored in the salad boxes at the bottom of the refrigerator.
- Soft fruits should be kept in the salad boxes, along with mushrooms, which are best kept in paper bags.
- To avoid cross-contamination, raw and cooked foods must be stored separately.
- Use all foods by the sell-by date – once opened, treat as cooked foods and use within two days.

General Rules

- Use all foods by the use-by date and store correctly. This applies to all foods: fresh, frozen, canned and dried. Potatoes are best if removed from polythene/plastic, stored in brown paper and kept in the cool and dark.
- Ensure that all food is thoroughly thawed before use, unless meant to be cooked from frozen.
- Cook all poultry thoroughly at the correct temperature (190°C/375°F/Gas Mark 5), ensuring that the juices run clear.
- Leave hot foods to cool thoroughly before placing in the refrigerator; cover while cooling.
- Do not re-freeze any thawed frozen foods unless cooked first.
- Date and label frozen food and use in rotation.
- Reheat foods thoroughly until piping hot. Remember to allow foods to stand when using the microwave and stir to distribute the heat.
- Microwaves vary according to make and wattage – always refer to manufacturers' instructions.
- Only reheat dishes once and always heat until piping hot.
- Ensure that eggs are fresh. If using for mayonnaise, soufflés or other dishes that use raw or semi-cooked egg, do not give to the vulnerable – the elderly, pregnant women, those with a recurring illness, toddlers and babies.
- When buying frozen foods, transport in freezer-insulated bags, placing in the freezer as soon as possible after purchase.
- Chilled foods, such as cold meats, cheese, fresh meat, fish and dairy products should be bought, taken home and placed in the refrigerator immediately. Do not keep in a warm car or room.
- Avoid buying damaged or unlabelled canned goods. Keep store cupboards clean, wiping down regularly and rotating the food.
- Flour, nuts, rice, pulses/legumes (peas, beans etc), grains and pasta should be checked regularly and, once opened, placed in airtight containers.
- Do not buy eggs or frozen or chilled foods that are damaged in any way.
- Keep dried herbs and ready-ground spices in a cool, dark place, not in a spice rack on the work surface. They quickly lose their pungency and flavour when exposed to light.

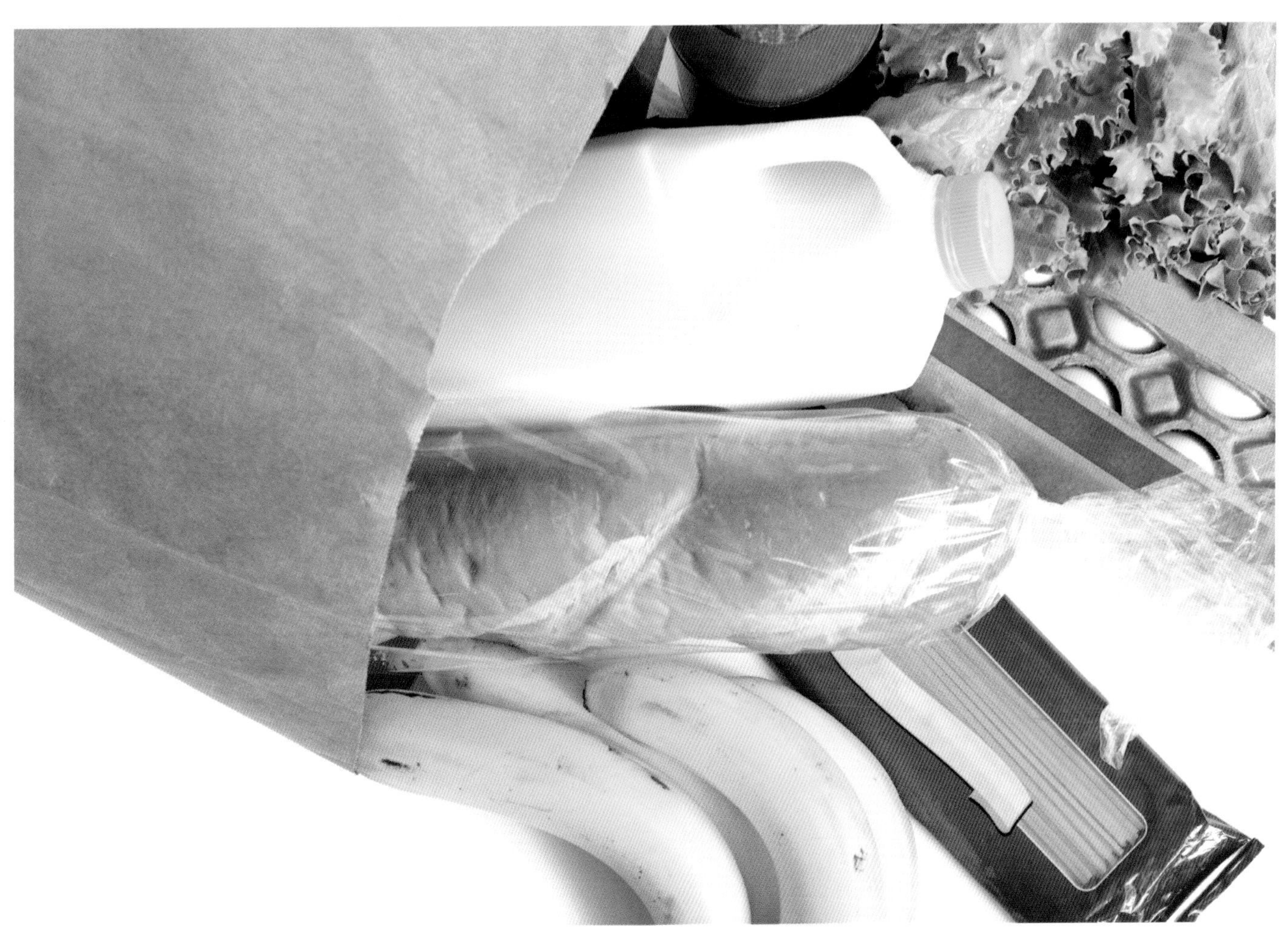

Useful Conversions

Liquid Measures

Metric, Imperial and US Cups/Quarts

2.5 ml	1/2 tsp	–	
5 ml	1 tsp	–	
15 ml	1 tbsp	–	
25 ml	1 fl oz	1/8 cup	2 tbsp
50 ml	2 fl oz	1/4 cup	3–4 tbsp
65 ml	2 1/2 fl oz	1/3 cup	5 tbsp
75–85 ml	3 fl oz	1/3 cup	6 tbsp
100 ml	3 1/2 fl oz	1/3 cup	7 tbsp
120 ml	4 fl oz	1/2 cup	8 tbsp
135 ml	4 1/2 fl oz	1/2 cup	9 tbsp
150 ml	5 fl oz	1/4 pint	2/3 cup
175 ml	6 fl oz	1/3 pint	scant 3/4 cup
200 ml	7 fl oz	1/3 pint	3/4 cup
225–50 ml	8 fl oz	3/8 pint	1 cup
275 ml	9 fl oz	1/2 pint	1 1/8 cups
300 ml	10 fl oz	1/2 pint	1 1/4 cups
350 ml	12 fl oz	2/3 pint	1 1/2 cups
400 ml	14 fl oz	5/8 pint	1 2/3 cups
450 ml	15 fl oz	3/4 pint	1 3/4 cups
475 ml	16 fl oz	7/8 pint	scant 2 cups
500 ml	18 fl oz	7/8 pint	2 cups
600 ml	20 fl oz	1 pint	2 1/2 cups
750 ml	26 fl oz	1 1/4 pints	3 1/4 cups
900 ml		1 1/2 pints	scant 1 quart
1 litre		1 3/4 pints	1 quart
1.1 litres		2 pints	1 1/4 quarts
1.2 litres		2 pints	1 1/4 quarts
1.25 litres		2 1/4 pints	1 1/3 quarts
1.3 litres		2 1/3 pints	1 1/3 quarts
1.4 litres		2 1/2 pints	1 1/2 quarts
1.5 litres		2 1/2 pints	1 2/3 quarts
1.6 litres		2 3/4 pints	1 3/4 quarts
1.7 litres		3 pints	1 3/4 quarts
1.8 litres		3 1/8 pints	1 7/8 quarts
1.9 litres		3 1/3 pints	2 quarts
2 litres		3 1/2 pints	2 quarts
2.25 litres		4 pints (1/2 gal)	2 3/8 quarts
2.5 litres		4 1/2 pints	2 2/3 quarts
2.75 litres		5 pints	3 quarts
3 litres		5 1/4 pints	3 quarts
4.5 litres		8 pints (1 gal)	scant 5 quarts

Temperature Conversion

–4°F	–20°C
5°F	–15°C
14°F	–10°C
23°F	–5°C
32°F	0°C
41°F	5°C
50°F	10°C
59°F	15°C
68°F	20°C
77°F	25°C
86°F	30°C
95°F	35°C
104°F	40°C
113°F	45°C
122°F	50°C
212°F	100°C

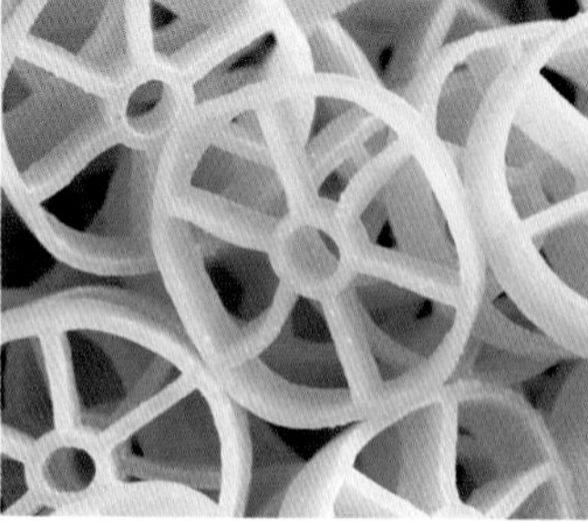

Dry Weights

Metric/Imperial

10 g	1/4 oz
15 g	1/2 oz
20 g	3/4 oz
25 g	1 oz
40 g	1 1/2 oz
50 g	2 oz
65 g	2 1/2 oz
75 g	3 oz
90 g	3 1/2 oz
100 g	3 1/2 oz
125 g	4–4 1/2 oz
150 g	5 oz
165 g	5 1/2 oz
175 g	6 oz
185 g	6 1/2 oz
200 g	7 oz
225 g	8 oz
250 g	9 oz
275 g	9 1/2 oz
300 g	10 oz
325 g	11 oz
350 g	12 oz
375 g	13 oz
400 g	14 oz
425 g	15 oz
450 g	1 lb

Oven Temperatures

Bear in mind that if using a fan oven you should reduce the stated temperature by around 20°C.

110°C	225°F	Gas Mark 1/4	Very slow (low) oven
120/130°C	250°F	Gas Mark 1/2	Very slow oven
140°C	275°F	Gas Mark 1	Slow oven
150°C	300°F	Gas Mark 2	Slow oven
160/170°C	325°F	Gas Mark 3	Moderate oven
180°C	350°F	Gas Mark 4	Moderate oven
190°C	375°F	Gas Mark 5	Moderately hot oven
200°C	400°F	Gas Mark 6	Moderately hot oven
220°C	425°F	Gas Mark 7	Hot oven
230°C	450°F	Gas Mark 8	Hot oven
240°C	475°F	Gas Mark 9	Very hot oven

Store Cupboard Essentials

Ingredients for a Healthy Lifestyle

The increasing emphasis on the importance of cooking healthy meals for your family means that modern lifestyles are naturally shifting towards lower-fat and cholesterol diets. Low-fat cooking has often been associated with the idea that reducing fat reduces flavour, but this simply is not the case, which is great news for those trying to eat healthily. Thanks to the increasing number of lower-fat ingredients now available in shops, there is no need to compromise on the choice of foods we eat.

The store cupboard is a good place to start when cooking healthy meals. Most of us have fairly limited cooking and preparation time available during the week, and choose to experiment at weekends. When time is of the essence, or friends arrive unannounced, it is a good idea to have some well thought-out basics in the cupboard, namely foods that are high in flavour whilst still being healthy.

As store cupboard ingredients keep reasonably well, it is worth making a trip to a speciality grocery shop. Our society's growing interest in recent years with travel and food from around the world has led us to seek out alternative ingredients with which to experiment and incorporate into our cooking. Consequently, supermarket chains have had to broaden their product range and often have a specialist range of imported ingredients from around the world.

If the local grocers or supermarket only carries a limited choice of products, do not despair. The internet offers freedom to food lovers. There are some fantastic food sites (both local and international) where food can be purchased and delivery arranged online.

When thinking about essentials, think of flavour, something that is going to add to a dish without increasing its fat content. It is worth spending a bit more money on these products to make flavoursome dishes that will help stop the urge to snack on fatty foods.

Store Cupboard Hints

There are many different types of store cupboard ingredients readily available – including myriad varieties of rice and pasta, which can provide much of the carbohydrate required in our daily diets. Store the ingredients in a cool, dark place and remember to rotate them. The ingredients will be safe to use for six months.

Bulgur wheat A cracked wheat that is often used in tabbouleh. Bulgur wheat is a good source of complex carbohydrate.

Couscous Now available in instant form, couscous just needs to be covered with boiling water, then forked. Couscous is a precooked wheat semolina. Traditional couscous needs to be steamed and is available from health food stores. This type of couscous contains more nutrients than the instant variety.

Dried fruit The ready-to-eat varieties are particularly good as they are plump, juicy and do not need to be soaked. They are fantastic when puréed into a compote, added to water and heated to make a pie filling and when added to stuffing mixtures. They are also good cooked with meats, rice or couscous.

Flours A useful addition (particularly cornflour/cornstarch, which can be used to thicken sauces). It is worth mentioning that wholemeal/whole-wheat flour should not be stored for too long at room temperature as the fats may turn rancid. While not strictly a flour, cornmeal is a very versatile low-fat ingredient that can be used when making dumplings and gnocchi.

Herbs and spices These are a must, so it is worth taking a look at the section on pages 21–22. Using herbs when cooking at home should reduce the temptation to buy ready-made sauces. Often these types of sauces contain large amounts of sugar and additives.

Noodles Also very useful and can accompany any Far Eastern dish. They are low in fat and also available in the wholemeal/whole-wheat variety. Rice noodles are available for those who have gluten-free diets; like pasta noodles, they provide slow-release energy to the body.

Pasta It is good to have a mixture of wholewheat and plain pasta as well as a wide variety of flavoured pastas. Whether fresh (it can also be frozen) or dried, pasta is a versatile ingredient with which to provide the body with slow-release energy. It comes in many different sizes and shapes; from the tiny tubettini (which can be added to soups to create a more substantial dish), to penne, fusilli, rigatoni and conchiglie, up to the larger cannelloni and lasagne sheets.

Pot and pearl barley Pot barley is the complete barley grain, whereas pearl barley has the outer husk removed. A high cereal diet can help to prevent bowel disorders and diseases.

Pulses/beans A vital ingredient for the store cupboard, pulses are easy to store, have a very high nutritional value and are great when added to soups, casseroles, curries and hot pots. Pulses also act as a thickener, whether flavoured or on their own. They come in two forms: either dried (in which case they generally need to be soaked overnight and then cooked before use – it is important to follow the instructions on the back of the packet), or canned, which is a convenient timesaver because the preparation of dried pulses can take a while. If buying canned pulses, try to buy the variety in water with no added salt or sugar. These simply need to be drained and rinsed before being added to a dish.

Kidney, borlotti, cannellini, butter and flageolet/lima beans, split peas and lentils all make tasty additions to any dish. Baked beans are a favourite with everyone and many shops now stock the organic variety, which have no added salt or sugar but are sweetened with fruit juice instead.

When boiling previously dried pulses, remember that salt should not be added as this will make the skins tough and inedible.

Puy lentils are a smaller variety. They often have mottled skins and are particularly good for cooking in slow dishes as they hold their shape and firm texture particularly well.

Rice Basmati and Thai fragrant rice are suited to Thai and Indian curries, the fine grains absorb the sauce and their delicate creaminess balances the pungency of the spices. Arborio is only one type of risotto rice – many are available, depending on whether the risotto is meant to accompany meat, fish or vegetable dishes. When cooked, rice swells to create a substantial low-fat dish. Easy-cook American rice, both plain and brown, is great for casseroles and for stuffing meat, fish and vegetables, as it holds its shape and firmness. Pudding rice can be used in a variety of ways to create an irresistible dessert.

Stock Good-quality stock is a must in low-fat cooking as it provides a good flavour base for many dishes. Many supermarkets now carry a variety of fresh and organic stocks, which, although need refrigeration, are probably one of the most time- and effort-saving ingredients available. There is also a fairly large range of dried stock, perhaps the best being bouillon, a high-quality form of stock (available in powder or liquid form) which can be added to any dish whether it be a sauce, casserole, pie or soup.

Sauce ingredients Many people favour meals that can be prepared and cooked in 30–45 minutes, so helpful ingredients that kick-start a sauce are great. A good-quality passata sauce or canned plum tomatoes can act as the foundation for any sauce, as can a good-quality green or red pesto. Other handy store cupboard additions include olive tapenade, mustard and anchovies. These have very distinctive tastes and are particularly flavoursome. Roasted red pepper sauce and sundried tomato paste, which tends to be sweeter and more intensely flavoured than regular tomato purée/paste, are also very useful.

Vinegar This is another worthwhile store cupboard essential, and with so many uses it is worth splashing out on really good-quality balsamic and wine vinegars.

Yeast extract This is also a good store cupboard ingredient, which can pep up sauces, soups and casseroles and adds a little substance, particularly to vegetarian dishes.

Other oils and flavours Eastern flavours offer a lot of scope where low-fat cooking is concerned. Flavourings such as fish sauce, soy sauce, red and green curry paste and Chinese rice wine all offer mouthwatering low-fat flavours to any dish.
For those who are incredibly short on time, or who rarely shop, it is now possible to purchase a selection of readily prepared freshly minced garlic, ginger and chilli (available in jars which can be kept in the refrigerator).

As well as these store cupboard additions, many shops and especially supermarkets provide a wide choice of foods. Where possible, invest in the leanest cut of meat and substitute saturated fats such as cream, butter and cheese with low-fat or half-fat alternatives.

Cooking Eggs

Boiled Eggs

Eggs should be boiled in gently simmering water. Remove the egg from the refrigerator at least 30 minutes before cooking. Bring a pan of water to the boil, then, once boiling, lower the heat to a simmer. Gently lower the egg into the water and cook for 3 minutes for lightly set, or 4 minutes for a slightly firmer set. Remove and lightly tap to stop the egg continuing to cook. Hard-boiled eggs should be cooked for 10 minutes then plunged into cold water and left until cold before shelling. Serve lightly boiled eggs with toast or buttered bread cut into fingers to use as dippers.

Fried Eggs

Place a little sunflower oil or butter in a frying pan. Break an egg into a cup or small jug. Carefully slip into the pan. Cook, spooning the hot oil or fat over the egg, for 3–4 minutes or until set to personal preference. Remove with a palette knife or fish slice. Serve with freshly grilled/broiled bacon or sausages or on toast with baked beans and tomatoes.

Poached Eggs

Half-fill a frying pan with water. Bring to a gentle boil, then reduce the heat to a simmer. Add either a little salt or a few drops of vinegar or lemon juice – this will help the egg to retain its shape. Break the egg into a cup or small jug and carefully slip into the simmering water. Lightly oiled round, plain pastry cutters can be used to contain the eggs, if preferred. Cover the pan with a lid and cook for 3–4 minutes or until set to personal preference. Once cooked, remove by draining with a slotted draining spoon or fish slice and serve. Alternatively, special poaching pans are available, if preferred. With these, half-fill the pan with water and place the tray with the egg containers on top. Place a little butter in the cups and bring to the boil. Swirl the melted butter around and carefully slip in the eggs. Cover with the lid and cook for 3–4 minutes. Serve either on hot buttered toast or on top of sliced ham or freshly cooked spinach.

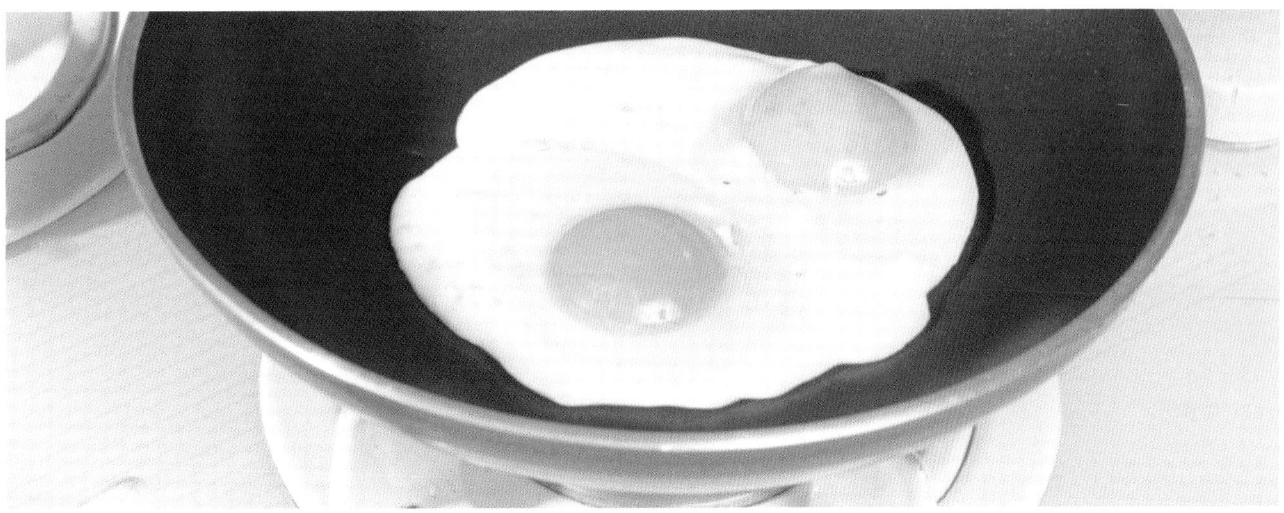

Scrambled Eggs

Melt 15 g/½ oz/1 tbsp butter in a small pan. Allowing two eggs per person, break the eggs into a small bowl and add 1 tablespoon milk and seasoning to taste. Whisk with a fork until blended, then pour into the melted butter. Cook over a gentle heat, stirring with a wooden spoon, until set and creamy. Serve on hot buttered toast with smoked salmon or stir in some freshly snipped chives or chopped tomatoes.

Omelettes

For a basic omelette, allow two eggs per person. Break the eggs into a small bowl, add seasoning to taste and 1 tablespoon milk. Whisk with a fork until frothy. Heat 2 teaspoons olive oil in a frying pan and, when hot, pour in the egg mixture. Cook gently, using a wooden spoon to bring the mixture from the edges of the pan to the centre and letting the uncooked egg mixture to flow to the edges. When the egg has set, cook without moving for an extra minute before folding the omelette into three and gently turning out on to a warmed serving plate. Take care not to overcook.

Cheese Omelette

Proceed as before, then sprinkle 25–40 g/1–1½ oz/¼–⅓ cup grated mature Cheddar cheese on top of the lightly set omelette. Cook for a further 2 minutes, or until the cheese starts to melt. If liked, place under a preheated grill/broiler for 2–3 minutes or until golden. Fold and serve.

Tomato Omelette

Proceed as for a plain omelette. After 2 minutes of cooking time, add 1 chopped tomato on top of the omelette. Cook as above until set.

Fine Herbs Omelette

Stir in 1 tablespoon finely chopped, fresh mixed herbs into the beaten eggs before cooking. Proceed as for a plain omelette.

Mushroom Omelette

Wipe and slice 50 g/2 oz/½ cup button mushrooms.
Heat 15 g/½ oz/1 tbsp butter in a small pan and cook the mushrooms for 2–3 minutes. Drain and reserve. Cook the omelette as above, adding the mushrooms once set.

Rice

Varieties

Rice is the staple food of many countries throughout the world. Every country and culture has its own repertoire of rice recipes – India, for example, has the aromatic biryani, Spain has the saffron-scented paella and Italy has the creamy risotto. Rice is grown on marshy, flooded land where other cereals cannot thrive and, because it is grown in so many different areas, there is a huge range of rice types.

Long-grain white rice Probably the most widely used type of rice. Long-grain white rice has been milled so that the husk, bran and germ are removed. Easy-cook long-grain white rice has been steamed under pressure before milling. Precooked rice, also known as parboiled or converted rice, is polished white rice that is half-cooked after milling, then dried again. It is quick to cook but has a bland flavour.

Long-grain brown rice Where the outer husk is removed, leaving the bran and germ behind. This retains more of the fibre, vitamins and minerals. It has a nutty, slightly chewy texture and takes longer to cook than white rice.

Basmati rice This slender long-grain rice, which may be white or brown, is grown in the foothills of the Himalayas. After harvesting, it is allowed to mature for a year, giving it a unique aromatic flavour, hence its name, which means fragrant.

Risotto rice Grown in the north of Italy, this is the only rice that is suitable for making risotto. The grains are plump and stubby and have the ability to absorb large quantities of liquid without becoming too soft, cooking to a creamy texture with a slight bite. There are two grades of risotto rice: superfino and fino. Arborio rice is the most widely sold variety of the former, but you may also find carnaroli, Roma and baldo in Italian delicatessens. Fino rice such as vialone nano has a slightly shorter grain, but the flavour is still excellent.

Valencia rice Traditionally used for Spanish paella, Valencia rice is soft and tender when ready. The medium-sized grains break down easily, so should be left unstirred during cooking to absorb the flavour of the stock and other ingredients.

Jasmine rice Also known as Thai fragrant rice, this long-grain rice has a delicate, almost perfumed aroma and flavour and has a soft, sticky texture.

Japanese sushi rice This is similar to glutinous rice in that it has a sticky texture. When mixed with rice vinegar, it is easy to roll up with a filling inside to make sushi.

Pudding rice This rounded, short-grain rice is ideal for rice desserts. The grains swell and absorb large quantities of milk during cooking, giving puddings a rich, creamy consistency.

Wild rice This is an aquatic grass grown in North America rather than a true variety of rice. The black grains are long and slender and after harvesting and cleaning they are toasted to remove the chaff and intensify the nutty flavour and slight chewiness. It is often sold as a mixture with long-grain rice.

Rice flour Raw rice can be finely ground to make rice flour, which may be used to thicken sauces (1 tablespoon will thicken 300 ml/½ pint/1¼ cups liquid) or in Asian desserts. It is also used to make rice noodles.

Buying and Storing Rice

Rice will keep for several years if kept in sealed packets. However, it is at its best when fresh. To ensure freshness, always buy rice from reputable shops with a good turnover and buy in small quantities. Once opened, store the rice in an airtight container in a cool, dry place to keep out moisture. Most rice (but not risotto) benefits from washing before cooking – tip into a sieve/strainer and rinse under cold running water until the water runs clear. This removes any starch still clinging to the grains.

Cooked rice will keep for up to two days if cooled and stored in a covered bowl in the refrigerator. If eating rice cold, serve within 24 hours – after this time it should be thoroughly re-heated.

Cooking Techniques

There are countless ways to cook rice, but much depends on the variety of rice being used, the dish being prepared and the desired results. Each variety of rice has its own characteristics. Some types of rice cook to light, separate grains, some to a rich, creamy consistency and some to a consistency where the grains stick together. Different types of rice have different powers of absorption. Long-grain rice will absorb three times its weight in water, whereas 25 g/1 oz/⅛ cup short-grain pudding rice can soak up a massive 300 ml/½ pint/1¼ cups liquid.

Cooking Long-grain Rice

The simplest method of cooking long-grain rice is to add it to plenty of boiling, salted water in a large saucepan. Allow 50 g/2 oz/¼ cup rice per person when cooking as an accompaniment. Rinse under cold running water until clear then tip into rapidly boiling water. Stir once, then, when the water returns to the boil, reduce the heat and simmer uncovered. Allow 10–12 minutes for white rice and 30–40 minutes for brown – check the packet for specific timings. The easiest way to test if rice is cooked is to bite a couple of grains – they should be tender but still firm. Drain immediately, then return to the pan with a little butter and herbs, if liked. Fluff up with a fork and serve. To keep the rice warm, put it in a bowl and place over a pan of barely simmering water. Cover the top of the bowl with a dishtowel until ready to serve.

Absorption Method

Cooking rice using the absorption method is also simple. Weigh out the quantity, then measure it by volume in a measuring jug – you will need 150 ml/¼ pint/⅔ cup for two people. Rinse the rice then tip into a large saucepan. If liked, cook the rice in a little butter or oil for 1 minute. Pour in two parts water or stock to one part rice, season with salt and bring to the boil. Cover, then simmer gently until the liquid is absorbed and the rice is tender. White rice will take 15 minutes to cook, whereas brown rice will take 35 minutes. If there is still a little liquid left when the rice is tender, uncover and cook for 1 minute until evaporated. Remove from the heat and leave, covered, for 4–5 minutes then fluff up before serving. This method is good for cooking jasmine and Valencia rice.

Oven-baked Method

The oven-baked method works by absorption too, but takes longer than cooking on the hob/stove top. For oven-baked rice for two, fry a chopped onion in 1 tablespoon olive oil in a 1.2 litre/2 pint/1¼ quart flameproof casserole dish until soft and golden. Add 75 g/3 oz/⅓ cup long-grain rice and cook for 1 minute, then stir in 300 ml/½ pint/1¼ cups stock – add a finely pared strip of lemon rind or bay leaf, if liked. Cover and bake in a preheated oven at 180°C/350°F/Gas Mark 4 for 40 minutes, or until the rice is tender and all the stock has been absorbed. Fluff up before serving.

Cooking in the Microwave

Place rinsed long-grain rice in a large, heatproof bowl. Add boiling water or stock, allowing 300 ml/½ pint/1¼ cups for 100 g/3½ oz/½ cup rice and 500 ml/18 fl oz/2 cups for 225 g/8 oz/1 cup rice. Add a pinch of salt and a knob of butter, if desired. Cover with pierced clingfilm/plastic wrap and cook on high for 3 minutes. Stir, re-cover and cook on medium for 12 minutes for white rice and 25 minutes for brown. Leave, covered, for 5 minutes before fluffing up and serving.

Cooking in a Pressure Cooker

Follow the quantities given for the absorption method and bring to the boil in the pressure cooker. Stir, cover and bring to a high 6.8 kg/15 lb pressure. Lower the heat and cook for 5 minutes if white rice or for 8 minutes for brown.

Cooking in a Rice Cooker

Follow the quantities given for the absorption method. Put the rice, salt and boiling water or stock in the cooker, return to the boil and cover. When all the liquid has been absorbed, the cooker will turn off automatically.

Health and Nutrition

Rice is low in fat and high in complex carbohydrates, which are absorbed slowly and help to maintain blood sugar levels. It is also a reasonable source of protein and provides many B vitamins and the minerals potassium and phosphorus. It is a gluten-free cereal, making it suitable for coeliacs. Brown rice is richer in nutrients and fibre than refined white rice.

Pasta

How to Make Pasta

Home-made pasta has a light, almost silky texture and is different from the fresh pasta that you can buy vacuum-packed in supermarkets. It is also easy to make and little equipment is needed, just a rolling pin and a sharp knife. If you make pasta regularly, it is perhaps worth investing in a pasta machine.

Basic Egg Pasta Dough

225 g/8 oz/2 cups type '00' pasta flour, plus extra for dusting
1 tsp salt, 2 eggs, plus 1 egg yolk
1 tbsp olive oil, 1–3 tsp cold water

Sift the flour and salt into a mound on a work surface and make a well in the middle, keeping the sides high so that the egg mixture will not trickle out when added. Beat the eggs, yolk, oil and 1 teaspoon water together. Add to the well, then gradually work in the flour, adding extra water if needed, to make a soft but not sticky dough. Knead on a lightly floured surface for 5 minutes, or until the dough is smooth and elastic. Wrap in clingfilm/plastic wrap and leave for 20 minutes at room temperature.

Using a Food Processor

Sift the flour and salt into a food processor fitted with a metal blade. Add the eggs, yolk, oil and water and pulse-blend until mixed and the dough begins to come together, adding extra water if needed. Knead for 1–2 minutes, then wrap and rest as before.

Rolling Pasta by Hand

Unwrap the pasta dough and cut in half. Work with just half at a time and keep the other half wrapped in clingfilm/plastic wrap. Place the dough on a lightly floured work surface, then flatten and roll out. Always roll away from you. Start from the centre, giving the dough a quarter turn after each rolling. Sprinkle a little more flour over the dough if it starts to get sticky. Continue rolling and turning until the dough is as thin as possible, ideally 3 mm/⅛ inch thick.

Rolling Pasta by Machine

Always refer to the manufacturers' instructions before using. Clamp the machine securely and attach the handle. Set the rollers at their widest setting and sprinkle with flour. Cut the pasta dough into four pieces. Wrap three of them in clingfilm/plastic wrap and reserve. Flatten the unwrapped dough slightly, then feed it through the rollers. Fold the strip of dough in three, rotate and feed through the rollers a second time. Continue to roll the dough, narrowing the roller setting by one notch every second time and flouring the rollers if the dough starts to get sticky. Only fold the dough the first time it goes through each roller width. If it is hard to handle, cut the strip in half and work with one piece at a time. Fresh pasta should be dried before cutting. Drape over a wooden pole for 5 minutes or place on a dishtowel sprinkled with a little flour for 10 minutes.

Shaping Up

For shaping freshly made pasta, have several lightly floured dishtowels ready.

Farfalle Use a fluted pasta wheel to cut the pasta sheets into rectangles 2.5 x 5 cm/1 x 2 inches. Pinch the long sides of each rectangle in the middle to make a bow. Spread on a floured dishtowel. Leave for 15 minutes.

Lasagne Trim the pasta sheets until neat and cut into lengths. Spread the sheets on a dishtowel sprinkled with flour.

Noodles If using a pasta machine, use the cutter attachment to produce tagliatelle or use a narrower one for spaghetti. To make by hand, sprinkle the rolled-out pasta with flour, then roll up like a Swiss roll and cut into thin slices. Unravel immediately after cutting. Leave over a wooden pole for 5 minutes to dry.

Ravioli Cut the rolled-out sheet of dough in half widthways. Cover one half. Brush the other sheet of dough with beaten egg. Place 1 teaspoon filling in even rows, at 4 cm/1½ inch intervals. Remove the clingfilm/plastic wrap from the reserved pasta sheet and, using a rolling pin, lift over the dough with the filling. Press down between the pockets to push out any air. Cut into squares. Leave on a floured dishtowel for 45 minutes before cooking.

Variations

Flavoured pastas are simple and there are many ways to change the flavour and colour of pasta.

Chilli Add 2 teaspoons crushed, dried red chillies to the egg mixture.

Herb Stir 3 tablespoons chopped fresh herbs into the flour.

Olive Blend 2 tablespoons black olive paste with the egg mixture and omit the water.

Porcini Soak 15 g/½ oz dried porcini mushrooms in boiling water for 20 minutes. Drain and squeeze out as much water as possible, then chop finely. Add to the egg mixture.

Spinach Chop 75 g/3 oz cooked fresh spinach finely. Add to the egg mixture.

Dried Pasta Varieties

Buckwheat A gluten-free pasta made from buckwheat flour.

Coloured and flavoured pasta Varieties are endless, the most popular being spinach and tomato. Others include beetroot/beet, herb, garlic, chilli, mushroom and black squid or cuttlefish ink.

Durum wheat pasta Most readily available and may be made with or without eggs. Look for 'durum wheat' or 'pasta di semola di grano duro' on the packet, as pastas made from soft wheat tend to become soggy when cooked.

Wholemeal/whole-wheat pasta Made with whole-wheat flour, this has a higher fibre content than ordinary pasta. Whole-wheat pasta takes longer to cook than the refined version.

Pasta Shapes

Long Pasta

Spaghetti Probably the best known type of pasta, spaghetti derives its name from the word 'spago' meaning string, which describes its round, thin shape perfectly.

Tagliatelle Most common type of ribbon noodle pasta. It is traditionally from Bologna, where it accompanies bolognese sauce (rather than spaghetti). Fettuccine is the Roman version of tagliatelle and is cut slightly thinner.

Short Pasta

There are two types of short pasta: 'secca' is factory-made from durum wheat and water and 'pasta all'uovo' is made with eggs. There are numerous different shapes and some of the most popular ones are listed below.

Conchiglie Pasta shapes resembling conch shells. Sizes vary from tiny to large. They may be smooth or ridged ('conchiglie rigate').

Eliche and fusilli These are twisted into the shape of a screw.

Farfalle Bow or butterfly shaped, often with crinkled edges.

Macaroni Known as elbow macaroni or maccheroni in Italy. A thin, quick-cook variety is also available.

Penne Slightly larger than macaroni, the ends of these tubes are cut and pointed like quills.

Pipe Curved, hollow pasta and often sold ridged as 'pipe rigate'.

Rigatoni Substantial, chunky, tubular pasta often used for baking.

Rotelle Thin, wheel-shaped pasta, often sold in packets of two or three colours.

Stuffed Pasta

Tortellini The most common variety, consisting of tiny, stuffed pieces of pasta. Larger ones are called tortelloni.

Cappelletti, ravioli and agnalotti These are sometimes sold dried, but are more often available fresh.

Fresh Pasta

Fresh pasta can be found in supermarkets and specialist shops. It is generally available in the same shapes as dried pasta.

How to Cook Perfect Pasta

Follow a few simple rules to ensure that your pasta is cooked to perfection every time:

1 Choose a large saucepan – there needs to be plenty of room for the pasta to move around so it does not stick together.

2 Cook the pasta in a large quantity of fast-boiling, well-salted water, ideally 4 litres/7 pints/4 quarts water and 1½–2 tablespoons salt for every 350–450 g/12 oz–1 lb pasta.

3 Tip in the pasta all at once, stir and cover. Return to a rolling boil, then remove the lid. Once it is boiling, lower the heat to medium-high and cook the pasta for the required time. It should be *al dente*, or tender but still firm to the bite.

4 Drain, reserving a little of the cooking water to stir into the drained pasta. This helps to thin the sauce, if necessary, and helps prevent the pasta sticking together as it cools.

Serving Quantities

As an approximate guide, allow 75–100 g/3–4 oz uncooked pasta per person. The amount will depend on whether the pasta is being served for a light or main meal and the type of sauce that it is being served with.

Herbs & Spices

In a culture where fast food, ready-made meals and processed foods are popular, homemade food can sometimes taste bland by comparison, due to the fact that the palate can quickly become accustomed to additives and flavour enhancers. The use of herbs and spices, however, can make all the difference in helping to make delicious homemade dishes.

Herbs are easy to grow and a garden is not needed as they can easily thrive on a small patio, window box or even on a windowsill. It is worth the effort to plant a few herbs, as they do not require much attention or nurturing. The reward will be a range of fresh herbs available whenever needed and fresh flavours that cannot be beaten to add to any dish that is being prepared.

While fresh herbs should be picked or bought as close as possible to the time of use, freeze-dried and dried herbs and spices will usually keep for around six months.

The best idea is to buy little and often and to store the herbs in airtight jars in a cool, dark cupboard. Fresh herbs tend to have a milder flavour than dried and equate to around 1 level tbsp fresh to 1 level tsp dried. As a result, quantities used in cooking should be altered accordingly. A variety of herbs and spices and their uses are listed below.

Allspice The dark allspice berries come whole or ground and have a flavour similar to that of cinnamon, cloves and nutmeg. Although not the same as mixed spices, allspice can be used with pickles, relishes, cakes and milk puddings, or whole in meat and fish dishes.

Aniseed Comes in whole seeds or ground. It has a strong aroma and flavour and should be used sparingly in baking and salad dressings.

Basil Best fresh but also available in dried form, basil can be used raw or cooked and works well in many dishes but is particularly well suited to tomato-based dishes and sauces, salads and Mediterranean dishes.

Bay leaves Available in fresh or dried form as well as ground. They make up part of a bouquet garni and are particularly delicious when added to meat and poultry dishes, soups, stews, vegetable dishes and stuffing. They also impart a spicy flavour to milk puddings and egg custards.

Caraway seeds These have a warm, sweet taste and are often used in breads and cakes, but are also delicious with cabbage dishes and pickles.

Cayenne The powdered form of a red chilli pepper said to be native to Cayenne. It is similar in appearance to paprika and can be used sparingly to add a fiery kick to many dishes.

Cardamom Has a distinctive sweet, rich taste. Can be bought whole in the pod, in seed form or ground. This sweet aromatic spice is delicious in curries, rice, cakes and biscuits/cookies and is great served with rice pudding and fruit.

Chervil Reminiscent of parsley and available either in fresh or dried form, chervil has a faintly sweet, spicy flavour and is particularly good in soups, cheese dishes, stews and with eggs.

Chilli Available whole, fresh, dried and in powdered form. Red chillies tend to be sweeter in taste than their green counterparts. They are particularly associated with Spanish and Mexican-style cooking and curries, but are also delicious with pickles, dips, sauces and in pizza toppings.

Chives Best used when fresh but also available in dried form, this member of the onion family is ideal for use when a delicate onion flavour is required. Chives are good with eggs, cheese, fish and vegetable dishes. They also work well as a garnish for soups, meat and vegetable dishes.

Cinnamon Comes in the form of reddish-brown sticks of bark from an evergreen tree and has a sweet, pungent aroma. Either whole or ground, cinnamon is delicious in cakes and milk puddings, particularly with apple, and is used in mulled wine and for preserving.

Cloves Mainly used whole, although available ground, cloves have a very warm, sweet, pungent aroma and can be used to stud roast ham and pork, in mulled wine and punch and when pickling fruit. When ground, they can be used in making mincemeat and in Christmas puddings and biscuits/cookies.

Coriander/cilantro Coriander seeds have an orangey flavour and are available whole or ground. Coriander is particularly delicious (whole or roughly ground) in curries, casseroles and as a pickling spice. Coriander/cilantro leaves are used both to flavour spicy aromatic dishes and as a garnish.

Cumin Also available ground or as whole seeds, cumin has a strong, slightly bitter flavour. It is one of the main ingredients in curry powder and complements many fish, meat and rice dishes.

Dill These leaves are available fresh or dried and have a mild flavour, while the seeds are slightly bitter. Dill is particularly good with salmon, new potatoes and in sauces. The seeds are good in pickles and vegetable dishes.

Fennel As whole seeds or ground, fennel has a fragrant, sweet aniseed flavour and is sometimes known as the fish herb because it complements fish dishes so well.

Ginger Comes in many forms but primarily as a fresh root and in dried, ground form, which can be used in baking, curries, pickles, sauces and Chinese cooking.

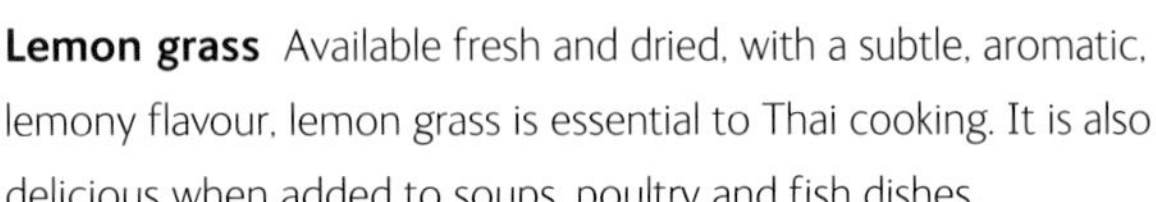

Lemon grass Available fresh and dried, with a subtle, aromatic, lemony flavour, lemon grass is essential to Thai cooking. It is also delicious when added to soups, poultry and fish dishes.

Mace The outer husk of nutmeg has a milder nutmeg flavour and can be used in pickles, cheese dishes, stewed fruits, sauces and hot punch.

Marjoram Often dried, marjoram has a sweet, slightly spicy flavour, which tastes fantastic when added to stuffing, meat or tomato-based dishes.

Mint Available fresh or dried, mint has a strong, sweet aroma that is delicious in a sauce or jelly to serve with lamb. It is great with fresh peas and new potatoes and an essential part of summer punch.

Nutmeg The large, whole seeds have a warm, sweet taste and complement custards/custard sauces, milk puddings, cheese dishes, parsnips and creamy soups.

Oregano These strongly flavoured dried leaves are similar to marjoram and are used extensively in Italian and Greek cooking.

Paprika Often comes in two varieties. One is quite sweet and mild and the other has a slight bite to it. Paprika is made from the fruit of the sweet pepper and is good in meat and poultry dishes as well as a garnish. The rule of buying herbs and spices little and often applies particularly to paprika, as unfortunately it does not keep particularly well.

Parsley The stems as well as the leaves of parsley can be used to complement most savoury dishes, as they contain the most flavour. They can also be used as a garnish.

Poppy seeds These small, grey-black coloured seeds impart a sweet, nutty flavour when added to biscuits/cookies, vegetable dishes, dressings and cheese dishes.

Rosemary Delicious fresh or dried, these small, needle-like leaves have a sweet aroma that is particularly good with lamb, stuffing and vegetables dishes. Also delicious when added to charcoal on the barbecue to give a piquant flavour to both meat and corn on the cob/corn ears.

Saffron Deep orange in colour, saffron is traditionally used in paella, rice and cakes but is also delicious with poultry. Saffron is the most expensive of all spices.

Sage Fresh or dried sage leaves have a pungent, slightly bitter taste that is delicious with pork and poultry, sausages, stuffing and with stuffed pasta when tossed in a little butter.

Sesame Sesame seeds have a nutty taste, especially when toasted, and are delicious in baking, on salads or with Far Eastern cooking.

Tarragon The fresh or dried leaves of tarragon have a sweet, aromatic taste that is particularly good with poultry, seafood, fish, creamy sauces and stuffing.

Thyme Available fresh or dried, thyme has a pungent flavour and is included in bouquet garni. It complements many meat and poultry dishes and stuffing.

Turmeric Obtained from the root of a lily from southeast Asia. This root is ground and has a brilliant yellow colour. It has a bitter, peppery flavour and is often combined for use in curry powder and mustard. Also delicious in pickles, relishes and dressings.

Meat

Both home-grown and imported meat is readily available from supermarkets, butchers, farm shops and markets. Home-grown meat is normally more expensive than imported meat, often brought into the country frozen. Meat also varies in price depending on the cut. The more expensive and tender meats are usually those cuts that exercised less. They need a minimal amount of cooking and are suitable for roasting, grilling/broiling, griddling, frying and stir-frying. The cheaper cuts need longer, slower cooking and are used in casseroles and for stewing. Meat plays an important part in most people's diet, offering an excellent source of protein, B vitamins and iron.

When choosing meat, it is important to buy from a reputable source and to choose the correct cut for the cooking method. Look for meat that is lean without an excess of fat, is a good colour and has no unpleasant odour. If in doubt about the suitability of a cut, ask the butcher, who should be happy to advise.

If buying frozen meat, allow to thaw before using. This is especially important for both pork and poultry. It is best to thaw meat slowly, lightly covered on the bottom shelf of the refrigerator. Use within 2–3 days of thawing, providing it has been kept in the refrigerator. If buying meat to freeze, do not freeze large joints in a home freezer as it will not be frozen quickly enough.

Store thawed or fresh meat out of the supermarket wrappings, on a plate, lightly covered with greaseproof or baking paper/parchment and then wrap with clingfilm/plastic wrap if liked. Do not secure the paper tightly round the meat, as it needs to breathe. Ensure that the raw meat juices do not drip on to cooked foods. The refrigerator needs to be at a temperature of 5°C/40°F. Fresh meat such as joints, chops and steaks can be stored for up to three days. Minced/ground meats, sausages and offal/variety meats should be stored for only one day.

Different cultures and religions affect the way the meat has been killed and the carcass cut. The following is a description of different cuts of meat. They may be called by different names depending on where you live.

Beef

When choosing beef, look for meat that is a good colour, with creamy yellow fat. There should be small flecks of fat (marbling) throughout, as this helps the meat to be tender. Avoid meat with excess gristle. Bright red beef means that the animal has been butchered recently, whereas meat that has a dark, almost purple, tinge is from meat that has been hung in a traditional manner. The darker the colour, especially with roasting joints, the more tender and succulent the beef will be.

Rib or fore rib (1) Suitable for roasting. Sold either on or off the bone. Look for meat that is marbled for tenderness and succulence.

Topside/Round (2) Suitable for pot roasting, roasting or braising. A lean, tender cut from the hindquarters.

Sirloin/Shortloin, Tenderloin, Top/Bottom Sirloin Suitable for roasting, grilling/broiling, frying or barbecuing. Sold either on or off the bone. A lean and tender cut from the back.

T-bone steak Suitable for grilling/broiling, griddling, barbecuing or roasting. A tender, succulent cut from the fillet end of the sirloin.

Top rib Suitable for pot roasting or braising. Sold on or off the bone.

Fillet steak Suitable for grilling/broiling, frying, barbecuing or griddling. A whole fillet is used to make Châteaubriand, some say the best of all cuts. The most tender and succulent cut with virtually no fat. Comes from the centre of the sirloin.

Rump/Shortloin, Tenderloin, Top/Bottom Sirloin (3) Suitable for grilling/broiling, frying, griddling or barbecuing. Not as tender as fillet of sirloin, but reputed to have more flavour.

Silverside/Round (4) Suitable for boiling and pot roasts. Used to be sold ready-salted but is now normally sold unsalted.

Flash-fry steaks (5) Suitable for grilling/broiling, griddling or frying. Cut from the silverside, thick flank or topside.

Braising steak (6) Chuck, blade or thick rib, ideal for all braising or stews. Sold either in pieces or ready diced.

Flank/Bottom Sirloin (7) Suitable for braising or stewing. A boneless cut from the mid- to hindquarters.

Minute steaks Suitable for grilling/broiling or griddling. A thin steak cut from the flank and beaten to flatten.

Skirt Suitable for stewing or making into mince. A boneless, rather gristly cut.

Brisket/Plate Suitable for slow or pot roasting. Sold boned and rolled and can be found salted.

Minced/ground beef Suitable for meat sauces such as bolognese and also burgers, shepherd's pie and moussaka. Normally cut from clod, skirt, neck, thin rib or flank. Can be quite fatty. Steaks can also be minced/ground to give a leaner result, if it is preferred.

Ox kidney Suitable for using in casseroles and stews. Strong flavour with hard central core that is discarded.

Oxtail Suitable for casseroles or braising. Normally sold cut into small pieces.

Lamb

Lamb is probably at its best in the spring, when the youngest lamb is available. It is tender to eat, with a delicate flavour, and its flesh is a paler pink than the older lamb, where the flesh is more red. The colour of the fat is also a good indication of age: young lamb fat is a very light, creamy colour. As the lamb matures, the fat becomes whiter and firmer. Imported lamb also has firmer, whiter fat. Lamb can be fatty, so take care when choosing. It used to be possible to buy mutton (lamb that is at least one year old), but this now tends to be available only in specialist outlets. It has a far stronger, almost gamey, flavour and the joints tend to be larger.

Leg (1) Suitable for roasting. Often sold as half legs and steaks cut from the fillet end. These can be grilled/broiled, griddled or barbecued. Steaks are very lean and need a little additional oil to prevent the meat from drying out.

Shank Suitable for braising. A cut off the leg.

Shoulder (2) Suitable for roasting. Can be sold boned, stuffed and rolled. Is fattier than the leg and has more flavour.

Loin (3) Suitable for roasting. Sold on or off the bone. Can be stuffed and rolled. Can also be cut into chops, often as double loin chops – suitable for grilling/broiling, griddling and barbecuing.

Noisette Suitable for grilling/broiling, griddling or barbecuing. A small boneless chop cut from the loin.

Valentine steak Suitable for grilling/broiling, griddling or barbecuing. Cut from a loin chop.

Chump chop (4) Suitable for grilling/broiling, griddling or barbecuing. Larger than loin chops and can be sold boneless.

Best end of neck (5) Suitable for roasting, grilling/broiling or griddling. Sold as a joint or cutlets.

Neck fillet Suitable for grilling/broiling or griddling. Sold whole or diced.

Middle and scrag end (6) Suitable for pot roasting, braising or stewing. A cheaper cut with a high ratio of fat and bone.

Breast (7) Suitable for pot roast if boned, stuffed and rolled. Can be marinated and grilled/broiled or barbecued.

Mince Suitable for burgers, pies, meatballs and for stuffing vegetables such as peppers. From various cuts and is often fatty.

Liver Suitable for pan frying or grilling/broiling. Milder than ox or pig liver and cheaper than calves' liver.

Kidney Suitable for grilling/broiling, pan frying or casseroles. Milder than ox or pig kidney and normally sold encased in suet, which is discarded.

Pork

Pork should be pale pink in colour and slightly marbled with small flecks of fat. There should be a layer of firm white fat with a thin elastic skin (rind), which can be scored before roasting to provide crackling. All cuts of pork are tender, as the pigs are slaughtered at an early age and are reared to be lean rather than fatty. Pork used to be well cooked, if not overcooked, due to the danger of the parasite trichina. This no longer applies, however, and it is now recommended that the meat is cooked less to keep it moist and tender.

Leg (1) Suitable for roasting. Sold either on or off the bone. Can be cut into chunks and braised or casseroled.

Steaks (2) Suitable for grilling/broiling, frying, griddling or barbecuing. A lean cut from the leg or the shoulder. Very tender but can be dry.

Fillet Sometimes called tenderloin and suitable for roasting, pan frying, griddling or barbecuing. A tender cut, often sold already marinated.

Loin (3) Suitable for roasting as a joint or cut into chops. Often sold with the kidney intact.

Shoulder (4) Suitable for roasting. Often referred to as hand and spring, and sold cubed for casseroles and stews. A fatty cut.

Spare ribs Suitable for barbecuing, casseroles and roasting. Sold either as 'Chinese', where thin ribs are marinated then cooked, or 'American Style' ribs, which are larger.

Escalope/cutlet Suitable for grilling/broiling, frying, griddling or barbecuing. Very lean and tender and requires very little cooking.

Minced/ground pork Suitable for burgers, meatballs or similar recipes. Often from the cheaper cuts and can be fatty.

Belly (5) Suitable for grilling/broiling or roasting. Can be salted before cooking. Is generally used to provide streaky bacon and is perhaps the fattiest cut of all.

Liver Suitable for casseroles or frying. Stronger than lamb or calves' liver.

Kidney Suitable for casseroles or frying. Often sold as part of a loin chop. Stronger than lambs' kidneys.

Poultry & Game

Poultry relates to turkey, chicken, poussin/game hen, duck and goose. Most is sold plucked, drawn and trussed. Due to extensive farming since the war, chicken in particular offers a good source of cheap meat. However, there is a growing movement to return to the more traditional methods of farming. Organically grown chickens offer a far more succulent bird with excellent flavour, although they tend to be more expensive. Both home-grown and imported poultry, fresh and frozen are available. When buying fresh poultry, look for plump birds with a flexible breast bone and no unpleasant odour or green tinge.

Frozen poultry should be rock hard with no ice crystals, as this could mean that the bird has thawed and been re-frozen. Avoid any produce where the packaging is damaged. When thawing, place in the refrigerator on a large plate and ensure that none of the juices drip on to other foods. Once thawed, remove all packaging, remove the giblets, if any, and store separately. Place on a plate and cover. Use within two days and ensure that the meat is thoroughly cooked and the juices run clear. Rest for 10 minutes before carving.

When storing fresh poultry, place on a plate and cover lightly, allowing air to circulate. Treat as thawed poultry: store for no longer than two days in the refrigerator, storing the giblets separately, and ensure that it is thoroughly cooked. Use within two days of cooking.

Poultry and game are low in saturated fat and provide a good source of protein as well as selenium, an antioxidant mineral. Remove the skin from poultry before eating if following a low-fat diet.

Poultry

Turkey Whole birds are suitable for roasting and traditionally served at Christmas and Thanksgiving. Various turkey cuts are eaten throughout the year, ranging from breast steaks, diced thigh, escalopes/cutlets, small whole breast fillets/halves, drumsticks, wings and minced/ground turkey. Specific cuts include:

Crown The whole bird with the legs removed.

Saddle Two turkey breast fillets/halves, boned with the wings inserted.

Butterfly The two breast fillets/halves.

Breast roll Boned breast meat, rolled and tied or contained in a net.

Chicken Suitable for all cooking: roasting, grilling/broiling, griddling, stewing, braising, frying and barbecuing. Also available in many different breeds and varieties, offering a good choice to the consumer. There are many cuts of chicken readily available: breast, wing and leg quarters, which are still on the bone, drumsticks, thighs, breast fillets/halves, escalopes (boneless, skinless portions), diced and stir-fry strips as well as minced/ground chicken.

Capon Suitable for roasting. These are young castrated cockerels and are normally bred for their excellent flavour.

Broilers These are older chickens that would be too tough to roast. Normally quite small birds, about 1.6 kg/3 ½ lb.

Poussin (pictured) Suitable for roasting, grilling/broiling or casseroles. These are young or spring chickens/game hens and are 4–6 weeks old. They can be bought whole or spatchcocked – this is where the bird is split through the breast, opened up and secured on skewers. One bird normally serves one person if small (450 g/1 lb) or two people if larger (900 g/2 lb).

Guinea fowl Suitable for roasting or casseroles. Available all year round, with a slightly gamey flavour. Most are sold ready for the table. When roasting, use plenty of fat or bacon as they can be dry.

Goose Suitable for roasting and often served as an alternative to turkey. Once dressed for the table, a goose will weigh around 4.5 kg/10 lb, but there is not much meat and this will serve around 6–8 people. It is very fatty, so pierce the skin well and roast on a trivet so the fat can be discarded or used for other cooking. Has a rich flavour, slightly gamey and a little like duck. Goose liver is highly prized and is used for foie gras.

Duck Suitable for roasting, grilling/broiling, griddling and casseroles. Ducklings between six weeks and three months old are normally used for the table; ducks are not normally eaten. Duck has an excellent flavour but it is a fatty bird, so cook on a trivet as for goose. Available fresh or frozen and on average weighs 1.75–2.75 kg/4–6 lb. Also available in cuts, as boneless breast fillets, ideal for grilling/broiling or griddling, and leg portions, suitable for casseroles. The meat is also used to make pâté. There are quite a few varieties available, with perhaps the most well known being the Aylesbury. Long Island/Pekin and Barbary are also popular varieties.

Game

Game describes birds or animals that are hunted, not farmed, although some, such as pheasant, quails and rabbits, are now being reared domestically. Most game has a stronger flavour than poultry and some is at its best when 'high' and smelling quite strong. Game is not as popular as most meat or poultry and is an acquired taste. When buying game, it is important to know its age, as this dictates the method of cooking. Normally sold oven-ready, it is advisable to buy from a reputable source who can guarantee the quality.

Pigeon Suitable for casseroles and stews, although the breast from young pigeons can be fried or grilled/broiled. Sometimes classified as poultry. Not widely available, mainly from licensed game sources.

Pheasant Suitable for roasting or casseroles. Breast, which can be grilled/broiled, is also available. Pheasant needs to be well hung to give the best flavour.

Rabbit Suitable for casseroles and stews and can be roasted or, if young, fried. Also makes excellent pies and fricassee. Sold whole or in portions, both with and without the bone, and available both fresh and frozen. Frozen rabbit often comes from China. If a milder flavour is preferred, soak in cold salted water for two hours before using. Generally regarded as country food and not served as haute cuisine.

Hare Suitable for casseroles. The most well-known recipe is Jugged Hare, where the blood is used to thicken the dish. Has a strong, gamey flavour. If a milder flavour is preferred, soak in cold water for up to 24 hours. Available from reputable game dealers.

Venison Suitable for roasting, grilling/broiling, casseroles or making into sausages. The saddle, haunch and shoulder are best for roasting, although the loin and fillet can also be used. All cuts benefit from marinating to help tenderize.

Other game Less widely available are partridge, grouse, quail, snipe and boar.

Fish

Preparing & Cooking Fish & Seafood

Requiring only minimal cooking, all fish is an excellent choice for speedy and nutritious meals. There are two categories of fish: white and oily (*see* pages 29 and 30). Seafood can be divided into three categories: shellfish, crustaceans and molluscs (*see* page 31).

Both types of fish are sold fresh or frozen as small whole fish, fillets or cutlets. Store as soon as possible in the refrigerator. Remove from the wrappings, place on a plate, cover lightly and store towards the top. Use within one day of purchase. If using frozen, thaw slowly in the refrigerator and use within one day of thawing.

Seafood should be eaten as fresh as possible. Live seafood gives the best flavour, as long as it is consumed on the day of purchase. If live is not available, buy from a reputable source and eat on the day of purchase, refrigerating until required. Clean all seafood thoroughly and, with mussels and clams, discard any that do not close when tapped lightly before cooking. After cooking, discard any that have not opened.

Cleaning Fish

When cleaning whole fish, first remove the scales. Using a round bladed knife, gently scrape the knife along the fish starting from the tail towards the head. Rinse frequently. To clean round fish, make a slit along the abdomen from the gills to the tail using a small, sharp knife and scrape out the innards. Rinse thoroughly.

For flat fish, open the cavity under the gills and remove the innards. Rinse. Remove the gills and fins and, if preferred, the tail and head. Rinse thoroughly in cold water and pat dry. Cutlet and fillets simply need lightly rinsing in cold water and patting dry.

Skinning Fish

For whole flat fish, clean and remove the fins as before. Make a small cut on the dark side of the fish across the tail and slip your thumb between the skin and flesh. Loosen the skin along the side. Holding the fish firmly with one hand, rip the skin off with the other. The white skin can be removed in the same way.

Round fish are normally cooked with the skin on but, if you do wish to skin them, start from the head and cut a narrow strip of skin along the backbone. Cut below the head and loosen the skin with the point of the knife. Dip your fingers in salt for a better grip and gently pull the skin down towards the tail. Take care not to break the flesh.

Filleting Fish

To fillet flat fish, use a sharp knife and make a cut along the line of bones. Insert the knife under the flesh and carefully cut it with long, sweeping strokes. Cut the first fillet from the left-hand side, working from head to tail. Turn the fish round and repeat, this time cutting from tail to head. Turn the fish over and repeat on this side.

For round fish, cut along the centre of the back to the bone and then cut along the abdomen. Cleanly remove the flesh with short, sharp strokes from the head downwards, pressing the knife against the bones. Turn the fish over and repeat. This is suitable for larger fish such as salmon.

To fillet herring and mackerel, discard the head, tail and fins and clean, reserving any roe if applicable. Place on a chopping board and gently press along the backbone to open fully and loosen the bone. Turn the fish over, ease the backbone up and remove, taking as many of the small bones as possible at the same time.

Basic Fish Recipes

Poached Fish

Clean the fish, remove scales if necessary and rinse thoroughly. Place in a large frying pan with 1 small peeled and sliced onion and carrot, 1 bay leaf, 5 peppercorns and a few parsley stalks. Pour over sufficient cold water to barely cover, then bring to the boil over a medium heat. Reduce the heat to a simmer, cover and cook gently for 8–10 minutes for fillets and 10–15 minutes for whole fish.

This method is suitable for fillets and small whole fish. When the fish is cooked, the flesh should yield easily when pierced with a round bladed knife, and the fish should look opaque.

Grilled/Broiled Fish

Line a grill rack with kitchen foil and preheat the grill to medium high just before grilling. Lightly rinse the fish, pat it dry and place on the foil-lined grill rack. Season with salt and pepper and brush lightly with a little oil. Cook under the grill for 8–10 minutes or until cooked, turning the heat down if the fish is cooking too quickly. Sprinkle with herbs or pour over a little melted butter or herb-flavoured olive oil to serve.

This method is suitable for fresh fish fillets (not smoked), sardines and other small whole fish. Make 3 slashes across whole fish before grilling.

Griddled Fish

Rinse the fish fillet, pat dry and, if desired, marinate in a marinade of your choice for 30 minutes. Heat a griddle pan until smoking and add the fish, skin-side down. Cook for 5 minutes, pressing the fish down with a fish slice. Turn the fish over and continue to cook for a further 4–5 minutes or until cooked to personal preference.

Types of Fish & Seafood

White Fish

White fish such as cod, haddock, plaice or coley are an excellent source of protein and have a low fat content. They also contain vitamin B12 and niacin, plus important minerals such as phosphorous, iodine, selenium and potassium.

Bass Sea fish. Suitable for grilling/broiling or frying. Large bass can be poached whole. Has very white flesh. At its best from May to August.

Sea bream/porgy Sea fish. Suitable for grilling, poaching and frying, can also be stuffed and baked or poached. Has white, firm flesh with a delicate flavour. At its best from June to December in the UK, or June to October in the USA.

Brill Sea fish. Suitable for grilling, baking or poaching and serving cold. Has firm flesh with a slight yellow tinge. At its best from April to August, but available all year, in the UK. Not fished in the USA.

Cod Sea fish. Also available smoked. Suitable for all types of cooking. Perhaps the most popular and versatile of all fish, with white flesh and a very delicate flavour. At its best from October to May but available all year round.

Coley/pollock Sea fish. Suitable for all types of cooking. One of the cheaper varieties of fish. Has a greyish-coloured flesh which turns slightly white on cooking. Available all year round in the UK, and in the USA depending on the variety.

Haddock Sea fish. Also available smoked. Suitable for all types of cooking. Has a firm, white flesh with a slightly stronger flavour than cod. At its best from September to February, but available all year round, in the UK. Available from June to October in the USA.

Hake Sea fish. Suitable for all methods of cooking. Has a firm, close-textured white flesh and is considered to have a better flavour than cod. At its best from June to January, but available all year round.

Halibut Sea fish. Suitable for all methods of cooking except deep frying. A large flat fish with excellent flavour. At its best from August to April but available all year round, in the UK. Available from March to November in the USA, depending on the variety.

John Dory Sea fish. Suitable for poaching or baking whole, or fillets can be cooked as for sole. Has a firm, white flesh with good flavour. Can be difficult to find. At its best from October to December, in the UK. Not fished in the USA.

Monkfish Sea fish. Suitable for all methods of cooking, including roasting. A firm, white fish with 'meaty' texture. A good substitute for lobster. Only the tail is eaten – the central bone is normally discarded and the two fillets are used. Available all year round.

Plaice or flounder Sea fish. The whole fish is suitable for grilling and pan frying, whilst fillets can be steamed, stuffed and rolled or used as goujons. A flat fish with distinctive dark grey/black skin with

red spots. Has soft, white flesh with a very delicate flavour. Available all year round.

Red mullet Sea fish. Suitable for grilling/broiling, frying or baking. Has a firm, white flesh and red skin. At its best from May to September.

Skate Sea fish. Suitable for grilling, frying or poaching. Only the wings are eaten and the bones are soft and gelatinous. A white fish with a delicate flavour. At its best from September to April.

Sole Sea fish. Suitable for frying or grilling. Has a firm yet delicate white skin with a delicious flavour. Available all year round. Dover sole is recognized by its dark grey/black skin and is considered by many to be the finest of the sole varieties. Lemon sole, which is more pointed. Witch and Torbay soles have the same qualities but the flavour is not as good.

Turbot Sea fish. Suitable for grilling or baking. Normally sold in cutlets, it has a creamy, white flesh with a delicious flavour which is reputed to be the best of all flat fish. At its best from March to August, in the UK. Not fished in the USA.

Whiting Sea fish. Suitable for all methods of cooking. Cooked whole or in fillets, it has a white, delicately flavoured flesh. Available all year round, depending on the variety.

Oily Fish

Oily fish such as sardines, mackerel, salmon and herring have a higher fat content than white fish but are an excellent source of Omega-3 polyunsaturated fatty acids, important in fighting heart disease, cancers and arthritis. Oily fish also contain niacin, B6, B12 and D vitamins and selenium, iodine, potassium and phosphorous minerals. The flavour is stronger and more robust, enabling stronger flavours such as chilli and garlic to be used. It is recommended that at least one portion of oily fish should be eaten each week.

Herring Sea fish. Suitable for frying, grilling/broiling or preserving in vinegar to make rollmops. A small fish with creamy-coloured flesh and fairly strong flavour, herrings contain many bones. At its best in spring and summer.

Mackerel Sea fish. Suitable for grilling and frying, whilst whole fish can be stuffed or baked. Has a distinctive bluish-coloured skin with blue/black lines and a creamy underside. At its best from late spring to early summer in the UK, or September to November in the USA.

Pilchard Sea fish. Normally sold canned but fresh pilchards are sometimes available. Similar to herring but smaller. Caught off the English Cornish coast all year round, as well as in South America.

Salmon Freshwater fish. The whole fish is suitable for poaching or baking to serve hot or cold. Fillets or cutlets can be fried, grilled, baked, steamed or barbecued. Farmed salmon has a milder flavour than wild, and the deep pink flesh is not as firm as that of wild salmon. The smaller wild salmon is much paler in colour, with a far superior flavour and texture. Nowadays farmed salmon is available all year round – wild salmon is at its best from February to August.

Sardine Sea fish. Suitable for grilling or frying. Sardines are young pilchards, sprats or herrings. Available all year round.

Sprat Sea fish. Suitable for frying or grilling. A small fish similar to herring and at its best from November to March. Not fished in the USA.

Brown trout Freshwater fish. Suitable for grilling or frying. The darker pink/red flesh is considered to be better than that of rainbow trout. At its best from March to September. Not fished in the USA.

Rainbow trout Freshwater fish. Suitable for grilling, frying, poaching and baking. Can be cooked whole or in fillets. Has a delicate pale pink flesh. Available all year round.

Salmon trout Freshwater fish. Suitable for poaching or baking whole. Cutlets or fillets can be fried, grilled or griddled. At its best from March to August. Treat as for salmon. Has a pinker flesh than salmon and the flavour is not as good.

Tuna Sea fish (mostly). Suitable for all methods of cooking. Does not count as an oily fish when canned. Available all year round.

Seafood

Crustaceans, such as lobsters, have hard shells which they shed and replace during their lifetime. Molluscs are animals that have hinged shells, such as scallops, or single shells, such as whelks. This term also includes cephalopods such as squid, cuttlefish and octopus.

Clams Available all year round but best in September. Usually eaten raw like oysters, or cook as for mussels.

Cockles Available all year round, but best in September. Normally eaten cooked. Eat plain with vinegar or use in recipes such as paella.

Crab Best from May to August, but also available canned and frozen. Normally sold ready-cooked either whole or as dressed crab.

Crayfish/crawfish Available from September to May. Resemble mini-lobsters and have a delicate flavour.

Mussels Best from September to March, but available most of the year due to farming. Normally sold live and can be eaten raw or cooked.

Oysters Available from September to April. Usually eaten raw on day of purchase, but can be cooked. Must be eaten absolutely fresh.

Dublin Bay prawns Small prawn-like lobster. Also known as langoustines and scampi (not to be confused with the fried prawns known as scampi). Available all year round. Sold live or cooked. Other large prawns are often confused for them.

Tiger prawns Available all year round, raw or cooked. Just one of many varieties of large prawns that are now imported. They are grey when raw and turn pink once cooked. Use within one day of purchasing if live or thawed.

Shrimp/prawns Available all year round, fresh or frozen. Shrimp are the smaller of the two and are not used as much in everyday cooking. Shrimp are brown in colour prior to cooking and prawns are grey, both turning pink once cooked.

Scallops Best from October to March, but available frozen all year. Usually sold live on the shell, but can be bought off the shell, often frozen. Scallops have a bright orange core which is edible. Serve cooked.

Squid/octopus Available all year round, sold fresh but previously frozen. Their black ink is often used in sauces and is also used to make black pasta.

Whelks Best from September to February. Usually sold cooked and shelled and served with vinegar.

Winkles/periwinkles Best from October to May in the UK, and May to November in the USA. Can be sold cooked or raw. Normally served cooked and with vinegar.

Vegetables & Salads

Vegetables add colour, texture, flavour and valuable nutrients to a meal. They play an important role in the diet, providing necessary vitamins, minerals and fibre. Vegetables are versatile: they can be served as an accompaniment to other dishes – they go well with meat, poultry and fish – or they can be used as the basis for the whole meal. There is a huge range of fresh vegetables on sale today in supermarkets, greengrocers and local markets. Also available is a growing selection of fresh organic produce, plus a wide variety of seasonal pick-your-own vegetables from specialist farms. For enthusiastic gardeners, a vast range of vegetable seeds are available. In addition, the increase in ethnic markets has introduced an extensive choice of exotic vegetables, such as chayote and breadfruit. With improved refrigeration and transport networks, vegetables are now flown around the world resulting in year-round availability.

Vegetables are classified into different groups: leaf vegetables; roots and tubers; beans, pods and shoots; bulb vegetables; fruit vegetables; brassicas; cucumbers and squashes; sea vegetables; and mushrooms.

Leaf Vegetables

This includes lettuce and other salad leaves, such as oakleaf, frisée, radicchio/chicory leaf, lamb's lettuce and lollo rosso as well as rocket/arugula, spinach, Swiss chard and watercress. These are available all year round as most are now grown under glass. Many leaf vegetables, such as watercress and spinach, are delicious cooked and made into soups.

Roots and Tubers

This group includes beetroot/beet, carrots, celeriac, daikon, Jerusalem artichokes, parsnips, potatoes, radish, salsify, scorzonera, sweet potatoes, swede/rutabaga, turnip and yam. Most are available all year round.

Beans, Pods and Shoots

This category includes all the beans, such as broad/fava beans, French/green beans, mangetout/snow peas and runner/string beans as well as peas and sweetcorn/corn, baby corn and okra. Shoots include asparagus, bamboo shoots, celery, chicory (root), fennel, globe artichokes and palm hearts. The majority are available all year round.

Bulb Vegetables

This is the onion family and includes all the different types of onion, from the common brown-skinned globe onion, Italian red onion and Spanish onion to shallots, pickling onions, pearl onions and spring onions/scallions. This category also includes leeks, chives and garlic. All are available throughout the year.

Fruit Vegetables

This group originates from hot climates like the Mediterranean, such as aubergines/eggplants, avocados, chilli peppers, sweet peppers and tomatoes. These are available all year round but are more plentiful in the summer.

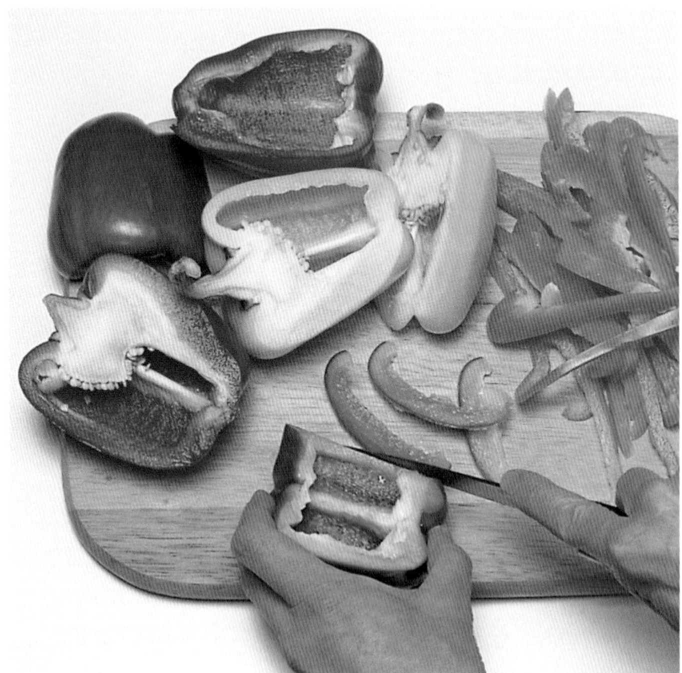

Brassicas

This is the cabbage family and includes all the different types of cabbage, broccoli, Brussels sprouts, cauliflower, curly kale, Chinese cabbage, pak choi/bok choy and purple sprouting broccoli. Some of the cabbages are only seasonal, such as Savoy cabbage and red cabbage, while summer cabbages are available only during the summer months.

Cucumbers and Squashes

These vegetables are members of the gourd family and include cucumbers, gherkins/pickles, pumpkins and other squashes. There are two types of squash – summer squashes, which include courgettes/zucchini, larger marrows and pattypan/white squashes, and winter squashes such as pumpkins and butternut, acorn, gem and spaghetti squashes. Courgettes/zucchini and cucumbers are available all through the year, but pumpkins and other winter squashes and marrow are seasonal.

Sea Vegetables

The vegetables from this group may be quite difficult to find in supermarkets. The most readily available are seaweed (normally available dried) and sea kale.

Mushrooms and Fungi

This category includes all the different types of mushroom: the cultivated button mushrooms, chestnut mushrooms, large portobello or flat mushrooms, oyster and shiitake mushrooms, as well as wild mushrooms such as ceps/porcini, morels, chanterelles and truffles. Cultivated mushrooms are available throughout the year but wild ones are only around from late summer. If you collect your own wild mushrooms, make sure you correctly identify them before picking, as some are very poisonous and can be fatal if eaten. Dried mushrooms are also available, including ceps, morels and oyster mushrooms. They add a good flavour to a dish, but need to be re-constituted before use.

Buying and Storage

When buying fresh vegetables, always look for ones that are bright and feel firm to the touch and avoid any that are damaged or bruised. Choose onions and garlic that are hard and not sprouting and avoid ones that are soft, as they may be damaged. Salad leaves and other leaf vegetables should be fresh, bright and crisp – do not buy any that are wilted, look limp or have yellow leaves. Vegetables such as peas and beans do not keep for very long, so try to eat them as soon as possible after buying or picking. Most vegetables can be stored in a cool, dry place that is frost-free, such as a larder or garage. Green vegetables, fruit vegetables and salad leaves should be kept in the salad drawer of the refrigerator, while root vegetables, tuber vegetables and winter squashes should be kept in a cool, dark place. Winter squashes can be kept for several months if stored correctly.

Preparation

Always clean vegetables thoroughly before using. Brush or scrape off any dirt and wash well in cold water. Wash lettuce and other salad leaves gently under cold running water and tear rather than cut the leaves. Dry thoroughly in a salad spinner or on kitchen paper/paper towels before use, otherwise the leaves tend to wilt. Spinach should be washed thoroughly to remove all traces of dirt. Cut off and discard any tough stalks and damaged leaves. Wash leaf vegetables and salad leaves well, then pull off and discard any tough stalks or outer leaves. Leeks need to be thoroughly cleaned before use to remove any grit and dirt. Most mushrooms just need wiping with a damp cloth. Prepare the vegetables just before cooking, as once peeled they lose nutrients. Do not leave them in water, as valuable water-soluble vitamins will be lost.

Cooking Techniques

Vegetables can be cooked in a variety of different ways, such as baking, barbecuing, blanching, boiling, braising, deep-frying, grilling/broiling, roasting, sautéing, steaming and stir-frying.

Boiling Always cook vegetables in a minimum amount of water and do not over-cook, or valuable nutrients will be lost. It is best to cut vegetables into even-sized pieces and briefly cook them in a small amount of water.

Blanching and parboiling These mean lightly cooking raw vegetables for a brief period of time, whether parboiling potatoes before roasting, cooking cabbage before braising or cooking leaf vegetables such as spinach. Spinach should be cooked in only the water clinging to its leaves for 2–3 minutes, or until wilted. Blanching is also used to remove skins easily from tomatoes. Cut a small cross in the top of the tomato and place in a heat-proof bowl. Cover with boiling water and leave for a few seconds, then drain and peel off the skin.

Braising This method is a slow way of cooking certain vegetables, notably cabbage and leeks. The vegetable is simmered for a long period of time in a small amount of stock or water.

Deep-frying This method is suitable for most vegetables except leafy ones. The vegetables can be cut into small pieces, coated in batter, then deep-fried briefly in hot oil.

Grilling/broiling For peppers, aubergines/eggplants and tomatoes, brush them with a little oil first, as they quickly dry out. To remove the skins from peppers/bell peppers, cut them in half lengthways and deseed. Place them skin-side up on the grill/broiler rack under a pre-heated hot grill/broiler and cook until the skins are blackened and blistered. Remove with tongs and place in a polythene/plastic bag, which will retain moisture. Seal and leave until the peppers/bell peppers are cool enough to handle. Once cool, remove from the bag and carefully peel away the blackened skin.

Roasting Suitable for vegetables such as fennel, courgettes/zucchini, pumpkin, squash, peppers, garlic, aubergines/eggplants and tomatoes. Cut the vegetables into even-sized chunks. Heat some oil in a roasting tin/pan in a preheated oven at 200°C/400°F/Gas Mark 6. Put the vegetables in the hot oil, baste, and roast in the oven for 30 minutes. Garlic can be split into different cloves or whole heads can be roasted. It is best not to peel them until cooked.

Steaming This is a great way to cook vegetables such as broccoli, cauliflower, beans, carrots, parsnips and peas. Fill a large saucepan with about 5 cm/2 inches water. Cut the vegetables into even-sized pieces, place in a metal steamer basket and lower into the saucepan, then cover and steam until tender. Alternatively, use a plate standing on a trivet in the pan. Do not let the water boil – it should just simmer. Once tender, refresh under cold running water. Asparagus is traditionally cooked in an asparagus steamer.

Health and Nutrition

Vegetables contain many essential nutrients and are especially high in vitamins A, B and C. They contain important minerals, in particular iron and calcium, and are also low in fat, high in fibre and have low cholesterol value. Red and orange vegetables, such as peppers and carrots, and dark green vegetables, such as broccoli, contain excellent anti-cancer properties as well as helping to prevent heart disease. Current healthy eating guidelines suggest that at least five portions of fruit and vegetables should be eaten per day, with vegetables being the more essential.

Sauces

White Pouring Sauce

Makes 300 ml/½ pint/1¼ cups

15 g/½ oz/1 tbsp butter or margarine
2 tbsp plain/all-purpose white flour
300 ml/½ pint/1¼ cups milk
salt and freshly ground black pepper

Melt the butter or margarine in a small saucepan and stir in the flour. Cook, stirring, over a gentle heat for 2 minutes, then draw off the heat and gradually stir in the milk. Return to the heat and cook, stirring with a wooden spoon, until the sauce thickens and coats the back of the spoon. Add seasoning to taste and use as required.

For a coating sauce, use 25 g/1 oz/¼ stick butter or margarine and 3 tablespoons flour to 300 ml/½ pint/1¼ cups liquid. Proceed as above.

For a binding sauce, use 50 g/2 oz/½ stick butter or margarine and 50 g/2 oz/½ cup flour to 300 ml/½ pint/1¼ cups liquid and proceed as above.

Cheese Sauce

Proceed as before, depending on which consistency is required, stirring in 1 tsp dried mustard powder with the flour. When the sauce has thickened, remove from the heat and stir in 50 g/2 oz mature Cheddar cheese, grated, or any other cheese of choice. Stir until melted.

Herb Sauce

Make a white sauce as before, then stir in 1 tbsp freshly chopped herbs, such as parsley, basil, oregano or a mixture of fresh herbs.

Mushroom Sauce

Make as before and lightly sauté 50 g/2 oz/1½ cups sliced mushrooms in 15 g/½ oz/1 tbsp butter for 3 minutes or until tender. Drain and stir into the prepared white sauce.

Bechamel Sauce

Makes 300 ml/½ pint/1¼ cups

Peel 1 small onion and place in a small saucepan together with a small piece of peeled carrot, a small celery stalk, 3 whole cloves and a few black peppercorns. Add 300 ml/½ pint/1¼ cups milk and bring slowly to just below boiling point. Remove from the heat, cover with a lid and leave to infuse for at least 30 minutes. When ready to use, strain off the milk and use to make a white sauce as before. If liked, 1–2 tablespoons single/light cream can be stirred in at the end of cooking.

Gravy

Makes 300 ml/½ pint/1¼ cups

When roasting meat, once the meat is cooked, remove from the roasting tin/pan, cover and keep warm. Pour off all but 2–3 tablespoons of the meat juices and heat on the hob. Stir in 2 tablespoons plain white/all-purpose flour and cook for 2 minutes, stirring the sediment that is left in the tin/pan into the gravy. Draw off the heat and gradually stir in 300 ml/½ pint/1¼ cups stock, according to the flavour of the meat. Return to the heat and cook, stirring, until the gravy comes to the boil and thickens. Add seasoning to taste and, if liked, a little port, wine or redcurrant jelly. Gravy browning can be added to give a darker colour.

If no meat juices are available, heat 2 tablespoons oil and stir in 1–2 tablespoons flour. Cook for 2 minutes then draw off the heat and stir in 300 ml/½ pint/1¼ cups stock of your choice. Return to the heat and cook, stirring, until thickened. Add seasoning, flavourings and gravy browning according to personal preference.

Tomato Sauce

Makes 450 ml/¾ pint/1¾ cups

1 tbsp olive or sunflower oil
1 small onion, peeled and finely chopped
1–2 garlic cloves, peeled and crushed
50 g/2 oz streaky bacon, chopped (optional)
4 ripe tomatoes, peeled if preferred, chopped or 400 g/14 oz can chopped tomatoes
1–2 tbsp tomato purée/paste
150 ml/¼ pint/⅔ cup vegetable stock
salt and freshly ground black pepper
1 tbsp freshly chopped oregano, marjoram or basil

Heat the oil in a saucepan and sauté the onion, garlic and bacon, if using, for 5 minutes. Add the chopped tomatoes and sauté for a further 5 minutes, stirring occasionally. Blend the tomato purée/paste with the stock then pour into the pan, add seasoning and herbs and bring to the boil. Cover with a lid, reduce the heat and simmer for 12–15 minutes or until a chunky sauce is formed. Blend in a food processor to form a slightly less chunky sauce, and then rub through a fine sieve/strainer if a smooth sauce is preferred. Adjust seasoning and use as required.

Curry Sauce

Makes 300 ml/½ pint/1¼ cups

1 tbsp sunflower oil
1 onion, peeled, chopped
2–4 garlic cloves, peeled and crushed
1 celery stalk, trimmed and chopped
1–2 red chillies, deseeded and chopped
1 tsp ground coriander
1 tsp ground cumin
½ tsp turmeric
1 tbsp plain/all-purpose white flour
450 ml/¾ pint/1¾ cups vegetable stock
salt and freshly ground black pepper
1 tbsp freshly chopped coriander/cilantro (optional)

Heat the oil in a saucepan and sauté the onion, garlic, celery and chillies for 5–8 minutes or until softened. Add the spices and continue to sauté for a further 3 minutes, stirring frequently. Sprinkle in the flour, cook for 2 minutes, then slowly add the stock and bring to the boil. Cover with a lid, reduce the heat and simmer for 15 minutes, stirring occasionally. Add seasoning to taste and stir in the chopped coriander/cilantro, if using. Use as required.

Apple Sauce

Makes 300 ml/½ pint/1¼ cups

450 g/1 lb Bramley/tart cooking apples, peeled, cored and chopped
15 g/½ oz/1 tbsp butter
2–3 tbsp sugar

Place all the ingredients with 2 tablespoons water in a saucepan and cook over a gentle heat for 10 minutes, or until the apples are tender, stirring occasionally. Take care that the apples do not burn on the base of the pan. Remove from the heat and either rub through a sieve/strainer to form a smooth purée or beat with the spoon to give a chunkier sauce. The apple sauce can be flavoured with 1 tablespoon finely grated orange or lemon rind and 2–3 whole cloves, which you should remove before serving. Alternatively, add 1 lightly bruised cinnamon stick (remove before serving).

Mint Sauce

Makes 120 ml/4 fl oz/½ cup

15 g/½ oz/¾ cup fresh mint
1 tbsp caster/superfine sugar
3–4 tbsp white wine vinegar or other vinegar of choice

Discard the stalks from the mint, rinse the leaves and dry. Finely chop and place in a sauceboat or small bowl. Pour over 3–4 tablespoons hot, but not boiling, water, then stir in the sugar until dissolved. Stir in the vinegar and use as required.

Cranberry Sauce

450 g/1 lb fresh or thawed frozen cranberries
150 ml/¼ pint/⅔ cup orange juice
50 g/2 oz/¼ cup light muscovado/golden brown sugar, or to taste
1–2 tbsp port (optional)

Rinse the cranberries and place in a saucepan with the orange juice and sugar. Place over a gentle heat and cook, stirring occasionally, for 12–15 minutes, or until the cranberries are soft and have popped. Remove from the heat and stir in the port, if using. Use as required.

French Dressing

Makes 175 ml/6 fl oz/¾ cup

½ tsp dried mustard powder
½–1 tsp caster/superfine sugar, or to taste
salt and freshly ground black pepper
3 tbsp white wine vinegar
120 ml/4 fl oz/½ cup extra virgin olive oil

Place all the ingredients in a screw top jar and shake vigorously. Use as required.

Other flavours can be made by substituting the vinegar: try raspberry, cider or balsamic vinegar with a little clear honey in place of the sugar. Replace the dried mustard powder with 1 teaspoon wholegrain mustard. Freshly chopped herbs can also be added to the dressing.

Mayonnaise

Makes 175 ml/6 fl ox/¾ cup

1 egg yolk
¼ tsp dried mustard powder
salt and freshly ground black pepper
½ tsp caster/superfine sugar
150 ml/¼ pint/⅔ cup extra virgin olive oil
1 tbsp white wine vinegar or lemon juice

Place the egg yolk in a bowl and stir in the mustard powder with a little seasoning and the sugar. Beat with a wooden spoon until blended, then gradually add the oil, drop by drop, stirring briskly with either a whisk or wooden spoon. If the mixture becomes too thick, beat in a little of the vinegar or lemon juice. When all the oil has been added, stir in the remaining vinegar or lemon juice and adjust the seasoning. Store, covered, in the refrigerator until required.

If the mayonnaise should curdle whilst being made, place a further egg in a separate bowl then slowly beat in the curdled mixture.

Tartare Sauce

Makes 175 ml/6 fl oz/¾ cup

150 ml/¼ pint/⅔ cup prepared mayonnaise
1 tbsp freshly chopped tarragon
1 tbsp freshly chopped parsley
1 tbsp capers, rinsed and chopped
1 tbsp finely chopped gherkins/pickles
1 tbsp lemon juice

Mix all the ingredients together. Place in a small bowl, cover and leave for at least 30 minutes for the flavours to blend.

Chocolate Sauce

Makes 150 ml/¼ pint/⅔ cup

100 g/3½ oz/4 squares plain dark/unsweetened chocolate
15 g/½ oz/1 tbsp butter
1 tsp golden or corn syrup
5 tbsp semi-skimmed/low-fat milk

Break the chocolate into small pieces and place in a small, heavy-based saucepan. Add the remaining ingredients and place over a gentle heat, stirring occasionally, until smooth. Pour into a small jug and use as required.

Butterscotch Sauce

Makes 300 ml/½ pint/1¼ cups

75 g/3 oz/⅓ cup light muscovado/golden brown sugar
1 tbsp golden or corn syrup
50 g/2 oz/½ stick butter
200 ml/7 fl oz/¾ cup single/light cream

Place the sugar, syrup and butter in a heavy-based saucepan and heat gently, stirring occasionally, until blended. Stir in the cream and continue to heat, stirring, until the sauce is smooth. Use as required.

Syrup Sauce

Makes 150 ml/¼ pint/⅔ cup

5 tbsp golden or corn syrup
2 tbsp lemon juice
1 tbsp arrowroot

Pour the syrup and lemon juice into a small pan and add 3 tablespoons water. Bring to the boil. Blend the arrowroot with 1 tablespoon water, then stir into the boiling syrup. Cook, stirring, until the sauce thickens and clears. Serve.

Lemon Sauce

Makes 150 ml/¼ pint/⅔ cup

grated rind of 1 large lemon, preferably unwaxed
5 tbsp fresh lemon juice, strained

2 tbsp caster/superfine sugar
1 tbsp arrowroot
knob of butter

Place the lemon rind and juice in a saucepan with 4 tablespoons water. Stir in the sugar and heat, stirring, until the sugar has dissolved. Bring to the boil. Blend the arrowroot with 1 tablespoon water, then blend into the boiling sauce. Cook, stirring, until the sauce thickens and clears. Add the butter and cook for a further 1 minute. Note that an orange can be used in place of the lemon, or a combination of the two.

Melba Sauce

Makes 300 ml/½ pint/1¼ cups

350 g/12 oz/2 cups fresh or thawed frozen raspberries
3 tbsp sugar, or to taste
1 tbsp lemon or orange juice

Clean the raspberries, if using fresh, then place all the ingredients and 4 tablespoons water in a heavy-based saucepan and place over a gentle heat. Bring to the boil, then reduce the heat and simmer for 5–8 minutes, or until the fruits are really soft. Remove from the heat, cool slightly, then blend in a food processor to form a purée. Rub through a fine sieve/strainer to remove the pips and use as required.

Jam/Jelly Sauce

Makes 150 ml/¼ pint/⅔ cup

4 tbsp jam/jelly, such as raspberry, apricot, strawberry or marmalade
150 ml/¼ pint/⅔ cup fruit juice or water
1 tbsp arrowroot
1 tbsp lemon juice

Place the jam/jelly and the fruit juice or water in a small pan and heat, stirring, until blended. Rub through a fine sieve/strainer to remove any pips, return to the pan and bring to the boil. Blend the arrowroot with the lemon juice and stir into the sauce. Cook, stirring, until the sauce thickens and clears. For a thicker sauce, use half the amount of fruit juice or water.

Custard

Makes 300 ml/½ pint/1¼ cups

300 ml/½ pint/1¼ cups milk
2 tbsp plain/all-purpose white flour
1 egg
few drops vanilla essence/extract
15 g/½ oz/1 tbsp butter
1–2 tbsp caster/superfine sugar, or to taste

Heat the milk to lukewarm. Sift the flour into a bowl, make a well in the centre and add the egg. Beat the egg into the flour, drawing the flour in from the sides of the bowl and slowly adding half the warmed milk. When all the flour has been incorporated, beat well to remove any lumps then stir in the remaining milk. Strain into a clean saucepan and place over a gentle heat and cook, stirring, until the sauce thickens and coats the back of the wooden spoon. Stir in the vanilla essence/extract, butter and sugar to taste. Stir until blended and use as required.

Stocks

Chicken Stock

Makes 900 ml/1½ pints/3¾ cups

1 cooked chicken carcass
1 onion, peeled, cut into wedges
1 large carrot, peeled, chopped
1 celery stalk, trimmed, chopped
1 bouquet garni
10 peppercorns
4 whole cloves, salt to taste

Remove any large pieces of meat from the carcass and use as required. Break the carcass into small pieces and place in a large saucepan. Add the vegetables, bouquet garni and spices with 1.2 litres/2 pints/1¼ quarts water and bring to the boil. Cover with a lid, reduce the heat and simmer for 2 hours. If the liquid is evaporating too quickly, reduce the heat under the pan. Cool, strain and allow to cool fully before storing, covered, in the refrigerator. Store for up to 3 days. Bring to the boil and simmer for 5 minutes before re-using. Freeze if desired in small, lidded, freezer-safe tubs.

Beef Stock

Makes 900 ml/1½ pints/3¾ cups

450 g/1 lb beef bones, chopped into small chunks
250 g/12 oz shin of beef, fat discarded, cut into small chunks
1 onion, peeled, cut into wedges
1 large carrot, peeled, cut into chunks
1 celery stalk, trimmed, chopped
1 bouquet garni
12 black peppercorns
salt to taste

Place the bones and beef in a roasting tin/pan and cook in an oven preheated to 200°C/400°F/Gas Mark 6 for 20, minutes or until sealed and browned. Remove, place in a large saucepan with the remaining ingredients and 1.2 litres/2 pints/1¼ quarts water and bring to the boil. cover with a lid, reduce the heat and simmer very gently for 4 hours. Strain and add salt to taste. Cool, then skim off any fat that rises to the surface. Store in the refrigerator for up to 3 days, boiling for 5 minutes before using. Alternatively, freeze in small, lidded, freezer-safe tubs.

Vegetable Stock

Makes 900 ml/1½ pints/3¾ cups

1 tbsp sunflower oil
1 onion, peeled, cut into wedges
1 large carrot, peeled, chopped
2 celery stalks, trimmed, chopped
1 small turnip, peeled, chopped (optional)
2 bay leaves
10 black peppercorns
3 whole cloves
salt to taste

Heat the oil in a large saucepan and sauté the vegetables for 8 minutes, stirring frequently. Add the bay leaves with the spices and 1.2 litres/2 pints/1¼ quarts water and bring to the boil. Cover with a lid, reduce the heat and simmer for 40 minutes. Strain the stock and add salt to taste. Cool, cover and store in the refrigerator for up to 3 days. Alternatively, freeze in small, lidded, freezer-safe tubs.

Fish Stock

Makes 600 ml/1 pint/2½ cups

fish bones or 1 cod's head
1 onion, peeled, cut into wedges
1 celery stalk, trimmed, chopped
1 bouquet garni
salt and freshly ground black pepper

Thoroughly wash the fish bones or cod's head and place in a large saucepan with the vegetables and bouquet garni. Add 900 ml/1½ pints/3¾ cups water and bring to the boil. Cover with a lid, reduce the heat and simmer for 30 minutes. Strain and add seasoning to taste, then cool and store in the refrigerator for up to 2 days, bringing to the boil and simmering steadily for 5 minutes before using. If desired, freeze in small, lidded, freezer-safe tubs.

Bouquet Garni

1 celery stalk
2 bay leaves
2 parsley sprigs
1 thyme sprig
1 sage sprig

Cut the celery stalk in half and rinse the herbs. Place the herbs on top of one piece of celery and place the second piece of celery on top. Tie securely and use as required.

Entertaining

There are many ways of entertaining friends and family and, whether it is an informal or formal occasion, there are some rules that can be applied to all entertaining that will help to make life easy for the host and hostess.

First of all, decide what kind of entertaining you wish to do: dinner party, supper, barbecue, picnic, cheese and wine party or even a disco. This will dictate how formal the event will be. These days, parties tend to be far more informal and relaxed than they once were, but even so it is still advisable to be guided by a few rules.

Make Life Easy

- Decide how many guests to invite and check their dietary requirements – are they vegetarian, do they have allergies to certain foods or have specific likes or dislikes?
- Choose the venue and menu and decide on the drinks to serve, ensuring that there are plenty of soft drinks for those driving.
- Make a shopping list ahead of time. This will allow for non-perishable foods to be bought early, as well as leaving time for a change of menu, if necessary.
- Check china, cutlery/silverware, glasses and table linen. Make sure that it is clean and you have sufficient for all the guests.
- If it helps, work out a time plan early on. This will enable you to cook ahead if possible, thus saving time and effort on the day.
- If trying a new recipe, it is advisable to cook it beforehand to ensure that it works and tastes good.
- Arrange flowers the day before. Ensure you have nibbles and appetizers to serve, and stock up on ice, mixer drinks, lemons and glasses. Make sure you have plenty of coffee, tea or other after-dinner drinks.

Menu Planning for Different Occasions

Drinks/Cocktail Parties

These are normally semi-informal and, unless you serve very expensive wines or Champagne, relatively cheap. Although food is not served as at an actual meal, it is a good idea to serve some light starters/first courses. This will help to offset too much alcohol. People tend to eat more than you might think and it is a good idea to offer at least four or five different snacks as well as nuts, crisps/chips and little biscuits/crackers. Try to offer at least two vegetarian choices.

Try serving bite-sized vol-au-vents/hollow pastries, filled with peeled prawns/shrimp in a flavoured mayonnaise or chicken and sweetcorn. Small squares of quiche are good, or try roasted peppers with blue cheese. Smoked salmon and asparagus rolls, in both white and brown bread, cocktail sausages on sticks with a sweet chilli dip and chicken satay on sticks with satay sauces are all fairly straightforward. Hand round either small napkins or plates so guests can take a few at a time and do not spill the food on themselves or your furniture.

Keep drinks simple – do not offer everything. People are quite happy with a limited choice; red or white wine and beer with plenty of soft drinks is perfectly acceptable, or in winter try a warming punch. Fruity punch or Pimm's in the summer is an ideal choice.

Formal Dinner Party

These take a little more planning, both in terms of which guests to invite and the food. When working out the invitations, ensure that all your guests will get on well together and that there is at least one thing they have in common. Always remember to check their dietary requirements. Dinner parties can consist of as many courses as wished. If offering more than three, ensure that all the courses complement each other and that the portions are not too large. Invite guests to arrive at least 30 minutes before you hope to sit down – this allows for guests arriving late.

Menus should be balanced: normally, the dinner should start with a soup or small appetizer, and fish can be served either as the main course or as a second course as a prelude to the meat or poultry. Cheese and dessert are served after the main course; it is a matter of personal preference which is served first.

Supper, Lunch or Brunch Parties

These are normally much more informal and spur-of-the-moment events. However, a little planning is an excellent idea so that the host or hostess does not spend the entire time dashing around, making both themselves and the guests stressed while trying to ensure that everyone enjoys the occasion.

Obviously, the menu will depend on the time of year and the ages of those involved. Younger people are more than happy with fast food such as pizza or baked chicken pieces, with plenty of crisps/chips and oven-baked chips/fries or a large bowl of pasta.

Try a theme for your party, such as Italian or Oriental. There are many excellent Chinese and pasta dishes in this book to choose from.

Barbecue Parties

Because the weather is not always reliable, barbecues have to be fairly impromptu, meaning that the food needs to be simple and adaptable. Depending on tastes, keep the food quick and easy to prepare – the best choices are steak, chicken pieces, small whole fish such as sardines, and sausages, all of which can be cooked whole or cut into cubes, skewered and marinated to make kebabs/kabobs. These cook quickly and will be ready in a very short time. Serve plenty of salads and bread. If cooking chicken portions that still contain the bones, it is advisable to cook them in the oven first and finish them on the barbecue to ensure that the chicken is thoroughly cooked through.

When barbecuing, it is vital that the food is cooked properly – semi-cooked sausages and chicken are one of the main causes of stomach upsets. If using a barbecue that uses coal, light it in plenty of time (at least 20 minutes before required) to allow the coals to reach the correct temperature before starting to cook. The coals should be white/grey in colour and coated in ash, and the flames should have died down to give a good, steady heat.

Eating outside often sharpens the appetite, so along with the meats serve plenty of bread or potatoes with assorted salads. Coleslaw and rice and pasta salads all work well. Keep desserts and drinks simple: fresh fruit, ice cream or cheese with wine or beer to drink.

Children's Parties

The highlight of any child's year is their birthday party and, to avoid tears, a little planning is a good idea. Many companies now offer a complete service so that the children can participate in an activity, such as skating, football or swimming, then the birthday tea is provided and all that is expected of the parents is to take and collect. This is by far one of the easiest and least stressful ways to celebrate their day, but can be expensive.

If that is not for you, above all keep it simple, whether you hold the party at home or in a local hall. First, decide on a date and venue and how long the party will be. Send out the invitations in plenty of time, stating clearly what time it will finish – most important for your sanity. Enlist the help of at least two other adults who are used to dealing with tears and tantrums. Decide on a few games, depending on age, such as pass the parcel or hot potato, pin the tail on the donkey, musical chairs or blind man's bluff. Clear away furniture and any breakable ornaments and ensure that no sharp objects are in easy reach of little fingers.

Serve the food in a separate room and keep it fairly plain. Too much rich food could result in a few children being ill. Go for simple sandwiches, small pieces of cheese with grapes, sausages, sausage rolls, crisps/chips, cup cakes and, of course, a birthday cake. Serve fruit juice to drink.

Many parties finish with the guests being issued with a goodie bag to take home. If you do this, keep it simple: a few sweets/some candy, a piece of birthday cake and two or three very small gifts is perfectly acceptable. There is no need to spend a lot of money on these.

Soups & Starters

Fuel your family with these nutritious, hearty soups. From classics, such as Tomato & Basil, to something new, like Coconut Chicken, there is something to suit every taste. The starter recipes can be served as healthy snacks, light lunches or appetizers – recipes such as Sweetcorn Fritters and Mixed Satay Sticks are so delicious you will look for any opportunity to make them.

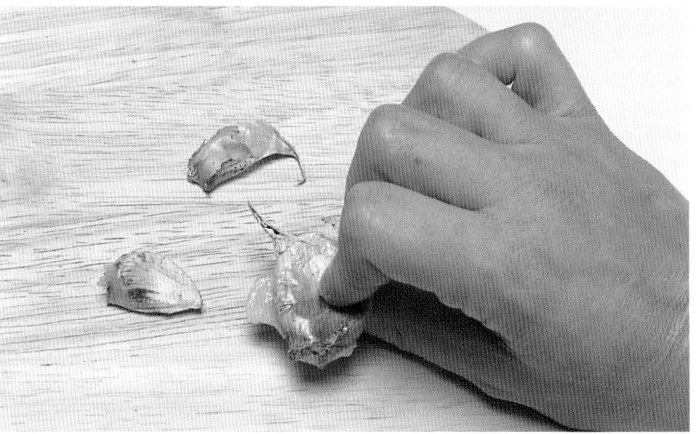

Tomato & Basil Soup

Serves 4

Ingredients

7 ripe tomatoes, cut in half
2 garlic cloves, unpeeled
1 tsp olive oil
1 tbsp balsamic vinegar
1 tbsp dark brown sugar
1 tbsp tomato puree/paste
300 ml/½ pint/1¼ cups vegetable stock
6 tbsp low-fat natural/plain yogurt
2 tbsp freshly chopped basil
salt and freshly ground black pepper
small basil leaves, to garnish

Preheat the oven to 200°C/400°F/Gas Mark 6. Evenly spread the tomatoes and garlic in a single layer in a large roasting tin/pan.

Mix the oil and vinegar together. Drizzle over the tomatoes and sprinkle with the dark brown sugar.

Roast the tomatoes in the preheated oven for 20 minutes until tender and lightly charred in places.

Remove from the oven and allow to cool slightly. When cool enough to handle, squeeze the softened flesh of the garlic from the papery skins. Place with the charred tomatoes in a nylon sieve/strainer over a saucepan.

Press the garlic and tomato through the sieve with the back of a wooden spoon. When all the flesh has been sieved, add the tomato puree/paste and vegetable stock to the pan. Heat gently, stirring occasionally.

In a small bowl, beat the yogurt and basil together and season to taste with salt and pepper. Stir the basil yogurt into the soup. Garnish with basil leaves and serve immediately.

Health Rating: 5 points

Carrot & Ginger Soup

Serves 4

Ingredients

4 slices bread, crusts removed
1 tsp yeast extract
2 tsp olive oil
1 onion, peeled and chopped
1 garlic clove, peeled and crushed
½ tsp ground ginger
6 carrots, peeled, chopped
1 litre/1¾ pints/1 quart vegetable stock
2.5 cm/1 inch piece root ginger, peeled and finely grated
salt and freshly ground black pepper
1 tbsp lemon juice

To garnish:
chives
lemon zest/rind

Preheat the oven to 180°C/350°F/Gas Mark 4. Roughly chop the bread. Dissolve the yeast extract in 2 tablespoons warm water and mix with the bread.

Spread the bread cubes over a lightly oiled baking sheet and bake for 20 minutes, turning halfway through. Remove from the oven and reserve.

Heat the oil in a large saucepan. Gently cook the onion and garlic for 3–4 minutes.

Stir in the ground ginger and cook for 1 minute to release the flavour.

Add the chopped carrots, then stir in the stock and the fresh ginger. Simmer gently for 15 minutes.

Remove from the heat and allow to cool a little. Blend until smooth, then season to taste with salt and pepper. Stir in the lemon juice. Garnish with the chives and lemon zest/rind and serve immediately with the garlic croutons.

Health Rating: 5 points

Rice & Tomato Soup

Serves 4

Ingredients

150 g/5 oz/heaping 3/4 cup easy-cook basmati rice
400 g can/1 3/4 cups chopped tomatoes
2 garlic cloves, peeled and crushed
grated zest/rind of 1/2 lime
2 tbsp extra virgin olive oil
1 tsp sugar
salt and freshly ground black pepper
300 ml/1/2 pint/1 1/4 cups vegetable stock or water

For the croutons:
2 tbsp prepared pesto sauce
2 tbsp olive oil
6 thin slices ciabatta bread, cut into 1 cm/1/2 inch cubes

Preheat the oven to 220°C/425°F/Gas Mark 7. Rinse and drain the basmati rice. Place the canned tomatoes with their juice in a large, heavy-based saucepan with the garlic, lime rind, oil and sugar. Season to taste with salt and pepper. Bring to the boil, then reduce the heat, cover and simmer for 10 minutes.

Add the boiling vegetable stock or water and the rice, then cook, uncovered, for a further 15–20 minutes or until the rice is tender. If the soup is too thick, add a little more water. Reserve and keep warm, if the croutons are not ready.

Meanwhile, to make the croutons, mix the pesto and olive oil in a large bowl. Add the bread cubes and toss until they are coated completely with the mixture. Spread on a baking sheet and bake in the preheated oven for 10–15 minutes, until golden and crisp, turning them over halfway through cooking.
Serve the soup immediately sprinkled with the warm croutons.

Health Rating: 4 points

Swede, Turnip, Parsnip & Potato Soup

Serves 4

Ingredients

2 large onions, peeled
25 g/1 oz/¼ stick butter
2 carrots, peeled and roughly chopped
175 g/6 oz/1 cup swede/rutabaga peeled and roughly chopped
125 g/4½ oz/¾ cup turnip peeled and roughly chopped
125 g/4½ oz/¾ cup parsnips peeled and roughly chopped
175 g/6 oz/1 cup potatoes peeled and roughly chopped
1 litre/1¾ pints/1 quart vegetable stock
½ tsp freshly grated nutmeg
salt and freshly ground black pepper
4 tbsp vegetable oil, for frying
120 ml/4 fl oz/½ cup double/heavy cream
warm crusty bread, to serve

Finely chop 1 of the onions. Melt the butter in a large saucepan and add the onion, carrots, swede/rutabaga, turnip, parsnips and potatoes. Cover and cook gently for about 10 minutes, without colouring. Stir occasionally during this time.

Add the stock and season to taste with the nutmeg, salt and pepper. Cover and bring to the boil, then reduce the heat and simmer gently for 15–20 minutes, or until the vegetables are tender. Remove from the heat and leave to cool for 30 minutes.

Heat the oil in a large, heavy-based frying pan. Finely chop the remaining onion, add to the frying pan and cook over a medium heat for 2–3 minutes, stirring frequently, until golden brown. Remove the fried onions with a slotted spoon and drain well on absorbent paper towels. As they cool, they will turn crispy.

Pour the cooled soup into a food processor or blender and process to form a smooth puree. Return to the cleaned pan, adjust the seasoning, then stir in the cream. Gently reheat and top with the crispy onions. Serve immediately with chunks of bread.

Health Rating: 3 points

Cream of Pumpkin Soup

Serves 4

Ingredients

4 tbsp olive oil
900 g/2 lb/6 cups pumpkin, peeled, deseeded and cut into 2.5 cm/1 inch cubes
1 large onion, peeled and finely chopped
1 leek, trimmed and finely chopped
1 carrot, peeled and diced
2 celery stalks, diced
4 garlic cloves, peeled and crushed
1.7 litres/3 pints/1 3/4 quarts water
salt and freshly ground black pepper
1/4 tsp freshly grated nutmeg
150 ml/1/4 pint/2/3 cup single/light cream
1/4 tsp cayenne pepper
warm herby bread, to serve

Heat the olive oil in a large saucepan and cook the pumpkin for 2–3 minutes, coating it completely with oil.

Add the onion, leek, carrot and celery to the saucepan with the garlic and cook, stirring, for 5 minutes, or until they have begun to soften. Cover the vegetables with the water and bring to the boil. Season with plenty of salt and pepper and the nutmeg, cover and simmer for 15–20 minutes, or until all of the vegetables are tender.

When the vegetables are tender, remove from the heat, cool slightly, then pour into a food processor or blender. Liquidize to form a smooth puree then pass through a sieve/strainer into a clean saucepan.

Adjust the seasoning to taste and add all but 2 tablespoons of the cream and enough water to obtain the desired consistency. Bring the soup to boiling point, add the cayenne pepper and serve immediately, swirled with cream and accompanied by warm herby bread.

Health Rating: 3 points

Cream of Spinach Soup

Serves 6–8

Ingredients

1 large onion, peeled and chopped
5 large, plump garlic cloves, peeled and chopped
2 potatoes, peeled and chopped
750 ml/1¼ pints/3¼ cups cold water
1 tsp salt
450 g/1 lb/1½ cups spinach, washed and large stems removed
50 g/2 oz/½ stick butter
3 tbsp plain/all-purpose flour
750 ml/1¼ pints/3¼ cups milk
½ tsp freshly grated nutmeg
freshly ground black pepper
6–8 tbsp crème fraîche/sour cream
warm focaccia bread, to serve

Place the onion, garlic and potatoes in a large saucepan and cover with the cold water. Add half the salt and bring to the boil. Cover and simmer for 15–20 minutes, or until the potatoes are tender. Remove from the heat and add the spinach. Cover and set aside for 10 minutes.

Slowly melt the butter in another saucepan, add the flour and cook over a low heat for about 2 minutes. Remove the saucepan from the heat and add the milk, a little at a time, stirring continuously. Return to the heat and cook, stirring continuously, for 5–8 minutes, or until the sauce is smooth and slightly thickened. Add the freshly grated nutmeg to taste.

Blend the cooled potato and spinach mixture in a food processor or blender to a smooth puree, then return to the saucepan and gradually stir in the white sauce. Season to taste with the remaining salt and some pepper and gently reheat, taking care not to allow the soup to boil.

Ladle into soup bowls and top with spoonfuls of crème fraîche/sour cream. Serve immediately with warm focaccia bread.

Health Rating: 3 points

Lettuce Soup

Serves 4

Ingredients

2 iceberg lettuces, quartered with hard core removed
1 tbsp olive oil
50 g/$^{1}/_{2}$ stick butter
125 g/$^{1}/_{2}$ cup spring onions/scallions, trimmed and chopped
1 tbsp freshly chopped parsley
1 tbsp plain/all-purpose flour
600 ml/1 pint/2$^{1}/_{2}$ cups chicken stock
salt and freshly ground black pepper
150 ml/$^{1}/_{4}$ pint/$^{2}/_{3}$ cup single/light cream
$^{1}/_{4}$ tsp cayenne pepper, to taste
thick slices of stale ciabatta bread
parsley sprig, to garnish

Bring a large saucepan of water to the boil and blanch the lettuce leaves for 3 minutes. Drain and dry thoroughly on absorbent paper towels, then shred with a sharp knife.

Heat the oil and butter in a clean saucepan and add the lettuce, spring onions/scallions and parsley and cook together for 3–4 minutes, or until very soft.

Stir in the flour and cook for 1 minute, then gradually pour in the stock, stirring throughout. Bring to the boil and season to taste with salt and pepper. Reduce the heat, cover and simmer gently for 10–15 minutes, or until soft.

Allow the soup to cool slightly, then either sieve or puree in a blender. Alternatively, leave the soup chunky. Stir in the cream, add more seasoning, to taste, if liked, then add the cayenne pepper.

Arrange the slices of ciabatta bread in a large soup dish or in individual bowls and pour the soup over the bread. Garnish with parsley sprigs and serve immediately.

Health Rating: 3 points

Classic Minestrone

Serves 6–8

Ingredients

25 g/1 oz/$^{1}/_{4}$ stick butter
3 tbsp olive oil
3 slices streaky/fatty bacon
1 large onion, peeled
1 garlic clove, peeled
1 celery stalk, trimmed
2 carrots, peeled
400 g/14 oz can chopped tomatoes
1.2 litres/2 pints/1$^{1}/_{4}$ quarts chicken stock
175 g/6 oz/2$^{1}/_{2}$ cups green cabbage, finely shredded
50 g/2 oz/$^{1}/_{2}$ cup French/green beans, trimmed and halved
3 tbsp frozen petits pois
50 g/2 oz spaghetti
salt and freshly ground black pepper
Parmesan cheese shavings, to garnish
crusty bread, to serve

Heat the butter and olive oil together in a large saucepan. Chop the bacon and add to the saucepan. Cook for 3–4 minutes, then remove with a slotted spoon and reserve.

Finely chop the onion, garlic, celery and carrots and add to the saucepan, one ingredient at a time, stirring well after each addition. Cover and cook gently for 8–10 minutes, until the vegetables are softened.

Add the chopped tomatoes, with their juice and the stock, bring to the boil, then cover the saucepan with a lid, reduce the heat and simmer gently for about 20 minutes.

Stir in the cabbage, beans, petits pois and spaghetti, broken into short pieces. Cover and simmer for a further 20 minutes, until all the ingredients are tender. Season to taste with salt and pepper.

Return the cooked bacon to the saucepan and bring the soup to the boil. Serve the soup immediately, with Parmesan shavings sprinkled on top and plenty of crusty bread.

Health Rating: 3 points

Pasta & Bean Soup

Serves 4–6

Ingredients

3 tbsp olive oil
2 celery stalks, trimmed and finely chopped
100 g/¾ cup prosciutto or prosciutto di speck, cut in to pieces
1 red chilli, deseeded and finely chopped
2 large potatoes, peeled and cut into 2.5 cm/1 inch cubes
2 garlic cloves, peeled and finely chopped
3 ripe plum tomatoes, skinned and chopped
1 x 400 g/14 oz can borlotti/cranberry beans, drained and rinsed
1 litre/1¾ pints/1 quart chicken or vegetable stock
100 g/1 cup pasta shapes
large handful basil leaves, torn
salt and freshly ground black pepper
shredded basil leaves, to garnish
crusty bread, to serve

Heat the olive oil in a heavy-based pan, add the celery and prosciutto and cook gently for 6–8 minutes, or until softened. Add the chopped chilli and potato cubes and cook for a further 10 minutes.

Add the garlic to the chilli and potato mixture and cook for 1 minute. Add the chopped tomatoes and simmer for 5 minutes. Stir in two thirds of the beans, then pour in the chicken or vegetable stock and bring to the boil.

Add the pasta shapes to the soup stock and return it to simmering point. Cook the pasta for about 10 minutes, or until *al dente*.

Meanwhile, place the remaining beans in a food processor or blender and blend with enough of the soup stock to make a smooth, thinnish puree.

When the pasta is cooked, stir in the pureed beans with the torn basil. Season the soup to taste with salt and pepper. Ladle into serving bowls, garnish with shredded basil and serve immediately with plenty of crusty bread.

Health Rating: 3 points

Tuna Chowder

Serves 4

Ingredients

2 tsp olive or sunflower oil
1 onion, peeled and finely chopped
2 celery stalks, trimmed and finely sliced
1 tbsp plain/all-purpose flour
600 ml/1 pint/2½ cups skimmed milk
200 g/7 oz can tuna in water
320 g/11 oz can sweetcorn in water, drained
2 tsp freshly chopped thyme
salt and freshly ground black pepper
pinch cayenne pepper
2 tbsp freshly chopped parsley

Heat the oil in a large, heavy-based saucepan. Add the onion and celery and cook gently for about 5 minutes, stirring from time to time until the onion is softened.

Stir in the flour and cook for about 1 minute to thicken. Draw the pan off the heat and gradually pour in the milk, stirring throughout.

Add the tuna and its liquid, the drained sweetcorn and the thyme. Mix gently, then bring to the boil. Cover and simmer for 5 minutes.

Remove the pan from the heat and season to taste with salt and pepper. Sprinkle the chowder with the cayenne pepper and chopped parsley. Divide into soup bowls and serve immediately.

Health Rating: 4 points

Sweetcorn & Crab Soup

Serves 4

Ingredients

450 g/1 lb fresh corn-on-the-cob
1.3 litres/2¼ pints/5½ cups chicken stock
2–3 spring onions/scallions, trimmed and finely chopped
1 cm/½ inch piece fresh root ginger, peeled and finely chopped
1 tbsp dry sherry or Chinese rice wine
2–3 tsp soy sauce
1 tsp light brown sugar
salt and freshly ground black pepper
2 tsp cornflour/cornstarch
225 g/½ lb white crabmeat, fresh or canned
1 medium/large egg white
1 tsp sesame oil
1–2 tbsp freshly chopped coriander/cilantro

Wash and dry the corn cobs. Using a sharp knife and holding the corn cobs at an angle to the cutting board, cut down along the cobs to remove the kernels, then scrape the cobs to remove any excess milky residue. Put the kernels and the milky residue into a large wok.

Add the chicken stock to the wok and place over a high heat. Bring to the boil, stirring and pressing some of the kernels against the side of the wok to squeeze out the starch to help thicken the soup. Simmer for 15 minutes, stirring occasionally.

Add the spring onions/scallions, ginger, sherry or Chinese rice wine, soy sauce and brown sugar to the wok and season to taste with salt and pepper. Simmer for a further 5 minutes, stirring occasionally.

Blend the cornflour with 1 tablespoon cold water to form a smooth paste and whisk into the soup. Return to the boil, then simmer over a medium heat until thickened. Add the crabmeat, stirring until blended. Beat the egg white with the sesame oil and stir into the soup in a slow, steady stream, stirring constantly. Stir in the chopped coriander and serve immediately.

Health Rating: 4 points

Coconut Chicken Soup

Serves 4

Ingredients

2 lemon grass stalks
3 tbsp vegetable oil
3 onions, peeled and finely sliced
3 garlic cloves, peeled and crushed
2 tbsp fresh root ginger, finely grated
2–3 kaffir lime leaves
$1^1/_2$ tsp turmeric
1 red pepper, deseeded and diced
400 ml/$13^1/_2$ fl oz can coconut milk
1.2 litres/2 pints/$1^1/_4$ quarts vegetable or chicken stock
275 g/9 oz/$1^1/_2$ cups easy-cook long-grain rice
275 g/9 oz cooked chicken meat
285 g/$9^1/_2$ oz can sweetcorn, drained
3 tbsp freshly chopped coriander/cilantro
1 tbsp Thai fish sauce
freshly chopped pickled chillies, to serve

Discard the outer leaves of the lemon grass stalks. Place on a chopping board and, using a rolling pin, pound gently to bruise; reserve.

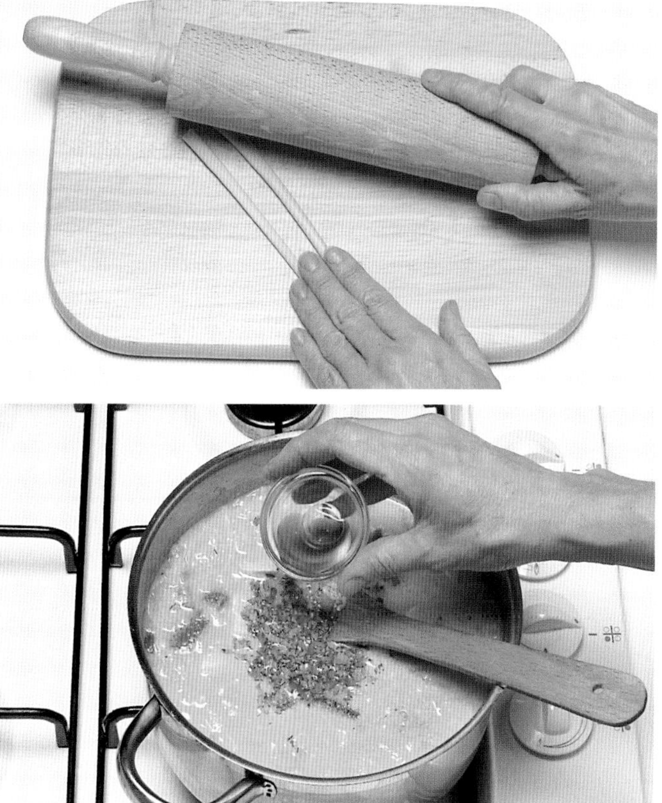

Heat the vegetable oil in a large saucepan and cook the onions over a medium heat for about 10–15 minutes until soft and beginning to change colour.

Lower the heat, stir in the garlic, ginger, lime leaves and turmeric and cook for 1 minute.

Add the red pepper, coconut milk, stock, lemon grass and rice. Bring to the boil, cover and simmer gently over a low heat for about 10 minutes.

Cut the chicken into bite-sized pieces, then stir into the soup with the sweetcorn and the freshly chopped coriander/cilantro. Add the Thai fish sauce to taste, then reheat gently, stirring frequently. Serve with a few chopped pickled chillies to sprinkle on top.

Health Rating: 3 points

Vietnamese Beef & Rice Noodle Soup

Serves 4–6

Ingredients

For the beef stock:

900 g/2 lb meaty beef bones
1 large onion, peeled and quartered
2 carrots, peeled and cut into chunks
2 celery stalks, trimmed and sliced
1 leek, washed and sliced into chunks
2 garlic cloves, unpeeled and lightly crushed
3 whole star anise
1 tsp black peppercorns

For the soup:

175 g/6 oz/2½ cups dried rice stick noodles
4–6 spring onions/scallions, trimmed and diagonally sliced
1 red chilli, deseeded and diagonally sliced
1 small bunch fresh coriander/cilantro
1 small bunch fresh mint
350 g/12 oz fillet steak, very thinly sliced
salt and freshly ground black pepper

Place all the ingredients for the beef stock into a large stock pot or saucepan and cover with cold water. Bring to the boil and skim off any scum that rises to the surface. Reduce the heat and simmer gently, partially covered, for 2–3 hours, skimming occasionally.

Strain into a large bowl and leave to cool, then skim off the fat. Chill in the refrigerator and, when cold, remove any fat from the surface. Pour 1.7 litres/3 pints/1¾ quarts of the stock into a large wok and reserve.

Cover the noodles with warm water and leave for 3 minutes, or until just softened. Drain, then cut into 10 cm/4 inch lengths.

Arrange the spring onions/scallions and chilli on a serving platter or large plate. Strip the leaves from the coriander/cilantro and mint and arrange them in piles on the plate. These are to be added to personal taste once served.

Bring the stock in the wok to the boil over a high heat. Add the noodles and simmer for about 2 minutes, or until tender. Add the beef strips and simmer for about 1 minute. Season to taste with salt and pepper. Ladle the soup with the noodles and beef strips into individual soup bowls and serve immediately, each person adding their own spring onions, chilli and herbs to taste.

Health Rating: 4 points

Aubergine Dip with Pitta Strips

Serves 4

Ingredients

4 pitta breads
2 large aubergines/eggplants
1 garlic clove, peeled
¼ tsp sesame oil
1 tbsp lemon juice
½ tsp ground cumin
salt and freshly ground black pepper
2 tbsp freshly chopped parsley
fresh salad leaves, to serve

Preheat the oven to 180°C/350°F/Gas Mark 4. On a chopping board, cut the pitta breads into strips. Spread the bread in a single layer on a large baking sheet. Cook in the preheated oven for 15 minutes until golden and crisp. Leave to cool on a wire cooling rack.

Trim the aubergines/eggplants, rinse lightly and reserve. Heat a griddle pan until almost smoking. Cook the aubergines and garlic for about 15 minutes. Turn the aubergines frequently, until very tender with wrinkled and charred skins. Remove from heat and leave to cool.

When the aubergines are cool enough to handle, cut in half and scoop out the cooked flesh and place in a food processor. Squeeze the softened garlic flesh from the papery skin and add to the aubergine. Blend the aubergine and garlic until smooth. Add the sesame oil, lemon juice and cumin and blend again to mix. Season to taste with salt and pepper; stir in the parsley. Serve with the pitta strips and mixed salad leaves.

Health Rating: 5 points

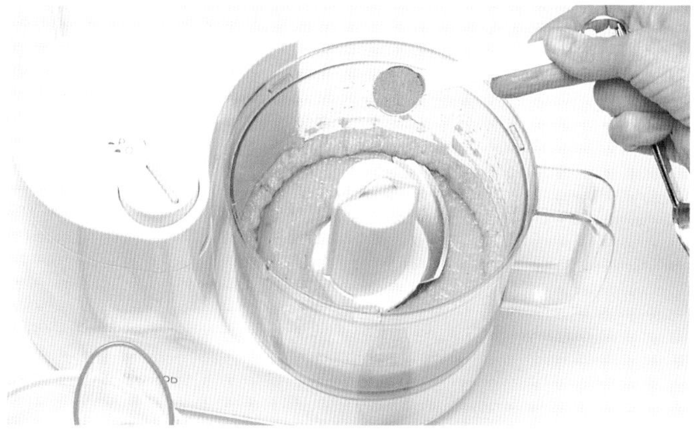

Courgette & Tarragon Tortilla

Serves 6

Ingredients

5–6 potatoes
3 tbsp olive oil
1 onion, peeled and thinly sliced
salt and freshly ground black pepper
1 courgette/zucchini, trimmed and thinly sliced
6 eggs
2 tbsp freshly chopped tarragon
tomato wedges, to serve

Peel the potatoes and slice thinly. Dry the slices in a clean dishtowel to get them as dry as possible. Heat the oil in a large heavy-based pan, add the onion and cook for 3 minutes. Add the potatoes with a little salt and pepper, then stir the potatoes and onion lightly to coat in the oil.

Reduce the heat to the lowest possible setting, cover and cook gently for 5 minutes. Turn the potatoes and onion over and continue to cook for a further 5 minutes. Give the pan a shake every now and again to ensure that the potatoes do not stick to the base or burn. Add the courgette/zucchini, then cover and cook for a further 10 minutes.

Beat the eggs and tarragon together and season to taste with salt and pepper. Pour the egg mixture over the vegetables and return to the heat. Cook on a low heat for up to 20–25 minutes, or until there is no liquid egg left on the surface of the tortilla.

Turn the tortilla over by inverting it on to a saucepan lid or a flat plate, then sliding it back into the pan. Return the pan to the heat and cook for a final 3–5 minutes, or until the underside is golden brown. If preferred, place the tortilla under a preheated grill/broiler for 4 minutes, or until set and golden brown on top. Cut into small squares and serve hot or cold with tomato wedges.

Health Rating: 3 points

Mozzarella Frittata with Tomato & Basil Salad

Serves 6

Ingredients

For the salad:
6 ripe but firm tomatoes, thinly sliced
2 tbsp fresh basil leaves
2 tbsp olive oil
1 tbsp fresh lemon juice
1 tsp caster/superfine sugar
freshly ground black pepper

For the frittata:
7 eggs, beaten
salt
300 g/10 oz/2 cups mozzarella cheese, grated
2 spring onions/scallions, trimmed and finely chopped
2 tbsp olive oil
warm crusty bread, to serve

To make the tomato and basil salad, place the tomatoes in a dish, tear up the basil leaves and sprinkle over. Make the dressing by whisking the olive oil, lemon juice and sugar together well. Season with black pepper before drizzling the dressing over the salad.

To make the frittata, preheat the grill/broiler to a high heat just before starting to cook. Place the eggs in a large bowl with plenty of salt and whisk. Stir the mozzarella into the egg with the finely chopped spring onions/scallions.

Heat the oil in a large, nonstick frying pan. Pour in the egg mixture, stirring with a wooden spoon to spread the ingredients evenly over the pan. Cook for 5–8 minutes, until the frittata is golden brown and firm on the underside. Place the whole pan under the preheated grill and cook for about 4–5 minutes, or until the top is golden brown. Slide the frittata on to a serving plate, cut into six large wedges and serve immediately with the tomato and basil salad and plenty of warm crusty bread.

Health Rating: 4 points

Sweet Potato Crisps with Mango Salsa

Serves 6

Ingredients

For the salsa:

1 large mango, peeled, stoned and cut into small cubes
8 cherry tomatoes, quartered
½ cucumber, peeled if preferred and finely diced
1 red onion, peeled and finely chopped
pinch sugar
1 red chilli, deseeded and finely chopped
2 tbsp rice vinegar
2 tbsp olive oil
grated zest/rind and juice of 1 lime

For the sweet potato crisps/chips:
450 g/1 lb/⅔ cup sweet potatoes, peeled and thinly sliced
vegetable oil, for deep-frying
sea salt
2 tbsp freshly chopped mint

To make the salsa, mix the mango with the tomatoes, cucumber and onion. Add the sugar, chilli, vinegar, oil and the lime rind and juice. Mix together, cover and leave for 45–50 minutes.

Soak the potatoes in cold water for 40 minutes to remove as much of the excess starch as possible. Drain and dry thoroughly in a clean dishtowel, or absorbent paper towels.

Heat the oil to 190°C/375°F in a deep-fryer. When at the correct temperature, place half the potatoes in the frying basket, then carefully lower the potatoes into the hot oil and cook for 4–5 minutes, or until they are golden brown, shaking the basket every minute so that they do not stick together.

Drain the potato crisps on absorbent paper towels, sprinkle with sea salt and place under a preheated moderate grill/broiler for a few seconds to dry out. Repeat with the remaining potatoes. Stir the mint into the salsa and serve with the potato crisps.

Health Rating: 2 points

Sweetcorn Fritters

Serves 4

Ingredients

4 tbsp groundnut/peanut oil
1 small onion, peeled and finely chopped
1 red chilli, deseeded and finely chopped
1 garlic clove, peeled and crushed
1 tsp ground coriander
325 g/11½ oz can sweetcorn
6 spring onions/scallions, trimmed and finely sliced
1 egg, lightly beaten
salt and freshly ground black pepper
3 tbsp plain/all-purpose flour
1 tsp baking powder
spring onion/scallion curls
Thai-style chutney, to serve

Heat 1 tablespoon of the oil in a frying pan, add the onion and cook gently for 7–8 minutes, or until beginning to soften. Add the chilli, garlic and ground coriander and cook for 1 minute, stirring continuously. Remove from the heat.

Drain the sweetcorn and tip into a mixing bowl. Lightly mash to break down the corn a little. Add the cooked onion mixture to the bowl with the spring onions/scallions and beaten egg. Season to taste with salt and pepper, then stir to mix together. Sift the flour and baking powder over the mixture and stir in.

Heat 2 tablespoons of the oil in a large frying pan. Drop 4 or 5 teaspoonfuls of the sweetcorn mixture into the pan and, using a spatula, flatten each to make a 1 cm/½ inch thick fritter.

Fry the fritters for 3 minutes, or until golden brown on the underside, turn over and fry for a further 3 minutes, or until cooked through and crisp.

Remove the fritters from the pan and drain on absorbent paper towels. Keep warm while cooking the remaining fritters, adding a little more oil if needed. Garnish with spring onion curls and serve immediately with a Thai-style chutney.

Health Rating: 2 points

Bruschetta with Pecorino, Garlic & Tomatoes

Serves 4

Ingredients

6 ripe but firm tomatoes
125 g/4½ oz/1¼ cup pecorino cheese, finely grated
1 tbsp oregano leaves, chopped
salt and freshly ground black pepper
3 tbsp olive oil
3 garlic cloves, peeled
8 slices flat Italian bread, such as focaccia
8 thin slices mozzarella cheese
marinated black olives, to serve

Preheat the grill/broiler and line the rack with foil just before cooking. Make a small cross in the tops of the tomatoes, then place in a small bowl and cover with boiling water. Leave to stand for 2 minutes, then drain and remove the skins. Cut into quarters, remove the seeds. Chop the flesh into small cubes.

Mix the tomato flesh with the pecorino cheese and 2 teaspoons of the fresh oregano and season to taste with salt and pepper. Add 1 tablespoon of the olive oil and mix thoroughly.

Crush the garlic and spread evenly over the slices of bread. Heat 2 tablespoons of the olive oil in a large frying pan and fry the bread slices until they are crisp and golden.

Place the fried bread on a lightly oiled baking sheet and spoon on the tomato and cheese topping. Place a little mozzarella on top and place under the preheated grill for 3–4 minutes, until golden and bubbling. Garnish with the remaining oregano, then arrange the bruschettas on a serving plate and serve immediately with the olives.

Health Rating: 3 points

Spaghettini with Lemon Pesto & Cheese & Herb Bread

Serves 4

Ingredients

1 small onion, peeled and grated
2 tsp freshly chopped oregano
1 tbsp freshly chopped parsley
75 g/3 oz/$^1/_3$ cup butter
125 g/4 oz/1$^1/_4$ cup pecorino cheese, grated
8 slices Italian flat bread
275 g/10 oz dried spaghettini
4 tbsp olive oil
1 large bunch basil, approximately 30 g/1 oz
75 g/3 oz/$^1/_2$ cup pine nuts
1 garlic clove, peeled and crushed
75 g/3 oz/$^3/_4$ cup Parmesan cheese, grated
finely grated zest/rind and juice of 2 lemons
salt and freshly ground black pepper
4 tsp butter

Preheat oven to 200°C/400°F/Gas Mark 6, 15 minutes before baking. Mix together the onion, oregano, parsley, butter and cheese. Spread the bread with the cheese mixture, place on a lightly oiled baking tray and cover with kitchen foil. Bake in the preheated oven for 10–15 minutes, then keep warm.

Add the spaghettini with 1 tablespoon olive oil to a large saucepan of fast-boiling, lightly salted water and cook for 3–4 minutes, or until *al dente*. Drain, reserving 2 tablespoons of the cooking liquor.

Blend the basil, pine nuts, garlic, Parmesan cheese, lemon rind and juice and remaining olive oil in a food processor or blender until a puree is formed. Season to taste with salt and pepper, then place in a saucepan.

Heat the lemon pesto very gently until piping hot, then stir in the pasta together with the reserved cooking liquor. Add the butter and mix together well.

Add plenty of black pepper to the pasta and serve immediately with the warm cheese and herb bread.

Health Rating: 3 points

Peperonata (Braised Mixed Peppers)

Serves 4

Ingredients

2 green peppers
1 red pepper
1 yellow pepper
1 orange pepper
1 onion, peeled
2 garlic cloves, peeled
2 tbsp olive oil
4 very ripe tomatoes
1 tbsp freshly chopped oregano
salt and freshly ground black pepper
150 ml/¼ pint/⅔ cup light chicken or vegetable stock
fresh oregano sprigs, to garnish
focaccia or flat bread, to serve

Remove the seeds from the peppers and cut into thin strips. Slice the onion into rings and chop the garlic cloves finely.

Heat the olive oil in a frying pan and fry the peppers, onions and garlic for 5–10 minutes, or until soft and lightly coloured. Stir continuously.

Make a cross on the tops of the tomatoes, then place in a bowl and cover with boiling water. Allow to stand for about 2 minutes. Drain, then remove the skins and seeds and chop the tomato flesh into cubes.

Add the tomatoes and oregano to the peppers and onion and season to taste with salt and pepper. Cover the pan and bring to the boil. Simmer gently for about 30 minutes, or until tender, adding the chicken or vegetable stock halfway through the cooking time.

Garnish with oregano sprigs and serve hot with plenty of freshly baked focaccia bread or lightly toasted slices of flat bread and pile a spoonful of peperonata on to each plate.

Health Rating: 5 points

Beetroot Ravioli with Dill Cream Sauce

Serves 4–6

Ingredients

For the pasta:

225 g/8 oz/1⅛ cups strong plain bread flour or type 00 pasta flour, plus extra for rolling
1 tsp salt
2 medium/large eggs; 1 medium/large egg yolk
1 tbsp extra virgin olive oil

For the filling:

1 tbsp olive oil
1 small onion, peeled and finely chopped
½ tsp caraway seeds
175 g/6 oz/1 cup cooked beetroot/beets, chopped
175 g/6 oz/¾ cup ricotta cheese
25 g/1 oz/½ cup fresh white breadcrumbs
1 medium/large egg yolk
2 tbsp grated Parmesan cheese
salt and freshly ground black pepper
4 tbsp walnut oil; 4 tbsp freshly chopped dill
1 tbsp green peppercorns, drained and roughly chopped
6 tbsp crème fraîche/sour cream

To make the pasta dough, sift the flour and salt into a large bowl, make a well in the centre and add the eggs and yolk, the oil and 1 teaspoon water. Gradually mix to form a soft but not sticky dough, adding a little more flour or water as necessary. Turn out on to a lightly floured surface and knead for 5 minutes, or until smooth and elastic. Wrap in clingfilm/plastic wrap and leave to rest at room temperature for about 30 minutes.

To make the filling, heat the olive oil in a large frying pan, add the onion and caraway seeds and cook over a medium heat for 5 minutes, or until the onion is softened and lightly golden. Stir in the beetroot and cook for 5 minutes. Blend the beetroot mixture in a food processor until smooth, then allow to cool.

Stir in the ricotta cheese, breadcrumbs, egg yolk and Parmesan cheese. Season the filling to taste with salt and pepper and reserve.

Divide the pasta dough into eight pieces. Roll out as for tagliatelle, but do not cut the sheets in half. Lay one sheet on a floured surface and place 5 heaped teaspoons of the filling 2.5 cm/1 inch apart.

Dampen around the heaps of filling and lay a second sheet of pasta over the top. Press around the heaps to seal. Cut into squares using a pastry wheel or sharp knife. Put the filled pasta shapes on to a floured dishtowel.

Bring a large pan of lightly salted water to a rolling boil. Drop the ravioli into the boiling water, return to the boil and cook for 3–4 minutes, until *al dente*.

Meanwhile, heat the walnut oil in a small pan, then add the chopped dill and green peppercorns. Remove from the heat, stir in the crème fraîche and season well.

Drain the cooked pasta thoroughly and toss with the sauce. Tip into warmed serving dishes and serve immediately.

Health Rating: 2 points

Spaghettini with Peas, Spring Onions & Mint

Serves 6

Ingredients

pinch saffron strands

700 g/1½ lb/4⅔ cups fresh peas or 350 g/12 oz/2¾ cups frozen petit pois, thawed

75 g/3 oz/⅓ cup unsalted butter, softened

6 spring onions/scallions, trimmed and finely sliced

salt and freshly ground black pepper

1 garlic clove, peeled and finely chopped

2 tbsp freshly chopped mint

1 tbsp freshly snipped chives

450 g/1 lb spaghettini

freshly grated Parmesan cheese, to serve

Soak the saffron in 2 tablespoons hot water while you prepare the sauce. Shell the peas if using fresh ones.

Heat 50 g/2 oz/¼ cup of the butter in a medium frying pan, add the spring onions/scallions and a little salt and cook over a low heat for 2–3 minutes, or until the onions have softened. Add the garlic, then the peas and 100 ml/3½ fl oz/1¼ cups water. Bring to the boil and cook for 5–6 minutes, or until the peas are just tender. Stir in the mint and keep warm.

Blend the remaining butter and the saffron water in a large warmed serving bowl and reserve.

Meanwhile, bring a large pan of lightly salted water to a rolling boil and add the spaghettini. Cook according to the packet instructions, or until *al dente*.

Drain thoroughly, reserving 2–3 tablespoons of the pasta cooking water. Tip into a warmed serving bowl, add the pea sauce and toss together gently. Season to taste with salt and pepper. Serve immediately with extra black pepper and grated Parmesan cheese.

Health Rating: 3 points

Vegetable Thai Spring Rolls

Serves 4

Ingredients

50 g/2 oz cellophane vermicelli
4 dried shiitake mushrooms
1 tbsp groundnut/peanut oil
2 carrots, peeled and cut into fine matchsticks
125 g/$4\frac{1}{2}$ oz/1 cup mangetout/snow peas, cut lengthways into fine strips
3 spring onions/scallions, trimmed and chopped
125 g/$4\frac{1}{2}$ oz/$\frac{1}{2}$ cup canned bamboo shoots, cut into matchsticks
1 cm/$\frac{1}{2}$ inch piece fresh root ginger, peeled and grated
1 tbsp light soy sauce
1 egg, separated
salt and freshly ground black pepper
20 spring roll wrappers
vegetable oil, for deep-frying
spring onion/scallion tassels, to garnish

Place the vermicelli in a bowl and pour over enough boiling water to cover. Leave to soak for 5 minutes, or until softened, then drain. Cut into 7.5 cm/3 inch lengths. Soak the shiitake mushrooms in almost-boiling water for 15 minutes, then drain, discard the stalks and slice thinly.

Heat a wok or large frying pan, add the nut oil and, when hot, add the carrots and stir-fry for 1 minute. Add the mangetout/snow peas and spring onions/scallions and stir-fry for 2–3 minutes, or until tender. Tip the vegetables into a bowl and leave to cool.

Stir the vermicelli and shiitake mushrooms into the cooled vegetables with the bamboo shoots, ginger, soy sauce and egg yolk. Season to taste with salt and pepper and mix thoroughly.

Brush the edges of a spring roll wrapper with a little beaten egg white. Spoon 2 teaspoons of the vegetable filling on to the wrapper, in a 7.5 cm/3 inch log shape 2.5 cm/1 inch from one edge. Fold the wrapper edge over the filling, then fold in the right and left sides. Brush the folded edges with more egg white and roll up neatly. Place on an oiled baking sheet, seam-side down, and make the rest of the spring rolls.

Heat the oil in a heavy-based saucepan or deep-fat fryer to 180°C/350°F. Deep-fry the spring rolls, six at a time, for 2–3 minutes, or until golden brown and crisp. Drain on absorbent paper towels. Arrange on a warmed platter. Garnish with spring onion tassels. Serve immediately.

Health Rating: 3 points

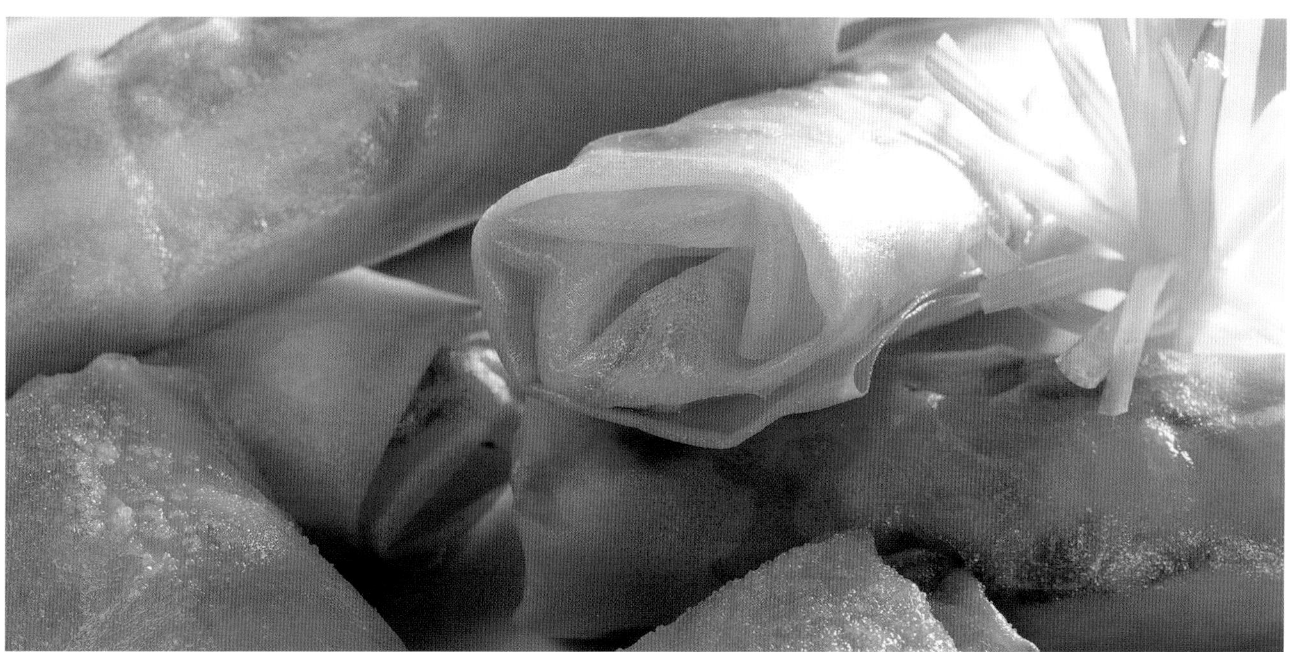

Fried Whitebait with Rocket Salad

Serves 4

Ingredients

450 g/1 lb whitebait/smelt, fresh or frozen
vegetable oil, for deep-frying
90 g/3½ oz/¾ cup plain/all-purpose flour
½ tsp cayenne pepper
salt and freshly ground black pepper

For the salad:
125 g/4½ oz/4 cups rocket/arugula leaves
8 cherry tomatoes, halved
½ cucumber, cut into cubes
3 tbsp olive oil
1 tbsp fresh lemon juice
½ tsp Dijon mustard
½ tsp caster/superfine sugar

If the fish are frozen, thaw completely then wipe dry with absorbent paper towels.

Start to heat the oil in a deep-fat fryer. Arrange the fish in a large, shallow dish and toss well in the flour, cayenne pepper and salt and pepper.

Deep-fry the fish in batches for 2–3 minutes, or until crisp and golden. Keep the cooked fish warm while deep-frying the remaining fish.

For the salad, arrange the leaves, tomatoes and cucumber on individual serving dishes. Whisk the olive oil and the remaining ingredients together and season lightly. Drizzle the dressing over the salad. Serve with the fish.

Health Rating: 2 points

Smoked Salmon Sushi

Serves 4

Ingredients

175 g/6 oz/⅞ cup sushi rice
2 tbsp rice vinegar
4 tsp caster/superfine sugar
½ tsp salt
2 sheets sushi nori
60 g/2½ oz smoked salmon
¼ cucumber, cut into fine strips

To serve:
wasabi
soy sauce
pickled ginger

Rinse the rice thoroughly in cold water, until the water runs clear, then place in a pan with 300 ml/½ pint/1¼ cups water. Bring to the boil and cover with a tight-fitting lid. Reduce to a simmer and cook gently for 10 minutes. Turn the heat off, but keep the pan covered, to allow the rice to steam for a further 10 minutes.

In a small saucepan, gently heat the rice vinegar, sugar and salt until the sugar has dissolved. When the rice has finished steaming, pour over the vinegar mixture and stir well to mix. Empty the rice out on to a large flat surface (a chopping board or large plate is ideal). Fan the rice to cool and to produce a shinier rice.

Lay one sheet of sushi nori on a sushi mat (if you do not have a sushi mat, improvise with a stiff piece of fabric that is a little larger than the sushi nori) and spread with half the cooled rice. Dampen the hands while doing this (this helps to prevent the rice from sticking to the hands). On the nearest edge, place half the salmon and half the cucumber strips.

Roll up the rice and smoked salmon into a tight Swiss roll-like shape. Dampen the blade of a sharp knife and cut the sushi into slices about 2 cm/¾ inch thick. Repeat with the remaining sushi nori, rice, smoked salmon and cucumber. Serve with wasabi, soy sauce and pickled ginger.

Health Rating: 5 points

Thai Fish Cakes

Serves 4

Ingredients

1 red chilli, deseeded and roughly chopped
4 tbsp roughly chopped fresh coriander/cilantro
1 garlic clove, peeled and crushed
2 spring onions/scallions, trimmed and roughly chopped
1 lemon grass stalk, outer leaves discarded, roughly chopped
75 g/3 oz prawns/shrimp, thawed if frozen
275 g/10 oz cod fillet, skinned, pin bones removed and cubed
salt and freshly ground black pepper
sweet chilli dipping sauce, to serve

Preheat the oven to 190°C/375°F/Gas Mark 5. Place the chilli, coriander/cilantro, garlic, spring onions/scallions and lemon grass in a food processor and blend together.

Pat the prawns/shrimp and cod dry with absorbent paper towels.

Add to the food processor and blend until the mixture is roughly chopped. Season to taste with salt and pepper and blend to mix.

Dampen your hands, then shape heaped tablespoons of the mixture into 12 small patties. Place the patties on a lightly oiled baking sheet and cook in the preheated oven for 12–15 minutes, or until piping hot and cooked through. Turn the patties over halfway through the cooking time.

Serve the fish cakes immediately, with the sweet chilli sauce for dipping.

Health Rating: 5 points

Sesame Prawn Toasts

Serves 4

Ingredients

125 g/4½ oz peeled cooked prawns/shrimp
1 tbsp cornflour/cornstarch
2 spring onions/scallions, peeled and roughly chopped
2 tsp freshly grated root ginger
2 tsp dark soy sauce
pinch Chinese five-spice powder
1 small/medium egg, beaten
salt and freshly ground black pepper
6 thin slices day-old white bread
5 tbsp sesame seeds
vegetable oil, for deep-frying
chilli sauce, to serve

Place the prawns/shrimp in a food processor or blender with the cornflour/cornstarch, spring onions/scallions, ginger, soy sauce and Chinese five-spice powder. Blend to a fairly smooth paste. Spoon into a bowl and stir in the beaten egg. Season to taste with salt and pepper.

Cut the crusts off the bread. Spread the prawn paste in an even layer on one side of each slice. Sprinkle over the sesame seeds and press down lightly. Cut each slice diagonally into four triangles, then place on a board and chill in the refrigerator for 30 minutes.

Pour oil into a heavy-based saucepan or deep-fat fryer so that it is one-third full. Heat until it reaches a temperature of 180°C/350°F. Cook the toasts in batches of five or six, carefully lowering them, seeded-side down, into the oil. Deep-fry for 2–3 minutes, or until lightly browned, then turn over and cook for 1 minute more. Using a slotted spoon, lift out the toasts and drain on absorbent paper towels. Keep warm while frying the remaining toasts. Arrange on a warmed platter and serve immediately with chilli sauce for dipping.

Health Rating: 3 points

Hoisin Chicken Pancakes

Serves 4

Ingredients

3 tbsp hoisin sauce
1 garlic clove, peeled and crushed
2.5 cm/1 inch piece root ginger, peeled and finely grated
1 tbsp soy sauce
1 tsp sesame oil
salt and freshly ground black pepper
4 skinless chicken thighs
½ cucumber, peeled (optional)
12 bought Chinese pancakes
6 spring onions/scallions, trimmed and cut lengthways into fine shreds
sweet chilli dipping sauce, to serve

Preheat the oven to 190°C/375°F/Gas Mark 5. In a nonmetallic bowl, mix the hoisin sauce with the garlic, ginger, soy sauce, sesame oil and seasoning.

Add the chicken thighs and turn to coat in the mixture. Cover loosely and leave in the refrigerator to marinate for 3–4 hours, turning the chicken from time to time.

Remove the chicken from the marinade and place in a roasting tin/pan. Reserve the marinade. Bake in the preheated oven for 30 minutes, basting occasionally with the marinade.

Cut the cucumber, if using, in half lengthways and remove the seeds by running a teaspoon down the middle to scoop them out. Cut into thin batons.

Place the pancakes in a steamer to warm, or heat according to packet instructions. Thinly slice the hot chicken and arrange on a plate with the shredded spring onions/scallions, cucumber and pancakes.

Place a spoonful of the chicken in the middle of each warmed pancake and top with pieces of cucumber, spring onion and a little dipping sauce. Roll up and serve immediately.

Health Rating: 5 points

Moo Shi Pork

Serves 4

Ingredients

175 g/6 oz pork fillet
2 tsp Chinese rice wine or dry sherry
2 tbsp light soy sauce
1 tsp cornflour/cornstarch
25 g/1 oz dried golden needles, soaked and drained
2 tbsp groundnut/peanut oil
3 medium/large eggs, lightly beaten
1 tsp freshly grated root ginger
3 spring onions/scallions, trimmed and thinly sliced
150 g/5 oz/1 cup bamboo shoots, cut into fine strips
salt and freshly ground black pepper
8 mandarin pancakes, steamed
hoisin sauce
fresh coriander/cilantro sprigs, to garnish

Cut the pork across the grain into 1 cm/½ inch slices, then cut into thin strips. Place in a bowl with the Chinese rice wine or sherry, soy sauce and cornflour/cornstarch. Mix well and reserve. Trim off the tough ends of the golden needles, then cut in half and reserve.

Heat a wok or large frying pan, add 1 tablespoon of the oil and, when hot, add the lightly beaten eggs and cook for 1 minute, stirring all the time, until scrambled. Remove and reserve. Wipe the wok clean with absorbent paper towels.

Return the wok to the heat, add the remaining oil and, when hot, transfer the pork strips from the marinade mixture to the wok, shaking off as much marinade as possible. Stir-fry for 30 seconds, then add the ginger, spring onions/scallions and bamboo shoots and pour in the marinade. Stir-fry for 2–3 minutes.

Return the scrambled eggs to the wok, season to taste with salt and pepper and stir for a few seconds until mixed well and heated through. Divide the mixture between the pancakes, drizzle each with 1 teaspoon hoisin sauce and roll up. Garnish and serve immediately.

Health Rating: 4 points

Crispy Pork Wontons

Makes 20

Ingredients

1 small onion, peeled and roughly chopped
2 garlic cloves, peeled and crushed
1 green chilli, deseeded and chopped
2.5 cm/1 inch piece fresh root ginger, peeled and roughly chopped
450 g/1 lb lean minced/ground pork
4 tbsp freshly chopped coriander/cilantro
1 tsp Chinese five-spice powder
salt and freshly ground black pepper
20 wonton wrappers
1 egg, lightly beaten
vegetable oil, for deep-frying
chilli sauce, to serve

Place the onion, garlic, chilli and ginger in a food processor and blend until very finely chopped. Add the pork, coriander/cilantro and Chinese five-spice powder. Season to taste with salt and pepper, then blend again briefly to mix. Divide the mixture into 20 equal portions and, with floured hands, shape each into a walnut-sized ball.

Brush the edges of a wonton wrapper with beaten egg, place a pork ball in the centre, then bring the corners to the centre and pinch together to make a pouch. Repeat with the remaining pork balls and wrappers.

Pour sufficient oil into a heavy-based saucepan or deep-fat fryer so that it is one-third full and heat to 180°C/350°F. Deep-fry the wontons in three or four batches for 3–4 minutes, or until cooked through, golden and crisp. Drain on absorbent paper towels. Serve the crispy pork wontons immediately, five per person, with some chilli sauce for dipping.

Health Rating: 1 point

Barbecue Pork Steamed Buns

Serves 12

Ingredients

For the buns:

175–200 g/6–7 oz/1½ –1¾ cups plain/all-purpose flour
1 tbsp easy-blend/instant yeast
120 ml/4 fl oz/½ cup milk
2 tbsp sunflower oil
1 tbsp sugar
½ tsp salt
spring onion/scallion tassels, to garnish
fresh green salad leaves, to serve

For the filling:

2 tbsp vegetable oil
1 small red pepper, deseeded and finely chopped
2 garlic cloves, peeled and finely chopped
225 g/8 oz cooked pork, finely chopped
50 g/2 oz/¼ cup light brown sugar
3 tbsp tomato ketchup
1–2 tsp hot chilli powder, or to taste

Put 75 g/3 oz/⅔ cup of the flour in a bowl and stir in the yeast.

Heat the milk, oil, sugar and salt in a small saucepan until warm, stirring until the sugar has dissolved. Pour into the bowl and, with an electric mixer, beat on a low speed for 30 seconds, scraping down the sides of the bowl, until blended. Beat at high speed for 3 minutes, then, with a wooden spoon, stir in as much of the remaining flour as possible until a stiff dough forms.

Shape the dough into a ball, place in a lightly oiled bowl and cover with clingfilm/plastic wrap. Leave for 1 hour in a warm place, or until doubled in size.

To make the filling, heat a wok, add the oil and, when hot, add the pepper and garlic. Stir-fry for 4–5 minutes. Add the remaining ingredients and bring to the boil, stir-frying for 2–3 minutes until thick and syrupy. Cool and reserve.

Punch down the dough and turn on to a lightly floured surface. Divide into 12 pieces and shape them into balls, then cover and leave to rest for 5 minutes. Roll each ball into a 7.5 cm/3 inch circle.

Place a heaped tablespoon of filling in the centre of each. Dampen the edges, then bring them up and around the filling, pinching together to seal. Place seam-side down on a small square of nonstick baking parchment. Continue with the remaining dough and filling. Leave to rise for 10 minutes.

Bring a large wok half-filled with water to the boil and place the buns in a lightly oiled Chinese steamer, without touching each other. Cover and steam for 20–25 minutes, then remove and cool slightly. Garnish with spring onion/scallion tassels and serve with salad leaves.

Health Rating: 2 points

Mixed Satay Sticks

Serves 4

Ingredients

12 large raw prawns/jumbo shrimp
350 g/12 oz/3/4 lb beef rump steak
1 tbsp lemon juice
1 garlic clove, peeled and crushed
pinch salt
2 tsp soft dark brown sugar
1 tsp ground cumin
1 tsp ground coriander
1/4 tsp ground turmeric
1 tbsp groundnut/peanut oil
fresh coriander/cilantro leaves, to garnish

For the spicy peanut sauce:
1 shallot, peeled and very finely chopped
1 tsp demerara/light brown sugar
50 g/2 oz/1/4 cup creamed coconut, chopped
pinch chilli powder
1 tbsp dark soy sauce
125 g/4 1/2 oz/1/2 cup crunchy peanut butter

Preheat the grill/broiler on high just before required. Soak eight bamboo skewers in cold water for at least 30 minutes. Peel the prawns/shrimp, leaving the tails on. Using a sharp knife, remove the black vein along the back of the prawns. Cut the beef into 1 cm/1/2 inch wide strips. Place the prawns and beef in separate bowls and sprinkle each with 1/2 tablespoon of the lemon juice.

Mix together the garlic, pinch of salt, sugar, cumin, coriander/cilantro, turmeric and oil to make a paste. Lightly brush over the prawns and beef. Cover and place in the refrigerator to marinate for at least 30 minutes. To make the sauce, pour 120 ml/4 fl oz/1/2 cup of water into a small saucepan, add the shallot and sugar. Heat gently until the sugar has dissolved. Stir in the creamed coconut and chilli powder. When melted, remove from the heat and stir in the peanut butter. Leave to cool slightly. Spoon into a serving dish.

Thread 3 prawns each on to four skewers. Divide the sliced beef between the remaining skewers. Cook the skewers under the preheated grill for 4–5 minutes, turning occasionally. The prawns should be opaque and pink, the beef browned on the outside but pink in the centre. Transfer to individual serving plates and garnish with a few fresh coriander leaves. Serve with the warm peanut sauce.

Health Rating: 2 points

Spicy Beef Pancakes

Serves 4

Ingredients

50 g/2 oz/2/5 cup plain/all-purpose flour
pinch salt, 1/2 tsp Chinese five-spice powder
1 large/extra-large egg yolk
150 ml/1/4 pint/2/3 cup milk
4 tsp sunflower oil
slices of spring onion/scallion, to garnish

For the spicy beef filling:
1 tbsp sesame oil, 4 spring onions/scallions, sliced
1 cm/1/2 inch piece fresh root ginger, peeled and grated
1 garlic clove, peeled and crushed
300 g/10 oz sirloin steak, trimmed and cut into strips
1 red chilli, deseeded and finely chopped
1 tsp sherry vinegar
1 tsp soft dark brown sugar
1 tbsp dark soy sauce

Health Rating: 2 points

Sift the flour, salt and Chinese five-spice powder into a bowl and make a well in the centre. Add the egg yolk and a little of the milk. Gradually beat in, drawing in the flour to make a smooth batter. Whisk in the rest of the milk.

Heat 1 teaspoon of the sunflower oil in a small heavy-based frying pan. Pour in just enough batter to thinly coat the base of the pan. Cook over a medium heat for 1 minute, or until the underside of the pancake is golden brown.

Turn or toss the pancake and cook for 1 minute, or until the other side of the pancake is golden brown. Make seven more pancakes with the remaining batter. Stack them on a warmed plate as you make them, with greaseproof paper between each pancake. Cover with kitchen foil and keep warm in a low oven.

Make the filling. Heat a wok or large frying pan, add the sesame oil and, when hot, add the spring onions/scallions, ginger and garlic and stir-fry for 1 minute. Add the beef strips, stir-fry for 3–4 minutes, then stir in the chilli, vinegar, sugar and soy sauce. Cook for 1 minute, then remove from the heat.

Spoon one eighth of the filling over one half of each pancake. Fold the pancakes in half, then fold in half again. Garnish with a few slices of spring onion and serve immediately.

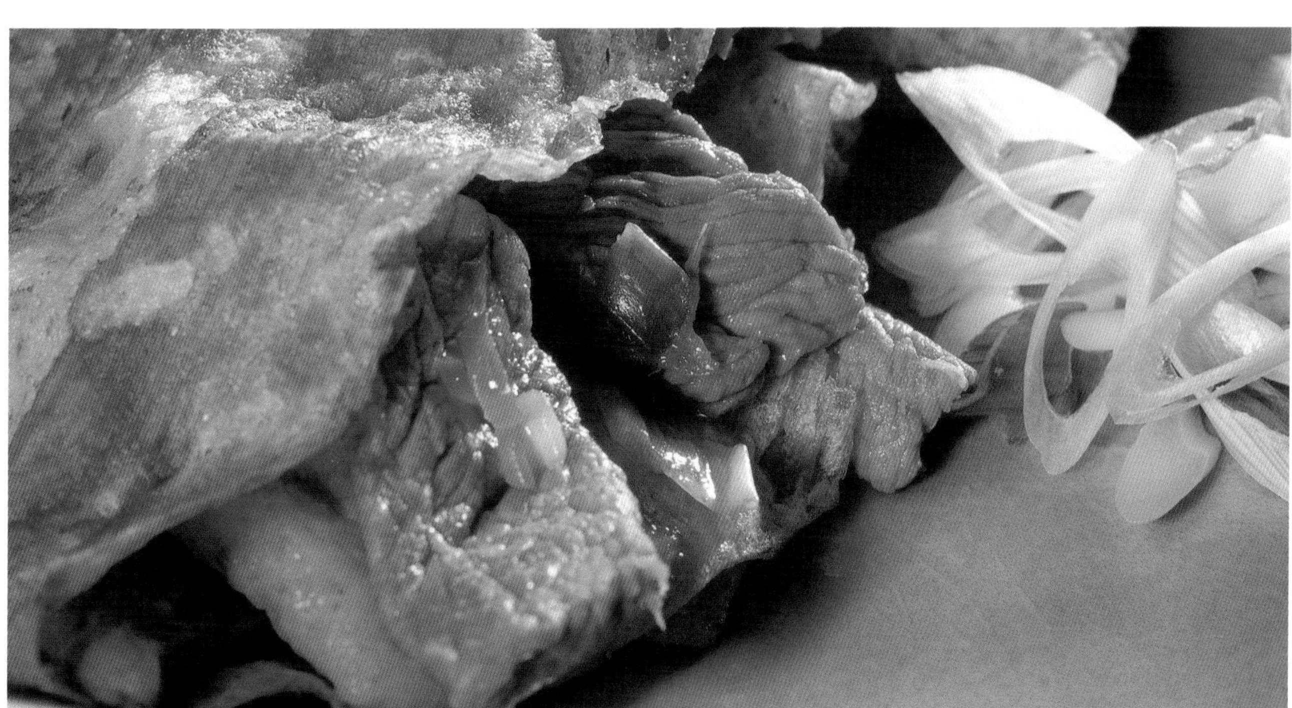

Fish & Shellfish

Whether stewed, steamed, roasted or grilled, fish and shellfish are easy and quick to cook. So, if you need to get a meal on the table in a hurry, one of these recipes may be the answer. Including family favourites, such as Battered Cod & Chunky Chips and Red Prawn Curry with Jasmine-scented Rice, even the fussiest eater will love these creations.

Ratatouille Mackerel

Serves 4

Ingredients

1 red pepper
1 tbsp olive oil
1 red onion, peeled
1 garlic clove, peeled and thinly sliced
2 courgettes/zucchini, trimmed and cut into thick slices
400 g/14 oz can chopped tomatoes
sea salt and freshly ground black pepper
4 x 275 g/10 oz small mackerel, cleaned and heads removed
spray of olive oil
lemon juice for drizzling
12 fresh basil leaves
couscous or rice mixed with chopped parsley, to serve

Preheat the oven to 190°C/375°F/Gas Mark 5. Cut the top off the red pepper, remove the seeds and membrane, then cut into chunks. Cut the red onion into thick wedges.

Heat the oil in a large pan and cook the onion and garlic for 5 minutes or until beginning to soften.

Add the pepper chunks and courgette/zucchini slices and cook for a further 5 minutes.

Pour in the chopped tomatoes with their juice and cook for a further 5 minutes. Season to taste with salt and pepper and pour into an ovenproof dish.

Season the fish with salt and pepper and arrange on top of the vegetables. Spray with a little olive oil and lemon juice. Cover and cook in the preheated oven for 20 minutes.

Remove the cover, add the basil leaves and return to the oven for a further 5 minutes. Serve immediately with couscous or rice mixed with parsley.

Health Rating: 5 points

Marinated Mackerel with Tomato & Basil Salad

Serves 3

Ingredients

3 mackerel, filleted
3 beef tomatoes, sliced
50 g/2 oz/2 cups watercress
2 oranges, peeled and segmented
75 g/3 oz/¾ cup sliced mozzarella cheese
2 tbsp basil leaves, shredded
fresh basil sprig, to garnish

For the marinade:
juice of 2 lemons; 4 tbsp olive oil; 4 tbsp basil leaves

For the dressing:
1 tbsp lemon juice
1 tsp Dijon mustard; 1 tsp caster/superfine sugar
salt and freshly ground black pepper
5 tbsp olive oil

Remove as many of the fine pin bones as possible from the mackerel fillets, lightly rinse and pat dry with absorbent paper towels and place in a shallow dish.

Blend the marinade ingredients together and pour over the mackerel. Make sure the marinade has covered the fish completely. Cover and leave in a cool place for at least 8 hours, but preferably overnight. As the fillets marinate, they will loose their translucency and look as if they are cooked.

Place the tomatoes, watercress, oranges and mozzarella cheese in a large bowl and toss. To make the dressing, whisk the lemon juice with the mustard, sugar and seasoning in a bowl. Pour half the dressing over the salad, toss again and then arrange on a serving platter. Remove the mackerel from the marinade, cut into bite-sized pieces and sprinkle with the shredded basil. Arrange on top of the salad, drizzle over the remaining dressing, scatter with basil leaves and garnish with a basil sprig. Serve.

Health Rating: 4 points

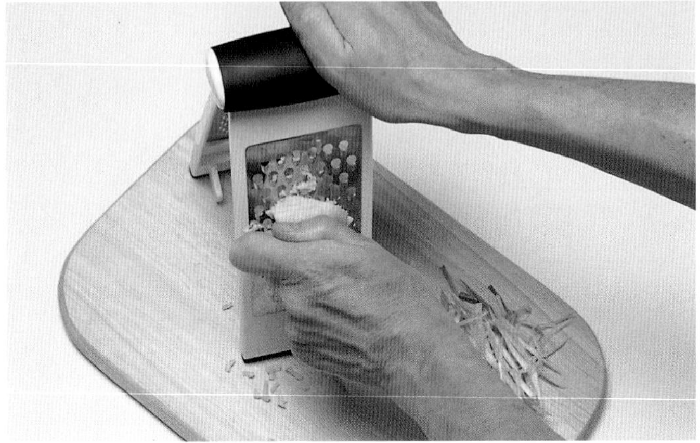

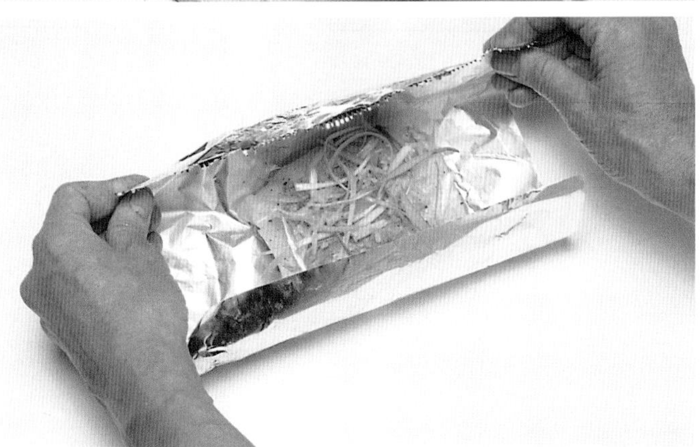

Gingered Cod Steaks

Serves 4

Ingredients

2.5 cm/1 inch piece fresh root ginger, peeled and coarsely grated
4 spring onions/scallions, cut into thin strips
2 tsp freshly chopped parsley
1 tbsp soft brown sugar
4 thick cod steaks, about 175 g/6 oz each
salt and freshly ground black pepper
25 g/1 oz/¼ stick butter
freshly cooked vegetables, to serve

Preheat the grill/broiler and line the rack with a layer of kitchen foil. Mix the ginger, spring onions/scallions, chopped parsley and sugar with 1 tablespoon water.

Wipe the fish steaks. Season to taste with salt and pepper. Place on four separate 20 x 20 cm/8 x 8 inch kitchen foil squares. Carefully spoon the spring onion and ginger mixture over the fish. Cut the butter into small cubes and place over the fish. Loosely fold the kitchen foil over the steaks to enclose the fish and to make a parcel.

Place under the preheated grill and cook for 10–12 minutes, or until the fish is cooked and the flesh has turned opaque.

Place the fish parcels on individual plates. Serve immediately with the freshly cooked vegetables.

Health Rating: 5 points

Battered Cod & Chunky Chips

Serves 4

Ingredients

1 tbsp fresh yeast
300 ml/½ pint/1¼ cups beer
225 g/8 oz/2 cups plain/all-purpose flour
1 tsp salt
700 g/1½ lb potatoes
450 ml/¾ pint/1¾ cups groundnut/peanut oil
4 cod fillets, about 225 g/8 oz each, skinned and boned
2 tbsp seasoned plain/all-purpose flour

To garnish:
lemon wedges
flat-leaf/Italian parsley sprigs

To serve:
tomato ketchup
vinegar

Dissolve the yeast with a little of the beer in a measuring jug and mix to a paste. Pour in the remaining beer, whisking all the time, until smooth. Place the flour and salt in a bowl and gradually pour in the beer mixture, whisking continuously, to make a thick, smooth batter. Cover the bowl and allow the batter to stand at room temperature for 1 hour.

Peel the potatoes and cut into thick slices. Cut each slice lengthways to make chunky chips/fries. Place them in a nonstick frying pan and heat, shaking the pan until all the moisture has evaporated. Turn them on to absorbent paper towels to dry off.

Heat the oil to 180°C/350°F, then fry the chips a few at a time for 4–5 minutes until crisp and golden. Drain on absorbent paper towels and keep warm.

Pat the cod fillets dry, then coat in the flour. Dip the floured fillets into the reserved batter. Fry for 2–3 minutes until cooked and crisp, then drain. Garnish with lemon wedges and parsley and serve immediately with the chips, tomato ketchup and vinegar.

Health Rating: 1 point

Spanish Omelette with Smoked Cod

Serves 3–4

Ingredients

3 tbsp sunflower oil
3 potatoes, peeled and diced
2 onions, peeled and cut into wedges
2–4 large garlic cloves, peeled and thinly sliced
1 large red pepper, deseeded, quartered and sliced
125 g/4½ oz smoked cod
salt and freshly ground black pepper
25 g/1 oz/¼ stick butter, melted
1 tbsp double/heavy cream
6 eggs, beaten
2 tbsp freshly chopped flat-leaf/Italian parsley
50 g/2 oz/½ cup grated mature Cheddar cheese

To serve:
crusty bread
tossed green salad

Heat the oil in a large, nonstick, heavy-based frying pan, add the potatoes, onions and garlic and cook gently for 10–15 minutes until golden brown, then add the red pepper and cook for 3 minutes.

Meanwhile, place the fish in a shallow frying pan and cover with water. Season to taste with salt and pepper and poach gently for 10 minutes. Drain and flake the fish into a bowl, pour in the melted butter and cream, adjust the seasoning and reserve.

When the vegetables are cooked, drain off excess oil and stir in the beaten eggs and parsley. Pour the fish mixture over the top and cook gently for 5 minutes, or until the eggs become firm.

Sprinkle the grated cheese over the top and place the pan under a preheated hot grill/broiler. Cook for 2–3 minutes until the cheese is golden and bubbling. Carefully slide the omelette on to a large plate and serve immediately with plenty of bread and salad.

Health Rating: 2 points

Fish Balls in Hot Yellow Bean Sauce

Serves 4

Ingredients

450 g/1 lb skinless white fish fillets, such as cod or haddock, cut into pieces
½ tsp salt
1 tbsp cornflour/cornstarch
2 spring onions/scallions, trimmed and chopped
1 tbsp freshly chopped coriander/cilantro
1 tsp soy sauce
1 medium/large egg white
freshly ground black pepper
tarragon sprig, to garnish
freshly cooked rice, to serve

For the yellow bean sauce:
75 ml/3 fl oz/⅓ cup fish or chicken stock
1–2 tsp yellow bean sauce
2 tbsp soy sauce
1–2 tbsp Chinese rice wine or dry sherry
1 tsp chilli bean sauce, or to taste
1 tsp sesame oil
1 tsp sugar (optional)

Put the fish pieces, salt, cornflour/cornstarch, spring onions/scallions, coriander/cilantro, soy sauce and egg white into a food processor.

Season to taste with pepper, then blend until a smooth paste forms, scraping down the sides of the food processor bowl occasionally.

With dampened hands, shape the mixture into 2.5 cm/1 inch balls. Transfer to a baking tray and chill in the refrigerator for at least 30 minutes.

Bring a large saucepan of water to simmering point. Working in two or three batches, drop in the fish balls and poach gently for 3–4 minutes, or until they float to the top. Transfer to absorbent kitchen paper to drain.

Put all the sauce ingredients in a wok or large frying pan and bring to the boil. Add the fish balls to the sauce and stir-fry gently for 2–3 minutes until piping hot. Transfer to a warmed serving dish, garnish with tarragon sprigs and serve immediately with freshly cooked rice.

Health Rating: 3 points

Barbecued Fish Kebabs

Serves 4

Ingredients

450 g/1 lb herring or mackerel fillets, cut into chunks
2 small red onions, peeled and quartered
16 cherry tomatoes
salt and freshly ground black pepper
couscous, to serve

For the sauce:
150 ml/¼ pint/⅔ cup fish stock
5 tbsp tomato ketchup
2 tbsp Worcestershire sauce
2 tbsp wine vinegar
2 tbsp brown sugar
2 drops Tabasco sauce
2 tbsp tomato puree/paste

Line a grill/broiler rack with a single layer of kitchen foil and preheat the grill at a high temperature 2 minutes before use. If using wooden skewers, soak in cold water for 30 minutes to prevent them burning.

Meanwhile, prepare the sauce. Put the fish stock, tomato ketchup, Worcestershire sauce, vinegar, sugar, Tabasco and tomato puree/paste in a small saucepan. Bring to the boil, then stir well, reduce the heat and leave to simmer for 5 minutes.

When ready to cook the kebabs, drain the skewers, if necessary, then thread the fish chunks, the quartered red onions and the cherry tomatoes alternately on to the skewers.

Season the kebabs to taste with salt and pepper and brush with the sauce. Cook under the preheated grill for 8–10 minutes, basting with the sauce occasionally during cooking. Turn the kebabs often to ensure that they are cooked thoroughly and evenly on all sides. Serve immediately with couscous.

Health Rating: 5 points

Citrus Monkfish Kebabs

Serves 4

Ingredients

For the marinade:
1 tbsp sunflower oil
finely grated rind and juice of 1 lime
1 tbsp lemon juice
1 fresh rosemary sprig, chopped
1 tbsp wholegrain mustard
1 garlic clove, peeled and crushed
salt and freshly ground black pepper

For the kebabs:
450 g/1 lb monkfish tail
8 raw tiger prawns/jumbo shrimp
1 small courgette/zucchini, trimmed and sliced
4 tbsp crème fraîche/sour cream

Health Rating: 5 points

Preheat the grill/broiler and line the rack with kitchen foil. Mix all the marinade ingredients together in a small bowl and reserve.

Using a sharp knife, cut down both sides of the monkfish tail. Remove the bone and discard. Cut away and discard any skin, then cut the monkfish into bite-sized cubes.

Peel the prawns/shrimp, leaving the tails intact and remove the thin black vein that runs down the back of each prawn. Place the fish and prawns in a nonmetallic shallow dish.

Pour the marinade over the fish and prawns. Cover lightly and leave to marinate in the refrigerator for 30 minutes. Spoon the marinade over the fish and prawns occasionally during this time. If using wooden skewers, soak them in cold water for 30 minutes, then drain.

Thread the cubes of fish, prawns and courgette/zucchini on to the skewers. Arrange on the grill rack then place under the preheated grill and cook for 5–7 minutes, or until cooked thoroughly and the prawns have turned pink. Occasionally brush with the remaining marinade and turn the kebabs during cooking. Mix 2 tablespoons of the marinade with the crème fraîche/sour cream and serve as a dip with the kebabs.

Roasted Monkfish with Vegetables

Serves 4

Ingredients

300 g/10 oz parsnips, peeled
350 g/12 oz sweet potatoes, peeled
300 g/10 oz carrots, peeled
2 onions, peeled
4–6 garlic cloves, peeled
salt and freshly ground black pepper
2 tbsp olive oil
2 small monkfish tails, about 900 g/2 lb total weight, or 4 monkfish fillets, about 700 g/1½ lb total weight
2–3 fresh rosemary sprigs
2 yellow peppers, deseeded
225 g/8 oz/1½ cups cherry tomatoes
2 tbsp freshly chopped parsley

Preheat the oven to 190°C/375°F/Gas Mark 5. Cut all the root vegetables, including the onions, into even-sized wedges and place in a roasting tin/pan. Reserve 2 garlic cloves and add the remainder to the roasting tin. Season to taste with salt and pepper and pour over 1 tablespoon of the oil. Turn the vegetables over until lightly coated in oil, then roast in the oven for 20 minutes.

Meanwhile, cut the monkfish tails into fillets. Using a sharp knife, cut down both sides of the central bone to form 2 fillets from each tail. Discard any skin or membrane, then rinse thoroughly. Make small incisions down the length of the monkfish fillets.

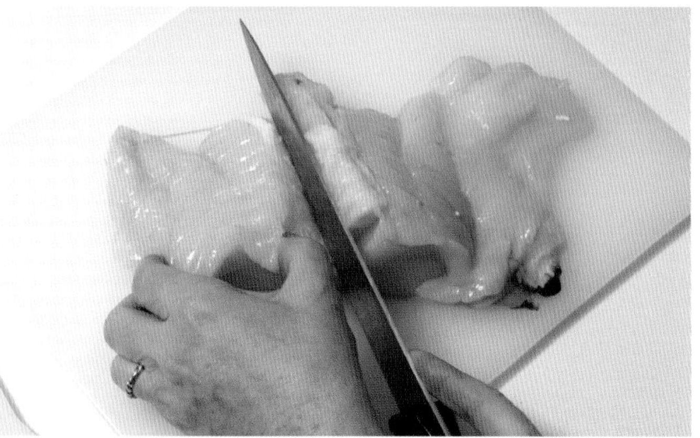

Cut the reserved garlic cloves into small slivers and break the rosemary into small sprigs. Insert the garlic and rosemary into the incisions in the fish.

Cut the peppers into strips, then add to the roasting tin together with the cherry tomatoes. Place the fish on top and drizzle with the remaining oil. Cook for a further 12–15 minutes, or until the vegetables and fish are thoroughly cooked. Serve sprinkled with chopped parsley.

Health Rating: 5 points

Coconut Fish Curry

Serves 4

Ingredients

2 tbsp sunflower oil
1 onion, peeled and very finely chopped
1 yellow pepper, deseeded and finely chopped
1 garlic clove, peeled and crushed; 1 tbsp mild curry paste
2.5 cm/1 inch piece root ginger, peeled and grated
1 red chilli, deseeded and finely chopped
400 ml/14 oz can coconut milk
700 g/1½ lb firm white fish, e.g. monkfish fillets, skinned and cut into chunks
225 g/8 oz/1⅓ cups basmati rice
1 tbsp freshly chopped coriander/cilantro
1 tbsp mango chutney
salt and freshly ground black pepper

To garnish:
lime wedges
fresh coriander/cilantro sprigs

To serve:
Greek/plain yogurt
warm naan bread

Put 1 tablespoon of the oil into a large frying pan and cook the onion, pepper and garlic for 5 minutes, or until soft. Add the remaining oil, curry paste, ginger and chilli and cook for a further minute.

Pour in the coconut milk and bring to the boil, reduce the heat and simmer gently for 5 minutes, stirring occasionally. Add the monkfish to the pan and continue to simmer gently for 5–10 minutes, or until the fish is tender, but not overcooked.

Meanwhile, cook the rice in a saucepan of boiling salted water for 15 minutes, or until tender. Drain the rice thoroughly and turn out into a serving dish.

Stir the chopped coriander/cilantro and chutney gently into the fish curry and season to taste with salt and pepper. Spoon the fish curry over the cooked rice, garnish with lime wedges and coriander sprigs and serve immediately with spoonfuls of Greek/plain yogurt and warm naan bread.

Health Rating: 2 points

Smoked Haddock Rösti

Serves 4

Ingredients

3–4 potatoes, peeled and coarsely grated
1 large onion, peeled and coarsely grated
2–3 garlic cloves, peeled and crushed
450 g/1 lb smoked haddock
1 tbsp olive oil
salt and freshly ground black pepper
finely grated zest/rind of ½ lemon
1 tbsp freshly chopped parsley
2 tbsp half-fat crème fraîche/sour cream
mixed salad leaves, to garnish
lemon wedges, to serve

Dry the potatoes in a clean dishtowel. Rinse the grated onion thoroughly in cold water, dry in a clean dishtowel and place in a bowl with the potatoes. Add the garlic and stir. Skin the smoked haddock and remove as many of the tiny pin bones as possible. Cut into thin slices and reserve.

Heat the oil in a nonstick frying pan. Add half the potatoes and press down firmly in the frying pan. Season to taste with salt and pepper.

Add a layer of fish and a sprinkling of lemon rind, parsley and a little black pepper. Top with the remaining potatoes and press down firmly. Cover with a sheet of kitchen foil and cook on the lowest heat for 25–30 minutes.

Preheat the grill/broiler 2–3 minutes before the end of the cooking time. Remove the kitchen foil and place the rösti under the grill to brown. Turn out on to a warmed serving dish and serve immediately with spoonfuls of crème fraîche/sour cream, mixed salad leaves and lemon wedges.

Health Rating: 3 points

Stir-fried Salmon with Peas

Serves 4

Ingredients

450 g/1 lb salmon fillet
salt, for sprinkling
6 slices streaky/fatty bacon
1 tbsp vegetable oil
50 ml/2 fl oz/¼ cup chicken or fish stock
2 tbsp dark soy sauce
2 tbsp Chinese rice wine or dry sherry
1 tsp sugar
75 g/3 oz/⅔ cup frozen peas, thawed
1–2 tbsp freshly shredded mint
1 tsp cornflour/cornstarch
fresh mint sprigs, to garnish
freshly cooked noodles, to serve

Wipe and skin the salmon fillet and remove any pin bones. Slice into 2.5 cm/1 inch strips, place on a plate and sprinkle with salt. Leave for 20 minutes, then pat dry with absorbent paper towels and reserve.

Remove any cartilage from the bacon, cut into small dice and reserve.

Heat a wok or large frying pan over a high heat, then add the oil and, when hot, add the bacon and stir-fry for 3 minutes, or until crisp and golden. Push to one side and add the strips of salmon. Stir-fry gently for 2 minutes, or until the flesh is opaque.

Pour the chicken or fish stock, soy sauce and Chinese rice wine or sherry into the wok, then stir in the sugar, peas and freshly shredded mint.

Blend the cornflour/cornstarch with 1 tablespoon water to form a smooth paste and stir into the sauce. Bring to the boil, reduce the heat and simmer for 1 minute, or until slightly thickened and smooth. Garnish and serve immediately with noodles.

Health Rating: 4 points

Salmon Fish Cakes

Serves 4

Ingredients

450 g/1 lb salmon fillet, skinned
salt and freshly ground black pepper
3 potatoes, peeled and cut into chunks
25 g/1 oz/¼ stick butter
1 tbsp milk
2 tomatoes, skinned, deseeded and chopped
2 tbsp freshly chopped parsley
75 g/3 oz/1¼ cups wholemeal breadcrumbs
25 g/1 oz/¼ cup grated Cheddar cheese
2 tbsp plain/all-purpose flour
2 eggs, beaten
3–4 tbsp vegetable oil

To serve:
ready-made raita
fresh mint sprigs

Place the salmon in a shallow frying pan and cover with water. Season to taste with salt and pepper and simmer for 8–10 minutes until the fish is cooked. Drain and flake into a bowl.

Boil the potatoes in lightly salted water until soft, then drain. Mash with the butter and milk until smooth. Add the potato to the bowl of fish and stir in the tomatoes and half the parsley. Adjust the seasoning to taste. Chill the mixture in the refrigerator for at least 2 hours to firm up.

Mix the breadcrumbs with the grated cheese and the remaining parsley. When the fish mixture is firm, form into eight flat cakes. First, lightly coat the fish cakes in the flour, then dip into the beaten egg, allowing any excess to drip back into the bowl. Finally, press into the breadcrumb mixture until well coated.

Heat a little of the oil in a frying pan and fry the fish cakes in batches for 2–3 minutes on each side until golden and crisp, adding more oil if necessary. Serve with raita garnished with mint sprigs.

Health Rating: 3 points

Salmon Noisettes with Fruity Sauce

Serves 4

Ingredients

4 x 125 g/4 oz salmon steaks
grated rind and juice of 2 lemons
grated rind and juice of 1 lime
3 tbsp olive oil
1 tbsp clear honey
1 tbsp wholegrain mustard
coarse sea salt and freshly ground black pepper
1 tbsp groundnut/peanut oil
125 g/4 oz mixed salad leaves, washed
1 bunch watercress, washed and thick stalks removed
250 g/9 oz/1⅔ cup baby plum tomatoes, halved

Using a sharp knife, cut the bone away from each salmon steak to create 2 salmon fillets. Repeat with the remaining salmon steaks. Shape the salmon fillets into noisettes and secure with fine string.

Mix together the citrus rinds and juices, olive oil, honey, wholegrain mustard, salt and pepper in a shallow dish. Add the salmon fillets and turn to coat. Cover and leave to marinate in the refrigerator for 4 hours, turning them occasionally in the marinade.

Heat the wok, then add the groundnut/peanut oil and heat until hot. Lift out the salmon noisettes, reserving the marinade. Add the salmon to the wok and cook for 6–10 minutes, turning once during cooking, until cooked and the fish is just flaking. Pour the marinade into the wok and heat through gently.

Mix together the salad leaves, watercress and tomatoes and arrange on serving plates. Top with the salmon noisettes and drizzle over any remaining warm marinade. Serve immediately.

Health Rating: 5 points

Salmon Parcels

Serves 4–6

Ingredients

4 salmon fillets, each about 150 g/5 oz in weight
5 cm/2 inch piece fresh root ginger, peeled and grated
1 red chilli, deseeded and sliced
1 green chilli, deseeded and sliced
2–3 garlic cloves, peeled and crushed
1 tbsp curry paste
4 tbsp sweet chilli sauce
few fresh coriander/cilantro sprigs

To serve:
lime wedges
new potatoes
steamed vegetables

Preheat the oven to 180°C/350°F/Gas Mark 4. Cut out 4 x 20.5 cm/8 inch squares of nonstick baking paper or foil. Lightly rinse the salmon and pat dry with absorbent paper towels. Place a salmon fillet on each square of paper.

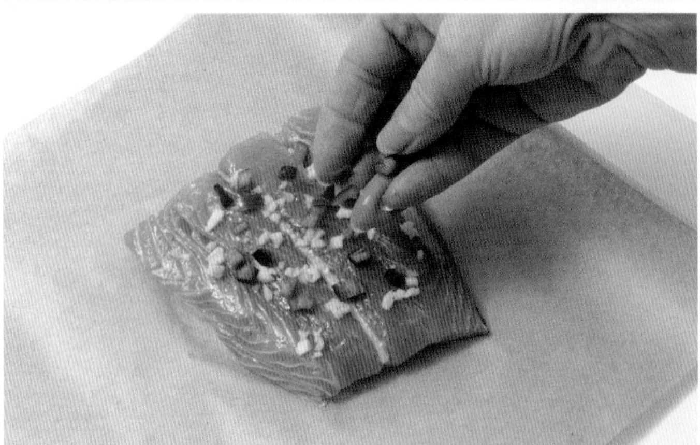

Sprinkle the fillets equally with the ginger, chillies and garlic. Blend the curry paste with the sweet chilli sauce and pour 1 tablespoon of the mixture over each salmon fillet. Top with fresh coriander/cilantro sprigs.

Fold the paper to completely encase the fillets and all the flavourings. Place in a roasting tin/pan or on a baking tray and cook in the preheated oven for 20 minutes.

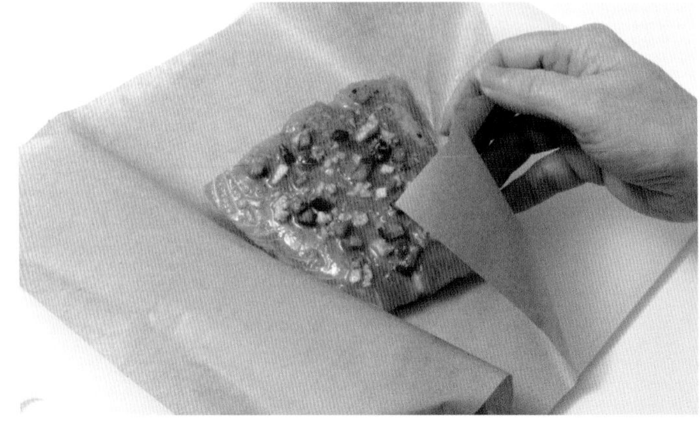

Place a parcel on each warmed dinner plate and let each person open up the parcels, so they can enjoy the pleasure of the spicy aroma. Serve with lime wedges, new potatoes and steamed vegetables.

Health Rating: 5 points

Chinese Five-spice Marinated Salmon

Serves 4

Ingredients

700 g/1½ lb skinless salmon fillet, cut into 2.5 cm/1 inch strips
2 medium/large egg whites
1 tbsp cornflour/cornstarch
vegetable oil, for frying
4 spring onions/scallions, cut diagonally into 5 cm/2 inch pieces
125 ml/4 fl oz/½ cup fish stock
lime or lemon wedges, to garnish

For the marinade:
3 tbsp soy sauce
3 tbsp Chinese rice wine or dry sherry
2 tsp sesame oil
1 tbsp soft brown sugar
1 tbsp lime or lemon juice
1 tsp Chinese five-spice powder
2–3 dashes hot pepper sauce

Combine the marinade ingredients in a shallow nonmetallic baking dish until well blended. Add the salmon strips and stir gently to coat. Leave to marinate in the refrigerator for 20–30 minutes.

Using a slotted spoon or fish slice, remove the salmon pieces, drain on absorbent paper towels and pat dry. Reserve the marinade.

Beat the egg whites with the cornflour/cornstarch to make a batter. Add the salmon strips and stir into the batter until coated completely.

Pour enough oil into a large wok to come 5 cm/2 inches up the side and place over a high heat. Working in two or three batches, add the salmon strips and cook for 1–2 minutes, or until golden. Remove from the wok with a slotted spoon and drain on absorbent kitchen paper. Reserve.

Discard the hot oil and wipe the wok clean. Add the marinade, spring onions/scallions and stock to the wok. Bring to the boil and simmer for 1 minute. Add the salmon strips and stir-fry gently until coated in the sauce. Spoon into a warmed shallow serving dish, garnish with the lime or lemon wedges and serve immediately.

Health Rating: 3 points

Teriyaki Salmon

Serves 4

Ingredients

450 g/1 lb salmon fillet, skinned
6 tbsp Japanese teriyaki sauce
1 tbsp rice wine vinegar
1 tbsp tomato puree/paste
dash of Tabasco sauce
2 tsp grated lemon zest
salt and freshly ground black pepper
4 tbsp groundnut/peanut oil
1 carrot, peeled and cut into matchsticks
125 g/4½ oz/1 cup mangetout/snow peas
125 g/4½ oz/1¾ cups oyster mushrooms, wiped

Using a sharp knife, cut the salmon into thick slices and place in a shallow dish. Mix together the teriyaki sauce, rice wine vinegar, tomato puree/paste, Tabasco sauce, lemon zest and seasoning.

Spoon the marinade over the salmon, then cover loosely and leave to marinate in the refrigerator for 30 minutes, turning the salmon or spooning the marinade occasionally over the salmon.

Heat a large wok, then add 2 tablespoons of the oil until almost smoking. Stir-fry the carrot for 2 minutes, then add the mangetout/snow peas and stir-fry for a further 2 minutes. Add the oyster mushrooms and stir-fry for 4 minutes, until softened. Using a slotted spoon, transfer the vegetables to four warmed serving plates and keep warm.

Remove the salmon from the marinade, reserving both the salmon and marinade. Add the remaining oil to the wok, heat until almost smoking, then cook the salmon for 4–5 minutes, turning once during cooking, or until the fish is just flaking. Add the marinade and heat through for 1 minute.

Serve immediately, with the salmon arranged on top of the vegetables and the marinade drizzled over.

Health Rating: 5 points

Sweet-and-sour Fish

Serves 4

Ingredients

1 small carrot, peeled and cut into julienne strips
1 small red or green pepper
125 g/4 oz/1 cup mangetout/snow peas, cut in half diagonally
125 g/4 oz/1 cup frozen peas, thawed
2–3 spring onions/scallions, trimmed and sliced diagonally into 5 cm/2 inch pieces
450 g/1 lb small thin skinless plaice/flounder fillets
1½–2 tbsp cornflour/cornstarch
vegetable oil, for frying
fresh coriander/cilantro sprigs, to garnish

For the sweet-and-sour sauce:
2 tsp cornflour/cornstarch
300 ml/½ pint/1¼ cups fish or chicken stock
4 cm/1½ inch piece fresh root ginger, peeled and finely sliced
2 tbsp soy sauce
2 tbsp rice wine vinegar or dry sherry
2 tbsp ketchup or tomato concentrate
2 tbsp Chinese rice vinegar or cider vinegar
1½ tbsp soft light brown sugar

Make the sauce. Place the cornflour/cornstarch in a saucepan and gradually whisk in the stock. Stir in the remaining sauce ingredients and bring to the boil, stirring, until the sauce thickens. Simmer for 2 minutes, then remove from the heat and reserve.

Bring a saucepan of water to the boil. Add the carrot, return to the boil and cook for 3 minutes. Add the pepper and cook for 1 minute. Add the mangetout/snow peas and peas and cook for 30 seconds. Drain, rinse under cold running water and drain again, then add to the sweet-and-sour sauce with the spring onions/scallions.

Using a sharp knife, make crisscross slashes across the top of each fish fillet, then lightly coat on both sides with the cornflour. Pour enough oil into a large wok to come 5 cm/2 inches up the side. Heat to 190°C/375°F, or until a cube of bread browns in 30 seconds. Fry the fish fillets, 2 at a time, for 3–5 minutes, or until crisp and golden, turning once. Using a fish slice, remove and drain on absorbent paper towels. Keep warm.

Bring the sweet-and-sour sauce to the boil, stirring constantly. Arrange the fish fillets on a warmed platter and pour over the hot sauce. Garnish with coriander/cilantro sprigs and serve immediately.

Health Rating: 4 points

Citrus-grilled Plaice

Serves 4

Ingredients

1 tsp sunflower oil
1 onion, peeled and chopped
1 orange pepper, deseeded and chopped
175 g/6 oz/¾ cup long-grain rice
150 ml/¼ pint/⅔ cup orange juice
2 tbsp lemon juice
250 ml/8 fl oz/1 cup vegetable stock
oil, for spraying
4 plaice/flounder fillets, skinned, 175 g/6 oz each
1 orange
1 lemon
25 g/1 oz/¼ stick half-fat butter or low-fat margarine
2 tbsp freshly chopped tarragon
salt and freshly ground black pepper
lemon wedges, to garnish

Heat the oil in a large frying pan. Fry the onion, pepper and rice for 2 minutes. Add the orange and lemon juice and bring to the boil. Reduce the heat, add half the stock. Simmer for 15–20 minutes, or until the rice is tender, adding the remaining stock as necessary.

Preheat the grill/broiler. Finely spray the base of the grill pan with oil. Put the plaice/flounder fillets in the base and reserve. Finely grate the orange and lemon zest/rind. Squeeze the juice from half of each fruit.

Melt the butter or margarine in a small saucepan. Add the grated rind, juice and half of the tarragon and use to baste the fish fillets.

Cook one side only of the fish under the preheated grill at a medium heat for 4–6 minutes, basting continuously. Once the rice is cooked, stir in the remaining tarragon and season to taste with salt and pepper. Garnish the fish with the lemon wedges and serve immediately with the rice.

Health Rating: 4 points

Goujons of Plaice with Tartare Sauce

Serves 4

Ingredients

75 g/3 oz/1¼ cup fresh white breadcrumbs
3 tbsp freshly grated Parmesan cheese
salt and freshly ground black pepper
1 tbsp dried oregano
1 medium/large egg
450 g/1 lb plaice/flounder fillets
300 ml/½ pint/1¼ cups vegetable oil, for deep frying
fat chips/fries, to serve

For the tartare sauce:
200 ml/7 fl oz/¾ cup prepared mayonnaise
50 g/2 oz/¼ cup gherkins/pickles, finely chopped
2 tbsp freshly snipped chives
1 garlic clove, peeled and crushed
2–3 tbsp capers, drained and chopped
pinch cayenne pepper
salt and freshly ground black pepper

Mix together the breadcrumbs, Parmesan cheese, seasoning and oregano on a large plate. Lightly beat the egg in a shallow dish. Then, using a sharp knife, cut the plaice/flounder fillets into thick strips.

Coat the plaice strips in the beaten egg, allowing any excess to drip back into the dish, then dip the strips into the breadcrumbs until well coated. Place the goujons on a baking sheet, cover and chill in the refrigerator for 30 minutes.

Meanwhile, to make the tartare sauce, mix together the mayonnaise, gherkins/pickles, chives, garlic, capers and cayenne pepper. Stir, then season to taste with salt and pepper. Place in a bowl, cover loosely and store in the refrigerator until required.

Pour the oil into a large wok. Heat to 190°C/375°F, or until a small cube of bread turns golden and crisp in about 30 seconds. Cook the plaice goujons in batches for about 4 minutes, turning occasionally, until golden. Using a slotted spoon, remove and drain on absorbent paper towels. Serve immediately with the tartare sauce and chips/fries.

Health Rating: 1 point

Tuna Fish Burgers

Serves 4

Ingredients

3–4 potatoes, peeled and cut into chunks
50 g/2 oz/½ stick butter
2 tbsp milk
400 g/14 oz can tuna in oil
1 spring onion/scallion, trimmed and finely chopped
1 tbsp freshly chopped parsley
salt and freshly ground black pepper
2 medium/large eggs, beaten
2 tbsp seasoned plain/all-purpose flour
125 g/4½ oz/2 cups fresh white breadcrumbs
4 tbsp vegetable oil
4 sesame seed baps/buns (optional)

To serve:
fat chips/fries
mixed salad
tomato chutney

Place the potatoes in a large saucepan, cover with boiling water and simmer until soft. Drain, then mash with 40 g/1½ oz/3 tbsp of the butter and the milk. Turn into a large bowl. Drain the tuna, discarding the oil, and flake into the bowl of potato. Stir well to mix.

Add the spring onion/scallion and parsley to the mixture and season to taste with salt and pepper. Add 1 tablespoon of the beaten egg to bind the mixture together. Chill in the refrigerator for at least 1 hour.

Shape the chilled mixture with your hands into four large burgers. First, coat the burgers with seasoned flour, then brush them with the remaining beaten egg, allowing any excess to drip back into the bowl. Finally, coat them evenly in the breadcrumbs, pressing the crumbs on with your hands, if necessary.

Heat a little of the oil in a frying pan and fry the burgers for 2–3 minutes on each side until golden, adding more oil if necessary. Drain on absorbent paper towels and serve hot in baps, if using, with chips/fries, mixed salad and chutney.

Health Rating: 2 points

Seared Tuna with Italian Salsa

Serves 4

Ingredients

4 tuna or swordfish steaks, about 175 g/6 oz each
salt and freshly ground black pepper
3 tbsp Pernod; 2 tbsp olive oil
zest and juice of 1 lemon; 2 tsp fresh thyme leaves
2 tsp fennel seeds, lightly roasted
4 sun-dried tomatoes, chopped
1 tsp dried chilli flakes
assorted salad leaves, to serve

For the salsa:
1 white onion, peeled and finely chopped
2 tomatoes, deseeded and sliced
2 tbsp freshly shredded basil leaves
1 red chilli, deseeded and finely sliced
3 tbsp extra virgin olive oil
2 tsp balsamic vinegar; 1 tsp caster/superfine sugar

Wipe the fish and season lightly with salt and pepper, then place in a shallow dish. Mix together the Pernod, olive oil, lemon zest and juice, thyme, fennel seeds, sun-dried tomatoes and chilli flakes and pour over the fish. Cover lightly and leave to marinate in a cool place for 1–2 hours, occasionally spooning the marinade over the fish.

Meanwhile, mix all the ingredients for the salsa together in a small bowl. Season to taste with salt and pepper, then cover and leave for about 30 minutes to allow all the flavours to develop.

Lightly oil a griddle pan and heat until hot. When the pan is very hot, drain the fish, reserving the marinade. Cook the fish for 3–4 minutes on each side, taking care not to overcook them – the tuna steaks should be a little pink inside. Pour any remaining marinade into a small saucepan, bring to the boil and boil for 1 minute. Serve the steaks hot with the marinade, chilled salsa and a few assorted salad leaves.

Health Rating: 5 points

Steamed Whole Trout with Ginger & Spring Onion

Serves 4

Ingredients

2 whole trout, gutted, with heads removed, 700 g/1½ lb each
coarse sea salt, for rubbing
2 tbsp groundnut/peanut oil
½ tbsp soy sauce
1 tbsp sesame oil
2 garlic cloves, peeled and thinly sliced
2.5 cm/1 inch piece fresh root ginger, peeled and cut into strips
2 spring onions/scallions, trimmed and thinly sliced diagonally

To garnish:
fresh chives
lemon slices

To serve:
freshly cooked rice
oriental salad

Wipe the fish inside and out with absorbent paper towels, then rub with salt inside and out. Leave for about 20 minutes. Pat dry with absorbent paper towels.

Set a steamer rack or inverted ramekin in a large wok and pour in enough water to come about 5 cm/2 inches up the side of the wok. Bring to the boil.

Brush a heatproof dinner plate with a little of the groundnut/peanut oil. Place the fish on the plate with the tails pointing in opposite directions. Place the plate on the rack, cover tightly and simmer over a medium heat for 10–12 minutes, or until tender and the flesh is opaque near the bone. Carefully transfer the plate to a heatproof surface. Divide the fish into four servings. Sprinkle with the soy sauce, keep warm.

Pour the water out of the wok and return to the heat. Add the remaining groundnut oil and sesame oil. When hot, add the garlic, ginger and spring onions/scallions. Stir-fry for 2 minutes, or until golden. Pour over the fish, garnish with chives and lemon slices. Serve with rice and an oriental salad.

Health Rating: 4 points

Grilled Red Mullet with Orange & Anchovy Sauce

Serves 4

Ingredients

2 oranges
4 x 175 g/6 oz red mullet, cleaned and descaled
salt and freshly ground black pepper
4 fresh rosemary sprigs
1 lemon, sliced
2 tbsp olive oil
2 garlic cloves, peeled and crushed
6 anchovy fillets in oil, drained and roughly chopped
2 tsp freshly chopped rosemary
1 tsp lemon juice

Preheat the grill/broiler and line the grill rack with kitchen foil just before cooking.

Peel the oranges with a sharp knife, over a bowl in order to catch the juice. Cut into thin slices and reserve. If necessary, make up the juice to 150 ml/¼ pint/⅔ cup with extra juice.

Place the fish on a chopping board and make two diagonal slashes across the thickest part of both sides of the fish. Season well, both inside and out, with salt and pepper. Tuck a rosemary sprig and a few lemon slices inside the cavity of each fish. Brush the fish with a little of the olive oil and then cook under the preheated grill for 4–5 minutes on each side. The flesh should just fall away from the bone.

Heat the remaining oil in a saucepan and gently fry the garlic and anchovies for 3–4 minutes. Do not allow to brown. Add the chopped rosemary and plenty of black pepper. The anchovies will be salty enough, so do not add any salt. Stir in the orange slices with their juice and the lemon juice. Simmer gently until heated through. Spoon the sauce over the red mullet and serve immediately.

Health Rating: 4 points

Fragrant Thai Swordfish with Peppers

Serves 4–6

Ingredients

550 g/1¼ lb swordfish, cut into 5 cm/2 inch strips
2 tbsp vegetable oil
2 lemon grass stalks, peeled, bruised and cut into 2.5 cm/1 inch pieces
2.5 cm/1 inch piece fresh root ginger, peeled and thinly sliced
4–5 shallots, peeled and thinly sliced
2–3 garlic cloves, peeled and thinly sliced
1 small red pepper, deseeded and thinly sliced
1 small yellow pepper, deseeded and thinly sliced
2 tbsp soy sauce
2 tbsp Chinese rice wine or dry sherry
1–2 tsp sugar
1 tsp sesame oil
1 tbsp Thai or Italian basil, shredded
salt and freshly ground black pepper
1 tbsp toasted sesame seeds

For the marinade:
1 tbsp soy sauce
1 tbsp Chinese rice wine or dry sherry
1 tbsp sesame oil
1 tbsp cornflour/cornstarch

Blend all the marinade ingredients together in a shallow, nonmetallic baking dish. Add the swordfish and spoon the marinade over the fish. Cover and leave to marinate in the refrigerator for at least 30 minutes.

Using a slotted spatula or spoon, remove the swordfish from the marinade and drain briefly on absorbent paper towels. Heat a wok or large frying pan, add the oil and, when hot, add the swordfish and stir-fry for 2 minutes, or until it begins to brown. Remove the swordfish and drain on absorbent paper towels.

Add the lemon grass, ginger, shallots and garlic to the wok and stir-fry for 30 seconds. Add the peppers, soy sauce, Chinese rice wine or sherry and sugar and stir-fry for 3–4 minutes.

Return the swordfish to the wok and stir-fry gently for 1–2 minutes, or until heated through and coated with the sauce. If necessary, moisten the sauce with a little of the marinade or some water.

Stir in the sesame oil and the basil and season to taste with salt and pepper. Tip into a warmed serving bowl, sprinkle with sesame seeds and serve immediately.

Health Rating: 4 points

Aromatic Sole

Serves 4–6

Ingredients

175 g/6 oz/⅞ cup Thai fragrant rice
8 sole fillets, about 350 g/12 oz total weight, skinned
3 tbsp groundnut/peanut oil
1 tsp cumin seeds, plus extra to garnish
1 tsp sesame seeds, plus extra to garnish
1 lemon grass stalk, bruised and outer leaves discarded
1 small cinnamon stick, bruised
4 cardamom pods, cracked
2 whole cloves
2–3 curry leaves
2.5 cm/1 inch piece fresh root ginger, peeled and grated
1 tbsp Madras/hot curry paste
400 ml/14 fl oz can coconut milk
100 g/3½ oz button mushrooms, wiped and sliced

Health Rating: 3 points

Cook the rice in a saucepan of boiling water for 12 minutes, or until cooked. Drain and reserve. Rinse the fish fillets and pat dry with absorbent paper towels and cut into strips. Reserve.

Heat 1 tablespoon of the oil in a nonstick frying pan, add a teaspoon each of the cumin and sesame seeds and fry for 30 seconds, or until they pop. Drain on paper towels and reserve.

Heat a further tablespoon oil in a wok or large saucepan, add the lemon grass, cinnamon stick, cardamom pods, cloves, curry leaves and grated ginger and gently stir-fry for 2 minutes. Add the curry paste and continue to cook gently for 2 minutes, stirring constantly. Take off the heat and gradually stir in the coconut milk. Half-fill the coconut milk can with water, then swirl to dislodge any coconut milk on the sides of the can and add to the pan. Bring to the boil, then reduce the heat and simmer for 10 minutes.

Heat the remaining oil in a small saucepan, add the mushrooms and cook for 2 minutes. Drain and add to the sauce with the sole. Continue to simmer for 5–8 minutes, or until the fish is tender. Spoon the rice into warmed serving dishes and ladle over the sole and coconut milk. Sprinkle with a few seeds and serve.

Chunky Halibut Casserole

Serves 6

Ingredients

50 g/2 oz/½ stick butter or margarine
2 large onions, peeled and sliced into rings
1 red pepper, deseeded and roughly chopped
3–4 potatoes, peeled and cut into small chunks
450 g/1 lb (about 3) courgettes/zucchini, trimmed and sliced
2 tbsp plain/all-purpose flour
1 tbsp paprika
2 tsp vegetable oil
300 ml/½ pint/1¼ cups white wine
150 ml/¼ pint/⅔ cup fish stock
400 g/14 oz can chopped tomatoes
2 tbsp freshly chopped basil
salt and freshly ground black pepper
450 g/1 lb halibut fillet, skinned and cut into 2.5 cm/1 inch cubes
fresh basil sprigs, to garnish
freshly cooked rice, to serve

Melt the butter or margarine in a large saucepan, add the onions and pepper and cook for 5 minutes, or until softened.

Rinse the potatoes lightly and shake dry. Add them to the onions and pepper in the saucepan. Add the courgettes/zucchini and cook, stirring frequently, for a further 2–3 minutes.

Sprinkle the flour, paprika and vegetable oil into the saucepan and cook, stirring continuously, for 1 minute. Pour in 150 ml/¼ pint/⅔ cup of the wine, with all the stock and the chopped tomatoes, and bring to the boil.

Add the basil to the casserole, season to taste with salt and pepper and cover. Simmer for 15 minutes, then add the halibut and the remaining wine and simmer very gently for a further 5–7 minutes, or until the fish and vegetables are just tender. Garnish with basil sprigs and serve immediately with freshly cooked rice.

Health Rating: 4 points

Mediterranean Fish Stew

Serves 4–6

Ingredients

4 tbsp olive oil
1 onion, peeled and finely sliced
5 garlic cloves, peeled and finely sliced
1 fennel bulb, trimmed and finely chopped
3 celery stalks, trimmed and finely chopped
400 g/14 oz can chopped tomatoes with herbs
1 tbsp freshly chopped oregano
1 bay leaf
zest and juice of 1 orange
1 tsp saffron strands
750 ml/1¼ pints/3 cups fish stock
3 tbsp dry vermouth
salt and freshly ground black pepper
225 g/8 oz thick haddock fillets
225 g/8 oz sea bass or bream fillets
225 g/8 oz raw tiger prawns/jumbo shrimp, peeled
crusty bread, to serve

Heat the olive oil in a large saucepan. Add the onion, garlic, fennel and celery and cook over a low heat for 15 minutes, stirring frequently, until the vegetables are soft and just beginning to turn brown.

Add the canned tomatoes with their juice, oregano, bay leaf, orange zest and juice and the saffron strands. Bring to the boil, then reduce the heat and simmer for 5 minutes. Add the fish stock and vermouth and season to taste with salt and pepper. Bring to the boil. Reduce the heat and simmer for 20 minutes.

Wipe or rinse the haddock and bass fillets. Remove as many bones as possible. Place on a chopping board and cut into 5 cm/2 inch cubes. Add to the saucepan and cook for 3 minutes. Add the prawns/shrimp and cook for a further 5 minutes. Adjust the seasoning to taste and serve with crusty bread.

Health Rating: 4 points

Quick Mediterranean Prawns

Serves 4

Ingredients

20 raw Mediterranean prawns/shrimp
3 tbsp olive oil
1 garlic clove, peeled and crushed
finely grated zest and juice of ½ lemon
fresh rosemary sprigs
lemon wedges, to garnish

For the pesto and sun-dried tomato dips:
150 ml/¼ pint Greek-style/plain yogurt
1 tbsp prepared pesto
150 ml/¼ pint crème fraîche/sour cream
1 tbsp sun-dried tomato paste
1 tbsp wholegrain mustard
salt and freshly ground black pepper

Remove the shells from the prawns/shrimp, leaving the tail shells. Using a small, sharp knife, remove the dark vein that runs along the backs of the prawns. Rinse and drain on paper towels.

Whisk 2 tablespoons of the oil with the garlic, lemon zest and juice in a small bowl. Bruise 1 rosemary sprig with a rolling pin and add to the bowl. Add the prawns, toss to coat, then cover and leave to marinate in the refrigerator until needed.

For the simple dips, mix the yogurt and pesto in one bowl and the crème fraîche/sour cream, tomato paste and mustard in another bowl. Season to taste with salt and pepper.

Heat a wok, add the remaining oil and swirl round to coat the sides. Remove the prawns from the marinade, leaving any juices and the rosemary behind. Add to the wok and stir-fry over a high heat for 3–4 minutes, or until the prawns are pink and just cooked through.

Remove the prawns from the wok and arrange on a platter. Garnish with lemon wedges and more fresh rosemary sprigs and serve hot or cold with the dips.

Health Rating: 2 points

Red Prawn Curry with Jasmine-scented Rice

Serves 4

Ingredients

1/2 tbsp coriander seeds
1 tsp cumin seeds
1 tsp black peppercorns
1/2 tsp salt
1–2 dried red chillies
2 shallots, peeled and chopped
3–4 garlic cloves
2.5 cm/1 inch piece fresh galangal or root ginger, peeled and chopped
1 kaffir lime leaf or 1 tsp kaffir lime rind
1/2 tsp red chilli powder
1/2 tbsp prawn/shrimp paste
1–1 1/2 lemon grass stalks, thinly sliced after removing outer leaves
750 ml/1 1/4 pints/3 1/4 cups coconut milk
1 red chilli, deseeded and thinly sliced
2 tbsp Thai fish sauce
2 tsp soft brown sugar
1 red pepper, deseeded and thinly sliced
550 g/1 1/4 lb large peeled tiger prawns/shrimp
2 fresh lime leaves, shredded (optional)
2 tbsp fresh mint leaves, shredded
2 tbsp Thai or Italian basil leaves, shredded
freshly cooked Thai fragrant rice, to serve

Using a pestle and mortar or a spice grinder, grind the coriander and cumin seeds, peppercorns and salt to a fine powder. Add the dried chillies one at a time and grind to a fine powder.

Place the shallots, garlic, galangal or ginger, kaffir lime leaf or rind, chilli powder and prawn/shrimp paste in a food processor. Add the ground spices and process until a thick paste forms.

Scrape down the bowl once or twice, adding a few drops of water if the mixture is too thick and not forming a paste. Stir in the lemon grass.

Transfer the paste to a large wok. Cook over a medium heat for 2–3 minutes, or until fragrant. Stir in the coconut milk, bring to the boil. Lower the heat and simmer for about 10 minutes. Add the chilli, fish sauce, sugar and red pepper and simmer for 15 minutes. Stir in the prawns/shrimp and cook for 5 minutes, or until the prawns are pink and tender. Stir in the shredded herbs, heat for a further minute and serve immediately with the cooked rice.

Health Rating: 3 points

Szechuan Chilli Prawns

Serves 4

Ingredients

450 g/1 lb raw tiger prawns/jumbo shrimp
2 tbsp groundnut/peanut oil
1 onion, peeled and sliced
1 red pepper, deseeded and cut into strips
1 small red chilli, deseeded and thinly sliced
2 garlic cloves, peeled and finely chopped
2–3 spring onions/scallions, trimmed and diagonally sliced
fresh coriander/cilantro sprigs or chilli flowers, to garnish
freshly cooked rice or noodles, to serve

For the chilli sauce:
1 tbsp cornflour/cornstarch
4 tbsp cold fish stock or water
2 tbsp soy sauce
2 tbsp sweet or hot chilli sauce, or to taste
2 tsp soft light brown sugar

Peel the prawns/shrimp, leaving the tails attached if you like. Using a sharp knife, remove the black vein along the backs of the prawns. Rinse and pat dry with absorbent paper towels.

Heat a wok or large frying pan, add the oil and, when hot, add the onion, pepper and chilli and stir-fry for 4–5 minutes, or until the vegetables are tender but retain a bite. Stir in the garlic and cook for 30 seconds. Using a slotted spoon, transfer to a plate and reserve.

Add the prawns to the wok and stir-fry for 1–2 minutes, or until they turn pink and opaque. Blend all the chilli sauce ingredients together in a bowl or measuring jug, then stir into the prawns. Add the reserved vegetables and bring to the boil, stirring constantly. Cook for 1–2 minutes, or until the sauce is thickened and the prawns and vegetables are well coated. Stir in the spring onions/scallions, tip on to a warmed platter. Garnish with coriander/cilantro sprigs or chilli flowers. Serve with rice or noodles.

Health Rating: 4 points

Coconut Seafood

Serves 4

Ingredients

2 tbsp groundnut/peanut oil
450 g/1 lb raw king prawns/jumbo shrimp, peeled
2 bunches spring onions/scallions, trimmed and thickly sliced
1 garlic clove, peeled and chopped
2.5 cm/1 inch piece fresh root ginger, peeled and cut into matchsticks
125 g/4½ oz/1 cup shiitake mushrooms, rinsed and halved
150 ml/¼ pint/⅔ cup dry white wine
200 ml/7 fl oz carton coconut cream
4 tbsp freshly chopped coriander/cilantro
salt and freshly ground black pepper
freshly cooked Thai fragrant rice

Heat a large wok, add the oil and heat until it is almost smoking, swirling the oil around the wok to coat the sides. Add the prawns/shrimp and stir-fry over a high heat for 4–5 minutes, or until browned on all sides. Using a slotted spoon, transfer the prawns to a plate and keep warm in a low oven.

Add the spring onions/scallions, garlic and ginger to the wok and stir-fry for 1 minute. Add the mushrooms and stir-fry for a further 3 minutes. Using a slotted spoon, transfer the mushroom mixture to a plate and keep warm in a low oven.

Add the wine and coconut cream to the wok, bring to the boil and boil rapidly for 4 minutes, until reduced slightly. Return the mushroom mixture and prawns to the wok, bring back to the boil, then simmer for 1 minute, stirring occasionally, until piping hot. Stir in the freshly chopped coriander/cilantro and season to taste with salt and pepper. Serve immediately with the freshly cooked Thai fragrant rice.

Health Rating: 2 points

Meat

Meat is an excellent source of protein, B vitamins and iron. Choose from this delicious selection of pork, lamb and beef recipes; for example, the Sausage & Apple Pot, Roast Leg of Lamb & Boulangere Potatoes or Chilli Beef. All provide a filling family feast for everyone to tuck into.

Jamaican Jerk Pork with Rice & Peas

Serves 4

Ingredients

2 onions, peeled and chopped
2 garlic cloves, peeled and crushed
4 tbsp lime juice
2 tbsp each treacle/molasses, soy sauce and chopped fresh root ginger
2 jalapeño chillies, deseeded and chopped
½ tsp ground cinnamon
¼ tsp each ground allspice and ground nutmeg
175 g/6 oz/1 cup dried red kidney beans, soaked overnight
4 pork loin chops, on the bone

For the rice:
1 tbsp vegetable oil
1 onion, peeled and finely chopped
1 celery stalk, trimmed and finely sliced
3 garlic cloves, peeled and crushed
2 bay leaves
225 g/8 oz/1¼ cups long-grain white rice
475 ml/18 fl oz/2 cups chicken or ham stock
fresh flat-leaf/Italian parsley sprigs, to garnish

To make the jerk pork marinade, puree the onions, garlic, lime juice, treacle/molasses, soy sauce, ginger, chillies, cinnamon, allspice and nutmeg together in a food processor until smooth. Put the pork chops into a nonmetallic dish and pour over the marinade, turning the chops to coat. Marinate in the refrigerator for at least 1 hour or overnight.

Drain the beans and place in a large saucepan with about 2 litres/3½ pints/2 quarts cold water. Bring to the boil and boil rapidly for 10 minutes. Reduce the heat, cover and simmer gently for 1 hour until tender, adding more water if necessary. When cooked, drain well and mash roughly.

Heat the oil for the rice in a saucepan with a tight-fitting lid and add the onion, celery and garlic. Cook gently for 5 minutes until softened. Add the bay leaves, rice and stock and stir. Bring to the boil, cover and cook very gently for 10 minutes. Add the beans and stir well again. Cook for a further 5 minutes, then remove from the heat.

Heat a griddle pan until almost smoking. Remove the pork chops from the marinade, scraping off any surplus, and add to the hot pan. Cook for 5–8 minutes on each side, or until cooked. Garnish with the parsley and serve immediately with the rice.

Health Rating: 2 points

Pork Sausages with Onion Gravy & Best-ever Mash

Serves 4

Ingredients

50 g/2 oz/$\frac{1}{2}$ stick butter
1 tbsp olive oil
2 large onions, peeled and thinly sliced
pinch sugar
1 tbsp freshly chopped thyme
1 tbsp plain/all-purpose flour
100 ml/3$\frac{1}{2}$ fl oz/$\frac{1}{3}$ cup Madeira
200 ml/7 fl oz/$\frac{3}{4}$ cup vegetable stock
8–12 good-quality butchers' pork sausages, depending on size

For the mashed potatoes:
6–8 floury potatoes, peeled
75 g/3 oz/$\frac{3}{4}$ stick butter
4 tbsp crème fraîche/sour cream
salt and freshly ground black pepper

Melt the butter with the oil and add the onions. Cover and cook gently for about 20 minutes until the onions have collapsed. Add the sugar and stir well. Uncover and continue to cook, stirring often, until the onions are very soft and golden. Add the thyme, stir well, then add the flour, stirring. Gradually add the Madeira and the stock. Bring to the boil and simmer gently for 10 minutes.

Meanwhile, put the sausages in a large frying pan and cook over a medium heat for 15–20 minutes, turning often, until golden brown and slightly sticky all over.

For the mashed potatoes, boil the potatoes in plenty of lightly salted water for 15–18 minutes until tender. Drain well and return to the saucepan. Put the saucepan over a low heat to allow the potatoes to dry thoroughly. Remove from the heat and add the butter, crème fraîche/sour cream and salt and pepper. Mash thoroughly. Serve the mashed potatoes topped with the sausages and onion gravy.

Health Rating: 1 point

Oven-roasted Vegetables with Sausages

Serves 4

Ingredients

2 medium aubergines/eggplants, trimmed
3 medium courgettes/zucchini, trimmed
4 tbsp olive oil
6 garlic cloves
8 Tuscany-style sausages
4 plum tomatoes
2 x 325 g/11 oz cans cannellini beans
salt and freshly ground black pepper
1 bunch fresh basil, torn into coarse pieces
4 tbsp Parmesan cheese, grated

Preheat oven to 200°C/400°F/Gas Mark 6, 15 minutes before cooking. Cut the aubergines/eggplants and courgettes/zucchini into bite-sized chunks. Place the olive oil in a large roasting tin/pan and heat in the preheated oven for 3 minutes, or until very hot. Add the aubergines, courgettes and garlic cloves, then stir until coated in the hot oil and cook in the oven for 10 minutes.

Remove the roasting tin from the oven and stir. Lightly prick the sausages, add to the roasting tin and return to the oven. Continue to roast for a further 20 minutes, turning once during cooking, until the vegetables are tender and the sausages are golden brown.

Meanwhile, roughly chop the plum tomatoes and drain the cannellini beans. Remove the sausages from the oven and stir in the tomatoes and cannellini beans. Season to taste with salt and pepper, then return to the oven for 5 minutes, or until heated thoroughly.

Scatter over the basil leaves and sprinkle with plenty of Parmesan cheese and extra freshly ground black pepper. Serve immediately.

Health Rating: 3 points

Sausage & Apple Pot

Serves 4

Ingredients

1 tbsp olive oil
1 onion, peeled and sliced
2–3 garlic cloves, peeled and sliced
2 celery stalks, trimmed and sliced
8 apple- and pork-flavoured thick sausages
300 g/10 oz/$^2/_3$ cups carrots, peeled and sliced
1 large cooking apple, peeled and sliced
300 g/10 oz/2$^2/_3$ cup courgettes/zucchini, trimmed and sliced
salt and freshly ground black pepper
600 ml/1 pint/2$^1/_2$ cups vegetable stock
2 tsp dried mixed herbs
450 g/1 lb (about 3) potatoes, peeled and grated
50 g/2 oz/$^1/_2$ cup Gruyère cheese, grated

Preheat the oven to 180°C/350°F/Gas Mark 4. Heat the oil in an ovenproof casserole dish (or frying pan, if preferred), add the onion, garlic and celery and fry for 5 minutes.

Push the vegetables to one side then add the sausages and cook, turning the sausages over, until browned.

If a frying pan has been used, transfer everything to a casserole dish. Arrange the onions over and around the sausages together with the carrots, apple and courgettes/zucchini. Season to taste with salt and pepper and pour over the stock. Sprinkle with the mixed herbs, cover with a lid and cook in the oven for 30 minutes.

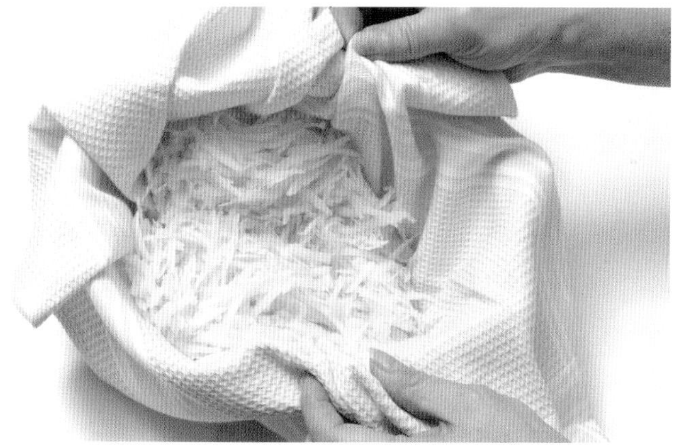

Meanwhile, soak the grated potatoes in a bowl of cold water for 10 minutes. Drain thoroughly, then place the potatoes on a clean dishtowel and squeeze to remove any excess moisture.

Remove the casserole dish from the oven and place the grated potatoes on top. Sprinkle with the grated cheese, then return to the oven and cook for 30 minutes, or until the vegetables are tender and the topping is crisp. Serve.

Health Rating: 3 points

Pork Chop Hotpot

Serves 4

Ingredients

4 pork chops
flour, for dusting
8–12 shallots, peeled
2 garlic cloves, peeled
50 g/2 oz (about 20) sun-dried tomatoes
2 tbsp olive oil
400 g/14 oz can plum tomatoes
150 ml/$^1/_4$ pint/$^2/_3$ cup red wine
150 ml/$^1/_4$ pint/$^2/_3$ cup chicken stock
3 tbsp tomato puree/paste
2 tbsp freshly chopped oregano
salt and freshly ground black pepper
fresh oregano leaves, to garnish

To serve:
freshly cooked new potatoes
French/green beans

Preheat the oven to 190°C/375°F/Gas Mark 5, 10 minutes before cooking. Trim the pork chops, removing any excess fat, wipe with a clean, damp cloth, then dust with a little flour and reserve.

Cut the shallots in half if large. Chop the garlic and slice the sun-dried tomatoes.

Heat the olive oil in a large casserole dish and cook the pork chops for about 5 minutes, turning occasionally during cooking, until browned all over. Using a slotted spoon, carefully lift out of the dish and reserve. Add the shallots and cook for 5 minutes, stirring occasionally.

Return the pork chops to the casserole dish and scatter with the garlic and sun-dried tomatoes, then pour over the can of tomatoes.

Blend the red wine, stock and tomato puree/paste together and add the chopped oregano. Season to taste with salt and pepper, then pour over the pork chops and bring to a gentle boil. Cover with a close-fitting lid and cook in the preheated oven for 1 hour, or until the pork chops are tender. Adjust the seasoning to taste, then scatter with a few oregano leaves and serve immediately with freshly cooked potatoes and French/green beans.

Health Rating: 4 points

Italian Meatballs in Tomato Sauce

Serves 4

Ingredients

For the tomato sauce:

4 tbsp olive oil
1 large onion, peeled and finely chopped
2 garlic cloves, peeled and chopped
400 g/14 oz can chopped tomatoes
1 tbsp sun-dried tomato paste
1 tbsp dried mixed herbs
150 ml/¼ pint/⅔ cup water
salt and freshly ground black pepper

For the meatballs:

450 g/1 lb fresh minced/ground pork
50 g/2 oz/1 cup fresh breadcrumbs
1 egg yolk
75 g/3 oz/¾ cup grated Parmesan cheese
20 small stuffed green olives

freshly snipped chives, to garnish
freshly cooked pasta, to serve

To make the tomato sauce, heat half the olive oil in a saucepan and cook half the chopped onion for 5 minutes until softened. Add the garlic, chopped tomatoes, sun-dried tomato paste, mixed herbs and water to the pan and season to taste with salt and pepper. Stir well until blended. Bring to the boil, then cover and simmer for 15 minutes.

To make the meatballs, place the pork, breadcrumbs, remaining onion, egg yolk and half the Parmesan in a large bowl. Season well and mix together with your hands. Divide the mixture into 20 balls.

Flatten one ball out in the palm of your hands, place an olive in the centre, then squeeze the meat around the olive to enclose completely. Repeat with the remaining mixture and olives. Place the meatballs on a baking sheet, cover with clingfilm/plastic wrap and chill in the refrigerator for 30 minutes.

Heat the remaining oil in a large frying pan and cook the meatballs for 8–10 minutes, turning occasionally, until golden brown. Pour in the sauce and heat through. Sprinkle with chives and the remaining Parmesan. Serve immediately with the freshly cooked pasta.

Health Rating: 3 points

Hoisin Pork

Serves 4

Ingredients

1.4 kg/3 lb piece lean belly pork, boned
sea salt, for rubbing
2 tsp Chinese five-spice powder
2 garlic cloves, peeled and chopped
1 tsp sesame oil
4 tbsp hoisin sauce
1 tbsp clear honey
assorted salad leaves, to garnish

Health Rating: 4 points

Preheat the oven to 200°C/400°F/Gas Mark 6, 15 minutes before cooking. Using a sharp knife, cut the pork skin in a criss-cross pattern, making sure not to cut all the way through into the flesh. Rub the salt evenly over the skin and leave to stand for 30 minutes.

Meanwhile, mix together the five-spice powder, garlic, sesame oil, hoisin sauce and honey until smooth. Rub the mixture evenly over the pork skin. Place the pork on a plate, cover and chill in the refrigerator to marinate for up to 6 hours.

Place the pork on a wire rack set inside a roasting tin/pan and roast in the preheated oven for 1–1¼ hours, or until the pork is very crisp and the juices run clear when pierced with a skewer.

Remove the pork from the heat, leave to rest for 15 minutes, then cut into strips. Arrange on a warmed serving platter. Garnish with salad leaves and serve immediately.

Pork with Tofu & Coconut

Serves 4

Ingredients

50 g/2 oz/⅓ cup unsalted cashew nuts
1 tbsp ground coriander
1 tbsp ground cumin
2 tsp hot chilli powder
2.5 cm/1 inch piece fresh root ginger, peeled and chopped
1 tbsp oyster sauce
4 tbsp groundnut/peanut oil
400 ml/14 fl oz can coconut milk
175 g/6 oz rice noodles
450 g/1 lb pork tenderloin, thickly sliced
1 red chilli, deseeded and sliced
1 green chilli, deseeded and sliced
1 bunch spring onions/scallions, trimmed and thickly sliced
3 tomatoes, roughly chopped
75 g/3 oz/⅓ cup tofu, drained
2 tbsp freshly chopped coriander/cilantro
2 tbsp freshly chopped mint
salt and freshly ground black pepper

Place the cashew nuts, ground coriander, cumin, chilli powder, ginger and oyster sauce in a food processor and blend until well ground.

Heat a wok or large frying pan, add 2 tablespoons of the oil and, when hot, add the cashew mixture and stir-fry for 1 minute. Stir in the coconut milk, bring to the boil, then simmer for 1 minute. Pour into a small jug and reserve. Wipe the wok clean.

Meanwhile, place the rice noodles in a bowl, cover with boiling water, leave to stand for 5 minutes, then drain thoroughly.

Reheat the wok, add the remaining oil and, when hot, add the pork and stir-fry for 5 minutes, or until browned all over. Add the chillies and spring onions/scallions and stir-fry for 2 minutes. Add the tomatoes and tofu to the wok with the noodles and coconut mixture and stir-fry for a further 2 minutes, or until heated through, being careful not to break up the tofu. Sprinkle with the chopped coriander/cilantro and mint, season to taste with salt and pepper and stir. Tip into a warmed serving dish and serve immediately.

Health Rating: 3 points

Cashew & Pork Stir-fry

Serves 4

Ingredients

450 g/1 lb pork tenderloin
4 tbsp soy sauce
1 tbsp cornflour/cornstarch
125 g/4 oz/1 cup unsalted cashew nuts
4 tbsp sunflower oil
450 g/1 lb/4 cups leeks, trimmed and shredded
2.5 cm/1 inch piece fresh root ginger, peeled and cut into matchsticks
2 garlic cloves, peeled and chopped
1 red pepper, deseeded and sliced
300 ml/½ pint/1¼ cups chicken stock
2 tbsp freshly chopped coriander/cilantro
freshly cooked noodles, to serve

Using a sharp knife, trim the pork, discarding any sinew or fat. Cut into 2 cm/¾ inch slices and place in a shallow dish. Blend the soy sauce and cornflour/cornstarch together until smooth and free from lumps, then pour over the pork. Stir until coated in the cornflour mixture, then cover with clingfilm/plastic wrap and leave to marinate in the refrigerator for at least 30 minutes.

Heat a nonstick frying pan until hot, add the cashew nuts and dry-fry for 2–3 minutes, or until toasted, stirring frequently. Transfer to a plate and reserve.

Heat a wok or large frying pan, add 2 tablespoons of the oil and, when hot, add the leeks, ginger, garlic and pepper and stir-fry for 5 minutes, or until softened. Using a slotted spoon, transfer to a plate and keep warm.

Drain the pork, reserving the marinade. Add the remaining oil to the wok and, when hot, add the pork and stir-fry for 5 minutes, or until browned. Return the reserved vegetables to the wok with the marinade and the stock. Bring to the boil, then simmer for 2 minutes, or until the sauce has thickened. Stir in the toasted cashew nuts and chopped coriander/cilantro and serve immediately with freshly cooked noodles.

Health Rating: 4 points

Pork Cabbage Parcels

Serves 4

Ingredients

8 large green cabbage leaves
1 tbsp vegetable oil
2 celery stalks, trimmed and chopped
1 carrot, peeled and cut into matchsticks
125 g/4 oz fresh minced/ground pork
50 g/2 oz/½ cup button mushrooms, wiped and sliced
1 tsp Chinese five-spice powder
50 g/2 oz/¼ cup cooked long-grain rice
juice of 1 lemon
1 tbsp soy sauce
150 ml/¼ pint/⅔ cup chicken stock

For the tomato sauce:
1 tbsp vegetable oil
1 bunch spring onions/scallions, trimmed and chopped
400 g/14 oz can chopped tomatoes
1 tbsp light soy sauce
1 tbsp freshly chopped mint
freshly ground black pepper

Preheat the oven to 180°C/350°F/Gas Mark 4, 10 minutes before cooking. To make the sauce, heat the oil in a heavy-based saucepan, add the spring onions/scallions and cook for 2 minutes, or until softened.

Add the tomatoes, soy sauce and mint to the saucepan, bring to the boil, cover, then simmer for 10 minutes. Season to taste with pepper. Reheat when required.

Meanwhile, blanch the cabbage leaves in a large saucepan of lightly salted water for 3 minutes. Drain and refresh under cold running water. Pat dry with absorbent paper towels and reserve.

Heat the oil in a small saucepan, add the celery, carrot and pork and cook for 3 minutes.

Add the mushrooms and cook for 3 minutes. Stir in the Chinese five-spice powder, rice, lemon juice and soy sauce and heat through.

Place some of the filling in the centre of each cabbage leaf and fold to enclose the filling. Place in a shallow ovenproof dish seam-side down. Pour over the stock and cook in the preheated oven for 30 minutes. Serve immediately with the reheated tomato sauce.

Health Rating: 5 points

Caribbean Pork

Serves 4

Ingredients

450 g/1 lb pork fillet, trimmed and cut into strips
2.5 cm/1 inch piece fresh root ginger, peeled and grated
2 garlic cloves, peeled and crushed
2 tbsp freshly chopped parsley
150 ml/¼ pint/⅔ cup orange juice
2 tbsp dark soy sauce
2 tbsp groundnut/peanut oil
1 large onion, peeled and sliced into wedges
1 large courgette/zucchini (about 225 g/8 oz), trimmed and cut into strips
1 orange pepper, deseeded and cut into strips
1 ripe but firm mango, peeled and pitted
freshly cooked rice to serve

Place the pork in a shallow dish. Sprinkle with the ginger, garlic and 1 tablespoon of the parsley. Blend together the orange juice, soy sauce and 1 tablespoon of the oil, then pour over the pork. Cover and chill in the refrigerator for 30 minutes, stirring occasionally. Remove the pork strips with a slotted spoon and reserve the marinade.

Heat the wok, pour in the remaining oil, stir-fry the pork for 3–4 minutes. Add the onion rings and the courgette/zucchini and pepper strips and cook for 2 minutes. Add the reserved marinade to the wok and stir-fry for a further 2 minutes.

Cut the mango flesh into strips, then stir it into the pork mixture. Continue to stir-fry until everything is piping hot. Garnish with the remaining parsley and serve immediately with plenty of freshly cooked rice.

Health Rating: 4 points

Sweet-&-Sour Pork

Serves 4

Ingredients

1 egg white
4 tsp cornflour/cornstarch
salt and freshly ground black pepper
450 g/1 lb pork fillet, trimmed and cut into cubes
300 ml/½ pint/1¼ cups groundnut/peanut oil
1 small onion, peeled and finely sliced
1 large carrot, peeled and cut into matchsticks
2.5 cm/1 inch piece fresh root ginger, peeled and cut into thin strips
150 ml/¼ pint/⅔ cup orange juice
150 ml/¼ pint/⅔ cup chicken stock
1 tbsp light soy sauce
220 g/7 oz can pineapple pieces, drained, with juice reserved
1 tbsp white wine vinegar
1 tbsp freshly chopped parsley
freshly cooked rice, to serve

In a bowl, whisk the egg white and cornflour/cornstarch with a little seasoning, then add the pork to the egg white mixture and stir until the cubes are well coated.

Heat the wok, then add the oil and heat until very hot before adding the pork and stir-frying for 30 seconds. Turn off the heat and continue to stir for 3 minutes. The meat should be white and sealed. Drain off the oil into a bowl and reserve; reserve the pork and wipe the wok clean.

Pour 2 teaspoons of the drained oil back into the wok and cook the onion, carrot and ginger for 2–3 minutes. Blend the orange juice with the chicken stock and soy sauce and make up to 300 ml/½ pint/1¼ cups with the reserved pineapple juice.

Return the pork to the wok with the juice mixture and simmer for 3–4 minutes. Stir in the pineapple pieces and vinegar. Heat through, sprinkle with the chopped parsley, serve with freshly cooked rice.

Health Rating: 4 points

Kerala Pork Curry

Serves 4–6

Ingredients

450 g/1 lb pork loin, trimmed
2 tbsp vegetable oil or ghee
1 tbsp desiccated/dried coconut
1 tsp mustard seeds
1 tsp fennel seeds
1 cinnamon stick, bruised
1 tsp ground cumin
1 tsp ground coriander
1–2 red chillies, deseeded and chopped
2–3 garlic cloves, peeled and chopped
2 onions, peeled and chopped
½ tsp saffron strands
300 ml/½ pint/1¼ cups coconut milk
150 ml/¼ pint/⅔ cup water
100 g/3½ oz/⅘ cup frozen peas
freshly cooked basmati rice, to serve

Cut the pork into small chunks and reserve. Heat 1 teaspoon of the oil or ghee in a frying pan, add the coconut and fry for 30 seconds, stirring, until lightly toasted. Reserve.

Add the remaining oil or ghee to the pan, add the seeds and fry for 30 seconds, or until they pop. Add the remaining spices and cook, stirring, for 2 minutes. Add the pork and fry for 5 minutes, or until sealed.

Add the chillies, garlic and onions and continue to fry for 3 minutes before stirring in the saffron strands. Stir, then pour in the coconut milk and water.

Bring to the boil then reduce the heat, cover and simmer, stirring occasionally, for 30 minutes. Add a little more water if the liquid is evaporating quickly. Turn the heat down slightly, then add the peas and cook for a further 10 minutes before serving with freshly cooked basmati rice.

Health Rating: 4 points

Vietnamese-style Braised Pork

Serves 4–6

Ingredients

550 g/1¼ lb pork tenderloin
2 tbsp vegetable oil
6 spring onions/scallions, trimmed and halved
5 cm/2 inch piece fresh root ginger, chopped
2 lemon grass stalks, bruised and outer leaves discarded
2–4 bird's eye chillies, deseeded
2 kaffir lime leaves
600 ml/1 pint/2½ cups chicken or vegetable stock
1 tbsp clear honey
salt and freshly ground black pepper
1 tbsp fish sauce, or to taste
1 tbsp freshly chopped coriander/cilantro

To serve:
freshly cooked fragrant rice
stir-fried vegetables

Trim the pork and cut into four portions. Heat the oil in a large saucepan or frying pan, add the pork and brown on all sides. Remove and reserve.

Place the reserved pork, spring onions/scallions, ginger, lemon grass, chillies and lime leaves in a clean saucepan and add the stock and honey. Bring to the boil, then reduce the heat and simmer for 30 minutes, or until tender.

Add salt and pepper to taste with the fish sauce, then serve the pork sprinkled with chopped coriander/cilantro on a bed of rice with the stir-fried vegetables.

Health Rating: 4 points

Braised Lamb with Broad Beans

Serves 4

Ingredients

700 g/1½ lb lamb, cut into large chunks
1 tbsp plain/all-purpose flour
1 onion
2 garlic cloves
1 tbsp olive oil
400 g/14 oz can chopped tomatoes with basil
300 ml/½ pint/1¼ cups lamb stock
2 tbsp freshly chopped thyme
2 tbsp freshly chopped oregano
salt and freshly ground black pepper
150 g/5 oz/1 cup frozen broad/fava beans
fresh oregano, to garnish
creamy mashed potatoes, to serve

Trim the lamb, discarding any fat or gristle, then place the flour in a polythene bag, add the lamb and toss until coated thoroughly. Peel and slice the onion and garlic and reserve.

Heat the olive oil in a heavy-based saucepan and, when hot, add the lamb and cook, stirring, until the meat is sealed and browned all over. Using a slotted spoon, transfer the lamb to a plate and reserve.

Add the onion and garlic to the saucepan and cook for 3 minutes, stirring frequently, until softened, then return the lamb to the saucepan.

Add the chopped tomatoes with their juice, the stock, the chopped thyme and oregano to the pan and season to taste with salt and pepper. Bring to the boil, then cover with a close-fitting lid, reduce the heat and simmer for 1 hour.

Add the broad/fava beans to the lamb and simmer for 20–30 minutes, or until the lamb is tender. Garnish with fresh oregano and serve with creamy mashed potatoes.

Health Rating: 3 points

Roast Leg of Lamb & Boulangère Potatoes

Serves 6

Ingredients

7 potatoes, peeled
1 large onion, peeled and finely sliced
salt and freshly ground black pepper
2 tbsp olive oil
50 g/2 oz/½ stick butter
200 ml/7 fl oz/¾ cup lamb stock
100 ml/3½ fl oz/⅓ cup milk
2 kg/4½ lb leg of lamb
2–3 fresh rosemary sprigs, plus extra to garnish
6 large garlic cloves, peeled and finely sliced
6 anchovy fillets, drained
fresh rosemary sprigs, to garnish

Preheat the oven to 230°C/450°F/Gas Mark 8. Finely slice the potatoes – a mandolin is the best tool for this. Layer the potatoes with the onion in a large roasting tin/pan, seasoning each layer with salt and pepper. Drizzle about 1 tablespoon of the olive oil over the potatoes and add the butter in small pieces. Pour in the lamb stock and milk. Set aside.

Make small incisions all over the lamb with the point of a small, sharp knife. Into each incision insert a small piece of rosemary, a sliver of garlic and a piece of anchovy fillet. Drizzle the lamb and its flavourings with the rest of the olive oil and season well. Place the meat directly on a shelf in the preheated oven. Position the pan of potatoes directly underneath to catch the juices during cooking. Roast for 20 minutes per 450 g/1 lb 2 oz (about 1 hour 40 minutes for a joint this size), reducing the oven temperature after 20 minutes to 200°C/400°F/Gas Mark 6.

When the lamb is cooked, remove from the oven and allow to rest for 10 minutes before carving. Meanwhile, increase the oven heat and cook the potatoes for a further 10–15 minutes to crisp up. Garnish with fresh rosemary sprigs and serve immediately with the lamb.

Health Rating: 2 points

Lancashire Hotpot

Serves 4

Ingredients

1 kg/2¼ lb middle end neck of lamb, divided into cutlets
2 tbsp vegetable oil
2 large onions, peeled and sliced
2 tsp plain/all-purpose flour
150 ml/¼ pint/⅔ cup vegetable or lamb stock
4–5 waxy potatoes, peeled and thickly sliced
salt and freshly ground black pepper
1 bay leaf
2 fresh thyme sprigs
1 tbsp melted butter
2 tbsp freshly chopped herbs, to garnish
freshly cooked green beans, to serve

Preheat the oven to 170°C/325°F/Gas Mark 3. Trim any excess fat from the lamb cutlets. Heat the oil in a frying pan and brown the cutlets in batches for 3–4 minutes. Remove with a slotted spoon and reserve.

Add the onions to the frying pan and cook for 6–8 minutes until softened and just beginning to colour, remove and reserve.

Stir in the flour and cook for a few seconds, then gradually pour in the stock, stirring well, and bring to the boil. Remove from the heat.

Spread the base of a large casserole dish with half the potato slices. Top with half the onions and season well with salt and pepper. Arrange the browned meat in a layer. Season again and add the remaining onions, bay leaf and thyme. Pour in the remaining liquid from the onions and top with remaining potatoes so that they overlap in a single layer. Brush the potatoes with the melted butter and season again.

Cover the saucepan and cook in the preheated oven for 2 hours, uncovering for the last 30 minutes to allow the potatoes to brown. Garnish with chopped herbs and serve immediately with green beans.

Health Rating: 2 points

Marinated Lamb Chops with Garlic-fried Potatoes

Serves 6

Ingredients

4 thick lamb chump chops
3 tbsp olive oil
4 potatoes, peeled and cut into 1 cm/½ inch dice
6 unpeeled garlic cloves
mixed salad or freshly cooked vegetables, to serve

For the marinade:
1 small bunch fresh thyme, leaves removed
1 tbsp freshly chopped rosemary
1 tsp salt
2 garlic cloves, peeled
rind and juice of 1 lemon
2 tbsp olive oil

Trim the chops of any excess fat, wipe with a clean damp cloth and reserve. To make the marinade, using a pestle and mortar, pound the thyme leaves and rosemary with the salt until pulpy. Add the garlic and continue pounding until crushed. Stir in the lemon rind and juice and the olive oil.

Pour the marinade over the lamb chops, turning them until they are well coated. Cover lightly and leave to marinate in the refrigerator for about 1 hour.

Meanwhile, heat the oil in a large, nonstick frying pan. Add the potatoes and garlic. Cook over a low heat for about 20 minutes, stirring occasionally. Increase the heat and cook for a further 10–15 minutes until golden. Drain on absorbent paper towels. Add salt to taste. Keep warm.

Heat a griddle pan until almost smoking. Add the lamb chops and cook for 3–4 minutes on each side until golden, but still pink in the middle. Serve with the potatoes and either a mixed salad or freshly cooked vegetables.

Health Rating: 2 points

Lamb with Stir-fried Vegetables

Serves 4

Ingredients

550 g/1¼ lb lamb fillet, trimmed and cut into strips
2.5 cm/1 inch piece fresh root ginger, peeled and cut into matchsticks
2 garlic cloves, peeled and chopped
4 tbsp soy sauce
2 tbsp dry sherry
2 tsp cornflour/cornstarch
4 tbsp groundnut/peanut oil
75 g/3 oz/½ cup French/green beans, trimmed and cut in half
2 carrots, peeled and cut into matchsticks
1 red and 1 yellow pepper, deseeded and cut into chunks
225 g/8 oz can water chestnuts, drained and halved
3 tomatoes, chopped
freshly cooked sticky rice in banana leaves, to serve (optional)

Place the lamb strips in a shallow dish. Mix together the ginger, half the garlic, the soy sauce and the sherry in a small bowl, stirring well. Pour over the lamb and stir until coated lightly. Cover with clingfilm/plastic wrap and leave to marinate for at least 30 minutes, occasionally spooning the marinade over the lamb.

Using a slotted spoon, lift the lamb from the marinade and place on a plate. Blend the cornflour/cornstarch and the marinade together until smooth, then reserve.

Heat a wok or large frying pan, add 2 tablespoons of the oil and, when hot, add the remaining garlic, French/green beans, carrots and peppers and stir-fry for 5 minutes. Using a slotted spoon, transfer the vegetables to a plate and keep warm.

Heat the remaining oil in the wok, add the lamb and stir-fry for 2 minutes, or until tender. Return the vegetables to the wok with the water chestnuts, tomatoes and reserved marinade mixture. Bring to the boil, then simmer for 1 minute. Serve immediately with freshly cooked sticky rice in banana leaves, if liked.

Health Rating: 3 points

Slow-roasted Lamb

Serves 6

Ingredients

1 leg of lamb, about 1.5 kg/3 lb in weight
2 tbsp vegetable oil
1 tsp fennel seeds
1 tsp cumin seeds
1 tsp ground coriander
1 tsp turmeric
2 garlic cloves, peeled and crushed
2 green chillies, deseeded and chopped
freshly cooked vegetables, to serve

For the potatoes:
550 g/1¼ lb potatoes, peeled
2 onions, peeled; 4 garlic cloves, peeled

Preheat the oven to 190°C/375°F/Gas Mark 5. Wipe the lamb with absorbent paper towels and make small slits over the lamb. Reserve.

Heat the oil in a frying pan, add the seeds and fry for 30 seconds, stirring. Add the remaining spices including the 2 garlic cloves and green chillies and cook for 5 minutes. Remove and use half to spread over the lamb.

Cut the potatoes into bite-sized chunks and the onions into wedges. Cut the garlic in half. Place in a roasting tin and cover with the remaining spice paste, then place the lamb on top.

Cook in the preheated oven for 1¼–1½ hours, or until the lamb and potatoes are cooked. Turn the potatoes over occasionally during cooking. Serve the lamb with the potatoes and freshly cooked vegetables.

Health Rating: 2 points

Lamb Passanda

Serves 4–6

Ingredients

550 g/1¼ lb lean lamb, such as leg steaks
2 tbsp vegetable oil or ghee
1 tsp ground cumin; 1 tsp ground coriander
1 tsp turmeric; ½ tsp fenugreek seeds
3 green cardamom pods, cracked
1 cinnamon stick, bruised; 3 whole cloves
5 cm/2 inch piece fresh root ginger, peeled and grated
1–2 green chillies, deseeded and finely chopped
2–4 garlic cloves, peeled and crushed
2 red onions, peeled and chopped
150 ml/¼ pint/⅔ cup natural/plain yogurt
250 ml/8 fl oz/1 cup water
85 ml/3 fl oz/⅓ cup coconut cream
1 green pepper, deseeded and cut into strips
50 g/2 oz/⅓ packed cup sultanas/golden raisins
3 tbsp ground almonds
25 g/1 oz/scant ¼ cup blanched almonds
25 g/1 oz/scant ¼ cup unsalted cashews, chopped

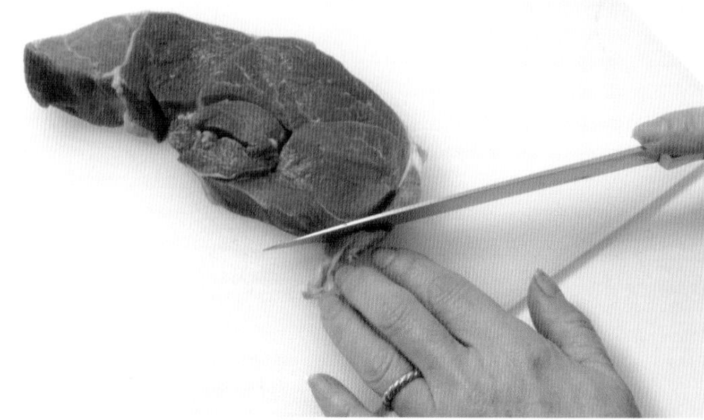

Discard any fat or gristle from the lamb, cut into thin strips and reserve. Heat the oil or ghee in a large frying pan, add the spices including the cinnamon and cloves and cook for 3 minutes.

Add the ginger, chillies, garlic, onions and meat and cook, stirring, until the meat is coated in the spices.

Stir in the yogurt then spoon into a bowl, cover and leave to marinate in the refrigerator for 15 minutes.

Clean the pan and return the meat mixture to it together with the water. Bring to the boil, then reduce the heat, cover and simmer for 15 minutes. Pour in the coconut cream and add the green pepper and sultanas/golden raisins. Stir in the ground almonds. Return to the boil, then reduce the heat and simmer for 20 minutes, or until the meat is tender. Spoon into a warmed serving dish, sprinkle with the nuts and serve.

Health Rating: 3 points

Lamb & Date Tagine

Serves 4

Ingredients

few saffron strands
1 tbsp olive oil
1 onion, peeled and cut into wedges
2–3 garlic cloves, peeled and sliced
550 g/1 1/4 lb lean lamb such as neck fillet, diced
1 cinnamon stick, bruised
1 tsp ground cumin
225 g/8 oz/1 3/4 cups carrots, peeled and sliced
350 g/12 oz/2 2/3 cups sweet potato, peeled and diced
900 ml/1 1/2 pints/scant 1 quart lamb or vegetable stock
salt and freshly ground black pepper
100 g/3 1/2 oz/1/2 cup dates (fresh or dried), pitted and halved
freshly prepared couscous, to serve

Place the saffron in a small bowl, cover with warm water and leave to infuse for 10 minutes. Heat the oil in a large, heavy-based pan, add the onion, garlic and lamb and fry for 8–10 minutes, or until sealed. Add the cinnamon stick and ground cumin and cook, stirring constantly, for a further 2 minutes.

Add the carrots and sweet potato, then add the saffron with the soaking liquid and the stock. Bring to the boil, season to taste with salt and pepper, then reduce the heat to a simmer. Cover with a lid and simmer for 45 minutes, stirring occasionally.

Add the dates and continue to simmer for a further 15 minutes. Remove the cinnamon stick, adjust the seasoning and serve with freshly prepared couscous.

Health Rating: 4 points

Steak & Kidney Stew

Serves 4

Ingredients

1 tbsp olive oil
1 onion, peeled and chopped
2–3 garlic cloves, peeled and crushed
2 celery stalks, trimmed and sliced
550 g/1¼ lb braising steak, trimmed and diced
100 g/3½ oz lambs' kidneys, cored and chopped
2 tbsp plain/all-purpose flour
1 tbsp tomato puree/paste
900 ml/1½ pints/scant 1 quart beef stock
salt and freshly ground black pepper
1 fresh bay leaf
300 g/10 oz/2⅓ cups carrots, peeled and sliced
350 g/12 oz baby new potatoes, scrubbed
350 g/12 oz/6 cups fresh spinach leaves, chopped

For the dumplings:
100 g/3½ oz/¾ cup self-raising flour
50 g/2 oz/⅖ cup shredded suet/lard
1 tbsp freshly chopped mixed herbs
2–3 tbsp water

Heat the oil in a large, heavy-based saucepan, add the onion, garlic and celery and fry for 5 minutes, or until browned. Remove from the pan with a slotted spoon and reserve.

Add the steak and kidneys to the pan and cook for 3–5 minutes, or until sealed, then return the onion mixture to the pan. Sprinkle in the flour and cook, stirring, for 2 minutes.

Take off the heat, stir in the tomato puree/paste, then the stock, and season to taste with salt and pepper. Add the bay leaf. Return to the heat and bring to the boil, stirring occasionally.

Add the carrots, then reduce the heat to a simmer and cover with a lid. Cook for 1¼ hours, stirring occasionally. Reduce the heat if the liquid is evaporating quickly. Add the potatoes and cook for a further 30 minutes.

Place the flour, suet and herbs in a bowl and add a little seasoning. Add the water and mix to a stiff mixture. Using a little extra flour, shape into eight small balls. Place the dumplings on top of the stew, cover with the lid and continue to cook for 15 minutes, or until the meat is tender and the dumplings are well risen and fluffy. Stir in the spinach and leave to stand for 2 minutes, or until the spinach has wilted.

Health Rating: 2 points

Beef Bourguignon

Serves 4

Ingredients

700 g/1½ lb braising steak, trimmed
225 g/8 oz piece of pork belly or lardons
2 tbsp olive oil
12 shallots, peeled
225 g/8 oz/1¾ cups carrots, peeled and sliced
2 garlic cloves, peeled and sliced
2 tbsp plain/all-purpose flour
3 tbsp brandy (optional)
150 ml/¼ pint/⅔ cup red wine, such as a Burgundy
450 ml/¾ pint/1¾ cups beef stock
1 bay leaf
salt and freshly ground black pepper
450 g/1 lb new potatoes, scrubbed
1 tbsp freshly chopped parsley, to garnish

Preheat the oven to 160°C/325°F/Gas Mark 3. Cut the steak and pork into small pieces and reserve. Heat 1 tablespoon of the oil in an ovenproof casserole dish (or frying pan, if preferred), add the meat and cook in batches for 5–8 minutes, or until sealed. Remove with a slotted spoon and reserve.

Add the remaining oil to the casserole dish/pan, then add the shallots, carrots and garlic and cook for 10 minutes. Return the meat to the casserole dish/pan and sprinkle in the flour. Cook for 2 minutes, stirring occasionally, before pouring in the brandy. Heat for 1 minute, then take off the heat and ignite.

When the flames have subsided, pour in the wine and stock. Return to the heat and bring to the boil, stirring constantly.

If a frying pan has been used, transfer everything to a casserole dish, add the bay leaf and season to taste with salt and pepper. Cover with a lid and cook in the oven for 1 hour.

Cut the potatoes in half. Remove the casserole dish from the oven and add the potatoes. Cook for a further 1 hour, or until the meat and potatoes are tender. Serve sprinkled with chopped parsley.

Health Rating: 2 points

Chilli Con Carne with Crispy-skinned Potatoes

Serves 4

Ingredients

2 tbsp vegetable oil, plus extra for brushing
1 large onion, peeled and finely chopped
1 garlic clove, peeled and finely chopped
1 red chilli, deseeded and finely chopped
450 g/1 lb chuck steak, finely chopped, or lean minced/ground beef
1 tbsp chilli powder
400 g/14 oz can chopped tomatoes
2 tbsp tomato puree/paste
400 g/14 oz can red kidney beans, drained and rinsed
4 large baking potatoes
coarse salt and freshly ground black pepper

To serve:
ready-made guacamole
sour cream

Preheat the oven to 150°C/300°F/Gas Mark 2. Heat the oil in a large flameproof casserole dish and add the onion. Cook gently for 10 minutes until soft and lightly browned. Add the garlic and chilli and cook briefly. Increase the heat. Add the beef and cook for a further 10 minutes, stirring occasionally, until browned.

Add the chilli powder and stir well. Cook for about 2 minutes, then add the chopped tomatoes and tomato puree/paste. Bring slowly to the boil. Cover and cook in the preheated oven for 1½ hours. Remove from the oven and stir in the kidney beans. Return to the oven for a further 15 minutes.

Brush a little vegetable oil all over the potatoes and rub on some coarse salt. Put the potatoes in the oven alongside the chilli.

Remove the chilli and potatoes from the oven. Cut a cross in each potato, squeeze to open slightly and season to taste with salt and pepper. Serve with the chilli, guacamole and sour cream.

Health Rating: 3 points

Grilled Steaks with Saffron Potatoes and Roast Tomatoes

Serves 4

Ingredients

700 g/1½ lb new potatoes, halved
few strands of saffron
300 ml/½ pint/1¼ cups vegetable or beef stock
1 small onion, peeled and finely chopped
75 g/3 oz/⅓ cup butter
salt and freshly ground black pepper
2 tsp balsamic vinegar
2 tbsp olive oil
1 tsp caster/superfine sugar
8 plum tomatoes, halved
4 boneless sirloin steaks, each weighing 225 g/8 oz
2 tbsp freshly chopped parsley, to garnish

Cook the potatoes in boiling salted water for 8 minutes and drain well. Return the potatoes to the saucepan along with the saffron, stock, onion and 25 g/1 oz/1¾ tbsp of the butter. Season to taste with salt and pepper and simmer, uncovered, for 10 minutes until the potatoes are tender.

Meanwhile, preheat the grill/broiler to medium. Mix together the vinegar, olive oil, sugar and seasoning. Arrange the tomatoes cut-side up in a foil-lined grill pan and drizzle over the dressing. Grill for 12–15 minutes, basting occasionally, until tender.

Melt the remaining butter in a frying pan. Add the steaks and cook for 4–8 minutes to taste and depending on thickness.

Arrange the potatoes and tomatoes in the centre of four serving plates. Top with the steaks along with any pan juices. Sprinkle over the parsley and serve immediately.

Health Rating: 3 points

Pan-fried Beef with Creamy Mushrooms

Serves 4

Ingredients

225 g/8 oz shallots (about 10), peeled
2 garlic cloves, peeled
2 tbsp olive oil
4 medallions of beef
4 plum tomatoes, rinsed and cut into eighths
125 g/4 oz/1¾ cups flat mushrooms, wiped and sliced
3 tbsp brandy
150 ml/¼ pint/⅔ cup red wine
salt and freshly ground black pepper
4 tbsp double/heavy cream

To serve:
baby new potatoes
freshly cooked green beans

Cut the shallots in half if large, then chop the garlic. Heat the oil in a large frying pan and cook the shallots for about 8 minutes, stirring occasionally, until almost softened. Add the garlic and beef and cook for 8–10 minutes, turning once during cooking, until the meat is browned all over. Using a slotted spoon, transfer the beef to a plate and keep warm.

Add the tomatoes and mushrooms to the pan and cook for 5 minutes, stirring frequently, until the mushrooms have softened.

Pour in the brandy and heat through. Draw the pan off the heat and carefully ignite. Allow the flames to subside. Pour in the wine, return to the heat and bring to the boil. Boil until reduced by one third. Draw the pan off the heat, season to taste with salt and pepper, add the cream and stir.

Arrange the beef on serving plates and spoon over the sauce. Serve with baby new potatoes and a few green beans.

Health Rating: 3 points

Fillet Steaks with Tomato & Garlic Sauce

Serves 4

Ingredients

700 g/1½ lb ripe tomatoes
2 garlic cloves
2 tbsp olive oil
2 tbsp freshly chopped basil
2 tbsp freshly chopped oregano
2 tbsp red wine
salt and freshly ground black pepper
75 g/3 oz/½ cup pitted black olives, chopped
4 fillet steaks, about 175 g/6 oz each in weight
freshly cooked vegetables, to serve

Make a small cross on the top of each tomato and place in a large bowl. Cover with boiling water and leave for 2 minutes. Using a slotted spoon, remove the tomatoes and skin carefully. Repeat until all the tomatoes are skinned. Place on a chopping board, cut into quarters, remove the seeds and roughly chop, then reserve.

Peel and chop the garlic. Heat half the olive oil in a saucepan and cook the garlic for 30 seconds. Add the chopped tomatoes with the basil, oregano and red wine and season to taste with salt and pepper. Bring to the boil, then reduce the heat, cover and simmer for 15 minutes, stirring occasionally, or until the sauce is reduced and thickened. Stir the olives into the sauce and keep warm while cooking the steaks.

Meanwhile, lightly oil a griddle pan or heavy-based frying pan with the remaining olive oil and cook the steaks for 2 minutes on each side to seal. Continue to cook the steaks for a further 2–4 minutes, depending on personal preference. Serve the steaks immediately with the garlic sauce and freshly cooked vegetables.

Health Rating: 3 points

Jerked Steaks

Serves 4–6

Ingredients

4 rump/sirloin steaks, about 100 g/4 oz each

For the jerk sauce:
1 tsp ground allspice
2 tbsp light muscovado/light brown sugar
1–2 garlic cloves, peeled and chopped
1 small red chilli, deseeded and chopped
few fresh thyme sprigs, leaves removed
1 tsp ground cinnamon
1/4 tsp freshly grated nutmeg
salt and freshly ground black pepper
1 tbsp soy sauce

For the mango relish:
1 ripe mango, peeled, stoned and finely chopped
6 spring onions/scallions, trimmed and chopped
1–2 garlic cloves, peeled and crushed
1 red chilli, deseeded and chopped
1 small, ripe but firm banana, peeled and chopped
1 tbsp lime juice
1 tbsp clear honey, warmed
50 g/2 oz/1/3 cup unsweetened chopped dates
1 tsp ground cinnamon

To serve:
salad
potato wedges

Blend all the ingredients for the jerk sauce, then rub over the steaks. Place on a plate, lightly cover and leave in the refrigerator for at least 30 minutes.

Mix together all the ingredients for the mango relish, cover and leave for 30 minutes to allow the flavours to develop.

When ready to cook, heat a griddle pan or heavy-based frying pan until hot and a few drops of water sizzle when dropped into the pan. Add the steaks and cook for 2–3 minutes on each side for rare, 3–4 minutes on each side for medium and 5–6 minutes on each side for well done.

Remove from the pan and serve with the prepared relish, salad and potato wedges.

Health Rating: 3 points

Veal Escalopes with Marsala Sauce

Serves 6

Ingredients

6 veal escalopes, about 125 g/4 oz each
lemon juice, for sprinkling
salt and freshly ground black pepper
6 sage leaves
6 slices prosciutto
2 tbsp olive oil
25 g/1 oz/¼ stick butter
1 onion, peeled and sliced
1 garlic clove, peeled and chopped
2 tbsp Marsala wine
4 tbsp double/heavy cream
2 tbsp freshly chopped parsley
sage leaves, to garnish
selection of freshly cooked vegetables, to serve

Place the veal escalopes between sheets of non-pvc clingfilm/plastic wrap and, using a mallet or rolling pin, pound lightly to flatten out thinly to about 5 mm/¼ inch thickness. Remove the clingfilm and sprinkle the veal escalopes with lemon juice, salt and black pepper.

Place a sage leaf in the centre of each escalope. Top with slice of prosciutto making sure it fits, then roll up the escalopes enclosing the prosciutto and sage leaves. Secure with a cocktail stick.

Heat the olive oil and butter in a large nonstick frying pan and fry the onions for 5 minutes, or until softened. Add the garlic and rolled escalopes and cook for about 8 minutes, turning occasionally, until the escalopes are browned all over.

Add the Marsala wine and cream to the pan and bring to the boil, cover and simmer for 10 minutes, or until the veal is tender. Season to taste, then sprinkle with the parsley. Discard the cocktail sticks and serve immediately with a selection of freshly cooked vegetables.

Health Rating: 2 points

Italian Beef Pot Roast

Serves 6

Ingredients

1.8 kg/4 lb brisket of beef
225 g/8 oz small onions, peeled
3 garlic cloves, peeled and chopped
2 celery stalks, trimmed and chopped
2 carrots, peeled and sliced
450 g/1 lb ripe tomatoes
300 ml/½ pint/1¼ cups Italian red wine
2 tbsp olive oil
300 ml/½ pint/1¼ cups beef stock
1 tbsp tomato puree/paste
2 tsp freeze-dried mixed herbs
salt and freshly ground black pepper
25 g/1 oz/¼ stick butter
3 tbsp plain/all-purpose flour
freshly cooked vegetables, to serve

Preheat oven to 150°C/300°F/Gas Mark 2, 10 minutes before cooking. Place the beef in a bowl. Add the onions, garlic, celery and carrots.

Place the tomatoes in a bowl and cover with boiling water. Allow to stand for 2 minutes and drain. Peel away the skins, discard the seeds and chop, then add to the beef mixture along with the red wine. Cover tightly and marinate in the refrigerator overnight.

Lift the marinated beef from the bowl and pat dry with absorbent paper towels. Heat the olive oil in a large casserole dish and cook the beef until it is browned all over, then remove from the dish.

Drain the vegetables from the marinade, reserving the marinade. Add the vegetables to the casserole dish and fry gently for 5 minutes, stirring occasionally, until all the vegetables are browned.

Return the beef to the casserole dish with the marinade, beef stock, tomato puree/paste and mixed herbs and season with salt and pepper. Bring to the boil, then cover and cook in the preheated oven for 3 hours.

Using a slotted spoon, transfer the beef and any large vegetables to a plate and leave in a warm place. Blend the butter and flour to form a paste. Bring the casserole juices to the boil, then gradually stir in small spoonfuls of the paste. Cook until thickened. Serve with the sauce and a selection of vegetables.

Health Rating: 4 points

Coconut Beef

Serves 4

Ingredients

450 g/1 lb beef rump or sirloin steak
4 tbsp groundnut/peanut oil
2 bunches spring onions/scallions, trimmed and thickly sliced
1 red chilli, deseeded and chopped
1 garlic clove, peeled and chopped
2 cm/1 inch piece fresh root ginger, peeled and cut into matchsticks
125 g/4 oz shiitake mushrooms
200 ml/7 fl oz/¾ cup coconut cream
150 ml/¼ pint/⅔ cup chicken stock
4 tbsp freshly chopped coriander/cilantro
salt and freshly ground black pepper
freshly cooked rice, to serve

Trim off any fat or gristle from the beef and cut into thin strips. Heat a wok or large frying pan, add 2 tablespoons of the oil and heat until just smoking. Add the beef and cook for 5–8 minutes, turning occasionally, until browned on all sides. Using a slotted spoon, transfer the beef to a plate and keep warm.

Add the remaining oil to the wok and heat until almost smoking. Add the spring onions/scallions, chilli, garlic and ginger and cook for 1 minute, stirring occasionally. Add the mushrooms and stir-fry for 3 minutes. Using a slotted spoon, transfer the mushroom mixture to a plate and keep warm.

Return the beef to the wok, pour in the coconut cream and stock. Bring to the boil and simmer for 3–4 minutes, or until the juices are slightly reduced and the beef is just tender.

Return the mushroom mixture to the wok and heat through. Stir in the chopped coriander/cilantro and season to taste with salt and pepper. Serve immediately with freshly cooked rice.

Health Rating: 3 points

Chilli Beef

Serves 4

Ingredients

550 g/1¼ lb beef rump steak
2 tbsp groundnut/peanut oil
2 carrots, peeled and cut into matchsticks
125 g/4 oz/1 cup mangetout/snow peas, shredded
125 g/4 oz/1⅔ cups beansprouts
1 green chilli, deseeded and chopped
2 tbsp sesame seeds
freshly cooked rice, to serve

For the marinade:
1 garlic clove, peeled and chopped
3 tbsp soy sauce
1 tbsp sweet chilli sauce
4 tbsp groundnut/peanut oil

Using a sharp knife, trim the beef, discarding any fat or gristle, then cut into thin strips and place in a shallow dish. Combine all the marinade ingredients in a bowl and pour over the beef. Turn the beef in the marinade until coated evenly, cover with clingfilm/plastic wrap and leave to marinate in the refrigerator for at least 30 minutes.

Heat a wok or large frying pan, add the groundnut/peanut oil and heat until almost smoking, then add the carrots and stir-fry for 3–4 minutes, or until softened. Add the mangetout/snow peas and stir-fry for a further 1 minute. Using a slotted spoon, transfer the vegetables to a plate and keep warm.

Lift the beef strips from the marinade, shaking to remove excess marinade. Reserve the marinade. Add the beef to the wok and stir-fry for 3 minutes, or until browned all over.

Return the stir-fried vegetables to the wok together with the beansprouts, chilli and sesame seeds and cook for 1 minute. Stir in the reserved marinade and stir-fry for 1–2 minutes, or until heated through. Tip into a warmed serving dish or spoon on to individual plates and serve immediately with freshly cooked rice.

Health Rating: 4 points

Beef Fajitas with Avocado Sauce

Serves 3–6

Ingredients

2 tbsp sunflower oil
450 g/1 lb beef fillet or rump steak, trimmed and cut into thin strips
2 garlic cloves, peeled and crushed
1 tsp ground cumin
$^1/_4$ tsp cayenne pepper
1 tbsp paprika
230 g/8 oz can chopped tomatoes
215 g/7$^1/_2$ oz can red kidney beans, drained
1 tbsp freshly chopped coriander/cilantro
1 avocado, peeled, pitted and chopped
1 shallot, peeled and chopped
1 large tomato, skinned, deseeded and chopped
1 red chilli, diced
1 tbsp lemon juice
6 large flour tortilla pancakes
3–4 tbsp sour cream
green salad, to serve

Heat the wok, add the oil, then stir-fry the beef for 3–4 minutes. Add the garlic and spices and continue to cook for a further 2 minutes. Stir the tomatoes into the wok, bring to the boil, cover and simmer gently for 5 minutes.

Blend the kidney beans in a food processor until slightly broken up, then add to the wok. Continue to cook for a further 5 minutes, adding 2–3 tablespoons water. The mixture should be thick and fairly dry. Stir in the chopped coriander/cilantro.

Mix the chopped avocado, shallot, tomato, chilli and lemon juice together. Spoon into a serving dish and reserve.

When ready to serve, warm the tortillas and spread with a little sour cream. Place a spoonful of the beef mixture on top, followed by a spoonful of the avocado sauce, then roll up. Repeat until all the mixture is used up. Serve immediately with a green salad.

Health Rating: 3 points

Beef with Paprika

Serves 4

Ingredients

700 g/1½ lb rump steak
3 tbsp plain/all-purpose flour
salt and freshly ground black pepper
1 tbsp paprika
350 g/12 oz/scant 2 cups long-grain rice
75 g/3 oz/⅓ cup butter
1 tsp oil
1 onion, peeled and thinly sliced into rings
225 g/8 oz/2½ cups button mushrooms, wiped and sliced
2 tsp dry sherry
150 ml/¼ pint/⅔ cup sour cream
2 tbsp freshly snipped chives
bundles of chives, to garnish

Beat the steak until very thin, then trim off and discard the fat and cut into thin strips. Season the flour with the salt, pepper and paprika, then toss the steak in the flour until coated.

Meanwhile, place the rice in a saucepan of boiling salted water and simmer for 15 minutes until tender, or according to packet directions. Drain the rice, then return to the saucepan, add one third of the butter, cover and keep warm.

Heat the wok, then add the oil and another ⅓ (25 g/1 oz) of the butter. When hot, stir-fry the meat for 3–5 minutes until sealed. Remove from the wok with a slotted spoon and reserve. Add the remaining butter to the wok and stir-fry the onion rings and button mushrooms for 3–4 minutes.

Add the sherry while the wok is very hot, then turn down the heat. Return the steak to the wok with the sour cream and seasoning to taste. Heat through until piping hot, then sprinkle with the snipped chives. Garnish with bundles of chives and serve immediately with the cooked rice.

Health Rating: 3 points

Vietnamese-style Aromatic Beef

Serves 4–6

Ingredients

550 g/1¼ lb stewing steak
2 tbsp vegetable oil
5 cardamom pods, cracked
1 cinnamon stick, bruised, 3 whole star anise
2 lemon grass stalks, bruised and outer leaves discarded
1 small green chilli, deseeded and chopped
1–2 tbsp medium-hot curry paste
2 red onions, peeled and cut into wedges
2 garlic cloves, peeled and sliced
450 ml/¾ pint/1¾ cups beef stock
150 ml/¼ pint/⅔ cup coconut milk
1 tbsp soy sauce
225 g/8 oz/1¾ cups carrots, peeled and sliced
175 g/6 oz/1⅔ cups sugar snap peas

Trim the meat, cut into bite-sized chunks and reserve. Heat the oil in a large heavy-based frying pan, add the cardamom pods, cinnamon stick, star anise and lemon grass and gently fry for 2 minutes. Add the chilli and continue to fry for a further 2 minutes.

Add the meat to the pan and stir-fry for 5 minutes, or until the meat is sealed.

Add the curry paste and the onions and garlic and fry for a further 5 minutes before stirring in the beef stock and coconut milk. Bring to the boil, then reduce the heat, cover and simmer for 1½ hours, stirring occasionally.

Add the soy sauce and carrots and continue to cook for a further 30 minutes.

Add the sugar snap peas and cook for 10 minutes, or until the meat and vegetables are tender. Remove the cinnamon stick and whole anise and serve.

Health Rating: 2 points

Poultry & Game

This chapter includes numerous delicious chicken and turkey dishes, including Lemon Chicken with Potatoes, Rosemary & Olives and Turkey & Tomato Tagine. You do not need to be adventurous to try some of the easy-to-follow game recipes; why not give cooking pheasant, guinea fowl or rabbit a go?

Braised Chicken in Beer

Serves 4

Ingredients

4 skinless chicken joints
125 g/4 oz/$^2/_3$ cup pitted dried prunes
2 bay leaves; 12 shallots; 2 tsp olive oil
125 g/4 oz/1$^1/_4$ cups small button mushrooms, wiped
1 tsp soft dark brown sugar
$^1/_2$ tsp wholegrain mustard
2 tsp tomato puree/paste
150 ml/$^1/_4$ pint/$^2/_3$ cup light ale
150 ml/$^1/_4$ pint/$^2/_3$ cup chicken stock
salt and freshly ground black pepper
2 tsp cornflour/cornstarch
2 tsp lemon juice
2 tbsp chopped fresh parsley
flat-leaf/Italian parsley, to garnish

To serve:
mashed potatoes
seasonal green vegetables

Preheat the oven to 170°C/325°F/Gas Mark 3. Cut each chicken joint in half and put in an ovenproof casserole dish with the prunes and bay leaves.

To peel the shallots, put in a small bowl and cover with boiling water. Drain them after 2 minutes and rinse under cold water until cool enough to handle. The skins should then peel away easily from the shallots.

Heat the oil in a large nonstick frying pan. Add the shallots and gently cook for about 5 minutes until beginning to colour.

Add the mushrooms to the pan and cook for a further 3–4 minutes until both the mushrooms and shallots are softened.

Sprinkle the sugar over the shallots and mushrooms, then add the mustard, tomato puree/paste, ale and chicken stock. Season to taste with salt and pepper and bring to the boil, stirring to combine. Carefully pour over the chicken. Cover the dish and cook in the preheated oven for 1 hour.

Blend the cornflour/cornstarch with the lemon juice and 1 tablespoon cold water and stir into the chicken casserole. Return the casserole to the oven for a further 10 minutes, or until the chicken is cooked and the vegetables are tender.

Remove the bay leaves and stir in the chopped parsley. Garnish the chicken with the flat-leaf/Italian parsley. Serve with the mashed potatoes and fresh green vegetables.

Health Rating: 3 points

Spicy Chicken Skewers with Mango Tabbouleh

Serves 4

Ingredients

400 g/14 oz chicken breast fillet
200 ml/7 fl oz/$^3/_4$ cup natural/plain low-fat yogurt
1 garlic clove, peeled and crushed
1 small red chilli, deseeded and finely chopped
$^1/_2$ tsp ground turmeric
finely grated zest and juice of $^1/_2$ lemon
fresh mint sprigs, to garnish

For the mango tabbouleh:
175 g/6 oz/1 cup bulgur wheat
1 tsp olive oil
juice of $^1/_2$ lemon
$^1/_2$ red onion, finely chopped
1 ripe mango, halved, stoned, peeled and chopped
$^1/_4$ cucumber, finely diced
2 tbsp freshly chopped parsley
2 tbsp freshly shredded mint
salt and freshly ground black pepper

If using wooden skewers, pre-soak them in cold water for at least 30 minutes. (This stops them from burning during grilling.) Cut the chicken into 5 x 1 cm/2 x $^1/_2$ inch strips and place in a shallow dish. Mix together the yogurt, garlic, chilli, turmeric, lemon rind and juice. Pour over the chicken and toss to coat. Cover and leave to marinate in the refrigerator for up to 8 hours.

To make the tabbouleh, put the bulgur wheat in a bowl. Pour over enough boiling water to cover. Put a plate over the bowl. Leave to soak for 20 minutes.

Whisk together the oil and lemon juice in a bowl. Add the red onion and leave to marinate for 10 minutes.

Drain the bulgur wheat and squeeze out any excess moisture in a clean dishtowel. Add to the red onion with the mango, cucumber and herbs and season to taste with salt and pepper. Toss together.

Thread the chicken strips on to eight wooden or metal skewers. While turning and brushing with the marinade, cook under a hot grill/broiler for 8 minutes, until the chicken is lightly browned and cooked through.

Spoon the tabbouleh on to individual plates. Arrange the chicken skewers on top and garnish with the mint sprigs. Serve warm or cold.

Health Rating: 4 points

Cheesy Chicken Burgers

Serves 6

Ingredients

1 tbsp sunflower oil
1 small onion, peeled and finely chopped
1 garlic clove, peeled and crushed
½ red pepper, deseeded and finely chopped
450 g/1 lb fresh minced/ground chicken
2 tbsp Greek/plain yogurt
50 g/2 oz/1 cup fresh brown breadcrumbs
1 tbsp freshly chopped herbs, such as parsley or tarragon
50 g/2 oz/½ cup Cheshire cheese, crumbled
salt and freshly ground black pepper

For the sweetcorn and carrot relish:
200 g/7 oz can sweetcorn, drained
1 carrot, peeled and grated
½ green chilli, deseeded and finely chopped
2 tsp cider vinegar
2 tsp light soft brown sugar

To serve:
wholemeal or granary rolls
lettuce
sliced tomatoes
mixed salad leaves

Preheat the grill/broiler. Heat the oil in a frying pan and gently cook the onion and garlic for 5 minutes. Add the red pepper and cook for 5 minutes. Transfer into a mixing bowl. Add the chicken, yogurt, breadcrumbs, herbs and cheese and season to taste with salt and pepper. Mix well.

Divide the mixture equally into six and shape into burgers. Cover and chill in the refrigerator for at least 20 minutes.

To make the relish, put all the ingredients in a small saucepan with 1 tablespoon water and heat gently, stirring occasionally, until all the sugar has dissolved. Cover and cook over a low heat for 2 minutes, then uncover and cook for a further minute, or until the relish is thick.

Place the burgers on a lightly oiled grill pan and grill under a medium heat for 8–10 minutes on each side, or until browned and completely cooked through.

Warm the rolls if liked, then split in half and fill with the burgers, lettuce, sliced tomatoes and the prepared relish. Serve immediately with the salad leaves.

Health Rating: 3 points

Chicken Basquaise

Serves 4–6

Ingredients

1.4 kg/3 lb chicken, cut into 8 pieces
2 tbsp plain/all-purpose flour
salt and freshly ground black pepper
3 tbsp olive oil
1 large onion, peeled and sliced
2 red peppers, deseeded and cut into thick strips
2 garlic cloves, peeled and crushed
150 g/5 oz spicy chorizo sausage cut into 1 cm/½ inch pieces
200 g/7 oz/1 heaping cup long-grain white rice
450 ml/¾ pint/1¾ cups chicken stock
1 tsp crushed dried chillies
½ tsp dried thyme
1 tbsp tomato puree/paste
125 g/4 oz Spanish air-dried ham, diced
12 black olives
2 tbsp freshly chopped parsley

Dry the chicken pieces well with absorbent paper towels. Put the flour in a polythene bag, season with salt and pepper and add the chicken pieces. Twist the bag to seal, then shake to coat the chicken pieces thoroughly.

Heat 2 tablespoons of the oil in a large heavy-based saucepan over a medium-high heat. Add the chicken pieces and cook for about 15 minutes, turning on all sides, until well browned. Using a slotted spoon, transfer to a plate.

Add the remaining olive oil to the saucepan, then add the onion and peppers. Reduce the heat to medium and cook, stirring frequently, until starting to colour and soften. Stir in the garlic and chorizo and continue to cook for a further 3 minutes. Add the rice and cook for about 2 minutes, stirring to coat with the oil, until the rice is translucent and golden.

Stir in the stock, crushed chillies, thyme, tomato puree/paste and salt and pepper and bring to the boil. Return the chicken to the saucepan, pressing gently into the rice. Cover and cook over a very low heat for about 45 minutes until the chicken and rice are cooked and tender.

Gently stir in the ham, black olives and half the parsley. Cover and heat for a further 5 minutes. Sprinkle with the remaining parsley and serve immediately.

Health Rating: 4 points

Chicken & New Potatoes on Rosemary Skewers

Serves 4

Ingredients

8 thick fresh rosemary stems, at least 23 cm/9 inches long
3–4 tbsp extra virgin olive oil
2 garlic cloves, peeled and crushed
1 tsp freshly chopped thyme
grated rind and juice of 1 lemon
salt and freshly ground black pepper
4 skinless chicken breast fillets
16 small new potatoes, peeled or scrubbed
8 very small onions or shallots, peeled
1 large yellow or red pepper, deseeded
lemon wedges, to garnish
parsley-flavoured cooked rice, to serve

Preheat the grill/broiler and line the grill rack with kitchen foil just before cooking. If using a barbecue, light at least 20 minutes before required. Strip the leaves from the rosemary stems, leaving about 5 cm/2 inches of soft leaves at the top. Chop the leaves coarsely and reserve. Using a sharp knife, cut the thicker woody ends of the stems to a point which can pierce the chicken pieces and potatoes. Blend the chopped rosemary, oil, garlic, thyme and lemon rind and juice in a shallow dish. Season to taste with salt and pepper.

Cut the chicken into 4 cm/1½ inch cubes, add to the flavoured oil and stir well. Cover and refrigerate for at least 30 minutes, turning occasionally.

Cook the potatoes in lightly salted boiling water for 10–12 minutes until just tender. Add the onions to the potatoes 2 minutes before the end of the cooking time. Drain, rinse under cold running water and leave to cool. Cut the pepper into 2.5 cm/1 inch squares.

Beginning with a piece of chicken and starting with the pointed end of the skewer, alternately thread equal amounts of chicken, potato, pepper and onion on to each rosemary skewer. Cover the leafy ends of the skewers with kitchen foil to stop them from burning. Do not thread the chicken and vegetables too closely together on the skewer or the chicken may not cook completely.

Cook the kebabs for 15 minutes, or until tender and golden, turning and brushing with either extra oil or the marinade. Remove the foil, garnish with lemon wedges and serve on rice.

Health Rating: 5 points

Slow Roast Chicken with Potatoes & Oregano

Serves 6

Ingredients

1.4–1.8 kg/3–4 lb oven-ready chicken, preferably free range
1 lemon, halved
1 onion, peeled and quartered
50 g/2 oz/½ stick butter, softened
salt and freshly ground black pepper
1 kg/2¼ lb potatoes, peeled and quartered
3–4 tbsp extra virgin olive oil
1 tbsp dried oregano, crumbled
1 tsp fresh thyme leaves
2 tbsp freshly chopped thyme
fresh sage leaves, to garnish

Preheat the oven to 200°C/400°F/Gas Mark 6. Rinse the chicken and dry well, inside and out, with absorbent paper towels.

Rub the chicken all over with the lemon halves, then squeeze the juice over it and into the cavity. Put the squeezed halves into the cavity with the quartered onion.

Rub the softened butter all over the chicken and season to taste with salt and pepper, then put it in a large roasting tin/pan, breast-side down.

Toss the potatoes in the oil, season with salt and pepper to taste and add the dried oregano and fresh thyme. Arrange the potatoes with the oil around the chicken and carefully pour 150 ml/¼ pt/⅔ cup water into one end of the pan (not over the oil). Roast in the preheated oven for 25 minutes.

Reduce the oven temperature to 190°C/375°F/Gas Mark 5 and turn the chicken breast-side up. Turn the potatoes, sprinkle over half the fresh herbs and baste the chicken and potatoes with the juices. Continue roasting for 1 hour, or until the chicken is cooked, basting occasionally.

If the liquid evaporates completely, add a little more water. The chicken is done when the juices run clear when the thigh is pierced with a skewer. Transfer the chicken to a carving board and rest for 5 minutes, covered with kitchen foil. Return the potatoes to the oven while the chicken is resting.

Carve the chicken into serving pieces and arrange on a large heatproof serving dish. Arrange the potatoes around the chicken and drizzle over any remaining juices. Sprinkle with the remaining herbs and serve.

Health Rating: 3 points

Saffron Roast Chicken with Crispy Onions

Serves 4–6

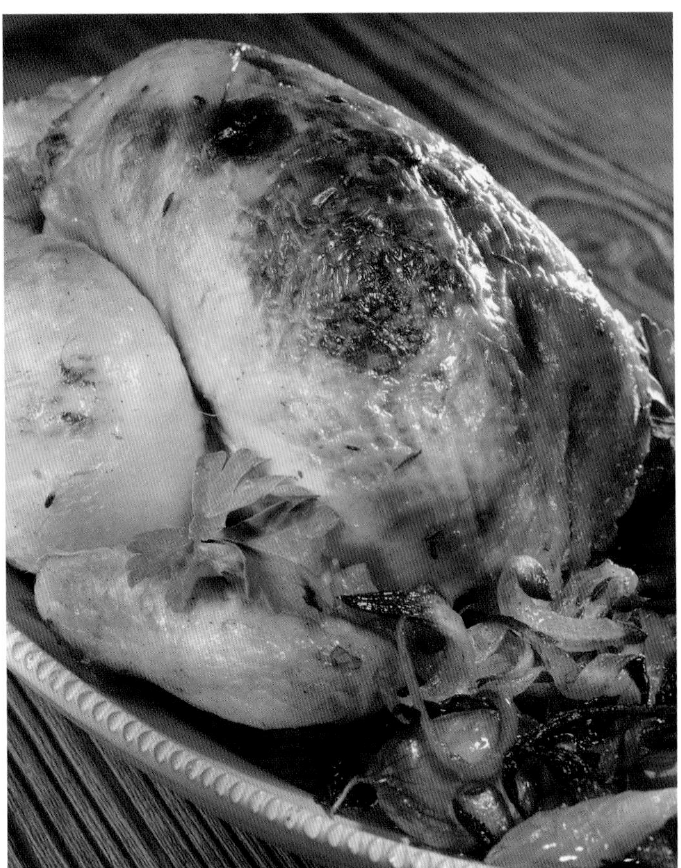

Ingredients

1.6 kg/3½ lb oven-ready chicken, preferably free range
75 g/3 oz/¾ stick butter, softened
1 tsp saffron strands, lightly toasted
grated rind of 1 lemon
2 tbsp freshly chopped flat-leaf/Italian parsley
2 tbsp extra virgin olive oil
450 g/1 lb/2½ cups onions, peeled and cut into thin wedges
8–12 garlic cloves, peeled
1 tsp cumin seeds
½ tsp ground cinnamon
50 g/2 oz/⅓ cup pine nuts
50 g/2 oz/⅓ cup sultanas/golden raisins
salt and freshly ground black pepper
fresh flat-leaf/Italian parsley sprig, to garnish

Preheat oven to 200°C/400°F/Gas Mark 6. Using your fingertips, gently loosen the skin from the chicken breast by sliding your hand between the skin and flesh. Cream together 50 g/2 oz/½ stick of the butter with the saffron threads, the lemon rind and half the parsley, until smooth. Push the butter under the skin. Spread over the breast and the top of the thighs with your fingers. Pull the neck skin to tighten the skin over the breast and tuck under the bird, then secure with a skewer or cocktail stick.

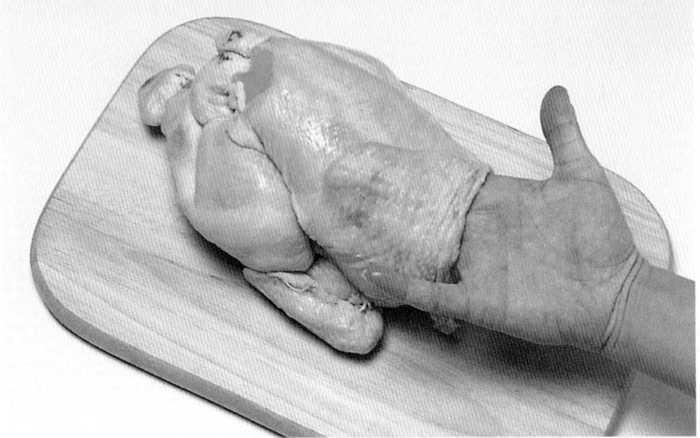

Heat the olive oil and remaining butter in a large heavy-based frying pan and cook the onions and garlic cloves for 5 minutes, or until the onions are soft. Stir in the cumin seeds, cinnamon, pine nuts and sultanas/golden raisins and cook for 2 minutes. Season to taste with salt and pepper and place in a roasting tin/pan.

Place the chicken, breast-side down, on the base of the onions and roast in the preheated oven for 45 minutes. Reduce the oven temperature to 170°C/325°F/Gas Mark 3. Turn the chicken breast-side up and stir the onions. Continue roasting until the chicken is a deep golden yellow and the onions are crisp.

Allow to rest for 10 minutes, then sprinkle with the remaining parsley. Before serving, garnish with a parsley sprig and serve immediately with the onions and garlic.

Health Rating: 3 points

Chicken Cacciatore

Serves 4

Ingredients

2–3 tbsp olive oil
125 g/4 oz pancetta or streaky/fatty bacon, diced
3 tbsp plain/all-purpose flour
salt and freshly ground black pepper
1.4–1.6 kg/3–3$^{1}/_{2}$ lb chicken, cut into 8 pieces
2 garlic cloves, peeled and chopped
125 ml/4 fl oz/$^{1}/_{2}$ cup red wine
400 g/14 oz can chopped tomatoes
150 ml/$^{1}/_{4}$ pint/$^{2}/_{3}$ cup chicken stock
12 small onions, peeled
1 bay leaf; 1 tsp brown sugar; 1 tsp dried oregano
1 green pepper, deseeded and chopped
225 g/8 oz/3 cups chestnut or field mushrooms, thickly sliced
2 tbsp freshly chopped parsley
freshly cooked tagliatelle, to serve

Heat 1 tablespoon of the olive oil in a large, deep frying pan and add the diced pancetta or bacon and stir-fry for 2–3 minutes, or until crisp and golden brown. Using a slotted spoon, transfer the pancetta or bacon to a plate and reserve.

Season the flour with salt and pepper, then use to coat the chicken. Heat the remaining oil in the pan and brown the chicken pieces on all sides for about 15 minutes. Remove from the pan and add to the bacon.

Stir the garlic into the pan and cook for about 30 seconds. Add the red wine and cook, stirring and scraping any browned bits from the base of the pan. Allow the wine to boil until it is reduced by half. Add the tomatoes, stock, onions, bay leaf, brown sugar and oregano and stir well. Season to taste. Return the chicken and bacon to the pan and bring to the boil. Cover and simmer for 30 minutes, then stir in the peppers and mushrooms and simmer for a further 15–20 minutes, or until the chicken and vegetables are tender and the sauce is reduced and slightly thickened. Stir in the chopped parsley and serve immediately with freshly cooked tagliatelle.

Health Rating: 3 points

Lemon Chicken with Potatoes, Rosemary & Olives

Serves 6

Ingredients

12 skinless, boneless chicken thighs
1 large lemon
125 ml/4 fl oz/½ cup extra virgin olive oil
6 garlic cloves, peeled and sliced
2 onions, peeled and thinly sliced
bunch of fresh rosemary
1.1 kg/2½ lb potatoes, peeled and cut into 4 cm/1½ inch pieces
salt and freshly ground black pepper
18–24 black olives, pitted

To serve:
steamed carrots
steamed courgettes/zucchini

Preheat oven to 200°C/400°F/Gas Mark 6, 15 minutes before cooking. Trim the chicken thighs and place in a shallow baking dish large enough to hold them in a single layer.

Remove the zest/rind from the lemon with a zester or, if using a peeler, cut into thin julienne strips. Reserve half and add the remainder to the chicken. Squeeze the lemon juice over the chicken, toss to coat well and leave to stand for 10 minutes. Add the remaining lemon zest or julienne strips, olive oil, garlic, onions and half of the rosemary sprigs. Toss gently and leave for about 20 minutes.

Cover the potatoes with lightly salted water and bring to the boil. Cook for 2 minutes, then drain well and add to the chicken. Season to taste with salt and pepper. Roast the chicken in the preheated oven for 50 minutes, turning frequently and basting, or until the chicken is cooked. Just before the end of cooking time, discard the rosemary and add fresh rosemary sprigs. Add the olives and stir. Serve immediately with steamed carrots and courgettes/zucchini.

Health Rating: 3 points

Chicken with Porcini Mushrooms

Serves 4

Ingredients

2 tbsp olive oil
4 boneless chicken breasts, preferably free range
2 garlic cloves, peeled and crushed
150 ml/¼ pint/⅔ cup dry vermouth or dry white wine
salt and freshly ground black pepper
25 g/1 oz/¼ stick butter
450 g/1 lb/4 cups porcini or wild mushrooms, thickly sliced
1 tbsp freshly chopped oregano
fresh basil sprigs, to garnish (optional)
freshly cooked rice, to serve

Health Rating: 3 points

Heat the olive oil in a large, heavy-based frying pan, then add the chicken breasts, skin-side down and cook for about 10 minutes, or until they are well browned. Remove the chicken breasts and reserve. Add the garlic, stir into the juices and cook for 1 minute.

Pour the vermouth or white wine into the pan and season to taste with salt and pepper. Return the chicken to the pan. Bring to the boil, reduce the heat to low and simmer for about 20 minutes, or until tender.

In another large frying pan, heat the butter and add the sliced porcini or wild mushrooms. Stir-fry for about 5 minutes, or until the mushrooms are golden and tender.

Add the porcini or wild mushrooms and any juices to the chicken. Season to taste, then add the chopped oregano. Stir together gently and cook for 1 minute longer. Transfer to a large serving plate and garnish with fresh basil sprigs, if desired. Serve immediately with rice.

Poached Chicken with Salsa Verde Herb Sauce

Serves 6

Ingredients

6 boneless chicken breasts, each about 175 g /6 oz
600 ml/1 pint/2½ cups chicken stock, preferably homemade

For the salsa verde:
2 garlic cloves, peeled and chopped
4 tbsp freshly chopped parsley
3 tbsp freshly chopped mint, 2 tsp capers
2 tbsp chopped gherkins/pickles (optional)
2–3 anchovy fillets in olive oil, drained and finely chopped (optional)
1 handful wild rocket/arugula leaves, chopped (optional)
2 tbsp lemon juice or red wine vinegar
125 ml/4 fl oz/½ cup extra virgin olive oil
salt and freshly ground black pepper
mint sprigs, to garnish
freshly cooked vegetables, to serve

Place the chicken breasts with the stock in a large frying pan and bring to the boil. Reduce the heat and simmer for 10–15 minutes, or until cooked. Leave to cool in the stock.

To make the salsa verde, switch the motor on a food processor, then drop in the garlic cloves and chop finely. Add the parsley and mint and, using the pulse button, pulse 2–3 times. Add the capers and, if using, add the gherkins/pickles, anchovies and rocket/arugula. Pulse 2–3 times until the sauce is evenly textured. With the machine still running, pour in the lemon juice or red wine vinegar, then add the olive oil in a slow, steady stream until the sauce is smooth. Season to taste with salt and pepper, then transfer to a large serving bowl and reserve.

Carve each chicken breast into thick slices and arrange on serving plates, fanning out the slices slightly. Spoon over a little of the salsa verde on to each chicken breast, garnish with mint sprigs and serve immediately with freshly cooked vegetables.

Health Rating: 4 points

Chicken Under a Brick

Serves 4–6

Ingredients

1.8 kg/4 lb free range corn-fed, oven-ready chicken
50 ml/2 fl oz olive oil
sea salt and freshly ground black pepper
tossed bitter salad leaves, to serve

To garnish:
fresh basil sprigs
chives

Rinse the chicken and dry well, inside and out. Using poultry shears or kitchen scissors, cut along each side of the backbone of the chicken and discard or use for stock. Place the chicken skin-side up on a work surface and, using the palm of your hand, press down firmly to break the breast bone and flatten the bird.

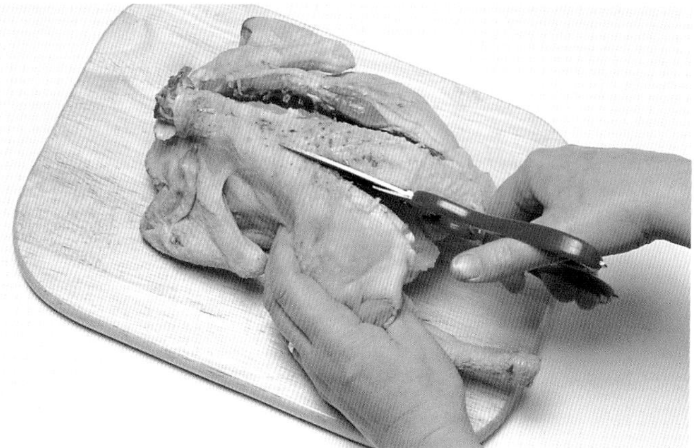

Turn the chicken breast-side up and use a sharp knife to slit the skin between the breast and thigh on each side. Fold the legs in and push the drumstick bones through the slits. Tuck the wing under; the chicken should be as flat as possible.

Heat the olive oil in a large, heavy-based frying pan until very hot, but not smoking. Place the chicken in the pan, skin-side down, and place a flat lid or plate directly on top of the chicken. Top with a brick (hence the name) or 2 kg/5 lb weight. Cook for 12–15 minutes, or until golden brown.

Remove the weights and lid and, using a pair of tongs, turn the chicken carefully, then season to taste with salt and pepper. Cover and weight the lid again, then cook for 12–15 minutes longer, until the chicken is tender and the juices run clear when a thigh is pierced with a sharp knife or skewer.

Transfer the chicken to a serving plate and cover loosely with kitchen foil to keep warm. Allow to rest for at least 10 minutes before carving. Garnish with basil sprigs and chives and serve with salad leaves.

Health Rating: 3 points

Chicken Marengo

Serves 4

Ingredients

2 tbsp plain/all-purpose flour
salt and freshly ground black pepper
4 skinless, boneless chicken breasts, cut into bite-sized pieces
4 tbsp olive oil
1 Spanish onion, peeled and chopped
1 garlic clove, peeled and chopped
400 g/14 oz can chopped tomatoes
2 tbsp sun-dried tomato paste
3 tbsp freshly chopped basil
3 tbsp freshly chopped thyme
125 ml/4 fl oz/½ cup dry white wine or chicken stock
350 g/12 oz/2¼ cups rigatoni
3 tbsp freshly chopped flat-leaf/Italian parsley

Season the flour with salt and pepper and toss the chicken in the flour to coat. Heat 2 tablespoons of the olive oil in a large frying pan and cook the chicken for 7 minutes, or until browned all over, turning occasionally. Remove from the pan using a slotted spoon and keep warm.

Add the remaining oil to the pan, add the onion and cook, stirring occasionally, for 5 minutes, or until softened and starting to brown. Add the garlic, tomatoes, tomato paste, basil and thyme.

Pour in the wine or chicken stock and season well. Bring to the boil. Stir in the chicken pieces and simmer for 15 minutes, or until the chicken is tender and the sauce has thickened.

Meanwhile, bring a large pan of lightly salted water to a rolling boil. Add the rigatoni and cook according to the packet instructions, or until *al dente*.

Drain the rigatoni thoroughly, return to the pan and stir in the chopped parsley. Tip the pasta into a warmed large serving dish or spoon on to individual plates. Spoon over the chicken sauce and serve immediately.

Health Rating: 3 points

Braised Chicken with Aubergine

Serves 4

Ingredients

3 tbsp vegetable oil
12 chicken thighs
2 large aubergines/eggplants, trimmed and cubed
4 garlic cloves, peeled and crushed
2 tsp freshly grated root ginger
900 ml/1½ pints/scant 1 quart vegetable stock
2 tbsp light soy sauce
2 tbsp Chinese preserved black beans
6 spring onions/scallions, trimmed and thinly sliced diagonally
1 tbsp cornflour/cornstarch
1 tbsp sesame oil
spring onion/scallion tassels, to garnish
freshly cooked noodles or rice, to serve

Heat a wok or large frying pan, add the oil and, when hot, add the chicken thighs and cook over a medium high heat for 5 minutes, or until browned all over. Transfer to a large plate and keep warm.

Add the aubergine/eggplant to the wok and cook over a high heat for 5 minutes, or until browned, turning occasionally. Add the garlic and ginger and stir-fry for 1 minute.

Return the chicken to the wok, pour in the stock and add the soy sauce and black beans. Bring to the boil, then simmer for 20 minutes, or until the chicken is tender. Add the spring onions/scallions after 10 minutes.

Blend the cornflour/cornstarch with 2 tablespoons water. Stir into the wok and simmer until the sauce has thickened. Stir in the sesame oil, heat for 30 seconds, then remove from the heat. Garnish with spring onion tassels and serve immediately with noodles or rice.

Health Rating: 3 points

Stir-fried Lemon Chicken

Serves 4

Ingredients

350 g/12 oz skinless, boneless chicken breast
1 large/extra-large egg white
5 tsp cornflour/cornstarch
3 tbsp vegetable or groundnut/peanut oil
150 ml/¼ pint/⅔ cup chicken stock
2 tbsp fresh lemon juice
2 tbsp light soy sauce
1 tbsp Chinese rice wine or dry sherry
1 tbsp sugar
2 garlic cloves, peeled and finely chopped
¼ tsp dried chilli flakes, or to taste

To garnish:
lemon rind strips
red chilli slices

Using a sharp knife, trim the chicken, discarding any fat, and cut into thin strips, about 5 cm/2 inches long and 1 cm/½ inch wide. Place in a shallow dish. Lightly whisk the egg white and 1 tablespoon of the cornflour/cornstarch together until smooth. Pour over the chicken strips and mix well until coated evenly. Leave to marinate in the refrigerator for at least 20 minutes.

When ready to cook, drain the chicken and reserve. Heat a wok or large frying pan, add the oil and, when hot, add the chicken and stir-fry for 1–2 minutes, or until the chicken has turned white. Using a slotted spoon, remove from the wok and reserve.

Wipe the wok and return to the heat. Add chicken stock, lemon juice, soy sauce, Chinese rice wine or sherry, sugar, garlic and chilli flakes and bring to the boil. Blend remaining cornflour with 1 tablespoon water and stir into the stock. Simmer for 1 minute.

Return the chicken to the wok and continue simmering for a further 2–3 minutes, or until the chicken is tender and the sauce has thickened. Garnish with lemon strips and red chilli slices. Serve immediately.

Health Rating: 3 points

Thai-stuffed Omelette

Serves 4

Ingredients

1 shallot, peeled and roughly chopped
1 garlic clove, peeled and roughly chopped
1 small red chilli, deseeded and roughly chopped
15 g/½ oz/1 cup coriander/cilantro leaves
pinch sugar
2 tsp light soy sauce
2 tsp Thai fish sauce
4 tbsp vegetable or groundnut/peanut oil
175 g/6 oz skinless, boneless chicken breast, finely sliced
½ small aubergine/eggplant, trimmed and diced
50 g/2 oz/⅔ cup button or shiitake mushrooms, wiped and sliced
½ small red pepper, deseeded and sliced
50 g/2 oz/⅓ cup fine green beans, trimmed and halved
2 spring onions/scallions, trimmed and thickly sliced
25 g/1 oz/⅙ cup peas, thawed if frozen
6 eggs
salt and freshly ground black pepper
fresh basil sprig, to garnish

Place the shallot, garlic, chilli, coriander/cilantro and sugar in the bowl of a spice grinder or food processor. Blend until finely chopped. Add the soy sauce, fish sauce and 1 tablespoon of the vegetable oil and blend briefly to mix into a paste. Reserve.

Heat a wok or large frying pan, add 1 tablespoon of the oil and, when hot, add the chicken and aubergine/eggplant and stir-fry for 3–4 minutes, or until golden. Add the mushrooms, red pepper, green beans and spring onions/scallions and stir-fry for 3–4 minutes, or until tender, adding the peas for the final 1 minute. Remove from the heat and stir in the reserved coriander paste. Reserve.

Beat the eggs in a bowl and season to taste with salt and pepper. Heat the remaining oil in a large nonstick frying pan and add the eggs, tilting the pan so that the eggs cover the bottom. Stir the eggs until they are starting to set all over, then cook for 1–2 minutes, or until firm and set on the bottom but still slightly soft on top.

Spoon the chicken and vegetable mixture on to one half of the omelette and carefully flip the other half over. Cook over a low heat for 2–3 minutes, or until the omelette is set and the chicken and vegetables are heated through. Garnish with a basil sprig and serve immediately.

Health Rating: 4 points

Pan-cooked Chicken with Thai Spices

Serves 4

Ingredients

4 kaffir lime leaves
5 cm/2 inch piece root ginger, peeled and chopped
300 ml/½ pint/1¼ cups chicken stock, boiling
4 x 175 g/6 oz chicken breasts
2 tsp groundnut/peanut oil
5 tbsp coconut milk, 1 tbsp fish sauce
2 red chillies, deseeded and finely chopped
225 g/8 oz/1¼ cup Thai jasmine rice
1 tbsp lime juice, 3 tbsp freshly chopped coriander/cilantro
salt and freshly ground black pepper

To garnish:
lime wedges
freshly chopped coriander/cilantro

Lightly bruise the kaffir lime leaves and put in a bowl with the chopped ginger. Pour over the chicken stock, cover and leave to infuse for 30 minutes.

Meanwhile, cut each chicken breast into two pieces. Heat the oil in a large nonstick frying pan or flameproof casserole dish and brown the chicken pieces for 2–3 minutes on each side. Strain the infused chicken stock into the pan. Half cover the pan with a lid and gently simmer for 10 minutes. Stir in the coconut milk, fish sauce and chopped chillies. Simmer uncovered for 5–6 minutes, or until the chicken is tender and cooked through and the sauce has reduced slightly.

Meanwhile, cook the rice in boiling salted water according to the packet instructions. Drain the rice thoroughly.

Stir the lime juice and chopped coriander/cilantro into the sauce. Season to taste with salt and pepper. Serve the chicken and sauce on a bed of rice. Garnish with wedges of lime and freshly chopped coriander and serve immediately.

Health Rating: 3 points

Red Chicken Curry

Serves 4

Ingredients

225 ml/8 fl oz/1 cup coconut cream
2 tbsp vegetable oil
2 garlic cloves, peeled and finely chopped
2 tbsp Thai red curry paste, 2 tbsp Thai fish sauce
2 tsp sugar
350 g/12 oz skinless chicken breast fillets, finely sliced
450 ml/¾ pint/1¾ cups chicken stock
2 lime leaves, shredded
chopped red chilli, to garnish
freshly boiled rice or steamed Thai fragrant rice, to serve

Health Rating: 2 points

Pour the coconut cream into a small saucepan and heat gently. Meanwhile, heat a wok or large frying pan and add the oil. When the oil is very hot, swirl the oil around the wok until it is lightly coated, then add the garlic and stir-fry for about 10–20 seconds, or until the garlic begins to brown. Add the curry paste and stir-fry for a few more seconds, then pour in the warmed coconut cream.

Cook the coconut cream mixture for 5 minutes, or until the cream has curdled and thickened. Stir in the fish sauce and sugar. Add the finely sliced chicken and cook for 3–4 minutes, or until the chicken has turned white.

Pour the stock into the wok, bring to the boil, then simmer for 1–2 minutes, or until the chicken is cooked through. Stir in the shredded lime leaves. Turn into a warmed serving dish, garnish with chopped red chilli and serve immediately with rice.

Green Chicken Curry

Serves 4

Ingredients

1 onion, peeled and chopped
3 lemon grass stalks, finely sliced and outer leaves discarded
2 garlic cloves, peeled and finely chopped
1 tbsp freshly grated root ginger
3 green chillies
zest and juice of 1 lime
2 tbsp groundnut/peanut oil
2 tbsp Thai fish sauce
6 tbsp freshly chopped coriander/cilantro
6 tbsp freshly chopped basil
450 g/1 lb skinless chicken breast fillets/halves, cut into strips
125 g/4½ oz/⅓ cup fine green beans, trimmed
400 ml/14 fl oz can coconut milk
fresh basil leaves, to garnish
freshly cooked rice, to serve

Place the onion, lemon grass, garlic, ginger, chillies, lime zest and juice, 1 tablespoon of the groundnut/peanut oil, the fish sauce, coriander/cilantro and basil in a food processor. Blend to form a smooth paste, which should be of a spoonable consistency. If the sauce looks thick, add a little water. Remove and reserve.

Heat the wok, add the remaining 1 tablespoon oil. When hot, add the chicken. Stir-fry for 2–3 minutes, until the chicken starts to colour. Add the green beans and stir-fry for a further minute. Remove the chicken and beans from the wok and reserve. Wipe the wok clean with absorbent paper towels.

Spoon the reserved green paste into the wok and heat for 1 minute. Add the coconut milk and whisk to blend. Return the chicken and beans to the wok and bring to the boil. Simmer for 5–7 minutes, or until the chicken is cooked. Sprinkle with basil leaves and serve immediately with freshly cooked rice.

Health Rating: 3 points

Aromatic Chicken Curry

Serves 4

Ingredients

125 g/4 oz/$^{2}/_{3}$ cup red lentils
2 tsp ground coriander
$^{1}/_{2}$ tsp cumin seeds
2 tsp mild curry paste
1 bay leaf
small strip lemon rind
600 ml/1 pint/2$^{1}/_{2}$ cups chicken or vegetable stock
8 skinless chicken thighs
175 g/6 oz/$^{3}/_{4}$ cup spinach leaves, rinsed and shredded
1 tbsp freshly chopped coriander/cilantro
2 tsp lemon juice
salt and freshly ground black pepper

To serve:
freshly cooked rice
low-fat natural/plain yogurt

Put the lentils in a sieve and rinse thoroughly under cold running water.

Dry-fry the ground coriander and cumin seeds in a large saucepan over a low heat for about 30 seconds. Stir in the curry paste.

Add the lentils to the saucepan with the bay leaf and lemon rind, then pour in the stock. Stir, then slowly bring to the boil. Turn down the heat, half-cover the pan with a lid and simmer gently for 5 minutes, stirring occasionally.

Secure the chicken thighs with cocktail sticks to keep their shape. Place in the pan and half-cover. Simmer for 15 minutes.

Stir in the shredded spinach and cook for a further 25 minutes, or until the chicken is very tender and the sauce is thick.

Remove the bay leaf and lemon rind. Stir in the coriander and lemon juice, then season to taste with salt and pepper. Serve immediately with the rice and a little natural yogurt.

Health Rating: 4 points

Chicken & Baby Vegetable Stir-fry

Serves 4

Ingredients

2 tbsp groundnut/peanut oil
1 small red chilli, deseeded and finely chopped
150 g/5 oz chicken breast or thigh meat, cut into cubes
2 baby leeks, trimmed and sliced
12 asparagus spears, halved
125 g/4½ oz/1 cup mangetout/snow peas, trimmed
125 g/4½ oz/1 cup baby carrots, trimmed and halved lengthways
125 g/4½ oz/¾ cup fine green beans, trimmed and diagonally sliced
125 g/4½ oz/1 cup baby sweetcorn, diagonally halved
50 ml/2 fl oz/¼ cup chicken stock
2 tsp light soy sauce
1 tbsp dry sherry
1 tsp sesame oil
toasted sesame seeds, to garnish

Heat a wok until very hot and add the oil. Add the chopped chilli and chicken and stir-fry for 4–5 minutes, or until the chicken is cooked and golden.

Increase the heat, add the leeks to the chicken and stir-fry for 2 minutes. Add the asparagus spears, mangetout/snow peas, baby carrots, green beans and baby sweetcorn. Stir-fry for 3–4 minutes, or until the vegetables soften slightly but still retain a slight crispness.

In a small bowl, mix together the chicken stock, soy sauce, dry sherry and sesame oil. Pour into the wok, stir and cook until heated through. Sprinkle with the toasted sesame seeds and serve immediately.

Health Rating: 4 points

Thai Coconut Chicken

Serves 4

Ingredients

1 tsp cumin seeds
1 tsp mustard seeds
1 tsp coriander seeds
1 tsp turmeric
1 bird's eye chilli, deseeded and finely chopped
1 tbsp freshly grated root ginger
2 garlic cloves, peeled and finely chopped
125 ml/4 fl oz/½ cup double/heavy cream
8 skinless chicken thighs
2 tbsp groundnut/peanut oil
1 onion, peeled and finely sliced
200 ml/7 fl oz/¾ cup coconut milk
salt and freshly ground black pepper
4 tbsp freshly chopped coriander/cilantro
2 spring onions/scallions, shredded, to garnish
freshly cooked Thai fragrant rice, to serve

Heat a wok and add the cumin, mustard and coriander seeds. Dry-fry over a low to medium heat for 2 minutes, or until the fragrance becomes stronger and the seeds start to pop. Add the turmeric and leave to cool slightly. Grind the spices using a pestle and mortar, or blend to a fine powder in a food processor.

Mix the chilli, ginger, garlic and the cream together in a small bowl, add the ground spices and mix. Place the chicken thighs in a shallow dish and spread the spice paste over the thighs.

Heat the wok over a high heat, add oil, and when hot, add the onion and stir-fry until golden brown. Add the chicken and spice paste. Cook for 5–6 minutes, stirring occasionally, until evenly coloured. Add the coconut milk and season with salt and pepper.

Simmer the chicken for 15–20 minutes, or until the thighs are cooked through, taking care not to allow the mixture to boil. Stir in the chopped coriander/cilantro and serve immediately with the freshly cooked rice sprinkled with shredded spring onions/scallions.

Health Rating: 1 point

Chicken & Cashew Nuts

Serves 4

Ingredients

450 g/1 lb skinless chicken breast fillets, cut into 1 cm/½ inch cubes
1 egg white, beaten
1 tsp salt
1 tsp sesame oil
2 tsp cornflour/cornstarch
300 ml/½ pint/1¼ cups groundnut/peanut oil, for deep-frying
2 tsp sunflower oil
50 g/2 oz/½ cup unsalted cashew nuts
4 spring onions/scallions, shredded
50 g/2 oz/½ cup mangetout/snow peas, diagonally sliced
1 tbsp Chinese rice wine
1 tbsp light soy sauce
shredded spring onions/scallions, to garnish
freshly steamed rice with fresh coriander/cilantro, to serve

Place the cubes of chicken in a large bowl. Add the beaten egg white, salt, sesame oil and cornflour/cornstarch. Mix well to ensure the chicken is coated thoroughly. Chill in the refrigerator for 20 minutes.

Heat the wok until very hot, add the groundnut/peanut oil. When hot, remove from the heat and add the chicken. Stir continuously to prevent the chicken from sticking to the wok. When the chicken turns white, after about 2 minutes, remove it using a slotted spoon and reserve. Discard the oil.

Wipe the wok clean and heat it again until very hot. Add the sunflower oil and heat. When hot, add the cashew nuts, spring onions/scallions and mangetout/snow peas and stir-fry for 1 minute. Add the rice wine and soy sauce. Return the chicken to the wok and stir-fry for 2 minutes. Garnish with shredded spring onions and serve with freshly steamed rice sprinkled with fresh coriander/cilantro.

Health Rating: 3 points

Steamed, Crispy Citrus Chicken

Serves 6

Ingredients

200 ml/7 fl oz/¾ cup light soy sauce
1 tbsp brown sugar
4 star anise
2 slices fresh root ginger, peeled
5 spring onions/scallions, trimmed and sliced
1 small orange, cut into wedges
1 lime, cut into wedges
1.1 kg/2½ lb oven-ready chicken
2 garlic cloves, peeled and finely chopped
2 tbsp Chinese rice wine
2 tbsp dark soy sauce
300 ml/½ pint/1¼ cups groundnut/peanut oil
orange slices, to garnish
freshly cooked steamed rice, to serve

Pour the light soy sauce and 200 ml/7 fl oz/¾ cup water into the wok and add the sugar and star anise. Bring to the boil over a gentle heat. Pour into a small bowl and leave to cool slightly. Wipe the wok clean with absorbent paper towels.

Put the ginger, 2 spring onions/scallions, orange and lime inside the cavity of the chicken. Place a rack in the wok. Pour in boiling water to a depth of 5 cm/2 inches. Put a piece of kitchen foil on the rack, place the chicken in the centre, then pour over the soy sauce mixture.

Cover the wok and steam gently for 1 hour–1 hour 10 minutes, or until the chicken is cooked through, pouring off excess fat from time to time. Add more water, if necessary. Leave the chicken to cool and dry for up to 3 hours, then cut the chicken into quarters.

Mix together the garlic, Chinese rice wine, dark soy sauce and remaining spring onions. Reserve. Dry the wok and heat again, then add the oil. When hot, shallow fry the chicken quarters for 4 minutes, or until golden and crisp. Do this 1 portion at a time. Remove and drain on absorbent paper towels.

When cool enough to handle, shred into bite-sized pieces and drizzle over the sauce. Garnish with slices of orange and serve with freshly steamed rice.

Health Rating: 3 points

Sticky-glazed Spatchcocked Poussins

Serves 4

Ingredients

2 poussins/game hens, each about 700 g/1½ lb
salt and freshly ground black pepper
4 kumquats, thinly sliced
assorted salad leaves, crusty bread or new potatoes, to serve

For the glaze:
zest of 1 small lemon, finely grated
1 tbsp lemon juice
1 tbsp dry sherry
2 tbsp clear honey
2 tbsp dark soy sauce
2 tbsp wholegrain mustard
1 tsp tomato puree/paste
½ tsp Chinese five-spice powder

Preheat the grill/broiler just before cooking. Place one of the poussins/game hens breast-side down on a board. Using poultry shears, cut down one side of the backbone. Cut down the other side of the backbone. Remove the bone.

Open out the poussin and press down hard on the breast bone with the heel of your hand to break it and to flatten the poussin.

Thread two skewers crossways through the bird to keep it flat, ensuring that each skewer goes through a wing and out through the leg on the opposite side. Repeat with the other bird. Season both sides of the bird with salt and pepper.

To make the glaze, mix together the lemon zest and juice, sherry, honey, soy sauce, mustard, tomato puree/paste and Chinese five-spice powder and use to brush all over the poussins.

Place the poussins skin-side down on a grill rack and grill under a medium heat for 15 minutes, brushing halfway through with more glaze. Turn the poussins over and grill for 10 minutes. Brush again with glaze and arrange the kumquat slices on top.

Grill for a further 15 minutes until well-browned and cooked through. If they start to brown too quickly, turn down the grill a little.

Remove the skewers and cut each poussin in half along the breastbone. Serve immediately with the salad, crusty bread or new potatoes.

Health Rating: 2 points

Potato-stuffed Roast Poussin

Serves 4

Ingredients

4 oven-ready poussins/game hens
salt and freshly ground black pepper
1 lemon, cut into quarters
4 large floury potatoes, peeled and cut into 4 cm/1½ inch pieces
1 tbsp freshly chopped thyme or rosemary
3–4 tbsp olive oil
4 garlic cloves, unpeeled and lightly smashed
8 slices streaky/fatty bacon or Parma ham/prosciutto
125 ml/4 fl oz/½ cup white wine
2 spring onions/scallions, trimmed and thinly sliced
2 tbsp double/heavy cream or crème fraîche/sour cream
lemon wedges, to garnish

Preheat the oven to 220°C/425°F/Gas Mark 7. Place a roasting tin/pan in the oven to heat. Rinse the poussin/game hen cavities and pat dry with absorbent paper towels. Season the cavities with salt and pepper and a squeeze of lemon. Push a lemon quarter into each cavity.

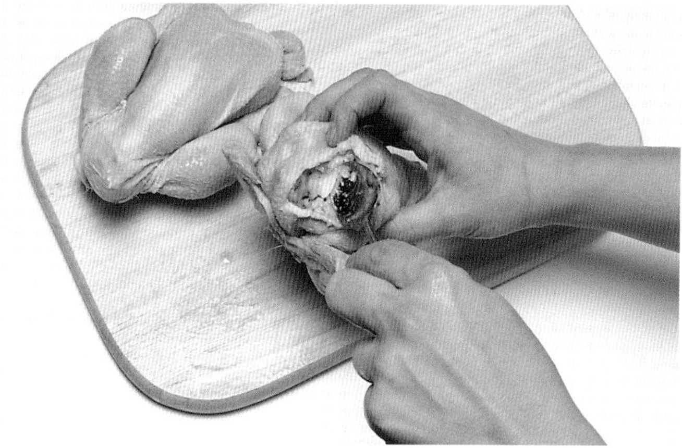

Put the potatoes in a saucepan of lightly salted water. Bring to the boil. Reduce the heat to low and simmer until just tender; do not overcook. Drain and cool slightly. Sprinkle the chopped herbs over the potatoes and drizzle with 2–3 tablespoons of the oil.

Spoon half the potatoes into the poussin cavities; do not pack too tightly. Rub each poussin with a little more oil and season with pepper. Carefully spoon 1 tablespoon oil into the hot roasting tin and add the poussins. Spoon the remaining potatoes around the edge and sprinkle over the garlic.

Roast the poussins in the preheated oven for 30 minutes, or until the skin is golden and beginning to crisp. Carefully lay the bacon or ham slices over the breast of each poussin. Roast for 15–20 minutes until crisp and the poussins are cooked through.

Transfer the poussins/hens and potatoes to a serving platter. Cover loosely with kitchen foil. Skim off the fat from the juices. Place the tin over a medium heat; add the wine and spring onions/scallions. Cook briefly, scraping the bits from the bottom of the tin. Whisk in the cream or crème fraîche/sour cream. Bubble for 1 minute, or until thickened. Garnish the poussins with lemon wedges. Serve with the creamy gravy.

Health Rating: 2 points

Spatchcocked Poussins with Garlic Sage Butter

Serves 4

Ingredients

For the herb butter:

6 large garlic cloves

150 g/5 oz/⅔ cup butter, softened

2 tbsp freshly snipped chives; 2 tbsp freshly chopped sage

grated rind and juice of 1 small lemon

salt and freshly ground black pepper

For the poussins:

4 spatchcocked poussins/game hens

2 tbsp extra virgin olive oil

To garnish:

chives

fresh sage leaves

To serve:

grilled polenta (*see* recipe page 209)

grilled tomatoes

Preheat the grill/broiler or light an outdoor charcoal grill and line the grill rack with kitchen foil just before cooking. Put the garlic cloves in a small saucepan and cover with cold water. Bring to the boil, then simmer for 5 minutes, or until softened. Drain and cool slightly. Cut off the root end of each clove and squeeze the softened garlic into a bowl.

Pound the garlic until smooth, then beat in the butter, chives, sage and lemon rind and juice. Season to taste with salt and pepper.

Using your fingertips, gently loosen the skin from each poussin/hen breast by sliding your hand between the skin and the flesh. Push one-quarter of the herb butter under the skin, spreading evenly over the breast and the top of the thighs. Pull the neck skin gently to tighten the skin over the breast and tuck under the bird. Repeat with the remaining birds and herb butter.

Thread two wooden skewers crossways through each bird, from one wing through the opposite leg, to keep the poussin flat. Repeat with the remaining birds, brush with the olive oil and season with salt and pepper.

Arrange the poussins on the foil-lined rack and grill for 25 minutes, turning occasionally, until golden and crisp and the juices run clear when a thigh is pierced with a sharp knife or skewer. (Position the rack about 12.5 cm/5 inches from the heat source or the skin will brown before the birds are cooked through.) Garnish with chives and sage leaves and serve immediately with grilled polenta and a few grilled tomatoes.

Health Rating: 2 points

Turkey & Tomato Tagine

Serves 4

Ingredients

For the meatballs:

450 g/1 lb fresh minced/ground turkey
1 small onion, peeled and very finely chopped
1 garlic clove, peeled and crushed
1 tbsp freshly chopped coriander/cilantro
1 tsp ground cumin
1 tbsp olive oil
salt and freshly ground black pepper

For the sauce:

1 onion, peeled and finely chopped
1 garlic clove, peeled and crushed
150 ml/¼ pint/⅔ cup turkey stock
400 g/14 oz can chopped tomatoes
½ tsp ground cumin
½ tsp ground cinnamon
pinch cayenne pepper
freshly chopped parsley
freshly chopped herbs, to garnish
freshly cooked couscous or rice, to serve

Preheat the oven to 190°C/375°F/Gas Mark 5. Put all the ingredients for the meatballs except the oil into a bowl and mix well. Season to taste with salt and pepper. Shape into 20 balls, about the size of walnuts. Put on a tray, cover lightly and chill in the refrigerator while making the sauce.

Put the onion and garlic in a pan with 125 ml/4 fl oz/½ cup of the stock. Cook over a low heat until all the stock has evaporated. Continue cooking for 1 minute, or until the onions begin to colour.

Add the remaining stock to the pan with the tomatoes, cumin, cinnamon and cayenne pepper. Simmer for 10 minutes, until slightly thickened and reduced. Stir in parsley and season to taste.

Heat the oil in a large nonstick frying pan and cook the meatballs in two batches until lightly browned all over. Lift the meatballs out with a slotted spoon and drain on absorbent paper towels.

Pour the sauce into a tagine or ovenproof casserole dish. Top with the meatballs, cover and cook in the preheated oven for 25–30 minutes, or until the meatballs are cooked through and the sauce is bubbling. Garnish with freshly chopped herbs and serve immediately on a bed of couscous or plain boiled rice.

Health Rating: 4 points

Turkey Escalopes with Apricot Chutney

Serves 4

Ingredients

4 x 175–225 g/6–8 oz turkey steaks
1 tbsp plain/all-purpose flour
salt and freshly ground black pepper
1 tbsp olive oil
flat-leaf/Italian parsley sprigs, to garnish
orange wedges, to serve

For the apricot chutney:
125 g/4 oz/1 cup no-need-to-soak dried apricots, chopped
1 red onion, peeled and finely chopped
1 tsp grated fresh root ginger
2 tbsp caster/superfine sugar
finely grated rind of ½ orange
125 ml/4 fl oz/½ cup fresh orange juice
125 ml/4 fl oz/½ cup ruby port
1 whole clove
1 tbsp freshly chopped coriander/cilantro

Put a turkey steak on to a sheet of non-pvc clingfilm/plastic wrap or nonstick baking parchment. Cover with a second sheet. Using a rolling pin, gently pound the turkey until the meat is flattened to about 5 mm/¼ inch thick. Repeat to make 4 escalopes.

Mix the flour with the salt and pepper and use to lightly dust the turkey escalopes. Put the escalopes on a board or baking tray and cover with a piece of non-pvc clingfilm or nonstick baking parchment. Chill in the refrigerator until ready to cook.

For the apricot chutney, put the apricots, onion, ginger, sugar, orange rind, orange juice, port and clove into a saucepan. Slowly bring to the boil and simmer, uncovered, for 10 minutes, stirring occasionally, until thick and syrupy. Remove the clove and stir in the chopped coriander.

Heat the oil in a pan and chargriddle the turkey escalopes, in two batches, if necessary, for 3–4 minutes on each side until golden brown and tender.

Spoon the chutney on to four individual serving plates. Place a turkey escalope on top of each spoonful of chutney. Garnish with parsley sprigs and serve immediately with orange wedges.

Health Rating: 5 points

Turkey Hash with Potato & Beetroot

Serves 4–6

Ingredients

2 tbsp vegetable oil
50 g/2 oz/½ stick butter
4 slices streaky/fatty bacon, diced or sliced
1 onion, peeled and finely chopped
450 g/1 lb/2¼ cups cooked turkey, diced
4 potatoes, cooked and sliced
2–3 tbsp freshly chopped parsley
2 tbsp plain/all-purpose flour
250 g/9 oz/1¾ cups diced cooked beetroot
green salad, to serve

In a large, heavy-based frying pan, heat the oil and half the butter over a medium heat until sizzling. Add the bacon and cook for 4 minutes, or until crisp and golden, stirring occasionally. Using a slotted spoon, transfer to a large bowl. Add the onion to the pan and cook for 3–4 minutes, or until soft and golden, stirring frequently.

Meanwhile, add the turkey, potatoes, parsley and flour to the cooked bacon in the bowl. Stir and toss gently, then fold in the diced beetroot.

Add half the remaining butter to the frying pan. Add the turkey vegetable mixture. Stir, then spread the mixture to cover the bottom of the frying pan evenly. Cook for 15 minutes, or until the underside is crisp and brown, pressing the hash firmly into a cake with a spatula. Remove from the heat.

Invert a large plate over the frying pan and, holding the plate and frying pan together with an oven glove, turn the hash out on to the plate. Heat the remaining butter in the pan, slide the hash back into the pan and cook for 4 minutes, or until crisp and brown on the other side. Invert on to the plate again and serve immediately with a green salad.

Health Rating: 3 points

Pheasant with Portabella Mushrooms & Red Wine Gravy

Serves 4

Ingredients

25 g/1 oz/¼ stick butter
1 tbsp olive oil
2 small pheasants (preferably hens)/game hens, rinsed, well dried and halved
8 shallots, peeled
300 g/11 oz/2¾ cups portabella/large mushrooms, thickly sliced
2–3 fresh thyme or rosemary sprigs, leaves stripped
300 ml/½ pint/1¼ cups Valpolicella or fruity red wine
300 ml/½ pint/1¼ cups hot chicken stock
1 tbsp cornflour/cornstarch
2 tbsp balsamic vinegar
2 tbsp redcurrant jelly, or to taste
2 tbsp freshly chopped flat leaf/Italian parsley
salt and freshly ground black pepper
fresh thyme sprigs, to garnish

Preheat the oven to 180°C/350°F/Gas Mark 4. Heat the butter and oil in a large saucepan or frying pan. Add the pheasant/hen halves and shallots, working in batches if necessary, and cook for 10 minutes or until golden on all sides, shaking the pan to glaze the shallots. Transfer to a casserole dish large enough to hold the pieces in a single layer.

Add the mushroom and thyme to the pan. Cook for 2–3 minutes, or until beginning to colour. Transfer to the dish with the pheasant halves.

Add the wine to the saucepan. Cook, stirring up any browned bits from the pan and allow to reduce by half. Pour in the stock, bring to the boil, then pour over the pheasant halves. Cover and braise in the preheated oven for 50 minutes, or until tender.

Remove the pheasant halves and vegetables to a wide, shallow serving dish.

Set the casserole dish over a medium-high heat. Skim off any surface fat, bring to the boil. Blend the cornflour/cornstarch with the vinegar. Stir into the sauce with the redcurrant jelly. Boil until the sauce is reduced and thickened slightly. Stir in the parsley. Season to taste with salt and pepper. Pour over the pheasant halves, garnish with fresh thyme sprigs. Serve immediately.

Health Rating: 3 points

Marinated Pheasant Breasts with Grilled Polenta

Serves 4

Ingredients

3 tbsp extra virgin olive oil
1 tbsp freshly chopped rosemary or sage leaves
1/2 tsp ground cinnamon
grated zest of 1 orange
salt and freshly ground black pepper
8 pheasant/game hen or wood pigeon breasts
600 ml/1 pint/2 1/2 cups water
125 g/4 1/2 oz/1 cup quick-cook polenta
25 g/1 oz/1/2 stick butter, diced
40 g/1 1/2 oz/1/2 cup grated Parmesan cheese
1–2 tbsp freshly chopped parsley
assorted salad leaves, to serve

Preheat the grill/broiler just before cooking. Blend 2 tablespoons of the olive oil with the rosemary or sage, cinnamon and orange zest and season to taste with salt and pepper.

Place the bird breasts in a large, shallow dish, pour over the flavoured oil and marinate until needed, turning occasionally.

Bring the water and 1 teaspoon salt to the boil in a large, heavy-based saucepan. Slowly whisk in the polenta in a thin, steady stream. Reduce the heat and simmer for 5–10 minutes, or until very thick, stirring constantly. Stir the butter, cheese, parsley and a little black pepper into the polenta.

Turn the polenta out on to a lightly oiled, nonstick baking sheet and spread into an even layer about 2 cm/3/4 inch thick. Leave to cool, then chill in the refrigerator for about 1 hour, or until the polenta is chilled.

Turn the cold polenta on to a work surface/countertop. Cut into 10 cm/4 inch squares. Brush with olive oil and arrange on a grill rack. Grill for 2–3 minutes on each side until crisp and golden, then cut each square into triangles and keep warm.

Transfer the marinated pheasant breasts to the grill rack and grill for 5 minutes, or until crisp and beginning to colour, turning once. Serve the pheasants immediately with the polenta triangles and salad leaves.

Health Rating: 3 points

Guinea Fowl with Calvados & Apples

Serves 4

Ingredients

4 skinless guinea fowl supremes/game hen breasts, each about 150 g/5 oz
1 tbsp plain/all-purpose flour
3 tsp sunflower oil
1 onion, peeled and finely sliced
1 garlic clove, peeled and crushed
1 tsp freshly chopped thyme
150 ml/¼ pint/⅔ cup dry cider
salt and freshly ground black pepper
3 tbsp Calvados brandy
fresh thyme sprigs, to garnish

For the caramelized apples:
15 g/½ oz/1 tbsp unsalted butter
2 red-skinned eating apples, quartered, cored and sliced
1 tsp sugar

Lightly dust the guinea fowl supremes/game hen breasts with the flour. Heat 2 teaspoons of the oil in a large, nonstick frying pan and cook the guinea fowl for 2–3 minutes on each side until browned. Remove from the pan and reserve.

Heat the remaining teaspoon of oil in the pan and add the onion and garlic. Cook over a medium heat for 10 minutes, stirring occasionally, until soft and just beginning to colour. Stir in the chopped thyme and cider.

Return the guinea fowl to the pan, season with salt and pepper and bring to a very gentle simmer. Cover and cook over a low heat for 15–20 minutes, or until the guinea fowl is tender. Remove the guinea fowl and keep warm. Turn up the heat and boil the sauce until thickened and reduced by half.

Meanwhile, prepare the caramelized apples. Melt the butter in a small, nonstick pan, add the apple slices in a single layer and sprinkle with the sugar. Cook until the apples are tender and beginning to caramelize, turning once.

Put the Calvados in a metal ladle or small saucepan and gently heat until warm. Carefully set alight with a match, let the flames die down, then stir into the sauce. Serve the guinea fowl with the sauce spooned over and garnished with the caramelized apples and fresh thyme sprigs.

Health Rating: 2 points

Duck with Berry Sauce

Serves 4

Ingredients

4 duck breast fillets, 175 g/6 oz each
salt and freshly ground black pepper
1 tsp sunflower oil

For the sauce:
juice of 1 orange
1 bay leaf, 3 tbsp redcurrant jelly
150 g/5 oz/$^{3}/_{4}$ cup fresh or frozen mixed berries
2 tbsp dried cranberries or cherries
$^{1}/_{2}$ tsp soft light brown sugar
1 tbsp balsamic vinegar
1 tsp freshly chopped mint
fresh mint sprigs, to garnish

To serve:
freshly cooked potatoes
freshly cooked green beans

Remove the skins from the duck breasts and season with a little salt and pepper. Brush a griddle pan with the oil, then heat on the stove until smoking hot. Place the duck in the pan. Cook over a medium-high heat for 5 minutes, or until well browned. Turn the duck and cook for 2 minutes. Lower the heat and cook for a further 5–8 minutes, or until cooked but still slightly pink in the centre. Remove from the pan and keep warm.

While the duck is cooking, make the sauce. Put the orange juice, bay leaf, redcurrant jelly, fresh or frozen and dried berries and sugar in a small griddle pan. Add any juices left in the duck griddle pan to the small pan. Slowly bring to the boil, lower the heat and simmer uncovered for 4–5 minutes until the fruit is soft. Remove the bay leaf. Stir in the vinegar and chopped mint and season to taste with salt and pepper.

Slice the duck breasts on the diagonal and arrange on serving plates. Spoon over the berry sauce and garnish with fresh mint sprigs. Serve immediately with the potatoes and green beans.

Health Rating: 2 points

Aromatic Duck Burgers on Potato Pancakes

Serves 4

Ingredients

700 g/1½ lb duck breast fillets
2 tbsp hoisin sauce
1 garlic clove, peeled and finely chopped
4 spring onions/scallions, trimmed and finely chopped
2 tbsp Japanese soy sauce
½ tsp Chinese five-spice powder
salt and freshly ground black pepper
freshly chopped coriander/cilantro, to garnish
extra hoisin sauce, to serve

For the potato pancakes:
4 floury potatoes
1 small onion, peeled and grated
1 small/medium egg, beaten
1 heaped tbsp plain/all-purpose flour

Peel off the thick layer of fat from the duck breasts and cut into small pieces. Put the fat in a small dry saucepan and set over a low heat for 10–15 minutes, or until the fat runs clear and the crackling goes crisp; reserve.

Cut the duck meat into pieces and blend in a food processor until coarsely chopped. Spoon into a bowl and add the hoisin sauce, garlic, half the spring onions/scallions, soy sauce and Chinese five-spice powder. Season to taste with salt and pepper and shape into four burgers. Cover and chill in the refrigerator for 1 hour.

To make the potato pancakes, grate the potatoes into a large bowl, squeeze out the water with your hands, then put on a clean dishtowel and twist the ends to squeeze out any remaining water. Return the potato to the bowl, add the onion and egg and mix well. Add the flour and salt and pepper. Stir to blend.

Heat 2 tablespoons of the clear duck fat in a large frying pan. Spoon the potato mixture into two to four patties and cook for 6 minutes, or until golden and crisp, turning once. Keep warm in the oven. Repeat with remaining mixture, adding duck fat as needed.

Preheat the grill/broiler and line the rack with kitchen foil. Brush the burgers with a little of the duck fat and grill for 6–8 minutes, or longer if wished, turning once.

Arrange one to two potato pancakes on a plate and top with a burger. Spoon a little hoisin sauce over, garnish with the remaining spring onions and coriander/cilantro and serve with some crackling on the side, if liked.

Health Rating: 2 points

Duck in Black Bean Sauce

Serves 4

Ingredients

450 g/1 lb skinless duck breast fillets
1 tbsp light soy sauce
1 tbsp Chinese rice wine or dry sherry
2.5 cm/1 inch piece fresh root ginger
3 garlic cloves
2 spring onions/scallions
2 tbsp Chinese preserved black beans
1 tbsp groundnut/peanut or vegetable oil
150 ml/$^1/_4$ pint/$^2/_3$ cup chicken stock
shredded spring onions/scallions, to garnish
freshly cooked noodles, to serve

Health Rating: 2 points

Using a sharp knife, trim the duck breasts, removing any fat. Slice thickly and place in a shallow dish. Mix together the soy sauce and Chinese rice wine or sherry and pour over the duck. Leave to marinate for 1 hour in the refrigerator, then drain and discard the marinade.

Peel the ginger and chop finely. Peel the garlic cloves and either chop finely or crush. Trim the root from the spring onions/scallions, discard the outer leaves and chop. Finely chop the black beans.

Heat a wok or large frying pan, add the oil and, when very hot, add the ginger, garlic, spring onions and black beans and stir-fry for 30 seconds. Add the drained duck and stir-fry for 3–5 minutes, or until the duck is browned.

Add the chicken stock to the wok, bring to the boil, then reduce the heat and simmer for 5 minutes, or until the duck is cooked and the sauce is reduced and thickened. Remove from the heat. Tip on to a bed of freshly cooked noodles, garnish with spring onion shreds and serve immediately.

Stir-fried Duck with Cashews

Serves 4

Ingredients

450 g/1 lb skinless duck breast
3 tbsp groundnut/peanut oil
1 garlic clove, peeled and finely chopped
1 tsp freshly grated root ginger
1 carrot, peeled and sliced
125 g/4 oz/1 cup mangetout/snow peas, trimmed
2 tsp Chinese rice wine or dry sherry
1 tbsp light soy sauce
1 tsp cornflour/cornstarch
50 g/2 oz/$^1/_3$ cup unsalted cashew nuts, roasted
1 spring onion/scallion, trimmed and finely chopped
1 spring onion/scallion, shredded
boiled or steamed rice, to serve

Trim the duck breasts, discarding any fat, and slice thickly. Heat a wok, add 2 tablespoons of the oil and, when hot, add the sliced duck breast. Cook for 3–4 minutes, or until sealed. Using a slotted spoon, remove from the wok and leave to drain on absorbent paper towels.

Wipe the wok clean and return to the heat. Add the remaining oil and, when hot, add the garlic and ginger. Stir-fry for 30 seconds, then add the carrot and mangetout/snow peas. Stir-fry for a further 2 minutes, then pour in the Chinese rice wine or sherry and soy sauce.

Blend the cornflour/cornstarch with 1 teaspoon water and stir into the wok. Mix well and bring to the boil. Return the duck slices to the wok and simmer for 5 minutes, or until the meat and vegetables are tender. Add the cashews, then remove the wok from the heat.

Sprinkle over the chopped and shredded spring onions/scallions and serve immediately with plain boiled or steamed rice.

Health Rating: 3 points

Crispy Roast Duck Legs with Pancakes

Serves 6

Ingredients

900 g/2 lbs/5½ cups plums, halved
25 g/1 oz/¼ stick butter; 2 star anise
1 tsp freshly grated root ginger
50 g/2 oz/¼ cup soft brown sugar
zest and juice of 1 orange
salt and freshly ground black pepper
4 duck legs
3 tbsp dark soy sauce
2 tbsp dark brown sugar
½ cucumber, cut into matchsticks
1 small bunch spring onions/scallions, trimmed and shredded
18 ready-made Chinese pancakes, warmed

Health Rating: 2 points

Preheat the oven to 220°C/425°F/Gas Mark 7, 15 minutes before cooking. Discard the stones from the plums. Place in a saucepan with the butter, star anise, ginger, brown sugar and orange zest and juice. Season to taste with pepper. Cook over a gentle heat until the sugar has dissolved. Bring to the boil, then reduce the heat and simmer for 15 minutes, stirring occasionally, until the plums are soft and the mixture is thick. Remove the star anise and leave to cool.

Using a fork, prick the duck legs all over. Place in a large bowl and pour boiling water over to remove some of the fat. Drain, pat dry on absorbent paper towels and leave until cold.

Mix together the soy sauce, dark brown sugar and ½ teaspoon salt. Generously rub this mixture over the duck legs. Transfer to a wire rack set over a roasting tin/pan and roast in the preheated oven for 30–40 minutes, or until well cooked and the skin is browned and crisp. Remove from the oven and leave to rest for 10 minutes.

Shred the duck meat, using a fork to hold the hot duck leg and another to remove the meat. Transfer to a warmed serving platter with the cucumber and spring onions/scallions. Serve immediately with the plum compote and warmed pancakes.

Duck in Crispy Wonton Shells

Serves 4

Ingredients

2 x 175 g/6 oz duck breasts
2 tbsp Chinese five-spice powder
2 tbsp Szechuan peppercorns
1 tsp whole black peppercorns
3 tbsp cumin seeds
5 tbsp sea salt
6 slices fresh root ginger
6 spring onions/scallions, roughly chopped
1 tbsp cornflour/cornstarch
1 litre/1$^{3}/_{4}$ pints/1 quart vegetable oil, for frying
16 wonton wrappers
5 cm/2 inch piece cucumber, cut into fine strips
125 ml/4 fl oz/$^{1}/_{2}$ cup hoisin sauce

Rinse the duck and dry thoroughly with absorbent paper towels. Place the Chinese five-spice powder, peppercorns, cumin seeds and salt in a pestle and mortar and crush. Rub the spice mix all over the duck. Wrap in clingfilm/plastic wrap and refrigerate for 24 hours.

Place a rack in a wok and pour in boiling water to a depth of 5 cm/2 inches. Place the duck breasts with the ginger slices and 3 chopped spring onions/scallions in a heatproof dish on top of the rack. Cover and steam for 40–50 minutes, or until the duck is cooked. Pour off any excess fat from time to time and add more water if necessary. Remove the duck and leave until cooled.

Dust the duck breasts with cornflour/cornstarch, shaking off the excess. Heat the wok, add the oil and, when almost smoking, deep-fry the duck for 8 minutes. Drain, then shred the meat into bite-sized pieces. Shred the remaining spring onions.

Reheat the oil until smoking. Working with one wonton at a time, insert two wooden skewers into each one, hold in a taco shape and lower into the oil. Hold in the oil until crisp and golden brown. Drain on absorbent paper towels. Repeat with the remaining wontons. Fill the wontons with the duck, topped with the spring onions, cucumber and hoisin sauce and serve immediately.

Health Rating: 2 points

Braised Rabbit with Red Peppers

Serves 4

Ingredients

1.1 kg/2½ lb rabbit pieces
125 ml/4 fl oz/½ cup olive oil
grated zest and juice of 1 lemon
2–3 tbsp freshly chopped thyme
salt and freshly ground black pepper
1 onion, peeled and thinly sliced
4 red peppers, deseeded and cut into 2.5 cm/1 inch pieces
2 garlic cloves, peeled and crushed
400 g/14 oz passata/bottled strained tomatoes
1 tsp brown sugar
freshly cooked polenta or creamy mashed potatoes, to serve

Place the rabbit pieces in a shallow dish with half the olive oil, the lemon zest and juice, thyme and some black pepper. Turn until well coated, cover and leave to marinate for about 1 hour.

Heat half the remaining oil in a large, heavy-based casserole dish, add the onion and cook for 5 minutes, then add the peppers and cook for a further 12–15 minutes, or until softened, stirring occasionally. Stir in the garlic, passata/bottled strained tomatoes and brown sugar and cook, covered, until soft, stirring occasionally.

Heat the remaining oil in a large frying pan, drain the rabbit, reserving the marinade, and pat the rabbit dry with absorbent paper towels. Add the rabbit to the pan and cook on all sides until golden. Transfer the rabbit to the casserole dish and mix to cover with the tomato sauce.

Add the reserved marinade to the frying pan and cook, stirring to loosen any browned bits from the pan. Add the marinade to the rabbit and stir gently. Cover the dish and simmer for 30 minutes, or until the rabbit is tender. Serve the rabbit and the vegetable mixture on a bed of polenta or creamy mashed potatoes.

Health Rating: 3 points

Vegetables & Salads

Get your family to eat their greens by whipping up some of these fantastic vegetable dishes; they will all enjoy the Marinated Vegetable Kebabs or the Winter Coleslaw. Vegetables add colour, texture and important nutrients to your diet and these recipes can be served either as a whole meal or as an accompaniment to other dishes, so why not experiment with one today?

Spiced Couscous & Vegetables

Serves 4

Ingredients

1 tbsp olive oil
1 large shallot, peeled and finely chopped
1 garlic clove, peeled and finely chopped
1 small red pepper, deseeded and cut into strips
1 small yellow pepper, deseeded and cut into strips
1 small aubergine/eggplant, diced
1 tsp each turmeric, ground cumin, ground cinnamon and paprika
2 tsp ground coriander
large pinch saffron strands
2 tomatoes, peeled, deseeded and diced
2 tbsp lemon juice
225 g/8 oz/1¼ cups couscous
225 ml/8 fl oz/1 cup vegetable stock
2 tbsp raisins
2 tbsp whole almonds
2 tbsp freshly chopped parsley
2 tbsp freshly chopped coriander/cilantro
salt and freshly ground black pepper

Heat the oil in a large frying pan, add the shallot and garlic and cook for 2–3 minutes until softened. Add the peppers and aubergine/eggplant and reduce the heat. Cook for 8–10 minutes until the vegetables are tender, adding a little water if necessary.

Test a piece of aubergine to ensure it is cooked through. Add all the spices and cook for a further minute, stirring.

Increase the heat and add the tomatoes and lemon juice. Cook for 2–3 minutes until the tomatoes have started to break down. Remove from the heat and leave to cool slightly.

Meanwhile, put the couscous into a large bowl. Bring the stock to the boil in a saucepan, then pour over the couscous. Stir well and cover with a clean dishtowel.

Leave to stand for 7–8 minutes until all the stock is absorbed and the couscous is tender. Uncover the couscous and fluff with a fork. Stir in the vegetable and spice mixture along with the raisins, almonds, parsley and coriander/cilantro. Season to taste with salt and pepper and serve.

Health Rating: 4 points

Black Bean Chilli with Avocado Salsa

Serves 4

Ingredients

250 g/9 oz/1½ cups black beans and black-eye beans, soaked overnight
2 tbsp olive oil
1 large onion, peeled and finely chopped
1 red pepper, deseeded and diced
2 garlic cloves, peeled and finely chopped
1 red chilli, deseeded and finely chopped
2 tsp chilli powder; 1 tsp ground cumin; 2 tsp ground coriander
400 g/14 oz can chopped tomatoes
450 ml/¾ pint/2 cups vegetable stock
1 small ripe avocado, diced
½ small red onion, peeled and finely chopped
2 tbsp freshly chopped coriander/cilantro
juice of 1 lime
1 small tomato, peeled, deseeded and diced
salt and freshly ground black pepper
25 g/1 oz dark chocolate

To garnish:

half-fat crème fraîche/sour cream
lime slices
coriander/cilantro sprigs

Drain the beans and place in a large saucepan with at least twice their volume of fresh water. Bring slowly to the boil, skimming off any froth that rises to the surface. Boil rapidly for 10 minutes, then reduce the heat and simmer for about 45 minutes, adding more water if necessary. Drain and reserve.

Heat the oil in a large saucepan and add the onion and pepper. Cook for 3–4 minutes until softened. Add the garlic and chilli. Cook for 5 minutes, or until the onion and pepper have softened. Add the chilli powder, cumin and coriander and cook for 30 seconds. Add the beans along with the tomatoes and stock. Bring to the boil and simmer uncovered for 40–45 minutes until the beans and vegetables are tender and the sauce has reduced.

Mix together the avocado, onion, fresh coriander/cilantro, lime juice and tomato. Season with salt and pepper and set aside. Remove the chilli from the heat. Break the chocolate into pieces. Sprinkle over the chilli. Leave for 2 minutes. Stir well. Garnish with crème fraîche/sour cream, lime and coriander. Serve with the avocado salsa.

Health Rating: 4 points

Roasted Mixed Vegetables with Garlic & Herb Sauce

Serves 4

Ingredients

1 large garlic bulb, halved horizontally
1 large onion, peeled and cut into wedges
4 small carrots, peeled and quartered
4 small parsnips, peeled
6 small potatoes, scrubbed and halved
1 fennel bulb, thickly sliced
4 fresh rosemary sprigs
4 fresh thyme sprigs
2 tbsp olive oil
salt and freshly ground black pepper
200 g/7 oz/1 cup low-fat cream cheese with herbs and garlic
4 tbsp milk
zest of ½ lemon
fresh thyme sprigs, to garnish

Preheat the oven to 220°C/425°F/Gas Mark 7. Put all the vegetables and herbs into a large roasting tin/pan. Add the oil, season well with salt and pepper and toss together to coat lightly in the oil. Cover with kitchen foil and roast in the preheated oven for 50 minutes.

Remove the kitchen foil and cook for a further 30 minutes until all the vegetables are tender and slightly charred. Remove the tin from the oven and allow to cool.

In a small saucepan, melt the low-fat cream cheese together with the milk and lemon zest. Remove the garlic from the roasting tin and squeeze the flesh into a bowl. Mash thoroughly, then add to the sauce. Heat through gently.

Season the vegetables to taste. Pour some sauce into small ramekins and garnish with 4 thyme sprigs. Serve the roasted vegetables with the sauce for dipping.

Health Rating: 4 points

Roasted Butternut Squash

Serves 4

Ingredients

2 small butternut squash
4 garlic cloves, peeled and crushed
1 tbsp olive oil
salt and freshly ground black pepper
1 tbsp walnut oil
4 leeks, trimmed, cleaned and thinly sliced
1 tbsp black mustard seeds
300 g/11 oz can cannellini beans, drained and rinsed
125 g/4½ oz/¾ cup fine French/green beans, halved
150 ml/¼ pint/⅔ cup vegetable stock
50 g/2 oz/1¼ cups rocket/arugula
2 tbsp freshly snipped chives
fresh chives, to garnish

To serve:
4 tbsp fromage frais/reduced-fat sour cream
mixed salad

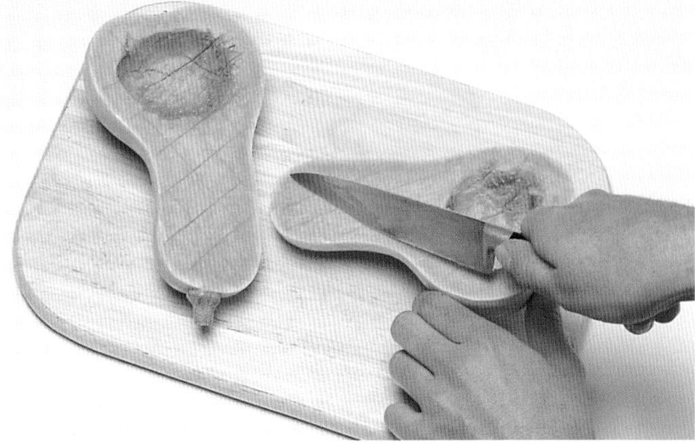

Preheat the oven to 200°C/400°F/Gas Mark 6. Cut the butternut squash in half lengthways and scoop out all of the seeds. Score the squash in a diamond pattern with a sharp knife. Mix the garlic with the olive oil and brush over the cut surfaces of the squash. Season well with salt and pepper. Put on a baking sheet and roast for 40 minutes until tender.

Heat the walnut oil in a saucepan and fry the leeks and mustard seeds for 5 minutes. Add the drained cannellini beans, French beans/green beans and vegetable stock. Bring to the boil and simmer gently for 5 minutes until the French beans are tender. Remove from the heat and stir in the rocket/arugula and chives. Season well.

Remove the squash from the oven. Allow to cool for 5 minutes. Spoon in bean mixture. Garnish with a few snipped chives. Serve with fromage frais/reduced-fat sour cream and a mixed salad.

Health Rating: 4 points

Mushroom Stew

Serves 4

Ingredients

15 g/½ oz/¼ cup dried porcini mushrooms
900 g/2 lb/9 cups assorted fresh mushrooms, wiped
2 tbsp good-quality virgin olive oil
1 onion, peeled and finely chopped
2 garlic cloves, peeled and finely chopped
1 tbsp fresh thyme leaves
pinch ground cloves
salt and freshly ground black pepper
700 g/1½ lb/4 cups tomatoes, peeled, deseeded and chopped
225 g/8 oz/2 cups instant polenta
600ml/1 pt/2½ cups vegetable stock
3 tbsp freshly chopped mixed herbs
parsley sprigs, to garnish

Health Rating: 4 points

Soak the porcini mushrooms in a small bowl of hot water for 20 minutes. Drain, reserving the porcini and their soaking liquor. Cut the fresh mushrooms in half and reserve.

In a saucepan, heat the oil and add the onion. Cook gently for 5–7 minutes until softened. Add the garlic, thyme and cloves and continue cooking for 2 minutes.

Add all the mushrooms and cook for 8–10 minutes until the mushrooms have softened, stirring often. Season to taste with salt and pepper and add the tomatoes and the reserved soaking liquid.

Simmer, partly-covered, over a low heat for about 20 minutes until thickened. Adjust the seasoning to taste.

Meanwhile, cook the polenta according to the packet instructions using the vegetable stock and stir in the herbs.

Ladle the mushrooms out, dividing between four dishes, and pour over the polenta. Garnish with the parsley and serve immediately.

Marinated Vegetable Kebabs

Serves 4

Ingredients

2 small courgettes/zucchini, cut into 2 cm/¾ inch pieces
½ green pepper, deseeded and cut into 2.5 cm/1 inch pieces
½ red pepper, deseeded and cut into 2.5 cm /1 inch pieces
½ yellow pepper, deseeded and cut into 2.5 cm/1 inch pieces
8 baby onions, peeled
8 button mushrooms
8 cherry tomatoes
freshly chopped parsley, to garnish
freshly cooked couscous, to serve

For the marinade:
1 tbsp light olive oil, 4 tbsp dry sherry
2 tbsp light soy sauce, 1 red chilli, deseeded and finely chopped
2 garlic cloves, peeled and crushed
2.5 cm/1 inch piece root ginger, peeled and finely grated

Place the courgettes/zucchini, peppers and baby onions in a pan of just-boiled water. Bring back to the boil and simmer for about 30 seconds, then drain and rinse the cooked vegetables in cold water and dry on absorbent paper towels.

Thread the cooked vegetables and the mushrooms and tomatoes alternately on to skewers and place in a large shallow dish.

Make the marinade by whisking all the ingredients together until thoroughly blended. Pour the marinade evenly over the kebabs, then chill in the refrigerator for at least 1 hour. Spoon the marinade over the kebabs occasionally during this time.

Place the kebabs in a hot griddle pan or on a hot barbecue and cook gently for 10–12 minutes. Turn the kebabs frequently and brush with the marinade when needed. When the vegetables are tender, sprinkle over the chopped parsley and serve immediately with couscous.

Health Rating: 4 points

Light Ratatouille

Serves 4

Ingredients

1 red pepper
2 courgettes/zucchini, trimmed
1 small aubergine/eggplant, trimmed
1 onion, peeled
2 ripe tomatoes
50 g/2 oz/¾ cup button mushrooms, wiped and halved or quartered
200 ml/7 fl oz/¾ cup tomato juice
1 tbsp freshly chopped basil
salt and freshly ground black pepper

Health Rating: 5 points

Deseed the peppers, remove the membrane with a small sharp knife and cut into small dice. Thickly slice the courgettes and cut the aubergine into small dice. Slice the onion into rings.

Place the tomatoes in boiling water until their skins begin to peel away. Remove the skins, cut into quarters and remove the seeds.

Place all the vegetables in a saucepan with the tomato juice and basil. Season to taste with salt and pepper. Bring to the boil, cover and simmer for 15 minutes, or until the vegetables are tender. Remove the vegetables with a slotted spoon and arrange in a serving dish.

Bring the liquid in the pan to the boil and boil for 20 seconds until it is slightly thickened. Season to taste with salt and pepper. Pass the sauce through a sieve to remove some of the seeds and pour over the vegetables. Serve the ratatouille hot or cold.

Sweet Potato Cakes with Tomato & Mango Salsa

Serves 4

Ingredients

700 g/1½ lb/4 cups sweet potatoes, peeled and cut into large chunks
salt and freshly ground black pepper
25 g/1 oz/¼ stick butter
1 onion, peeled and chopped
1 garlic clove, peeled and crushed
pinch freshly grated nutmeg
1 egg, beaten
50 g/2 oz/⅓ cup quick-cook polenta
2 tbsp sunflower oil

For the salsa:
1 ripe mango, peeled, stoned and diced
6 cherry tomatoes, cut into wedges
4 spring onions/scallions, trimmed and thinly sliced
1 red chilli, deseeded and finely chopped
finely grated rind and juice of ½ lime
2 tbsp freshly chopped mint
1 tsp clear honey
salad leaves, to serve

Steam or cook the sweet potatoes in lightly salted boiling water for 15–20 minutes, until tender. Drain well, then mash until smooth.

Melt the butter in a saucepan. Add the onion and garlic. Cook gently for 10 minutes until soft. Add to the mashed sweet potato and season with the nutmeg, salt and pepper. Stir together until mixed thoroughly. Leave to cool.

Shape the mixture into four oval potato patties, about 2.5 cm/1 inch thick. Dip first in the beaten egg, allowing the excess to fall back into the bowl, then coat in the polenta. Refrigerate for at least 30 minutes.

Meanwhile, mix together all the ingredients for the salsa. Spoon into a serving bowl and cover with clingfilm/plastic wrap. Leave at room temperature to allow the flavours to develop.

Heat the oil in a frying pan and cook the potato cakes for 4–5 minutes on each side. Serve with the salsa and salad leaves.

Health Rating: 4 points

Chunky Vegetable & Fennel Goulash with Dumplings

Serves 4

Ingredients

2 fennel bulbs, weighing about 450 g/1 lb
2 tbsp sunflower oil
1 large onion, peeled and sliced
1½ tbsp paprika
1 tbsp plain/all-purpose flour
300 ml/½ pint/1¼ cups vegetable stock
400 g/14 oz can chopped tomatoes
450 g/1 lb potatoes, peeled and cut into 2.5 cm/1 inch chunks
125 g/4 oz/1¼ cups small button mushrooms
salt and freshly ground black pepper

For the dumplings:
1 tbsp sunflower oil
1 small onion, peeled and finely chopped
1 egg
3 tbsp milk
3 tbsp freshly chopped parsley
125 g/4 oz/2 cups fresh white breadcrumbs

Cut the fennel bulbs in half widthways. Thickly slice the stalks and cut the bulbs into eight wedges.

Heat the oil in a large saucepan or flameproof casserole dish. Add the onion and fennel and cook gently for 10 minutes until soft. Stir in the paprika and flour.

Remove from the heat and gradually stir in the stock. Add the chopped tomatoes, potatoes and mushrooms. Season to taste with salt and pepper. Bring to the boil, reduce the heat and simmer for 20 minutes.

Meanwhile, make the dumplings. Heat the oil in a frying pan and gently cook the onion for 10 minutes, until soft. Leave to cool for a few minutes.

In a bowl, beat the egg and milk together, then add the onion, parsley and breadcrumbs and season to taste. With damp hands, form the breadcrumb mixture into 12 round dumplings, each about the size of a walnut.

Arrange the dumplings on top of the goulash. Cover and cook for a further 15 minutes, until the dumplings are cooked and the vegetables are tender. Serve immediately.

Health Rating: 3 points

Creamy Vegetable Korma

Serves 4–6

Ingredients

2 tbsp ghee or vegetable oil
1 large onion, peeled and chopped
2 garlic cloves, peeled and crushed
2.5 cm/1 inch piece root ginger, peeled and grated
4 cardamom pods
2 tsp ground coriander
1 tsp ground cumin
1 tsp ground turmeric
finely grated rind and juice of $^1/_2$ lemon
50 g/2 oz/$^1/_2$ cup ground almonds
400 ml/14 fl oz/1$^3/_4$ cups vegetable stock
450 g/1 lb/4 cups potatoes, peeled and diced
450 g/1 lb mixed vegetables, such as cauliflower, carrots and turnip, cut into chunks
150 ml/$^1/_4$ pt/$^2/_3$ cup double/heavy cream
3 tbsp freshly chopped coriander/cilantro
salt and freshly ground black pepper
naan bread, to serve

Heat the ghee or oil in a large saucepan. Add the onion and cook for 5 minutes. Stir in the garlic and ginger and cook for a further 5 minutes, or until soft and just beginning to colour.

Stir in the cardamom, ground coriander, cumin and turmeric. Continue cooking over a low heat for 1 minute, stirring.

Stir in the lemon rind and juice and almonds. Blend in the vegetable stock. Slowly bring to the boil, stirring occasionally.

Add the potatoes and vegetables. Bring back to the boil, then reduce the heat, cover and simmer for 35–40 minutes, or until the vegetables are just tender. Check after 25 minutes and add a little more stock if needed.

Slowly stir in the cream and chopped coriander/cilantro. Season to taste with salt and pepper. Cook very gently until heated through, but do not boil. Serve immediately with naan bread.

Health Rating: 3 points

Thai–style Cauliflower & Potato Curry

Serves 4

Ingredients

9–12 new potatoes, peeled, halved or quartered
350 g/12 oz/1¼ cups cauliflower florets
3 garlic cloves, peeled and crushed
1 onion, peeled and finely chopped
40 g/1½ oz/½ cup ground almonds
1 tsp ground coriander
½ tsp ground cumin
½ tsp turmeric
3 tbsp groundnut/peanut oil
salt and freshly ground black pepper
50 g/2 oz/6 tbsp creamed coconut, broken into small pieces
200 ml/7 fl oz/¾ cup vegetable stock
1 tbsp mango chutney
fresh coriander/cilantro sprigs, to garnish
freshly cooked long-grain rice, to serve

Bring a saucepan of lightly salted water to the boil, add the potatoes and cook for 15 minutes, or until just tender. Drain and leave to cool. Boil the cauliflower for 2 minutes, then drain and refresh under cold running water. Drain again and reserve.

Meanwhile, blend the garlic, onion, ground almonds and spices with 2 tablespoons of the oil and salt and pepper to taste in a food processor until a smooth paste is formed. Heat a wok, add the remaining oil and, when hot, add the spice paste and cook for 3–4 minutes, stirring continuously.

Dissolve the creamed coconut in 6 tablespoons boiling water and add to the wok. Pour in the stock, cook for 2–3 minutes, then stir in the cooked potatoes and cauliflower.

Stir in the mango chutney and heat through for 3–4 minutes, or until piping hot. Tip into a warmed serving dish, garnish with coriander/cilantro sprigs and serve immediately with freshly cooked rice.

Health Rating: 3 points

Pumpkin & Chickpea Curry

Serves 4

Ingredients

1 tbsp vegetable oil
1 small onion, peeled and sliced
2 garlic cloves, peeled and finely chopped
2.5 cm/1 inch piece root ginger, peeled and grated
1 tsp ground coriander
½ tsp ground cumin
½ tsp ground turmeric
¼ tsp ground cinnamon
2 tomatoes, chopped
2 red bird's eye chillies, deseeded and finely chopped
450 g/1 lb pumpkin or butternut squash flesh, cubed
1 tbsp hot curry paste
300 ml/½ pint/1¼ cups vegetable stock
1 large firm banana
400 g/14 oz can chickpeas, drained and rinsed
salt and freshly ground black pepper
1 tbsp freshly chopped coriander/cilantro sprigs, to garnish
rice or naan bread, to serve

Heat 1 tablespoon of the oil in a saucepan and add the onion. Fry gently for 5 minutes until softened.

Add the garlic, ginger and spices and fry for a further minute. Add chopped tomatoes and chillies and cook for another minute.

Add the pumpkin and curry paste and fry gently for 3–4 minutes before adding the stock.

Stir well, bring to the boil and simmer for 20 minutes until the pumpkin is tender.

Thickly slice the banana and add to the pumpkin along with the chickpeas. Simmer for a further 5 minutes.

Season to taste with salt and pepper and add the chopped coriander. Serve immediately, garnished with coriander sprigs and some rice or naan bread.

Health Rating: 4 points

Vegetables Braised in Olive Oil & Lemon

Serves 4

Ingredients

pared rind and juice of ½ lemon
4 tbsp olive oil
1 bay leaf
1 large thyme sprig
150 ml/¼ pint/⅔ cup water
4 spring onions/scallions, trimmed and chopped
175 g/6 oz/1½ cups button/white mushrooms
175 g/6 oz/2 cups broccoli florets
175 g/6 oz/2 cups cauliflower florets
1 courgette/zucchini, sliced diagonally
2 tbsp freshly snipped chives
salt and freshly ground black pepper
lemon zest, to garnish

Put the pared lemon rind and juice into a large saucepan. Add the olive oil, bay leaf, thyme and the water. Bring to the boil. Add the spring onions/scallions and mushrooms. Top with the broccoli and cauliflower florets, adding them so that the stalks are submerged in the water and the tops are just above it. Cover and simmer for 3 minutes.

Scatter the courgettes/zucchini on top, so that they are steamed rather than boiled. Cook, covered, for a further 3–4 minutes until all the vegetables are tender.

Using a slotted spoon, transfer the vegetables from the liquid into a warmed serving dish.

Increase the heat and boil rapidly for 3–4 minutes, or until the liquid is reduced to about 8 tablespoons. Remove the lemon rind, bay leaf and thyme sprig and discard.

Stir the chives into the reduced liquid, season to taste with salt and pepper and pour over the vegetables. Sprinkle with lemon zest and serve immediately.

Health Rating: 3 points

Stuffed Tomatoes with Grilled Polenta

Serves 4

Ingredients

For the polenta:

300 ml/½ pint/1¼ cups vegetable stock
salt and freshly ground black pepper
50 g/2 oz/½ cup quick-cook polenta
15 g/½ oz/1 tbsp butter

For the stuffed tomatoes:

4 large tomatoes
1 tbsp olive oil; 1 garlic clove, peeled and crushed
1 bunch spring onions/scallions, trimmed and finely chopped
2 tbsp freshly chopped parsley
2 tbsp freshly chopped basil
2 slices Parma ham/prosciutto, cut into thin slivers
50 g/2 oz/1 cup fresh white breadcrumbs
snipped chives, to garnish

Preheat the grill/broiler just before cooking. To make the polenta, pour the stock into a saucepan. Add a pinch of salt and bring to the boil. Pour in the polenta in a fine stream, stirring all the time. Simmer for about 15 minutes, or until very thick. Stir in the butter and add a little pepper. Turn the polenta out on to a chopping board and spread to a thickness of just over 1 cm/½ inch. Cool, cover with clingfilm/plastic wrap and chill in the refrigerator for 30 minutes.

To make the stuffed tomatoes, cut the tomatoes in half, then scoop out the seeds and press through a fine sieve to extract the juices. Season the insides of the tomatoes with salt and pepper and reserve.

Heat the olive oil in a saucepan and gently fry the garlic and spring onions/scallions for 3 minutes. Add the tomatoes' juices, bubble for 3–4 minutes until most of the liquid has evaporated. Stir in the herbs, Parma ham and a little black pepper with half the breadcrumbs. Spoon into the hollowed out tomatoes and reserve.

Cut the polenta into 5 cm/2 inch squares, then cut each in half diagonally to make triangles. Put the triangles on a piece of kitchen foil on the grill rack and grill for 4–5 minutes on each side until golden. Cover and keep warm.

Grill the tomatoes under a medium-hot grill for about 4 minutes – any exposed Parma ham will become crisp. Sprinkle with the remaining breadcrumbs and grill for 1–2 minutes, or until the breadcrumbs are golden brown. Garnish with snipped chives and serve immediately with the grilled polenta.

Health Rating: 3 points

Spinach Dumplings with Rich Tomato Sauce

Serves 4

Ingredients

For the sauce:
2 tbsp olive oil
1 onion, peeled and chopped
1 garlic clove, peeled and crushed
1 red chilli, deseeded and chopped
150 ml/¼ pint/⅔ cup dry white wine
400 g/14 oz can chopped tomatoes
pared strip of lemon rind
salt and freshly ground black pepper

For the dumplings:
450 g/1 lb/10 cups fresh spinach
50 g/2 oz/¼ cup ricotta cheese
25 g/1 oz/½ cup fresh white breadcrumbs
25 g/1 oz/¼ cup grated Parmesan cheese
1 egg yolk
¼ tsp freshly grated nutmeg
5 tbsp plain/all-purpose flour
2 tbsp olive oil, for frying
fresh basil leaves, to garnish
freshly cooked tagliatelle, to serve

To make the tomato sauce, heat the olive oil in a large saucepan and fry the onion gently for 5 minutes. Add the garlic and chilli and cook for a further 5 minutes until softened.

Stir in the wine, chopped tomatoes and lemon rind. Bring to the boil, cover and simmer for 20 minutes, then uncover and simmer for 15 minutes, or until the sauce has thickened. Remove the lemon rind and season to taste with salt and pepper.

To make spinach dumplings, wash the spinach and remove any tough stalks. Cover and cook in a large saucepan over a low heat with just the water clinging to the leaves. Drain, then squeeze out all excess water. Finely chop and put in a large bowl. Add the ricotta, breadcrumbs, Parmesan cheese and egg yolk to the spinach. Season with nutmeg and salt and pepper.

Mix together and shape into 20 walnut-sized balls. Toss the spinach balls in the flour.

Heat the olive oil in a large nonstick frying pan and fry the balls gently for 5–6 minutes, carefully turning occasionally. Garnish with fresh basil leaves and serve immediately with the tomato sauce and tagliatelle.

Health Rating: 3 points

Venetian Style Vegetables & Beans

Serves 4

Ingredients

250 g/9 oz/1½ cups dried pinto beans
3 fresh parsley sprigs
1 fresh rosemary sprig
2 tbsp olive oil
200 g/7 oz can chopped tomatoes
2 shallots, peeled

For the vegetable mixture:
1 large red onion, peeled
1 large white onion, peeled
1 carrot, peeled
2 celery stalks, trimmed
3 tbsp olive oil
3 bay leaves
1 tsp sugar
3 tbsp red wine vinegar
salt and freshly ground black pepper

Put the beans in a bowl, cover with plenty of cold water and leave to soak for at least 8 hours, or overnight. Drain and rinse the beans. Put in a large saucepan with 1.2 litres/2 pints/1¼ quarts cold water. Tie the parsley and rosemary in muslin and add to the beans with the olive oil.

Boil rapidly for 10 minutes, then lower the heat and simmer for 20 minutes with the saucepan half covered. Stir in the tomatoes and shallots and simmer for a further 10–15 minutes, or until the beans are cooked.

Meanwhile, slice the red and white onions into rings, then finely dice the carrot and celery. Heat the olive oil in a saucepan and cook the onions over a very low heat for about 10 minutes. Add the carrot, celery and bay leaves to the saucepan and cook for a further 10 minutes, stirring frequently, until the vegetables are tender. Sprinkle with sugar, stir and cook for 1 minute. Stir in the vinegar. Cook for 1 minute, then remove the saucepan from the heat.

Drain the beans through a fine sieve, discarding all the herbs, then add the beans to the onion mixture and season well with salt and pepper. Mix gently, tip the beans into a large serving bowl. Leave to cool, then serve at room temperature.

Health Rating: 4 points

Vegetable Frittata

Serves 2

Ingredients

6 eggs
2 tbsp freshly chopped parsley; 1 tbsp freshly chopped tarragon
25 g/1 oz/$^{1}/_{4}$ cup finely grated pecorino or Parmesan cheese
freshly ground black pepper
175 g/6 oz/1$^{1}/_{4}$ cups tiny new potatoes
2 small carrots, peeled and sliced
125 g/4$^{1}/_{2}$ oz/1$^{1}/_{4}$ cups broccoli, cut into small florets
1 courgette/zucchini, about 125 g/4$^{1}/_{2}$ oz/$^{3}/_{4}$ cup, sliced
2 tbsp olive oil
4 spring onions/scallions, trimmed and thinly sliced

To serve: mixed green salad; crusty Italian bread

Preheat the grill/broiler just before cooking. Lightly beat the eggs with the parsley, tarragon and half the cheese. Season to taste with black pepper and reserve. (Salt is not needed as the pecorino is very salty.)

Bring a large saucepan of lightly salted water to the boil. Add the new potatoes and cook for 8 minutes. Add the carrots and cook for 4 minutes, then add the broccoli florets and the courgette/zucchini and cook for a further 3–4 minutes, or until all the vegetables are barely tender. Drain well.

Heat the oil in a 20.5 cm/8 inch heavy-based frying pan. Add the spring onions/scallions and cook for 3–4 minutes, or until softened. Add all the vegetables and cook for a few seconds, then pour in the beaten egg mixture. Stir gently for about a minute. Cook for a further 1–2 minutes, or until the bottom of the frittata is set and golden brown.

Place the pan under a hot grill for 1 minute, or until almost set and just beginning to brown. Sprinkle with the remaining cheese and grill for a further 1 minute, or until it is lightly browned. Loosen the edges and slide out of the pan. Cut into wedges and serve hot or warm with a mixed green salad and crusty Italian bread.

Health Rating: 3 points

Mixed Vegetables Stir-fry

Serves 4

Ingredients

2 tbsp groundnut/peanut oil
4 garlic cloves, peeled and finely sliced
2.5 cm/1 inch piece fresh root ginger, peeled and finely sliced
75 g/3 oz/¾ cup broccoli florets
50 g/2 oz/heaping ½ cup mangetout/snowpeas, trimmed
1 carrot, peeled and cut into matchsticks
1 green pepper, deseeded and cut into strips
1 red pepper, deseeded and cut into strips
1 tbsp soy sauce
1 tbsp hoisin sauce
1 tsp sugar
salt and freshly ground black pepper
4 spring onions/scallions, trimmed and shredded, to garnish

Heat a wok, add the oil and, when hot, add the garlic and ginger slices and stir-fry for 1 minute.

Add the broccoli florets to the wok, stir-fry for 1 minute, then add the mangetout/snow peas, carrots and the green and red peppers and stir-fry for a further 3–4 minutes, or until tender but still crisp.

Blend the soy sauce, hoisin sauce and sugar in a small bowl. Stir well, season to taste with salt and pepper and pour into the wok. Transfer the vegetables to a warmed serving dish. Garnish with shredded spring onions/scallions and serve immediately with a selection of other Thai dishes.

Health Rating: 5 points

Vegetable Tempura

Serves 4–6

Ingredients

125 g/4 oz/1 cup rice flour
75 g/3 oz/$^2/_3$ cup plain/all-purpose flour
4 tsp baking powder
1 tbsp dried mustard powder
2 tsp semolina
salt and freshly ground black pepper
300 ml/$^1/_2$ pint groundnut/peanut oil
125 g/4 oz/1 heaping cup courgette/zucchini, trimmed and thickly sliced
125 g/4 oz/1 cup mangetout/snow peas
125 g/4 oz/1 cup baby sweetcorn
4 small red onions, peeled and quartered
1 large red pepper, deseeded and cut into 2.5 cm/1 inch wide strips
light soy sauce, to serve

Sift the rice flour and the plain/all-purpose flour into a large bowl, then sift in the baking powder and dried mustard powder.

Stir the semolina into the flour mixture and season to taste with salt and pepper. Gradually beat in 300 ml/$^1/_2$ pint/1$^1/_4$ cups cold water to produce a thin coating batter. Leave to stand at room temperature for 30 minutes.

Heat a wok or large frying pan, add the oil and heat to 180°C/350°F. Working in batches and using a slotted spoon, dip the vegetables in the batter until well coated, then drop them carefully into the hot oil. Cook each batch for 2–3 minutes, or until golden. Drain on absorbent paper towels and keep warm while cooking the remaining batches.

Transfer the vegetables to a warmed serving platter and serve immediately with the light soy sauce to use as a dipping sauce.

Health Rating: 4 points

Coconut-baked Courgettes

Serves 4

Ingredients

3 tbsp groundnut/peanut oil
1 onion, peeled and finely sliced
4 garlic cloves, peeled and crushed
$^1/_2$ tsp chilli powder
1 tsp ground coriander
6–8 tbsp desiccated/dried coconut
1 tbsp tomato puree/paste
700 g/1$^1/_2$ lb/6 cups courgettes/zucchini, thinly sliced
freshly chopped parsley, to garnish

Health Rating: 4 points

Preheat the oven to 180°C/350°F/Gas Mark 4, 10 minutes before cooking. Lightly oil a large, shallow ovenproof gratin dish. Heat a wok, add the oil and, when hot, add the onion and stir-fry for 2–3 minutes, or until softened. Add the garlic, chilli powder and coriander and stir-fry for 1–2 minutes.

Pour 300 ml/$^1/_2$ pint/1$^1/_4$ cups cold water into the wok and bring to the boil. Add the coconut and tomato puree/paste and simmer for 3–4 minutes; most of the water will evaporate at this stage. Spoon 4 tablespoons of the spice and coconut mixture into a small bowl and reserve.

Stir the courgettes/zucchini into the remaining spice and coconut mixture, coating well. Spoon the courgettes into the oiled gratin dish and sprinkle the reserved spice and coconut mixture evenly over the top. Bake, uncovered, in the preheated oven for 15–20 minutes, or until golden. Garnish with chopped parsley and serve immediately.

Vegetable & Coconut Stew

Serves 4–6

Ingredients

2 tbsp vegetable oil or ghee
1 tsp cumin seeds
1 cinnamon stick, bruised
3 whole cloves
3 cardamom pods, bruised
$^1/_2$–1 tsp chilli powder
8 shallots, peeled and halved
2–3 garlic cloves, peeled and finely chopped
225 g/8 oz/2 cups potatoes, peeled and cut into chunks
$^1/_2$ butternut squash, about 350 g/12 oz in weight, peeled, deseeded and cut into chunks
225 g/8 oz/1$^3/_4$ cups carrots, peeled and chopped
200 ml/7 fl oz/$^3/_4$ cup water
300 ml/$^1/_2$ pint/1$^1/_4$ cups coconut milk
225 g/8 oz/1$^1/_2$ cups French/green beans, trimmed and chopped
400 g/14 oz can red kidney beans, drained and rinsed
4–6 spring onions/scallions, trimmed and finely chopped

Heat the oil or ghee in a large saucepan, add the seeds, cinnamon stick, cloves, cardamom pods and chilli powder and fry for 30 seconds, or until the seeds pop.

Add the shallots, garlic, potatoes, squash and carrots and stir until the vegetables are coated in the flavoured oil. Add the water, bring to the boil, then reduce the heat, cover and simmer for 15 minutes.

Pour in the coconut milk and add the chopped beans and kidney beans. Stir well, then cook for a further 10 minutes. Sprinkle with the chopped spring onions and serve.

Health Rating: 4 points

Vegetable & Lentil Casserole

Serves 4

Ingredients

225 g/8 oz/1$^1/_4$ cups Puy lentils
1–2 tbsp olive oil
1 onion, peeled and chopped
2–3 garlic cloves, peeled and crushed
300 g/10 oz/2$^1/_3$ cups carrots, peeled and cut into chunks
3 celery stalks, trimmed and sliced
350 g/12 oz/2$^1/_2$ cups butternut squash, peeled, seeds removed and diced
1 litre/1$^3/_4$ pints/1 quart vegetable stock
salt and freshly ground black pepper
few fresh oregano sprigs, plus extra to garnish
1 large red pepper, deseeded and chopped
2 courgettes/zucchini, trimmed and sliced
150 ml/$^1/_4$ pint/$^2/_3$ cup sour cream, to serve

Preheat the oven to 160°C/325°F/Gas Mark 3. Pour the lentils out on to a plate and look through them for any small stones, then rinse the lentils and reserve.

Heat the oil in a large ovenproof casserole dish (or a deep frying pan, if preferred), add the onion, garlic, carrots and celery and fry for 5 minutes, stirring occasionally.

Add the squash and lentils. Pour in the stock and season to taste with salt and pepper. Add the oregano sprigs and bring to the boil.

If a frying pan has been used, transfer everything to a casserole dish. Cover with a lid and cook in the oven for 25 minutes.

Remove the casserole dish from the oven, add the red pepper and courgettes/zucchini and stir. Return the casserole to the oven and cook for a further 20 minutes, or until all the vegetables are tender. Adjust the seasoning, garnish with oregano sprigs and serve with sour cream on the side.

Health Rating: 4 points

Three Bean Tagine

Serves 4

Ingredients

few saffron strands
2–3 tbsp olive oil
1 small aubergine/eggplant, trimmed and diced
1 onion, peeled and chopped
350 g/12 oz/$2\frac{2}{3}$ cups sweet potatoes, peeled and diced
225 g/8 oz/$1\frac{3}{4}$ cups carrots, peeled and chopped
1 cinnamon stick, bruised
$1\frac{1}{2}$ tsp ground cumin
salt and freshly ground black pepper
600 ml/1 pint/$2\frac{1}{2}$ cups vegetable stock
2 fresh mint sprigs
200 g/7 oz can red kidney beans, drained
300 g/10 oz can haricot beans, drained
300 g/10 oz can flageolet beans, drained
100 g/$3\frac{1}{2}$ oz/$\frac{3}{4}$ cup ready-to-eat dried apricots, chopped
1 tbsp freshly chopped mint, to garnish

Place warm water into a small bowl and sprinkle with saffron strands. Leave to infuse for at least 10 minutes.

Heat the oil in a large heavy-based saucepan, add the aubergine/eggplant and onion and fry for 5 minutes before adding the sweet potatoes, carrots, cinnamon stick and ground cumin. Cook, stirring, until the vegetables are lightly coated in the cumin. Add the saffron with the soaking liquid and season to taste with salt and pepper. Pour in the stock and add the mint sprigs.

Rinse the beans, add to the pan and bring to the boil. Reduce the heat, cover with a lid and simmer for 20 minutes. Add the apricots and cook, stirring occasionally, for a further 10 minutes, or until the vegetables are tender. Adjust the seasoning to taste, then serve sprinkled with chopped mint.

Health Rating: 4 points

Seared Scallop Salad

Serves 4

Ingredients

12 king (large) scallops
1 tbsp low-fat spread or butter
2 tbsp orange juice
2 tbsp balsamic vinegar
1 tbsp clear honey
2 ripe pears, washed
125 g/4 oz/6¼ cups rocket/arugula
125 g/4 oz/4 cups watercress
50 g/2 oz/½ cup walnuts
freshly ground black pepper

Health Rating: 3 points

Clean the scallops, removing the thin black vein from around the white meat and coral. Rinse thoroughly and dry on absorbent paper towels. Cut each into two or three thick slices, depending on the scallop size.

Heat a griddle pan or heavy-based frying pan, then, when hot, add the low-fat spread or butter and allow to melt. Once melted, sear the scallops for 1 minute on each side, or until golden. Remove from the pan and reserve.

Briskly whisk together the orange juice, balsamic vinegar and honey to make the dressing and reserve.

With a small, sharp knife, carefully cut the pears into quarters, core, then cut into chunks. Mix the rocket/arugula leaves, watercress, pear chunks and walnuts. Pile on to serving plates and top with the scallops. Drizzle over the dressing and grind over plenty of black pepper. Serve immediately.

Smoked Mackerel & Potato Salad

Serves 4

Ingredients

½ tsp dry mustard powder
1 large/extra-large egg yolk
salt and freshly ground black pepper
150 ml/¼ pint/⅔ cup sunflower oil
1–2 tbsp lemon juice
450 g/1 lb baby new potatoes
25 g/1 oz/¼ stick butter
350 g/12 oz/¾ lb smoked mackerel fillets
4 celery stalks, trimmed and finely chopped
3 tbsp creamed horseradish
150 ml/¼ pint/⅔ cup crème fraîche/sour cream
1 little gem/romaine lettuce, rinsed and roughly torn
8 cherry tomatoes, halved

Place the mustard powder and egg yolk in a small bowl with salt and pepper and whisk until blended. Add the oil, drop by drop, into the egg mixture, whisking continuously. When the mayonnaise is thick, add the lemon juice, drop by drop, until a smooth, glossy consistency is formed. Reserve.

Cook the potatoes in boiling salted water until tender, then drain. Cool slightly, then cut into halves or quarters, depending on size. Return to the saucepan and toss in the butter.

Remove the skin from the mackerel fillets and flake into pieces. Add to the potatoes in the saucepan, together with the celery.

Blend 4 tablespoons of the mayonnaise with the horseradish and crème fraîche/sour cream. Season to taste with salt and pepper, then add to the potato and mackerel mixture and stir lightly.

Arrange the lettuce and tomatoes on four serving plates. Pile the smoked mackerel mixture on top of the lettuce, grind over a little pepper and serve with the remaining mayonnaise.

Health Rating: 3 points

Mediterranean Feast

Serves 4

Ingredients

1 small iceberg/head of 1 lettuce
225 g/8 oz/1½ cups French/green beans
225 g/8 oz baby new potatoes, scrubbed
4 eggs
1 green pepper
1 onion, peeled
200 g/7 oz can tuna in water, drained and flaked into small pieces
50 g/2 oz/½ cup low-fat hard cheese, cut into small cubes
8 ripe but firm cherry tomatoes, quartered
50 g/2 oz/⅓ cup black pitted olives, halved
freshly chopped basil, to garnish

For the lime vinaigrette:
3 tbsp light olive oil
2 tbsp white wine vinegar
4 tbsp lime juice
grated rind of 1 lime
1 tsp Dijon mustard
1–2 tsp caster/superfine sugar
salt and freshly ground black pepper

Cut the lettuce into four and remove the hard core. Tear into bite-sized pieces and arrange on a large serving platter or four individual plates.

Cook the French/green beans in boiling salted water for 8 minutes and the potatoes for 10 minutes, or until tender. Drain and rinse in cold water until cool, then cut both the beans and potatoes in half with a sharp knife.

Boil the eggs for 10 minutes, then rinse thoroughly under a cold running tap until cool. Remove the shells under water and cut each egg into four. Remove the seeds from the pepper and cut into thin strips and finely chop the onion.

Arrange the beans, potatoes, eggs, pepper and onion on top of the lettuce. Add the tuna, cheese and tomatoes. Sprinkle the olives over and garnish with the basil.

To make the vinaigrette, place all the ingredients in a screw-topped jar and shake vigorously until everything is thoroughly mixed. Spoon 4 tablespoons over the top of the prepared salad and serve the remainder separately.

Health Rating: 4 points

Bulgur Wheat Salad with Minty Lemon Dressing

Serves 4

Ingredients

125 g/4½ oz/⅔ cup bulgur wheat
125 g/4½ oz/1 cup baby sweetcorn
3 ripe but firm tomatoes
10 cm/4 inch piece cucumber, diced
2 shallots, peeled and finely chopped

For the dressing:
grated rind of 1 lemon
3 tbsp lemon juice
3 tbsp freshly chopped mint
2 tbsp freshly chopped parsley
1–2 tsp clear honey
2 tbsp sunflower oil
salt and freshly ground black pepper

Place the bulgur wheat in a saucepan and cover with boiling water. Simmer for about 10 minutes, then drain thoroughly and turn into a serving bowl.

Steam the baby sweetcorn over a pan of boiling water for 10 minutes, or until tender. Drain and slice into thick chunks.

Cut a cross on the top of each tomato and place in boiling water until their skins start to peel away. Remove the skins and the seeds and cut the tomatoes into small cubes.

Make the dressing by briskly whisking all the ingredients in a small bowl until well mixed. When the bulgur wheat has cooled a little, add all the prepared vegetables and stir in the dressing. Season to taste with salt and pepper and serve.

Health Rating: 4 points

Chinese Salad with Soy & Ginger Dressing

Serves 4

Ingredients

1 head Chinese leaves/cabbage
200 g/7 oz can water chestnuts, drained
6 spring onions/scallions, trimmed
4 ripe but firm cherry tomatoes
125 g/4½ oz/1 cup mangetout/snow peas
125 g/4½ oz/¾ cup beansprouts
2 tbsp freshly chopped coriander/cilantro

For the soy and ginger dressing:
2 tbsp sunflower oil
4 tbsp light soy sauce
2.5 cm/1 inch piece root ginger, peeled and finely grated
zest and juice of 1 lemon
salt and freshly ground black pepper
crusty white bread, to serve

Rinse and finely shred the Chinese leaves/cabbage and place in a serving dish. Slice the water chestnuts into small slivers and cut the spring onions/scallions diagonally into 2.5 cm/1 inch lengths, then split lengthways into thin strips. Cut the tomatoes in half, then slice each half into three wedges and reserve.

Simmer the mangetout/snow peas in boiling water for 2 minutes until beginning to soften, then drain and cut in half diagonally.

Arrange the water chestnuts, spring onions, mangetout, tomatoes and beansprouts on top of the shredded Chinese leaves. Garnish with the freshly chopped coriander/cilantro.

Make the dressing by whisking all the ingredients together in a small bowl until mixed thoroughly. Serve the salad with the dressing and with some crusty white bread.

Health Rating: 5 points

Warm Leek & Tomato Salad

Serves 4

Ingredients

450 g/1 lb baby leeks
2 ripe but firm tomatoes
2 shallots, peeled and cut into thin wedges

Honey and lime dressing:
2 tbsp clear honey
grated rind of 1 lime
4 tbsp lime juice
1 tbsp light olive oil
1 tsp Dijon mustard
salt and freshly ground black pepper

To garnish:
freshly chopped tarragon
freshly chopped basil

Trim the leeks so that they are all the same length. Place in a steamer over a pan of boiling water and steam for 8 minutes, or until just tender, then drain thoroughly and arrange in a shallow dish.

Make a cross in the tops of the tomatoes, place in a bowl and cover them with boiling water until the skins start to peel away. Remove from the bowl and carefully remove the skins.

Cut the tomatoes into quarters and remove the seeds, then chop into small dice. Spoon over the top of the leeks together with the shallots.

In a small bowl, make the dressing by whisking the honey, lime rind, lime juice, olive oil, mustard and salt and pepper together. Pour 3 tablespoons of the dressing over the leeks and tomatoes and garnish with the tarragon and basil. Serve while the leeks are still warm, with the remaining dressing served separately.

Health Rating: 5 points

Winter Coleslaw

Serves 6

Ingredients

175 g/6 oz white cabbage
1 red onion, peeled
175 g/6 oz (about 2½) carrots, peeled
175 g/6 oz (1 head) celeriac, peeled
2 celery stalks, trimmed
75 g/3 oz/½ cup sultanas/golden raisins

Yogurt and herb dressing:
150 ml/¼ pint/⅔ cup natural yogurt
1 garlic clove, peeled and crushed
1 tbsp lemon juice
1 tsp clear honey
1 tbsp freshly snipped chives

Remove the hard core from the cabbage with a small knife and shred the cabbage finely. Slice the onion finely and coarsely grate the carrot. Place the raw vegetables in a large bowl and mix together.

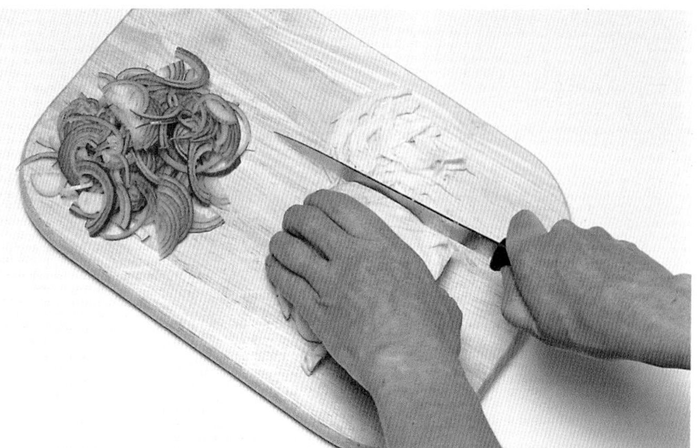

Cut the celeriac into thin strips and simmer in boiling water for about 2 minutes. Drain the celeriac and rinse thoroughly with cold water. Chop the celery and add to the bowl with the celeriac and sultanas/golden raisins and mix well.

Make the yogurt and herb dressing by briskly whisking the yogurt, garlic, lemon juice, honey and chives together.

Pour the dressing over the top of the salad.
Stir the vegetables thoroughly to coat evenly and serve.

Health Rating: 4 points

Carrot, Celeriac & Sesame Seed Salad

Serves 6

Ingredients

225 g/8 oz (1 head) celeriac
225 g/8 oz (about 2) carrots, peeled
50 g/2 oz/5 tbsp seedless raisins
2 tbsp sesame seeds
freshly chopped parsley, to garnish

Lemon and chilli dressing:
grated rind of 1 lemon
4 tbsp lemon juice
2 tbsp sunflower oil
2 tbsp clear honey
1 red bird's eye chilli, deseeded and finely chopped
salt and freshly ground black pepper

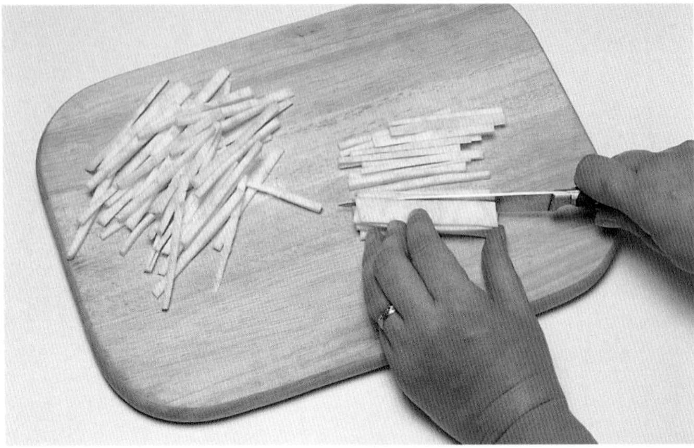

Slice the celeriac into thin matchsticks. Place in a small saucepan of boiling salted water and boil for 2 minutes.

Drain and rinse the celeriac in cold water and place in a mixing bowl. Finely grate the carrot. Add the carrot and the raisins to the celeriac in the bowl.

Place the sesame seeds under a hot grill/broiler or dry-fry in a frying pan for 1–2 minutes until golden brown, then leave to cool.

Make the dressing by whisking together the lemon rind, lemon juice, oil, honey, chilli and seasoning or by shaking thoroughly in a screw-topped jar.

Pour 2 tablespoons of the dressing over the salad and toss well. Turn into a serving dish and sprinkle over the toasted sesame seeds and chopped parsley. Serve the remaining dressing separately.

Health Rating: 5 points

Indonesian Salad with Peanut Dressing

Serves 4

Ingredients

225 g/8 oz (about 4) new potatoes, scrubbed
1 large carrot, peeled and cut into matchsticks
125 g/4½ oz/¾ cup French/green beans, trimmed
225 g/8 oz tiny cauliflower florets
125 g/4½ oz/¾ cup cucumber, cut into matchsticks
75 g/3 oz/1½ cups fresh beansprouts
3 eggs, hard-boiled and quartered

For the peanut dressing:
2 tbsp sesame oil
1 garlic clove, peeled and crushed
1 red chilli, deseeded and finely chopped
150 g/5 oz/⅔ cup crunchy peanut butter
6 tbsp hot vegetable stock
2 tsp soft light brown sugar
2 tsp dark soy sauce
1 tbsp lime juice

Cook the potatoes in a saucepan of boiling salted water for 15–20 minutes until tender. Remove with a slotted spoon and thickly slice into a large bowl. Keep saucepan of water boiling.

Add the carrot, beans and cauliflower to the water, return to the boil and cook for 2 minutes, or until just tender. Drain and refresh under cold running water, then drain well. Add to the potatoes with the cucumber and beansprouts.

To make the dressing, gently heat the sesame oil in a small saucepan. Add the garlic and chilli and cook for a few seconds, then remove from the heat. Stir in the peanut butter. Stir in the stock, a little at a time. Add the remaining ingredients and mix together to make a thick, creamy dressing.

Divide the vegetables between four plates and arrange the eggs on top. Drizzle the dressing over the salad and serve immediately.

Health Rating: 4 points

Baby Roast Potato Salad

Serves 4

Ingredients

350 g/12 oz (about 16) small shallots
sea salt and freshly ground black pepper
900 g/2 lb small even-sized new potatoes
2 tbsp olive oil
2 medium courgettes/zucchini
2 fresh rosemary sprigs
175 g/6 oz/$1\frac{1}{4}$ cups cherry tomatoes
150 ml/$\frac{1}{4}$ pt/$\frac{2}{3}$ cup sour cream
2 tbsp freshly snipped chives
$\frac{1}{4}$ tsp paprika

Preheat the oven to 200°C/400°F/Gas Mark 6. Trim the shallots, but leave the skins on. Put in a saucepan of lightly salted boiling water with the potatoes and cook for 5 minutes; drain. Separate the shallots and plunge them into cold water for 1 minute.

Put the oil on a baking sheet lined with kitchen foil or in a roasting tin/pan and heat for a few minutes. Peel the skins off the shallots – they should now come away easily. Add to the baking sheet or roasting tin with the potatoes and toss in the oil to coat. Sprinkle with a little sea salt. Roast the potatoes and shallots in the preheated oven for 10 minutes.

Meanwhile, trim the courgettes/zucchini, halve lengthways and cut into 5 cm/2 inch chunks. Add to the baking sheet or roasting tin, toss to mix and cook for 5 minutes.

Pierce the tomato skins with a sharp knife. Add to the sheet or tin with the rosemary and cook for a further 5 minutes, or until all the vegetables are tender. Remove the rosemary and discard. Grind a little black pepper over the vegetables.

Spoon into a wide serving bowl. Mix together the sour cream and chives and drizzle over the vegetables just before serving.

Health Rating: 3 points

Mixed Salad with Anchovy Dressing & Ciabatta Croutons

Serves 4

Ingredients

1 small head endive
1 small head chicory
1 fennel bulb
400 g/14 oz can artichokes, drained and rinsed
½ cucumber
125 g/4½ oz/1 cup cherry tomatoes
75 g/3 oz/½ cup black olives

For the anchovy dressing:
50 g/2 oz can anchovy fillets
1 tsp Dijon mustard
1 small garlic clove, peeled and crushed
4 tbsp olive oil
1 tbsp lemon juice
freshly ground black pepper

For the ciabatta croutons:
2 thick slices ciabatta bread
2 tbsp olive oil

Divide the endive and chicory into leaves and reserve some of the larger ones. Arrange the smaller leaves in a wide salad bowl. Cut the fennel bulb in half from the stalk to the root end, then cut across in fine slices. Quarter the artichokes, then quarter and slice the cucumber and halve the tomatoes. Add to the salad bowl with the olives.

To make the dressing, drain the anchovies and whizz in a blender with the mustard, garlic, olive oil, lemon juice, 2 tablespoons hot water and black pepper, until smooth and thickened.

To make the croutons, cut the bread into 1 cm/½ inch cubes. Heat the oil in a frying pan, add the bread cubes and fry for 3 minutes, turning frequently until golden. Remove and drain on absorbent paper towels.

Drizzle half the anchovy dressing over the prepared salad and toss to coat. Arrange the reserved endive and chicory leaves around the edge, then drizzle over the remaining dressing. Scatter over the croutons and serve immediately.

Health Rating: 4 points

Rice

From risotto, to rice cakes to rice-filled peppers, rice is a versatile and popular ingredient. This chapter offers a whole range of rice recipes including Paella and Spring Vegetable & Herb Risotto. Including tasty, easy-to-cook dishes from around the world, make rice part of your family's meal.

Fish Roulades with Rice & Spinach

Serves 4

Ingredients

4 x 175 g/6 oz skinless lemon sole
salt and freshly ground black pepper
1 tsp fennel seeds
75 g/3 oz/$^2/_5$ cup long-grain rice, cooked
150 g/5 oz/1 heaping cup white crab meat, fresh or canned
125 g/4 oz/4$^1/_4$ cups baby spinach, washed and trimmed
5 tbsp dry white wine
5 tbsp half-fat crème fraîche/sour cream
2 tbsp freshly chopped parsley, plus extra to garnish
asparagus spears, to serve

Wipe each fish fillet with either a clean damp cloth or paper towels. Place on a chopping board, skinned side up and season lightly with salt and black pepper.

Place the fennel seeds in a pestle and mortar and crush lightly. Transfer to a small bowl and stir in the cooked rice. Drain the crab meat thoroughly. Add to the rice mixture and mix lightly.

Lay 2–3 spinach leaves over each fillet and top with a quarter of the crab meat mixture. Roll up and secure with a cocktail stick if necessary. Place into a large pan and pour over the wine. Cover and cook on a medium heat for 5–7 minutes, or until cooked.

Remove the fish from the cooking liquor and transfer to a serving plate and keep warm. Stir the crème fraîche/sour cream into the cooking liquor and season to taste. Heat for 3 minutes, then stir in the chopped parsley.

Spoon the sauce on to the base of a plate. Cut each roulade into slices and arrange on top of the sauce. Serve with freshly cooked asparagus spears.

Health Rating: 3 points

Seafood Risotto

Serves 4

Ingredients

50 g/2 oz/½ stick butter
2 shallots, peeled and finely chopped
1 garlic clove, peeled and crushed
350 g/12 oz/2 cups Arborio/risotto rice
150 ml/¼ pint/⅔ cup white wine
600 ml/1 pint/2½ cups fish or vegetable stock, heated
125 g/4½ oz/¾ cup large prawns/shrimp
50 g/2 oz/½ cup smoked salmon trimmings
290 g/10 oz can baby clams
2 tbsp freshly chopped parsley
freshly grated Parmesan cheese

To serve:
green salad
crusty bread

Melt the butter in a large heavy-based saucepan, add the shallots and garlic and cook for 2 minutes until slightly softened. Add the rice and cook for 1–2 minutes, stirring continuously, then pour in the wine and boil for 1 minute.

Pour in half the hot stock, bring to the boil, cover the saucepan and simmer gently for 15 minutes, adding the remaining stock a little at a time. Continue to simmer for 5 minutes, or until the rice is cooked and all the liquid is absorbed.

Meanwhile, prepare the fish by peeling the prawns/shrimp and removing the heads and tails. Drain the clams and discard the liquid. Cut the smoked salmon trimmings into thin strips.

When the rice has cooked, stir in the prawns, smoked salmon strips, clams and half the chopped parsley, then heat through for 1–2 minutes until everything is piping hot. Turn into a serving dish, sprinkle with the remaining parsley and the Parmesan cheese and serve immediately with a green salad and crusty bread.

Health Rating: 3 points

Smoked Haddock Kedgeree

Serves 4

Ingredients

450 g/1 lb smoked haddock fillets
50 g/2 oz/½ stick butter
1 onion, peeled and finely chopped
2 tsp mild curry powder
175 g/6 oz/1 cup long-grain rice
450 ml/¾ pint/1¾ cups fish or vegetable stock, heated
2 large/extra-large eggs, hard-boiled and shelled
2 tbsp freshly chopped parsley
2 tbsp whipping cream (optional)
salt and freshly ground black pepper
pinch cayenne pepper

Place the haddock in a shallow frying pan and cover with 300 ml/½ pint/1¼ cups water. Simmer gently for 8–10 minutes, or until the fish is cooked. Drain, then remove all the skin and bones from the fish and flake into a dish. Keep warm.

Melt the butter in a saucepan and add the chopped onion and curry powder. Cook, stirring, for 3–4 minutes, or until the onion is soft, then stir in the rice. Cook for a further minute, stirring continuously, then stir in the hot stock.

Cover and simmer gently for 15 minutes, or until the rice has absorbed all the liquid. Cut the eggs into quarters or eighths and add half to the mixture with half the parsley.

Carefully fold in the cooked fish to the mixture and add the cream, if using. Season to taste with salt and pepper. Heat the kedgeree through briefly until piping hot.

Transfer the mixture to a large dish and garnish with the remaining egg quarters or eighths and the parsley and serve with a pinch of cayenne pepper. Serve immediately.

Health Rating: 3 points

Paella

Serves 6

Ingredients

450 g/1 lb live mussels
4 tbsp olive oil
6 medium-sized chicken thighs
1 onion, peeled and finely chopped
1 garlic clove, peeled and crushed
225 g/8 oz/¾ cup tomatoes, skinned, deseeded and chopped
1 red and 1 green pepper, deseeded and chopped
125 g/4½ oz/⅔ cup frozen peas
1 tsp paprika, ½ tsp turmeric
450 g/1 lb/2¼ cups Arborio/risotto rice
900 ml/1½ pints/3¾ cups chicken stock, warmed
175 g/6 oz/1 cup large peeled prawns/shrimp
salt and freshly ground black pepper
2 limes; 1 lemon; 1 tbsp freshly chopped basil
whole cooked unpeeled prawns/shrimp, to garnish

Rinse the mussels under cold running water, scrubbing well to remove any grit and barnacles, then pull off the hairy 'beards'. Tap any open mussels sharply with a knife, and discard if they refuse to close. Heat the oil in a paella pan or large heavy-based frying pan and cook the chicken thighs for 10–15 minutes until golden. Remove and keep warm.

Fry the onion and garlic in the remaining oil in the pan for 2–3 minutes, then add the tomatoes, peppers, peas and paprika and cook for a further 3 minutes. Add the rice to the pan and return the chicken with the turmeric and half the stock. Bring to the boil and simmer, gradually adding more stock as it is absorbed. Cook for 20 minutes, or until most of the stock has been absorbed and the rice is almost tender.

Put the mussels in a large saucepan with 5 cm/2 inches boiling salted water. Cover and steam for 5 minutes. Discard any unopened shells, then stir into the rice with the prawns/shrimp. Season with salt and pepper. Heat through for 2–3 minutes until piping hot. Squeeze the juice from one of the limes over the paella. Cut the remaining lime and the lemon into wedges and arrange on top. Sprinkle with basil, garnish with prawns and serve.

Health Rating: 3 points

Pea & Prawn Risotto

Serves 6

Ingredients

450 g/1 lb whole raw prawns/shrimp
125 g/4 oz/1 stick plus 1 tbsp butter
1 red onion, peeled and chopped
4 garlic cloves, peeled and finely chopped
225 g/8 oz/1 heaping cup Arborio/risotto rice
150 ml/¼ pint/⅔ cup dry white wine
1.1 litres/2 pints/1 quart vegetable or fish stock
375 g/13 oz/2½ cups frozen peas
4 tbsp freshly chopped mint
salt and freshly ground black pepper

Peel the prawns/shrimp and reserve the heads and shells. Remove the black vein from the back of each prawn, then wash and dry on absorbent paper towels. Melt half the butter in a large frying pan, add the prawns' heads and shells and fry, stirring occasionally, for 3–4 minutes, or until golden. Strain the butter, discard the heads and shells and return the butter to the pan.

Add half of the remaining butter to the pan and fry the onion and garlic for 5 minutes until softened but not coloured. Add the rice and stir the grains in the butter for 1 minute, until they are coated thoroughly. Add the white wine and boil rapidly until the wine is reduced by half.

Bring the stock to a gentle simmer and add to the rice, a ladleful at a time. Stir constantly, adding the stock as it is absorbed, until the rice is creamy, but still has a bite in the centre.

Melt the remaining butter and stir-fry the prawns for 3–4 minutes. Stir into the rice, along with all the pan juices and the peas. Add the chopped mint and season to taste with salt and pepper. Cover the pan and leave the prawns to infuse for 5 minutes before serving.

Health Rating: 3 points

Prawn Fried Rice

Serves 4

Ingredients

knob of butter
4 medium/large eggs, beaten
4 tbsp groundnut/peanut oil
1 bunch spring onions/scallions, trimmed and finely shredded
125 g/4 oz cooked ham, diced
350 g/12 oz large cooked prawns/shrimp, thawed if frozen, and peeled
125 g/4 oz/1 cup peas, thawed if frozen
450 g/1 lb/3 cups cooked long-grain rice
2 tbsp dark soy sauce
1 tbsp sherry
salt and freshly ground black pepper
1 tbsp freshly shredded coriander/cilantro

Heat a wok, lightly grease with the butter and, when melted, pour in half the beaten eggs. Cook for 4 minutes, stirring frequently, until the egg has set, forming an omelette. Using a fish slice, lift the omelette from the wok and roll up into a sausage shape. When cool, using a sharp knife, slice the omelette into thin rings, then reserve.

Wipe the wok clean with absorbent paper towels and heat it. Add the oil and heat until just smoking. Add the shredded spring onions/scallions, the ham, prawns/shrimp and peas and stir-fry for 2 minutes, or until heated through thoroughly. Add the cooked rice and stir-fry for a further 2 minutes.

Stir in the remaining beaten eggs and stir-fry for 3 minutes, or until the egg has set. Stir in the soy sauce and sherry and season to taste with salt and pepper, then heat until piping hot. Add the omelette rings and gently stir through the mixture, making sure not to break up the omelette rings. Sprinkle with the freshly shredded coriander/cilantro and serve immediately.

Health Rating: 2 points

Nasi Goreng

Serves 4

Ingredients

7 large shallots, peeled
1 red chilli, deseeded and roughly chopped
2 garlic cloves, peeled and roughly chopped
4 tbsp sunflower oil
2 tsp each tomato puree/paste and Indonesian sweet soy sauce (katjap manis)
225 g/8 oz/$^2/_3$ cup long-grain white rice
125 g/4 oz/1 cup French/green beans, trimmed
3 medium/large eggs, beaten
pinch sugar
salt and freshly ground black pepper
225 g/8 oz/1$^2/_3$ cups cooked ham, shredded
225 g/8 oz cooked peeled prawns/shrimp, thawed if frozen
6 spring onions/scallions, trimmed and thinly sliced
1 tbsp light soy sauce
3 tbsp freshly chopped coriander/cilantro

Roughly chop 1 of the shallots and place with the red chilli, garlic, 1 tablespoon of the oil, tomato puree/paste and sweet soy sauce in a food processor and blend until smooth, then reserve. Boil the rice in plenty of salted water for 6–7 minutes until tender, adding the French/green beans after 4 minutes. Drain well and leave to cool.

Beat the eggs with the sugar and a little salt and pepper. Heat a little of the oil in a small nonstick frying pan and add about one third of the egg mixture. Swirl to coat the base of the pan thinly and cook for about 1 minute until golden. Flip and cook the other side briefly before removing from the pan. Roll the omelette and slice thinly into strips. Repeat with the remaining egg to make three omelettes.

Thinly slice the remaining shallots, then heat a further 2 tablespoons of the oil in a clean frying pan. Add the shallots to the pan and cook for 8–10 minutes over a medium heat until golden and crisp. Drain on absorbent paper towels and reserve.

Add the remaining 1 tablespoon oil to a large wok or frying pan and fry the chilli paste over a medium heat for 1 minute. Add the cooked rice and beans and stir-fry for 2 minutes. Add the ham and prawns/shrimp and continue stir-frying for a further 1–2 minutes. Add the omelette slices, half the fried shallots, the spring onions, soy sauce and chopped coriander. Stir-fry for a further minute until heated through. Spoon on to serving plates and garnish with the remaining crispy shallots. Serve immediately.

Health Rating: 2 points

Pork Loin stuffed with Orange & Hazelnut Rice

Serves 4

Ingredients

15 g/½ oz/1 tbsp butter
1 shallot, peeled and finely chopped
50 g/2 oz/¼ cup long-grain brown rice
175 ml/6 fl oz/scant ¾ cup vegetable stock
½ orange
25 g/1 oz/⅛ cup ready-to-eat dried prunes, pitted and chopped
25 g/1 oz/scant ¼ cup hazelnuts, roasted and roughly chopped
1 small/medium egg, beaten
1 tbsp freshly chopped parsley
salt and freshly ground black pepper
450 g/1 lb boneless pork tenderloin or fillet, trimmed

To serve:
steamed courgettes/zucchini
steamed carrots

Preheat the oven to 190°C/375°F/Gas Mark 5, 10 minutes before required. Heat the butter in a small saucepan, add the shallot and cook gently for 2–3 minutes until softened. Add the rice and stir well for 1 minute. Add the stock, stir well and bring to the boil. Cover tightly and simmer gently for 30 minutes until the rice is tender and all the liquid is absorbed. Leave to cool.

Grate the orange rind and reserve. Remove the white pith and chop the orange flesh finely. Mix together the orange rind and flesh, prunes, hazelnuts, cooled rice, egg and parsley. Season to taste with salt and pepper.

Cut the fillet in half, then, using a sharp knife, split the pork fillet lengthways almost in two, forming a pocket, leaving it just attached. Open out the pork and put between two pieces of clingfilm/plastic wrap. Flatten using a meat mallet until about half its original thickness. Spoon the filling into the pocket and close the fillet over. Tie along the length with kitchen string at regular intervals.

Put the pork fillet in a small roasting tray and cook in the top of the preheated oven for 25–30 minutes, or until the meat is just tender. Remove from the oven and allow to rest for 5 minutes. Slice into rounds and serve with steamed courgettes/zucchini and carrots.

Health Rating: 4 points

New Orleans Jambalaya

Serves 6–8

Ingredients

For the seasoning mix:

2 dried bay leaves
1 tsp salt
2 tsp cayenne pepper, or to taste
2 tsp dried oregano
1 tsp each ground white and black pepper, or to taste

3 tbsp vegetable oil
125 g/4 oz/1 cup ham, chopped
225 g/8 oz (about 4 links) smoked pork sausage, cut into chunks
2 large onions, peeled and chopped
4 celery stalks, trimmed and chopped
2 green peppers, deseeded and chopped
2 garlic cloves, peeled and finely chopped
350 g/12 oz raw chicken, diced
400 g/14 oz can chopped tomatoes
600 ml/1 pint/2½ cups fish stock
400 g/14 oz/2 heaping cups long-grain white rice
4 spring onions/scallions, trimmed and coarsely chopped
275 g/10 oz raw prawns/shrimp, peeled
250 g/9 oz/2 scant cups white crab meat

Mix all the seasoning ingredients together in a small bowl and reserve.

Heat 2 tablespoons of the oil in a large flameproof casserole dish over a medium heat. Add the ham and sausage and cook, stirring often, for 7–8 minutes until golden. Remove from the pan and reserve.

Add the remaining onions, celery and peppers to the casserole dish and cook for about 4 minutes, or until softened, stirring occasionally. Stir in the garlic, then, using a slotted spoon, transfer all the vegetables to a plate and reserve with the sausage.

Add the chicken pieces to the casserole dish and cook for about 4 minutes, or until beginning to colour, turning once. Stir in the seasoning mix and turn the pieces to coat well. Return the sausage and vegetables to the casserole dish and stir well. Add the chopped tomatoes, with their juice, and the stock and bring to the boil.

Stir in the rice and reduce the heat to low. Cover and simmer for 12 minutes. Uncover, stir in the spring onions/scallions and prawns/shrimp and cook, covered, for a further 4 minutes. Add the crab and gently stir in. Cook for 2–3 minutes, or until the rice is tender. Remove from the heat, cover and leave to stand for 5 minutes before serving.

Health Rating: 2 points

Leek & Ham Risotto

Serves 4

Ingredients

1 tbsp olive oil
2 tbsp butter
1 medium onion, peeled and finely chopped
4 leeks, trimmed and thinly sliced
1½ tbsp freshly chopped thyme
350 g/12 oz/1¾ cups Arborio/risotto rice
1.4 l/2¼ pts/5½ cups vegetable or chicken stock, heated
225 g/8 oz/1⅔ cup cooked ham, chopped or finely shredded
175 g/6 oz/1¼ cup peas, thawed if frozen
50 g/2 oz/½ cup Parmesan cheese, grated
salt and freshly ground black pepper

Heat the oil and half the butter together in a large saucepan. Add the onion and leeks and cook over a medium heat for 6–8 minutes, stirring occasionally, until soft and beginning to colour. Stir in the thyme and cook briefly.

Add the rice and stir well. Continue stirring over a medium heat for about 1 minute until the rice is glossy. Add a ladleful or two of the stock and stir well until the stock is absorbed. Continue adding stock, a ladleful at a time and stirring well between additions, until about two thirds of the stock has been added. (Risotto should take about 15 minutes to cook, so taste it after this time – the rice should be creamy with just a slight bite to it. If it is not quite ready, continue adding the stock, a little at a time, and cook for a few more minutes. Stop as soon as it tastes ready as you do not have to add all of the liquid.)

Add the ham and peas to the saucepan of rice. Continue adding ladlefuls of stock, as described in step 2, until the rice is tender and the ham is heated through thoroughly.

Add the remaining butter, sprinkle over the Parmesan cheese and season to taste with salt and pepper. When the butter has melted and the cheese has softened, stir well to incorporate. Taste and adjust the seasoning, then serve immediately.

Health Rating: 2 points

Lamb Pilaf

Serves 4

Ingredients

2 tbsp vegetable oil
25 g/1 oz/¼ cup flaked or slivered almonds
1 medium onion, peeled and finely chopped
1 medium carrot, peeled and finely chopped
1 celery stalk, trimmed and finely chopped
350 g/12 oz lean lamb, cut into chunks
¼ tsp ground cinnamon; ¼ tsp chilli flakes
2 large tomatoes, skinned, deseeded and chopped
grated rind of 1 orange
350 g/12 oz/2 cups easy-cook brown basmati rice
600 ml/1 pint/2½ cups vegetable or lamb stock
2 tbsp freshly snipped chives
3 tbsp freshly chopped coriander/cilantro
salt and freshly ground black pepper

To garnish:
lemon slices; fresh coriander/cilantro sprigs

Preheat the oven to 140°C/275°F/Gas Mark 1. Heat the oil in a flameproof casserole dish with a tight-fitting lid and add the almonds. Cook for about 1 minute until just starting to brown, stirring often. Add the onion, carrot and celery and cook gently for a further 8–10 minutes until soft and lightly browned.

Increase the heat and add the lamb. Cook for a further 5 minutes until the lamb has changed colour. Add the ground cinnamon and chilli flakes and stir briefly before adding the tomatoes and orange rind.

Stir and add the rice, then the stock. Bring slowly to the boil and cover tightly. Transfer to the preheated oven and cook for 30–35 minutes until the rice is tender and the stock is absorbed.

Remove from the oven and leave to stand for 5 minutes before stirring in the chives and coriander/cilantro. Season to taste with salt and pepper. Garnish with the lemon slices and fresh coriander sprigs and serve immediately.

Health Rating: 3 points

Chicken Creole

Serves 4

Ingredients

450 g/1 lb skinless chicken breast fillets
1–2 tbsp olive oil
225 g/8 oz/2 cups leeks, trimmed and sliced
1 onion, peeled and chopped
3–4 garlic cloves, peeled and chopped
200 g/7 oz/1 heaping cup long-grain rice
½ tsp cayenne pepper; 1½ tsp paprika
1½ tsp dried oregano; 1½ tsp dried thyme
225 g/8 oz1¼ cups ripe tomatoes, chopped
900 ml/1½ pints/scant 1 quart chicken stock
175 g/6 oz/1¾ cups okra, trimmed and sliced

Lightly rinse the chicken and pat dry on absorbent paper towels. Cut the chicken into thin strips. Heat 1 tablespoon of the oil in a deep frying pan, add the chicken and fry for 5–7 minutes, or until sealed. Remove with a slotted spoon and reserve.

Add the remaining oil, if necessary, then add the leeks, onion, garlic and rice and cook, stirring constantly, for 5 minutes. Add all the spices and herbs and cook for a further 5 minutes.

Return the chicken to the pan and add the chopped tomatoes. Add half the stock and bring to the boil. Reduce the heat to a simmer and cook for 25 minutes, adding more stock if necessary. Stir in the okra and cook for a further 10 minutes, then serve.

Health Rating: 4 points

Persian Chicken Pilaf

Serves 4–6

Ingredients

2–3 tbsp vegetable oil
700 g/1½ lb skinless boneless chicken pieces (breast and thighs), cut into 2.5 cm/1 inch pieces
2 medium onions, peeled and coarsely chopped
1 tsp ground cumin
200 g/7 oz/1 heaping cup long-grain white rice
1 tbsp tomato puree/paste
1 tsp saffron strands
salt and freshly ground black pepper
100 ml/3½ fl oz/⅓ cup pomegranate juice
900 ml/1½ pints/scant 1 quart chicken stock
125 g/4 oz/1 cup ready-to-eat dried apricots or prunes, halved
2 tbsp raisins
2 tbsp freshly chopped mint or parsley
pomegranate seeds, to garnish (optional)

Heat the oil in a large heavy-based saucepan over a medium-high heat. Cook the chicken pieces, in batches, until lightly browned. Return all the browned chicken to the saucepan.

Add the onions to the saucepan, reduce the heat to medium and cook for 3–5 minutes, stirring frequently, until the onions begin to soften. Add the cumin and rice and stir to coat the rice. Cook for about 2 minutes until the rice is golden and translucent. Stir in the tomato puree/paste and the saffron strands, then season to taste with salt and pepper.

Add the pomegranate juice and stock and bring to the boil, stirring once or twice. Add the apricots or prunes and raisins and stir gently. Reduce the heat to low and cook for 30 minutes until the chicken and rice are tender and the liquid is absorbed.

Turn into a shallow serving dish and sprinkle with the chopped mint or parsley. Serve immediately, garnished with pomegranate seeds, if using.

Health Rating: 3 points

Creamy Chicken & Rice Pilaf

Serves 4–6

Ingredients

350 g/12 oz/2 cups basmati rice
salt and freshly ground black pepper
50 g/2 oz/½ stick butter
100 g/3½ oz/1 cup flaked/slivered almonds
75 g/3 oz/⅔ cup unsalted shelled pistachio nuts
4–6 skinless chicken breast fillets, each cut into 4
2 tbsp vegetable oil
2 onions, peeled and thinly sliced
2 garlic cloves, peeled and finely chopped
2.5 cm/1 inch piece fresh root ginger, finely chopped
6 green cardamom pods, lightly crushed
4–6 whole cloves
2 bay leaves
1 tsp ground coriander
½ tsp cayenne pepper, or to taste
225 ml/8 fl oz/1 cup natural/plain yogurt
225 ml/8 fl oz/ 1 cup double/heavy cream
225 g/8 oz/1½ cups seedless green grapes, halved if large
2 tbsp freshly chopped coriander/cilantro or mint

Bring a saucepan of lightly salted water to the boil. Gradually pour in the rice, return to the boil, then simmer for about 12 minutes until tender. Drain, rinse under cold water and reserve.

Heat the butter in a large, deep frying pan over a medium-high heat. Add the almonds and pistachios and cook for about 2 minutes, stirring constantly, until golden. Using a slotted spoon, transfer to a plate.

Add the chicken pieces to the pan and cook for about 5 minutes, or until golden, turning once. Remove from the pan and reserve.

Add the oil to the pan and cook the onions for 10 minutes, or until golden, stirring frequently. Stir in the garlic, ginger and spices and cook for 2–3 minutes, stirring. Add 2–3 tablespoons of the yogurt and cook, stirring, until the moisture evaporates. Continue adding the yogurt in this way until it is used up.

Return the chicken and nuts to the pan and stir. Stir in 125 ml/4 fl oz/½ cup of boiling water and season to taste with salt and pepper. Cook, covered, over a low heat for 10 minutes until the chicken is tender.

Stir in the cream, grapes and half the herbs. Gently fold in the rice. Heat through for 5 minutes and sprinkle with the remaining herbs, then serve.

Health Rating: 2 points

Chicken & White Wine Risotto

Serves 4–6

Ingredients

2 tbsp oil
125 g/4 oz/1 stick plus 1 tbsp unsalted butter
2 shallots, peeled and finely chopped
300 g/11 oz/$1\frac{1}{2}$ cups Arborio/risotto rice
600 ml/1 pint/$2\frac{1}{2}$ cups dry white wine
750 ml/$1\frac{1}{4}$ pints/$3\frac{1}{4}$ cups chicken stock, heated
350 g/12 oz skinless chicken breast fillets, thinly sliced
50 g/2 oz/$\frac{1}{2}$ cup Parmesan cheese, grated
2 tbsp freshly chopped dill or parsley
salt and freshly ground black pepper

Heat the oil and half the butter in a large heavy-based saucepan over a medium-high heat. Add the shallots and cook for 2 minutes, or until softened, stirring frequently. Add the rice and cook for 2–3 minutes, stirring frequently, until the rice is translucent and well coated.

Pour in half the wine; it will bubble and steam rapidly. Cook, stirring constantly, until the liquid is absorbed. Add a ladleful of the hot stock and cook until the liquid is absorbed. Carefully stir in the chicken.

Continue adding the stock, about half a ladleful at a time, allowing each addition to be absorbed before adding the next; never allow the rice to cook dry. This process should take about 20 minutes. The risotto should have a creamy consistency and the rice should be tender but firm to the bite.

Stir in the remaining wine and cook for 2–3 minutes. Remove from the heat and stir in the remaining butter with the Parmesan cheese and half the chopped herbs. Season to taste with salt and pepper. Spoon into warmed shallow bowls and sprinkle each with the remaining chopped herbs. Serve immediately.

Health Rating: 2 points

Fruity Rice-stuffed Poussins

Serves 6

Ingredients

For the rice stuffing:

225 ml/8 fl oz/1 cup port
125 g/4½ oz/¾ cup raisins
125 g/4½ oz/1 cup ready-to-eat dried apricots, chopped
2 tbsp olive oil; 1 onion, peeled and finely chopped
1 celery stalk, trimmed and finely sliced
2 garlic cloves, peeled and chopped
1½ tsp mixed spice
1 tsp each dried oregano and mint or basil
225 g/8 oz/2 cups unsweetened canned chestnuts, chopped
200 g/7 oz/1 heaping cup long-grain white rice, cooked
grated rind and juice of 2 oranges
350 ml/12 fl oz/1½ cups chicken stock
50 g/2 oz/½ cup walnut halves, lightly toasted and chopped
2 tbsp each freshly chopped mint and parsley
salt and freshly ground, black pepper

6 oven-ready poussins/game hens
50 g/2 oz/½ stick butter, melted

To garnish:
fresh herbs
orange wedges

Preheat the oven to 180°C/350°F/Gas Mark 4. To make the stuffing, place the port, raisins and apricots in a bowl and leave for 15 minutes. Heat the oil in a large saucepan. Add the onion and celery and cook for 3–4 minutes. Add the garlic, mixed spice, herbs and chestnuts and cook for 4 minutes, stirring occasionally. Add the rice, half the orange rind and juice and the stock and simmer for 5 minutes until most of the liquid is absorbed.Drain the raisins and apricots, reserving the port. Stir into the rice with the walnuts, mint, parsley and seasoning and cook for 2 minutes. Remove and cool.

Rinse the poussin/game hen cavities, pat dry and season with salt and pepper. Lightly fill the cavities with the stuffing, then tie the legs together, tucking in the tail. Form any extra stuffing into balls.

Place in roasting tins/pans with the stuffing balls and brush with melted butter. Drizzle over the remaining butter, orange rind and juice and port. Roast in the preheated oven for 50 minutes, or until golden and cooked, basting every 15 minutes. Transfer to a platter, cover with kitchen foil and rest. Pour over any pan juices. Garnish with herbs and orange wedges and serve with the stuffing.

Health Rating: 2 points

Turkey & Pesto Rice Roulades

Serves 4

Ingredients

125 g/4 oz/¾ cup cooked white rice, at room temperature
1 garlic clove, peeled and crushed
1–2 tbsp Parmesan cheese, grated
2 tbsp prepared pesto sauce
2 tbsp pine nuts, lightly toasted and chopped
4 turkey steaks, each weighing about 150 g/5 oz
salt and freshly ground black pepper
4 slices Parma ham/prosciutto
2 tbsp olive oil
50 ml/2 fl oz/¼ cup white wine
25 g/1 oz/¼ stick unsalted butter, chilled

To serve:
freshly cooked spinach
freshly cooked pasta

Put the rice in a bowl and add the garlic, Parmesan cheese, pesto and pine nuts. Stir to combine the ingredients, then reserve.

Place the turkey steaks on a chopping board and, using a sharp knife, cut horizontally through each steak, without cutting right through. Open up the steaks and cover with baking parchment. Flatten slightly by pounding with a meat mallet or rolling pin. Season each steak with salt and pepper. Divide the stuffing equally among the steaks, spreading evenly over one half. Fold the steaks in half to enclose the filling, then wrap each steak in a slice of Parma ham/prosciutto and secure with cocktail sticks.

Heat the oil in a large frying pan over medium heat. Cook the steaks for 5 minutes, or until golden on one side. Turn and cook for a further 2 minutes. Push the steaks to the side and pour in the wine. Allow the wine to bubble and evaporate. Add the butter, a little at a time, whisking constantly, until the sauce is smooth. Discard the cocktail sticks, then serve the steaks drizzled with the sauce and serve with spinach and pasta.

Health Rating: 2 points

Fried Ginger Rice with Soy Glazed Duck

Serves 4–6

Ingredients

2 duck breasts, skinned and diagonally cut into thin slices
2–3 tbsp Japanese soy sauce
1 tbsp mirin (sweet rice wine) or sherry
2 tbsp brown sugar
5 cm/2 inch piece fresh root ginger, peeled and finely chopped
4 tbsp groundnut/peanut or vegetable oil
2 garlic cloves, peeled and crushed
300 g/11 oz/1⅔ cups long-grain brown rice
900 ml/1½ pints/scant 1 quart chicken stock
freshly ground black pepper
125 g/4 oz/scant 1 cup lean ham, diced
175 g/6 oz/1½ cups mangetout/snow peas, diagonally cut in half
8 spring onions/scallions, trimmed and thinly sliced diagonally
1 tbsp freshly chopped coriander/cilantro
sweet or hot chilli sauce, to taste (optional)
fresh coriander/cilantro sprigs, to garnish

Put the duck slices in a bowl with 1 tablespoon of the soy sauce, the mirin, 1 teaspoon of the sugar and one third of the ginger; stir. Leave to stand.

Heat 2 tablespoons of the oil in a large heavy-based saucepan. Add the garlic and half the remaining ginger and stir-fry for 1 minute. Add the rice and cook for 3 minutes, stirring constantly, until translucent.

Stir in all but 125 ml/4 fl oz/½ cup of the stock with 1 teaspoon of the soy sauce and bring to the boil. Season with pepper. Reduce the heat to very low and simmer, covered, for 25–30 minutes until the rice is tender and the liquid is absorbed. Cover and leave to stand.

Heat the remaining oil in a large frying pan or wok. Drain the duck strips and add to the frying pan. Stir-fry for 2–3 minutes until just coloured. Add 1 tablespoon soy sauce and the remaining sugar and cook for 1 minute until glazed. Transfer to a plate and keep warm.

Stir in the ham, mangetout/snow peas, spring onions/scallions, the remaining ginger and the chopped coriander/cilantro. Add the remaining stock and duck marinade and cook until the liquid is almost reduced. Fork in the rice and a little chilli sauce to taste (if using); stir well. Turn into a serving dish and top with the duck. Garnish with coriander sprigs and serve immediately.

Health Rating: 2 points

Spring Vegetable & Herb Risotto

Serves 2–3

Ingredients

1 litre/1¾ pints/1 quart vegetable stock
125 g/4½ oz/½ cup asparagus tips, trimmed
125 g/4½ oz/1 cup baby carrots, scrubbed
50 g/2 oz/½ cup peas, fresh or frozen
50 g/2 oz/½ cup fine French/green beans, trimmed
1 tbsp olive oil; 1 onion, peeled and finely chopped
1 garlic clove, peeled and finely chopped
2 tsp freshly chopped thyme
225 g/8 oz/1 heaping cup Arborio/risotto rice
150 ml/¼ pint/⅔ cup white wine
1 tbsp each freshly chopped basil, chives and parsley
zest of ½ lemon; 3 tbsp crème fraîche/sour cream
salt and freshly ground black pepper

Bring the vegetable stock to the boil in a large saucepan and add the asparagus, baby carrots, peas and beans. Bring the stock back to the boil and remove the vegetables at once using a slotted spoon. Rinse under cold running water. Drain again and reserve. Keep the stock hot.

Heat the oil in a large, deep frying pan and add the onion. Cook over a medium heat for 4–5 minutes until starting to brown. Add the garlic and thyme and cook for a further few seconds. Add the rice and stir well for 1 minute until the rice is hot and coated in oil.

Add the white wine and stir constantly until the wine is almost completely absorbed by the rice. Begin adding the stock a ladleful at a time, stirring well and waiting until the last ladleful has been absorbed before stirring in the next. Add the vegetables after using about half of the stock. Continue until all the stock is used. This will take 20–25 minutes. The rice and vegetables should both be tender. Remove the pan from the heat. Stir in the herbs, lemon zest and crème fraîche/sour cream. Season to taste with salt and pepper and serve immediately.

Health Rating: 3 points

Vegetable Biryani

Serves 4

Ingredients

2 tbsp vegetable oil, plus a little extra for brushing
2 large onions, peeled and thinly sliced lengthways
2 garlic cloves, peeled and finely chopped
2.5 cm/1 inch piece fresh root ginger, peeled and finely grated
1 small carrot, peeled and cut into sticks
1 small parsnip, peeled and diced
1 small sweet potato, peeled and diced
1 tbsp medium curry paste
225 g/8 oz/1¼ cups basmati rice
4 ripe tomatoes, peeled, deseeded and diced
600 ml/1 pint/2½ cups vegetable stock
175 g/6 oz/1¾ cups cauliflower florets (white and/or Romanesco)
50 g/2 oz/⅓ cup peas, thawed if frozen
salt and freshly ground black pepper

To garnish:
roasted cashew nuts
raisins
fresh coriander/cilantro leaves

Preheat the oven to 200°C/400°F/Gas Mark 6. Put 1 tablespoon of the vegetable oil in a large bowl with the onions and toss to coat. Lightly brush or spray a nonstick baking sheet with a little more oil. Spread half the onions on the baking sheet and cook at the top of the preheated oven for 25–30 minutes, stirring regularly, until golden and crisp. Remove from the oven and reserve for the garnish.

Meanwhile, heat a large flameproof casserole dish over a medium heat and add the remaining oil and onions. Cook for 5–7 minutes until softened and starting to brown. Add a little water if they start to stick. Add the garlic and ginger and cook for another minute, then add the carrot, parsnip and sweet potato. Cook the vegetables for a further 5 minutes. Add the curry paste and stir for 1 minute until everything is coated, then stir in the rice and tomatoes. After 2 minutes, add the stock and stir well. Bring to the boil, cover and simmer over a very gentle heat for about 10 minutes.

Add the cauliflower and peas and cook for 8–10 minutes, or until the rice is tender. Season to taste with salt and pepper. Serve garnished with the crispy onions, cashew nuts, raisins and coriander/cilantro.

Health Rating: 4 points

Brown Rice Spiced Pilaf

Serves 4

Ingredients

1 tbsp vegetable oil
1 tbsp blanched almonds, flaked or chopped
1 onion, peeled and chopped
1 carrot, peeled and diced
225 g/8 oz/2 cups flat mushrooms, thickly sliced
1/4 tsp cinnamon
large pinch dried chilli flakes
50 g/2 oz/1/2 cup dried apricots, roughly chopped
25 g/1 oz/2 tbsp currants
350 g/12 oz/1 1/2 cups brown basmati rice
zest of 1 orange
900 ml/1 1/2 pints/3 3/4 cups vegetable stock
2 tbsp freshly chopped coriander/cilantro
2 tbsp freshly snipped chives
salt and freshly ground black pepper
snipped chives, to garnish

Preheat the oven to 200°C/400°F/Gas Mark 6. Heat the oil in a large flameproof casserole dish and add the almonds. Cook for 1–2 minutes until just browning – be careful as the nuts will burn very easily.

Add the onion and carrot. Cook for 5 minutes until softened and starting to turn brown. Add the mushrooms and cook for a further 5 minutes, stirring often.

Add the cinnamon and chilli flakes and cook for about 30 seconds before adding the apricots, currants, rice and orange zest. Stir together well and add the stock. Bring to the boil, cover tightly and transfer to the preheated oven. Cook for 45 minutes until the rice and vegetables are tender.

Stir the coriander/cilantro and chives into the pilaf and season to taste with salt and pepper. Garnish with the extra chives and serve immediately.

Health Rating: 4 points

Warm Fruity Rice Salad

Serves 4

Ingredients

175 g/6 oz/1 cup mixed basmati and wild rice
125 g/4 oz skinless chicken breast
300 ml/½ pint/1¼ cups chicken or vegetable stock
125 g/4 oz/1 cup ready-to-eat dried apricots
125 g/4 oz/⅔ cup ready-to-eat dried dates
3 celery stalks

For the dressing:
2 tbsp sunflower oil; 1 tbsp white wine vinegar
4 tbsp lemon juice; 1–2 tsp clear honey, warmed
1 tsp Dijon mustard; freshly ground black pepper

To garnish:
6 spring onions/scallions
fresh coriander/cilantro sprigs

Place the rice in a pan of boiling salted water and cook for 15–20 minutes, or until tender. Rinse thoroughly with boiling water and reserve.

Meanwhile, wipe the chicken and place in a shallow saucepan with the stock. Bring to the boil, cover and simmer for about 15 minutes, or until the chicken is cooked thoroughly and the juices run clear. Leave the chicken in the stock until cool enough to handle, then cut into thin slices.

Chop the apricots and dates into small pieces. Peel any tough membranes from the outside of the celery and chop into dice. Fold apricots, dates, celery and sliced chicken into the warm rice.

Make the dressing by whisking all the ingredients together in a small bowl until mixed thoroughly. Pour 2–3 tablespoons over the rice and stir in gently and evenly. Serve the remaining dressing separately. Trim and chop the spring onions/scallions. Sprinkle the spring onions over the top of the salad and garnish with the coriander/cilantro sprigs. Serve while still warm.

Health Rating: 3 points

Rice Nuggets in Herby Tomato Sauce

Serves 4

Ingredients

600 ml/1 pint/2½ cups vegetable stock
1 bay leaf; 175 g/6 oz/scant 1 cup Arborio/risotto rice
50 g/2 oz/½ cup Cheddar cheese, grated
1 egg yolk; 1 tbsp plain/all-purpose flour
2 tbsp freshly chopped parsley
salt and freshly ground black pepper
grated Parmesan cheese, to serve

For the herby tomato sauce:
1 tbsp olive oil; 1 onion, peeled and thinly sliced
1 garlic clove, peeled and crushed
1 small yellow pepper, deseeded and diced
400 g/14 oz can chopped tomatoes
1 tbsp freshly chopped basil

Pour the stock into a large saucepan. Add the bay leaf. Bring to the boil, add the rice, stir, then cover and simmer for 15 minutes.

Uncover, reduce the heat to low and cook for a further 5 minutes until the rice is tender and all the stock is absorbed, stirring frequently towards the end of cooking time. Leave to cool.

Stir the cheese, egg yolk, flour and parsley into the rice. Season to taste, then shape into 20 walnut-sized balls. Cover and refrigerate.

To make the sauce, heat the oil in a large frying pan and cook the onion for 5 minutes. Add the garlic and pepper and cook for a further 5 minutes, until soft. Stir in the chopped tomatoes and simmer gently for 3 minutes. Stir in the chopped basil and season to taste. Add the rice nuggets to the sauce and simmer for a further 10 minutes, or until the rice nuggets are cooked through and the sauce has reduced a little. Spoon on to serving plates and serve hot, sprinkled with grated Parmesan cheese.

Health Rating: 2 points

Calypso Rice with Curried Bananas

Serves 4

Ingredients

2 tbsp sunflower oil
1 medium onion, peeled and finely chopped
1 garlic clove, peeled and crushed
1 red chilli, deseeded and finely chopped
1 red pepper, deseeded and chopped
225 g/8 oz/1$^1/_4$ cups basmati rice
juice of 1 lime
350 ml/12 fl oz/1$^1/_2$ cups vegetable stock
200 g/7 oz can black-eye beans/peas, drained and rinsed
2 tbsp freshly chopped parsley
salt and freshly ground black pepper
coriander/cilantro sprigs, to garnish

For the curried bananas:
4 green bananas
2 tbsp sunflower oil
2 tsp mild curry paste
200 ml/7 fl oz/$^3/_4$ cup coconut milk

Heat the oil in a large frying pan and gently cook the onion for 10 minutes until soft. Add the garlic, chilli and red pepper and cook for 2–3 minutes.

Rinse the rice under cold running water, then add to the pan and stir. Pour in the lime juice and stock, bring to the boil, cover and simmer for 12–15 minutes, or until the rice is tender and the stock is absorbed.

Stir in the black-eye beans/peas and chopped parsley and season to taste with salt and pepper. Leave to stand, covered, for 5 minutes before serving, to allow the beans to warm through.

While the rice is cooking, make the curried green bananas. Remove the skins from the bananas – they may need to be cut off with a sharp knife. Slice the flesh thickly. Heat the oil in a frying pan and cook the bananas, in two batches, for 2–3 minutes, or until lightly browned.

Pour the coconut milk into the pan and stir in the curry paste. Simmer, uncovered, over a low heat for 8–10 minutes, or until the bananas are very soft and the coconut milk slightly reduced.

Spoon the rice on to warmed serving plates, garnish with coriander/cilantro and serve immediately with the curried bananas.

Health Rating: 2 points

Aduki Bean & Rice Burgers

Serves 4

Ingredients

2½ tbsp sunflower oil
1 medium onion, peeled and very finely chopped
1 garlic clove, peeled and crushed
1 tsp curry paste
225 g/8 oz/1¼ cups basmati rice
400 g/14 oz can aduki beans, drained and rinsed
250 ml/8 fl oz/1 cup vegetable stock
125 g/4 oz/½ cup firm tofu, crumbled
1 tsp garam masala
2 tbsp freshly chopped coriander/cilantro
salt and freshly ground black pepper

For the carrot raita:
2 large carrots, peeled and grated
½ cucumber, cut into tiny dice
150 ml/¼ pint Greek/plain yogurt

To serve:
wholemeal buns
tomato slices
lettuce leaves

Heat 1 tablespoon of the oil in a saucepan and gently cook the onion for 10 minutes until soft. Add the garlic and curry paste and cook for a few more seconds. Stir in the rice and beans.

Pour in the stock, bring to the boil and simmer for 12 minutes, or until all the stock has been absorbed – do not lift the lid for the first 10 minutes of cooking. Reserve.

Lightly mash the tofu. Add to the rice mixture with the garam masala, coriander/cilantro, salt and pepper. Mix. Shape the mixture into eight burgers. Chill in the refrigerator for 30 minutes.

Meanwhile, make the raita. Mix together the carrots, cucumber and Greek/plain yogurt. Spoon into a small bowl and chill in the refrigerator until ready to serve.

Heat the remaining oil in a large frying pan. Fry the burgers, in batches if necessary, for 4–5 minutes on each side, or until lightly browned. Serve in the buns with tomato slices and lettuce. Accompany with the raita.

Health Rating: 3 points

Thai Rice Cakes with Mango Salsa

Serves 4

Ingredients

225 g/8 oz/$^{2}/_{3}$ cup Thai fragrant rice
400 g/14 oz can coconut milk
1 lemon grass stalk, bruised
2 kaffir lime leaves, shredded
1 tbsp vegetable oil, plus extra for deep frying
1 garlic clove, peeled and finely chopped
1 tsp freshly grated root ginger
1 red pepper, deseeded and finely chopped
2 red chillies, deseeded and finely chopped
1 medium/large egg, beaten
25 g/1 oz/$^{1}/_{4}$ cup dried breadcrumbs

For the mango salsa:
1 large mango, peeled, stoned and finely chopped
1 small red onion, peeled and finely chopped
2 tbsp freshly chopped coriander/cilantro
2 tbsp freshly chopped basil
juice of 1 lime

Wash the rice in several changes of water until the water stays relatively clear. Drain, place in a saucepan with a tight fitting lid and add the coconut milk, lemon grass and lime leaves. Bring to the boil, cover and cook over the lowest possible heat for 10 minutes. Turn off the heat and leave to stand for 10 minutes, without lifting the lid.

Heat the wok, then add 1 tablespoon oil and, when hot, add the garlic, ginger, red pepper and half the chillies. Stir-fry for 1–2 minutes until just softened, then place in a large bowl.

When the rice is cooked, turn into the mixing bowl and add the egg. Season to taste with salt and pepper and mix together well. Put the breadcrumbs into a shallow dish. Form the rice mixture into eight cakes and coat them in the breadcrumbs. Chill the cakes in the refrigerator for 30 minutes.

Meanwhile, make the mango salsa. In a bowl, mix together the mango, red onion, coriander/cilantro, basil, lime juice and remaining red chilli and reserve.

Fill a clean wok about one-third full of vegetable oil. Heat to 190°C/375°F, or until a cube of bread browns in 30 seconds. Cook the rice cakes, one or two at a time, for 2–3 minutes until golden and crisp. Drain on paper towels. Serve with the salsa.

Health Rating: 1 point

Wild Rice Dolmades

Serves 4–6

Ingredients

6 tbsp olive oil; 2½ tbsp pine nuts
175 g/6 oz/1¾ cups mushrooms, wiped and finely chopped
4 spring onions/scallions, trimmed and finely chopped
1 garlic clove, peeled and crushed
50 g/2 oz/⅓ cup cooked wild rice
2 tsp freshly chopped dill; 2 tsp freshly chopped mint
salt and freshly ground black pepper
16–24 prepared medium vine/grape leaves
about 300 ml/½ pint/1¼ cups vegetable stock

To garnish:
lemon wedges; fresh dill sprigs

Heat 1 tbsp of the oil in a frying pan and gently cook the pine nuts for 2–3 minutes, stirring frequently, until golden. Remove from the pan and reserve.

Add 1½ tablespoons oil to the pan and gently cook the mushrooms, spring onions/scallions and garlic for 7–8 minutes until very soft. Stir in the rice, herbs, salt and pepper.

Put a heaped teaspoon of stuffing in the centre of each leaf (if the leaves are small, put two together, overlapping slightly). Fold over the stalk end, then the sides, and roll up to make a neat parcel. Continue until all the stuffing is used.

Arrange the stuffed leaves close together, seam-side down, in a large saucepan, drizzling each with a little of the remaining oil. There will be several layers. Pour over enough stock to cover.

Put an inverted plate over the dolmades to stop them unrolling during cooking. Bring to the boil, then simmer very gently for 3 minutes. Cool in the saucepan.

Transfer the dolmades to a serving dish. Cover and chill in the refrigerator before serving. Sprinkle with the pine nuts and garnish with lemon and dill. Serve.

Health Rating: 3 points

Wild Mushroom Risotto

Serves 4

Ingredients

15 g/½ oz dried porcini mushrooms
1.1 litres/2 pints/1¼ quarts vegetable stock
75 g/3 oz/¾ stick butter; 1 tbsp olive oil
1 onion, peeled and chopped
2–4 garlic cloves, peeled and chopped
1–2 red chillies, deseeded and chopped
225 g/8 oz/2¼ cups wild mushrooms, wiped and halved
125 g/4½ oz/1¼ cups button mushrooms, wiped and sliced
350 g/12 oz/1¾ cups Arborio/risotto rice
175 g/6 oz/1 cup cooked prawns/shrimp, peeled (optional)
150 ml/¼ pint/⅔ cup white wine
salt and freshly ground black pepper
1 tbsp lemon zest
1 tbsp freshly snipped chives; 2 tbsp freshly chopped parsley

Soak the porcini in 300 ml/½ pint/1¼ cups of very hot but not boiling water for 30 minutes. Drain, reserving the mushrooms and the soaking liquid. Pour the stock into a saucepan and bring to the boil, then reduce the heat to keep it simmering.

Melt the butter and oil in a large, deep frying pan, add the onion, garlic and chillies and cook gently for 5 minutes. Add the wild and button mushrooms with the drained porcini and continue to cook for 4–5 minutes, stirring frequently.

Stir in the rice and cook for 1 minute. Strain the reserved soaking liquid and stir into the rice with a little of the hot stock. Cook gently, stirring frequently, until the liquid is absorbed. Continue to add most of the stock, a ladleful at a time, stirring after each addition, until the rice is tender and the risotto looks creamy.

Add the prawns/shrimp, if using, and wine along with the last additions of stock. When the prawns are hot and all the liquid is absorbed, season to taste with salt and pepper. Remove from the heat and stir in the lemon zest, chives and parsley, reserving some for the garnish. Garnish and serve.

Health Rating: 2 points

Risi e Bisi

Serves 4

Ingredients

700 g/1½ lb/5 cups peas, thawed if frozen
25 g/1 oz/¼ stick unsalted butter
1 tsp olive oil
3 rashers pancetta or unsmoked back bacon, chopped
1 small onion, peeled and finely chopped
1 garlic clove, peeled and finely chopped
1.3 litres/2¼ pints/1⅓ quarts vegetable stock
pinch caster/superfine sugar
1 tsp lemon juice; 1 bay leaf
200 g/7 oz/1 cup Arborio/risotto rice
3 tbsp freshly chopped parsley
50 g/2 oz/½ cup Parmesan cheese, finely grated
salt and freshly ground black pepper

To garnish:
fresh parsley sprig
julienne strips of orange rind

Shell the peas, if using fresh ones. Melt the butter and olive oil together in a large heavy-based saucepan. Add the chopped pancetta or bacon, the chopped onion and garlic and gently fry for about 10 minutes, or until the onion is softened and is just beginning to colour.

Pour in the vegetable stock, then add the caster/superfine sugar, lemon juice and bay leaf. Add the fresh peas, if using. Bring the mixture to a fast boil.

Add the rice, stir and simmer, uncovered, for about 20 minutes, or until the rice is tender. Occasionally stir the mixture gently while it cooks. If using frozen petits pois, stir them into the rice about 2 minutes before the end of the cooking time.

When the rice is cooked, remove the bay leaf and discard. Stir in 2½ tablespoons of the chopped parsley and the grated Parmesan cheese. Season to taste with salt and pepper. Transfer the rice to a large serving dish. Garnish with the remaining chopped parsley, a fresh parsley sprig and julienne strips of orange rind. Serve immediately while piping hot.

Health Rating: 3 points

Rice-filled Peppers

Serves 4

Ingredients

8 ripe tomatoes; 2 tbsp olive oil
1 onion, peeled and chopped
1 garlic clove, peeled and crushed
$^1/_2$ tsp dark muscovado/brown sugar
125 g/4$^1/_2$ oz/$^3/_4$ cup cooked long-grain rice
1 tbsp freshly chopped oregano
50 g/2 oz/$^1/_3$ cup pine nuts, toasted
salt and freshly ground black pepper
2 large red and 2 large yellow peppers

To serve:
mixed salad
crusty bread

Preheat the oven to 200°C/400°F/Gas Mark 6. Put the tomatoes in a small bowl and pour over boiling water to cover. Leave for 1 minute, then drain. Plunge the tomatoes into cold water to cool, then peel off the skins. Quarter, remove the seeds and chop.

Heat the olive oil in a frying pan and cook the onion gently for 10 minutes until softened. Add the garlic, chopped tomatoes and sugar. Gently cook the tomato mixture for 10 minutes until thickened. Remove from the heat and stir the rice, oregano and pine nuts into the sauce. Season to taste with salt and pepper.

Halve the peppers lengthways, cutting through and leaving the stem on. Remove the seeds and cores, then put the peppers in a lightly oiled roasting tin/pan cut-side down and cook in the preheated oven for about 10 minutes.

Turn the peppers so they are cut-side up. Spoon in the filling, then cover with kitchen foil. Return to the oven for 15 minutes, or until the peppers are very tender, removing the kitchen foil for the last 5 minutes to allow the tops to brown a little. Serve half a red pepper and half a yellow pepper per person with a mixed salad and plenty of warmed, crusty bread.

Health Rating: 3 points

Roast Butternut Squash Risotto

Serves 4

Ingredients

1 butternut squash
2 tbsp olive oil
1 garlic bulb, cloves separated but unpeeled
15 g/½ oz/1 tbsp unsalted butter
280 g/10 oz/1½ cups risotto rice
large pinch saffron strands
150 ml/¼ pint/⅔ cup dry white wine
1 litre/1¾ pints/1 quart vegetable stock
1 tbsp freshly chopped parsley
1 tbsp freshly chopped oregano
50 g/2 oz/½ cup Parmesan cheese, finely grated
salt and freshly ground black pepper
fresh oregano sprigs, to garnish
extra Parmesan cheese, to serve

Preheat the oven to 190°C/375°F/Gas Mark 5. Cut the butternut squash in half, thickly peel, then scoop out the seeds and discard. Cut the flesh into 2 cm/¾ inch cubes.

Pour the oil into a large roasting tin/pan and heat in the preheated oven for 5 minutes. Add the butternut squash and garlic cloves. Turn in the oil to coat, then roast in the oven for about 25–30 minutes, or until golden brown and very tender, turning the vegetables halfway through cooking time.

Melt the butter in a large saucepan. Add the rice and stir over a high heat for a few seconds. Add the saffron and the wine and bubble fiercely until almost totally reduced, stirring frequently. At the same time, heat the stock in a separate saucepan and keep at a steady simmer.

Reduce the heat under the rice to low. Add a ladleful of stock to the saucepan and simmer, stirring, until absorbed. Continue adding the stock in this way until the rice is tender. This will take about 20 minutes and it may not be necessary to add all the stock.

Turn off the heat, stir in the herbs, Parmesan cheese and seasoning. Cover and leave to stand for 2–3 minutes. Quickly remove the skins from the roasted garlic. Add to the risotto with the butternut squash and mix gently. Garnish with oregano sprigs and serve immediately with Parmesan cheese.

Health Rating: 4 points

Broad Bean & Artichoke Risotto

Serves 4

Ingredients

275 g/10 oz/1 3/4 cups frozen broad/fava beans
400 g/14 oz can artichoke hearts, drained
1 tbsp sunflower oil
150 ml/1/4 pint/2/3 cup dry white wine
900 ml/1 1/2 pints/scant 1 quart vegetable stock
25 g/1 oz/1/4 stick butter
1 onion, peeled and finely chopped
200 g/7 oz/1 cup Arborio rice
finely grated zest/rind and juice of 1 lemon
50 g/2 oz Parmesan cheese, grated
salt and freshly ground black pepper
freshly grated Parmesan cheese, to serve

Cook the beans in a saucepan of lightly salted boiling water for 4–5 minutes, or until just tender. Drain and plunge into cold water. Peel off the tough outer skins, if liked. Pat the artichokes dry on absorbent paper towels and cut each in half lengthways through the stem end. Cut each half into three wedges.

Heat the oil in a large saucepan and cook the artichokes for 4–5 minutes, turning occasionally, until they are lightly browned. Remove and reserve. Bring the wine and stock to the boil in a separate frying pan. Keep them barely simmering while making the risotto.

Melt the butter in a large frying pan, add the onion and cook for 5 minutes until beginning to soften. Add the rice and cook for 1 minute, stirring. Pour in a ladleful of the hot wine and stock, simmer gently, stirring frequently, until the stock is absorbed. Continue to add the stock in this way for 20–25 minutes, until the rice is just tender and the risotto creamy and soft. Add the beans, artichokes and lemon zest/rind and juice. Gently mix in, cover and leave to warm through for 1–2 minutes. Stir in the Parmesan cheese and season to taste with salt and pepper. Serve sprinkled with extra Parmesan cheese.

Health Rating: 4 points

Pasta

Pasta is one of the simplest, fastest and most convenient ingredients available – these dishes are delicious too! It will take no time to cook recipes such as Spaghetti alla Puttanesca or Singapore Noodles. For more substantial meals, this chapter also includes dishes such as Spaghetti Bolognese and Traditional Lasagne – classics that the whole family will enjoy.

Spaghetti alle Vongole

Serves 4

Ingredients

1.8 kg/4 lb small fresh clams
6 tbsp dry white wine
2 tbsp olive oil
1 small onion, peeled and finely chopped
2 garlic cloves, peeled and crushed
400 g/14 oz spaghetti
2 tbsp freshly chopped parsley
2 tbsp freshly chopped or torn basil
salt and freshly ground black pepper
oregano leaves, to garnish

Soak clams in lightly salted cold water 8 hours before required, changing the water once or twice. Scrub the clams, removing any that have broken shells or remain open when tapped.

Place clams in a large saucepan and pour in the wine. Cover with a tight-fitting lid and cook over a medium heat for 5–6 minutes, shaking the pan occasionally, until the shells have opened.

Strain the clams and cooking juices through a sieve lined with muslin and reserve. Discard clams that have remained unopened.

Heat the olive oil in a saucepan and fry the onion and garlic gently for 10 minutes, or until very soft.

Meanwhile, bring a large pan of lightly salted water to a rolling boil. Add the spaghetti and cook according to the packet instructions, or until *al dente*.

Add the cooked clams to the onions and garlic and pour in the reserved cooking juices. Bring to the boil, then add the parsley and basil and season to taste with salt and black pepper.

Drain the spaghetti thoroughly. Return to the pan and add the clams with their sauce. Toss together gently, then tip into a large warmed serving bowl or into individual bowls. Serve immediately, sprinkled with oregano leaves.

Health Rating: 2 points

Spaghetti alla Puttanesca

Serves 4

Ingredients

4 tbsp olive oil
50 g/2 oz can anchovy fillets in olive oil, drained and coarsely chopped
2 garlic cloves, peeled and finely chopped
½ tsp crushed dried chillies
400 g/14 oz can chopped plum tomatoes
125 g/4½ oz/1 cup pitted black olives, cut in half
2 tbsp capers, rinsed and drained
1 tsp freshly chopped oregano
1 tbsp tomato puree/paste
salt and freshly ground black pepper
400 g/14 oz spaghetti
2 tbsp freshly chopped parsley

Heat the olive oil in a large frying pan, add the anchovies and cook, stirring with a wooden spoon and crushing the anchovies until they disintegrate. Add the garlic and dried chillies and cook for 1 minute, stirring frequently.

Add the tomatoes, olives, capers, oregano and tomato paste and cook, stirring occasionally, for 15 minutes, or until the liquid has evaporated and the sauce is thickened. Season the tomato sauce to taste with salt and pepper.

Meanwhile, bring a large pan of lightly salted water to a rolling boil. Add the spaghetti and cook according to the packet instructions, or until *al dente*.

Drain the spaghetti thoroughly, reserving 1–2 tablespoons of the cooking water. Return the spaghetti with the reserved water to the pan. Pour the tomato sauce over the spaghetti, add the chopped parsley and toss to coat. Tip into a warmed serving dish or spoon on to individual plates and serve immediately.

Health Rating: 3 points

Pasta & Mussels in Tomato & Wine Sauce

Serves 4

Ingredients

900 g/2 lb fresh live mussels
1 bay leaf
150 ml/¼ pint/⅔ cup light red wine
1 tbsp unsalted butter
1 tbsp olive oil
1 red onion, peeled and thinly sliced
2 garlic cloves, peeled and crushed
550 g/1¼ lb/3 cups ripe tomatoes, skinned, deseeded and chopped
400 g/14 oz/2½ cups fiochetti or penne
3 tbsp freshly chopped or torn basil
salt and freshly ground black pepper
basil leaves, to garnish
crusty bread, to serve

Scrub the mussels and remove any beards. Discard any that do not close when lightly tapped. Place in a large pan with the bay leaf and pour in the wine. Cover with a tight-fitting lid and steam, shaking the pan occasionally, for 3–4 minutes, or until the mussels open. Remove the mussels with a slotted spoon, discarding any that have not opened, and reserve. Strain the cooking liquid through a muslin-lined sieve and reserve.

Melt the butter with the oil in a large saucepan and gently cook the onion and garlic for 10 minutes until soft. Add the reserved cooking liquid and the tomatoes and simmer, uncovered, for 6–7 minutes, or until very soft and the sauce has reduced slightly.

Meanwhile, bring a large pan of lightly salted water to a rolling boil. Add the pasta and cook according to the packet instructions, or until *al dente*. Drain the pasta thoroughly and return to the pan. Add the mussels, removing the shells if you prefer, with the tomato sauce. Stir in the basil and season to taste with salt and pepper. Toss together gently. Tip into warmed serving bowls, garnish with basil leaves and serve with crusty bread.

Health Rating: 3 points

Tuna Cannelloni

Serves 4

Ingredients

1 tbsp olive oil
6 spring onions/scallions, trimmed and finely sliced
1 sweet Mediterranean red pepper, deseeded and finely chopped
200 g/7 oz can tuna in brine
250 g/9 oz tub ricotta or quark cheese
zest and juice of 1 lemon
1 tbsp freshly snipped chives
salt and freshly ground black pepper
8 dried cannelloni tubes
1 medium/large egg, beaten
125 g/4 oz/¼ cup cottage cheese
150 ml/¼ pt/½ cup natural/plain yogurt
pinch freshly grated nutmeg
50 g/2 oz/¼ cup mozzarella cheese, grated
tossed green salad, to serve

Preheat oven to 180°C/375°F/Gas Mark 5, 10 minutes before cooking. Heat the olive oil in a frying pan and cook the spring onions/scallions and pepper until soft. Remove from the pan with a slotted draining spoon and place in a large bowl.

Drain the tuna, then stir into the spring onions and pepper. Beat the ricotta cheese with the lemon zest and juice and the snipped chives and season to taste with salt and pepper until soft and blended. Add to the tuna and mix together. If the mixture is still a little stiff, add a little extra lemon juice.

With a teaspoon, carefully spoon the mixture into the cannelloni tubes, then lay the filled tubes in a lightly oiled shallow ovenproof dish. Beat the egg, cottage cheese, yogurt and nutmeg together and pour over the cannelloni. Sprinkle with the grated mozzarella cheese and bake in the preheated oven for 15–20 minutes, or until the topping is golden brown and bubbling. Serve immediately with a tossed green salad.

Health Rating: 2 points

Pappardelle with Smoked Haddock & Blue Cheese Sauce

Serves 4

Ingredients

350 g/12 oz smoked haddock
2 bay leaves, 300 ml/½ pint/1¼ cups milk
400 g/14 oz pappardelle or tagliatelle
25 g/1 oz/¼ stick butter
25 g/1 oz/¼ cup plain/all-purpose flour
150 ml/¼ pint/⅔ cup single/light cream or extra milk
125 g/4½ oz Dolcelatte cheese or Gorgonzola, cut into small pieces
¼ tsp freshly grated nutmeg
salt and freshly ground black pepper
40 g/1½ oz/⅓ cup toasted walnuts, chopped
1 tbsp freshly chopped parsley

Place the smoked haddock in a saucepan with 1 bay leaf and pour in the milk. Bring to the boil slowly, cover and simmer for 6–7 minutes, or until the fish is opaque. Remove and roughly flake the fish, discarding the skin and any bones. Strain the milk and reserve.

Bring a large pan of lightly salted water to a rolling boil. Add the pasta and cook according to the packet instructions, or until *al dente*.

Meanwhile, place the butter, flour and single cream, or milk if preferred, in a pan and stir to mix. Stir in the reserved warm milk and add the remaining bay leaf. Bring to the boil, whisking all the time until smooth and thick. Gently simmer for 3–4 minutes, stirring frequently. Discard the bay leaf. Add the cheese to the sauce. Heat gently, stirring until melted. Add the flaked haddock and season to taste with nutmeg and salt and pepper.

Drain the pasta thoroughly and return to the pan. Add the sauce and toss gently to coat, taking care not to break up the flakes of fish. Tip into a warmed serving bowl, sprinkle with toasted walnuts and parsley and serve immediately.

Health Rating: 2 points

Seared Salmon & Lemon Linguine

Serves 4

Ingredients

4 small skinless salmon fillets, each about 75 g/3 oz
2 tsp sunflower oil
½ tsp mixed or black peppercorns, crushed
400 g/14 oz linguine
15 g/½ oz/1 tbsp unsalted butter
1 bunch spring onions/scallions, trimmed and shredded
300 ml/½ pint/1¼ cups sour cream
zest of 1 lemon, finely grated
50 g/2 oz/½ cup freshly grated Parmesan cheese
1 tbsp lemon juice
pinch salt

To garnish:
dill sprigs
lemon slices

Brush the salmon fillets with the sunflower oil, sprinkle with crushed peppercorns and press on firmly and reserve.

Bring a large pan of lightly salted water to a rolling boil. Add the linguine and cook according to the packet instructions, or until *al dente*.

Meanwhile, melt the butter in a saucepan and cook the shredded spring onions/scallions gently for 2–3 minutes, or until soft. Stir in the sour cream and the lemon zest and remove from the heat.

Preheat a griddle or heavy-based frying pan until very hot. Add the salmon and sear for 1½–2 minutes on each side. Remove from the pan and allow to cool slightly.

Bring the sour cream sauce to the boil and stir in the Parmesan cheese and lemon juice. Drain the pasta thoroughly and return to the pan. Pour over the sauce and toss gently to coat. Spoon the pasta on to warmed serving plates and top with the salmon fillets. Serve immediately with dill sprigs and lemon slices.

Health Rating: 2 points

Hot Prawn Noodles with Sesame Dressing

Serves 4

Ingredients

600 ml/1 pint/2½ cups vegetable stock
350 g/12 oz Chinese egg noodles
1 tbsp sunflower oil
1 garlic clove, peeled and very finely chopped
1 red chilli, deseeded and finely chopped
3 tbsp sesame seeds
3 tbsp dark soy sauce
2 tbsp sesame oil
175 g/6 oz (about 30 medium) shelled cooked prawns/shrimp
3 tbsp freshly chopped coriander/cilantro
freshly ground black pepper
fresh coriander/cilantro sprigs, to garnish

Pour the vegetable stock into a large saucepan and bring to the boil. Add the egg noodles, stir once, then cook according to the packet instructions, usually about 3 minutes.

Meanwhile, heat the sunflower oil in a small frying pan. Add the chopped garlic and chilli and cook gently for a few seconds. Add the sesame seeds and cook, stirring continuously, for 1 minute, or until golden.

Add the soy sauce, sesame oil and prawns/shrimp to the frying pan. Continue cooking for a few seconds until the mixture is just starting to bubble, then remove immediately from the heat.

Drain the noodles thoroughly and return to the pan. Add the prawns in the dressing mixture and the chopped coriander/cilantro and season to taste with black pepper. Toss gently to coat the noodles with the hot dressing.

Tip into a warmed serving bowl or spoon on to individual plates and serve immediately, garnished with fresh coriander sprigs.

Health Rating: 3 points

Smoked Mackerel & Pasta Frittata

Serves 4

Ingredients

25 g/1 oz/¼ cup tricolore pasta spirals or shells
225 g/8 oz smoked mackerel (or salmon)
6 medium/large eggs; 3 tbsp milk
2 tsp wholegrain mustard; 2 tbsp freshly chopped parsley
salt and freshly ground black pepper
25 g/1 oz/¼ stick unsalted butter
6 spring onions/scallions, trimmed and diagonally sliced
50 g/2 oz/⅓ cup frozen peas, thawed
75 g/3 oz/¾ cup mature Cheddar cheese, grated

To serve:
green salad; warm crusty bread

Preheat the grill/broiler to high just before cooking. Bring a pan of lightly salted water to a rolling boil. Add the pasta and cook according to the packet instructions, or until *al dente*. Drain thoroughly and reserve.

Remove the skin from the mackerel and break the fish into large flakes, discarding any bones, and reserve.

Place the eggs, milk, mustard and parsley in a bowl and whisk together. Season with just a little salt and plenty of freshly ground black pepper and reserve.

Melt the butter in a large heavy-based frying pan. Cook the spring onions/scallions gently for 3–4 minutes until soft. Pour in the egg mixture, add the drained pasta, peas and half of the mackerel.

Gently stir the mixture in the pan for 1–2 minutes, or until beginning to set. Stop stirring and cook for about 1 minute until the underneath is golden brown.Scatter the remaining mackerel over the frittata, followed by the grated cheese. Place under the preheated grill for about 1½ minutes, or until golden brown and set. Cut into wedges and serve immediately with salad and crusty bread.

Health Rating: 2 points

Creamy Coconut Seafood Pasta

Serves 4

Ingredients

400 g/14 oz egg tagliatelle
1 tsp sunflower oil
1 tsp sesame oil
4 spring onions/scallions, trimmed and diagonally sliced
1 garlic clove, peeled and crushed
1 red chilli, deseeded and finely chopped
2.5 cm/1 inch piece fresh root ginger, peeled and grated
150 ml/$^1/_4$ pint/$^2/_3$ cup coconut milk
100 ml/3$^1/_2$ fl oz/$^1/_3$ cup double/heavy cream
225 g/8 oz/2 cups cooked, peeled tiger prawns/jumbo shrimp
185 g/6$^1/_2$ oz/1$^1/_2$ cups fresh white crab meat
2 tbsp freshly chopped coriander/cilantro, plus sprigs
salt and freshly ground black pepper

Bring a large pan of lightly salted water to a rolling boil. Add the pasta and cook according to the packet instructions, or until *al dente*.

Meanwhile, heat the sunflower oil and sesame oil together in a saucepan. Add the spring onions/scallions, garlic, chilli and ginger and cook for 3–4 minutes, or until softened.

Blend the coconut milk and cream together in a jug. Add the prawns/shrimp and crab meat to the pan and stir over a low heat for a few seconds to heat through. Gradually pour in the coconut cream, stirring all the time.

Stir the chopped coriander/cilantro into the seafood sauce and season to taste with salt and pepper. Continue heating the sauce gently until piping hot, but do not allow to boil.

Drain the pasta thoroughly and return to the pan. Add the seafood sauce and gently toss together to coat the pasta. Tip into a warmed serving dish or spoon on to individual plates. Serve immediately, garnished with fresh coriander sprigs.

Health Rating: 2 points

Fettuccine with Sardines & Spinach

Serves 4

Ingredients

120 g/3½ oz can sardines in olive oil
400 g/14 oz fettuccine or tagliarini
40 g/1½ oz/⅓ stick butter
2 tbsp olive oil
50 g/2 oz/1 cup one-day-old white breadcrumbs
1 garlic clove, peeled and finely chopped
50 g/2 oz/½ cup pine nuts
125 g/4 oz/1½ cups chestnut mushrooms, wiped and sliced
125 g/4 oz/1½ cups baby spinach leaves, rinsed
150 ml/¼ pint/⅔ cup crème fraîche/sour cream
zest/rind of 1 lemon, finely grated
salt and freshly ground black pepper

Drain the sardines and cut in half lengthways. Remove the bones, then cut the fish into 2.5 cm/1 inch pieces and reserve.

Bring a large pan of lightly salted water to a rolling boil. Add the pasta and cook according to packet instructions, or until *al dente*.

Melt half the butter with the olive oil in a large saucepan, add the breadcrumbs and fry, stirring, until they begin to turn crisp. Add the garlic and pine nuts and continue to cook until golden brown. Remove from the pan and reserve. Wipe the pan clean.

Melt the remaining butter in the pan, add the mushrooms and cook for 4–5 minutes, or until soft. Add the spinach and cook, stirring, for 1 minute, or until beginning to wilt. Stir in the crème fraîche/sour cream and lemon rind and bring to the boil. Simmer gently until the spinach is just cooked. Season the sauce to taste with salt and pepper.

Drain the pasta thoroughly and return to the pan. Add the spinach sauce and sardine pieces and gently toss together. Tip into a warmed serving dish. Sprinkle with the toasted breadcrumbs and pine nuts and serve immediately.

Health Rating: 2 points

Spaghetti Bolognese

Serves 4

Ingredients

3 tbsp olive oil
50 g/2 oz/¼ cup chopped unsmoked streaky/fatty bacon with rind removed
1 small onion, peeled and finely chopped
1 carrot, peeled and chopped
1 celery stalk, trimmed and chopped
2 garlic cloves, peeled and crushed
1 bay leaf
500 g/1 lb 2 oz minced/ground beef
400 g/14 oz can chopped tomatoes
2 tbsp tomato puree/paste
150 ml/¼ pint/⅔ cup red wine
150 ml/¼ pint/⅔ cup beef stock
salt and freshly ground black pepper
450 g/1 lb spaghetti
freshly grated Parmesan cheese, to serve

Heat the olive oil in a large heavy-based pan, add the bacon and cook for 5 minutes, or until slightly coloured. Add the onion, carrot, celery, garlic and bay leaf and cook, stirring, for 8 minutes, or until the vegetables are soft.

Add the minced/ground beef to the pan and cook, stirring with a wooden spoon to break up any lumps, for 5–8 minutes, or until browned.

Stir the tomatoes and tomato puree/paste into the beef and pour in the wine and stock. Bring to the boil, then lower the heat and simmer for at least 40 minutes, stirring occasionally. The longer you cook the sauce, the more intense the flavour will be. Season to taste with salt and pepper and remove the bay leaf.

Meanwhile, bring a large pan of lightly salted water to a rolling boil, add the spaghetti and cook for about 8 minutes, or until *al dente*. Drain and arrange on warmed serving plates. Top with the prepared Bolognese sauce and serve immediately sprinkled with grated Parmesan cheese.

Health Rating: 3 points

Traditional Lasagne

Serves 4

Ingredients

450 g/1 lb lean minced/ground beef
175 g/6 oz/¾ cup pancetta or smoked streaky bacon, chopped
1 large onion, peeled and chopped
2 celery stalks, trimmed and chopped
125 g/4 oz/1 cup button mushrooms, wiped and chopped
2 garlic cloves, peeled and chopped
100 g/3½ oz/1 cup plain/all-purpose flour
300 ml/½ pint/1¼ cups beef stock
1 tbsp freeze-dried mixed herbs
5 tbsp tomato puree/paste
salt and freshly ground black pepper
75 g/3 oz/½ stick butter
1 tsp English mustard powder
pinch freshly grated nutmeg
900 ml/1½ pints/scant 1 quart milk
125 g/4 oz/1¼ cups Parmesan cheese, grated
125 g/4 oz/1 cup Cheddar cheese, grated
8–12 precooked lasagne sheets

To serve:
crusty bread
fresh green salad leaves

Preheat oven to 200°C/400°F/Gas Mark 6, 15 minutes before cooking. Cook the beef and pancetta in a large saucepan for 10 minutes, stirring to break up any lumps. Add the onion, celery and mushrooms and cook for 4 minutes, or until softened slightly.

Stir in the garlic and 1 tablespoon of the flour, then cook for 1 minute. Stir in the stock, herbs and tomato puree/paste. Season to taste with salt and pepper. Bring to the boil, then cover, reduce the heat and simmer for 45 minutes.

Meanwhile, melt the butter in a small saucepan and stir in the remaining flour, mustard powder and nutmeg until well blended. Cook for 2 minutes. Remove from the heat and gradually blend in the milk until smooth. Return to the heat and bring to the boil, stirring, until thickened. Gradually stir in half the Parmesan and Cheddar cheeses until melted. Season to taste.

Spoon half the meat mixture into the base of a large ovenproof dish. Top with a single layer of pasta. Spread over half the sauce and scatter with half the cheese. Repeat layers, finishing with cheese. Bake in the preheated oven for 30 minutes, or until the pasta is cooked and the top is golden brown and bubbly. Serve immediately with crusty bread and a green salad.

Health Rating: 1 point

Cannelloni

Serves 4

Ingredients

2 tbsp olive oil
175 g/6 oz/$^3/_4$ cup fresh minced/ground pork
75 g/3 oz/$^2/_3$ cup chicken livers, chopped
1 small onion, peeled and chopped
1 garlic clove, peeled and chopped
175 g/6 oz/1 cup frozen spinach, thawed and chopped
1 tbsp freeze-dried oregano
pinch freshly grated nutmeg
salt and freshly ground black pepper
175 g/6 oz/$^3/_4$ cup ricotta or quark cheese
25 g/1 oz/$^1/_4$ stick butter
25 g/1 oz/$^1/_4$ cup plain/all-purpose flour
600 ml/1 pt/2$^1/_2$ cups milk
600 ml/1 pt/2$^1/_2$ cups ready-made tomato sauce
16 precooked cannelloni tubes
50 g/2 oz/$^1/_2$ cup Parmesan cheese, grated
green salad, to serve

Preheat oven to 190°C/375°F/Gas Mark 5, 10 minutes before cooking. Heat the olive oil in a frying pan and cook the pork and chicken livers for about 5 minutes, stirring occasionally, until browned all over. Break up any lumps if necessary with a wooden spoon.

Add the onion and garlic and cook for 4 minutes until softened. Add the spinach, oregano and nutmeg and season to taste with salt and pepper. Cook until all the liquid has evaporated, then remove the pan from the heat and allow to cool. Stir in the ricotta or quark cheese.

Meanwhile, melt the butter in a small saucepan and stir in the plain flour to form a roux. Cook for 2 minutes, stirring occasionally. Remove from the heat and blend in the milk until smooth. Return to the heat and bring to the boil, stirring until the sauce has thickened. Reserve.

Spoon a thin layer of the tomato sauce on the base of a large ovenproof dish. Divide the pork filling between the cannelloni tubes. Arrange on top of the tomato sauce. Spoon over the remaining tomato sauce.

Pour over the white sauce and sprinkle with the Parmesan cheese. Bake in the preheated oven for 30–35 minutes, or until the cannelloni is tender and the top is golden brown. Serve immediately with a green salad.

Health Rating: 2 points

Spaghetti & Meatballs

Serves 4

Ingredients

400 g/14 oz can chopped tomatoes
1 tbsp tomato puree/paste
1 tsp chilli sauce
1/4 tsp brown sugar
salt and freshly ground black pepper
350 g/12 oz spaghetti
75g/3 oz/3/4 cup Cheddar cheese, grated, plus extra to serve
freshly chopped parsley, to garnish

For the meatballs:
450 g/1 lb/5 cups lean minced/ground pork or beef
125 g/4 1/2 oz/2 cups fresh breadcrumbs
1 large onion, peeled and finely chopped
1 egg, beaten
1 tbsp tomato puree/paste
2 tbsp freshly chopped parsley
1 tbsp freshly chopped oregano

Preheat the oven to 200°C/400°F/Gas Mark 6, 15 minutes before using. Place the chopped tomatoes, tomato puree/paste, chilli sauce and sugar in a saucepan. Season to taste with salt and pepper and bring to the boil. Cover and simmer for 15 minutes, then cook, uncovered, for a further 10 minutes, or until the sauce has reduced and thickened.

Meanwhile, make the meatballs. Place the meat, breadcrumbs and onion in a food processor. Blend until all the ingredients are well mixed. Add the beaten egg, tomato puree, parsley and oregano and season to taste. Blend again.

Shape the mixture into small balls, about the size of a plum, and place on an oiled baking tray. Cook in the preheated oven for 25–30 minutes, or until browned and cooked.

Meanwhile, bring a large pan of lightly salted water to a rolling boil. Add the pasta and cook according to the packet instructions, or until *al dente*.

Drain the pasta and return to the pan. Pour over the tomato sauce and toss gently to coat the spaghetti. Tip into a warmed serving dish and top with the meatballs. Garnish with chopped parsley and serve immediately with grated cheese.

Health Rating: 3 points

Chorizo with Pasta in a Tomato Sauce

Serves 4

Ingredients

25 g/1 oz/¼ stick butter
2 tbsp olive oil
2 large onions, peeled and finely sliced
1 tsp soft brown sugar
2 garlic cloves, peeled and crushed
225 g/8 oz chorizo, sliced
1 chilli, deseeded and finely sliced
400 g/14 oz can chopped tomatoes
1 tbsp sun-dried tomato paste
150 ml/¼ pint/⅔ cup red wine
salt and freshly ground black pepper
450 g/1 lb/4 cups rigatoni
freshly chopped parsley, to garnish

Melt the butter with the olive oil in a large heavy-based pan. Add the onions and sugar and cook over a very low heat, stirring occasionally, for 15 minutes, or until soft and starting to caramelize.

Add the garlic and chorizo to the pan and cook for 5 minutes. Stir in the chilli, chopped tomatoes and tomato paste and pour in the wine. Season well with salt and pepper. Bring to the boil, cover, reduce the heat and simmer for 30 minutes, stirring occasionally. Remove the lid and simmer for a further 10 minutes, or until the sauce starts to thicken.

Meanwhile, bring a large pan of lightly salted water to a rolling boil. Add the pasta and cook according to the packet instructions, or until *al dente*. Drain the pasta, reserving 2 tablespoons of the water, and return to the pan.

Add the chorizo sauce with the reserved cooking water and toss gently until the pasta is evenly covered. Tip into a warmed serving dish, sprinkle with the parsley and serve immediately.

Health Rating: 2 points

Prosciutto & Gruyère Carbonara

Serves 4

Ingredients

3 medium/large egg yolks
50 g/2 oz/½ cup Gruyère cheese, grated
2 tbsp olive oil
2 garlic cloves, peeled and crushed
2 shallots, peeled and finely chopped
200 g/7 oz/1½ cups prosciutto ham, cut into strips
4 tbsp dry vermouth
salt and freshly ground black pepper
450 g/1 lb spaghetti
1 tbsp butter
1 tbsp freshly shredded basil leaves
basil sprigs, to garnish

Place the egg yolks with 6 tablespoons of the Gruyère cheese in a bowl and mix lightly until well blended, then reserve.

Heat the olive oil in a large pan and cook the garlic and shallots for 5 minutes, or until golden brown. Add the prosciutto ham, then cook for a further 1 minute. Pour in the dry vermouth and simmer for 2 minutes, then remove from the heat. Season to taste with salt and pepper and keep warm.

Meanwhile, bring a large pan of lightly salted water to a rolling boil. Add the pasta and cook according to the packet instructions, or until *al dente*. Drain thoroughly, reserving 4 tablespoons of the water, and return the pasta to the pan.

Remove from the heat, then add the egg and cheese mixture with the butter to the pasta; toss lightly until coated. Add the prosciutto mixture and toss again, adding the reserved pasta water, if needed, to moisten. Season to taste and sprinkle with the remaining Gruyère cheese and the shredded basil leaves. Garnish with basil sprigs and serve immediately.

Health Rating: 2 points

Moroccan Penne

Serves 4

Ingredients

1 tbsp sunflower oil
1 red onion, peeled and chopped
2 garlic cloves, peeled and crushed
1 tbsp coriander seeds
¼ tsp cumin seeds
¼ tsp freshly grated nutmeg
450 g/1 lb/5 cups lean minced/ground lamb
1 aubergine/eggplant, trimmed and diced
400 g/14 oz can chopped tomatoes
300 ml/½ pint/1¼ cups vegetable stock
125 g/4½ oz/½ cup ready-to-eat apricots, chopped
12 black olives, pitted
salt and freshly ground black pepper
350 g/12 oz/3 cups penne
1 tbsp toasted pine nuts, to garnish

Preheat the oven to 200°C/400°F/Gas Mark 6, 15 minutes before using. Heat the sunflower oil in a large flameproof casserole dish. Add the chopped onion and fry for 5 minutes, or until softened.

Using a pestle and mortar, pound the garlic, coriander seeds, cumin seeds and grated nutmeg together into a paste. Add to the onion and cook for 3 minutes.

Add the minced/ground lamb to the casserole dish and fry, stirring with a wooden spoon, for 4–5 minutes, or until the meat has broken up and browned. Add the aubergine/eggplant to the meat and fry for 5 minutes. Stir in the chopped tomatoes and vegetable stock and bring to the boil. Add apricots and olives, season well with salt and pepper. Return to the boil, lower the heat and simmer for 15 minutes.

Add the penne to the casserole dish, stir well, then cover and place in the preheated oven. Cook for 10 minutes, then stir and return to the oven, uncovered, for a further 15–20 minutes, or until the pasta is *al dente*. Remove from the oven, sprinkle with toasted pine nuts and serve immediately.

Health Rating: 2 points

Sausage & Redcurrant Pasta Bake

Serves 4

Ingredients

450 g/1 lb (about 7–8) good-quality thick pork sausages
2 tsp sunflower oil
25 g/1 oz/¼ stick butter
1 onion, peeled and sliced
2 tbsp plain/all-purpose white flour
450 ml/¾ pint/1¾ cups chicken stock
150 ml/¼ pint/⅔ cup port or good quality red wine
1 tbsp freshly chopped thyme leaves, plus sprigs to garnish
1 bay leaf
4 tbsp redcurrant jelly
salt and freshly ground black pepper
350 g/12 oz/2¼ cups fresh penne
75 g/3 oz/¾ cup Gruyère cheese, grated

Preheat the oven to 220°C/425°F/Gas Mark 7, 15 minutes before cooking. Prick the sausages, place in a shallow ovenproof dish and toss in the sunflower oil. Cook in the oven for 25–30 minutes, or until golden brown.

Meanwhile, melt the butter in a frying pan, add the sliced onion and fry for 5 minutes, or until golden brown. Stir in the flour and cook for 2 minutes. Remove the pan from the heat and gradually stir in the chicken stock with the port or red wine.

Return the pan to the heat and bring to the boil, stirring continuously, until the sauce starts to thicken. Add the thyme, bay leaf and redcurrant jelly and season well with salt and pepper. Simmer the sauce for 5 minutes.

Bring a large pan of salted water to a rolling boil, add the pasta and cook for about 4 minutes, or until *al dente*. Drain thoroughly and reserve.

Lower the oven temperature to 200°C/400°F/Gas Mark 6. Remove the sausages from the oven, drain off any excess fat and return the sausages to the dish. Add the pasta.

Pour over the sauce, removing the bay leaf, and toss together. Sprinkle with the Gruyère cheese and return to the oven for 15–20 minutes, or until bubbling and golden brown. Serve immediately, garnished with thyme sprigs.

Health Rating: 2 points

Lamb Arrabbiata

Serves 4

Ingredients

4 tbsp olive oil
450 g/1 lb lamb fillets, cubed
1 large onion, peeled and sliced
4 garlic cloves, peeled and finely chopped
1 red chilli, deseeded and finely chopped
400 g/14 oz can chopped tomatoes
175 g/6 oz/1½ cups pitted black olives, halved
150 ml/¼ pint/⅔ cup white wine
salt and freshly ground black pepper
280 g/10 oz/2½ cups farfalle pasta
knob butter
4 tbsp freshly chopped parsley, plus 1 tbsp to garnish

Health Rating: 2 points

Heat 2 tablespoons of the olive oil in a large frying pan and cook the lamb for 5–7 minutes, or until sealed. Remove from the pan using a slotted spoon and reserve.

Heat the remaining oil in the pan, add the onion, garlic and chilli and cook until softened. Add the tomatoes, bring to the boil, then simmer for 10 minutes.

Return the browned lamb to the pan with the olives and pour in the wine. Bring the sauce back to the boil, reduce the heat, then simmer, uncovered, for 15 minutes until the lamb is tender. Season to taste with salt and pepper.

Meanwhile, bring a large pan of lightly salted water to a rolling boil. Add the pasta and cook according to the packet instructions, or until *al dente*. Drain the pasta, toss in the butter, then add to the sauce and mix lightly. Stir in 4 tablespoons of the chopped parsley, then tip into a warmed serving dish. Sprinkle with the remaining parsley and serve immediately.

Creamed Lamb & Wild Mushroom Pasta

Serves 4

Ingredients

25 g/1 oz/$^{2}/_{3}$ cup dried porcini
450 g/1 lb/4 cups pasta shapes
25 g/1 oz/$^{1}/_{4}$ stick butter
1 tbsp olive oil
350 g/12 oz lamb neck fillet, thinly sliced
1 garlic clove, peeled and crushed
225 g/8 oz/2$^{1}/_{2}$ cups chestnut/crimini mushrooms, wiped and sliced
4 tbsp white wine
125 ml/4 fl oz/$^{1}/_{2}$ cup double/heavy cream
salt and freshly ground black pepper
1 tbsp freshly chopped parsley, to garnish
freshly grated Parmesan cheese, to serve

Place the porcini in a small bowl and cover with almost-boiling water. Leave to soak for 30 minutes. Drain the porcini, reserving the soaking liquid. Chop the porcini finely. Bring a large pan of lightly salted water to a rolling boil. Add the pasta and cook according to the packet instructions, or until *al dente*.

Meanwhile, melt the butter with the olive oil in a large frying pan and fry the lamb to seal. Add the garlic, mushrooms and prepared porcini and cook for 5 minutes, or until just soft. Add the wine and the reserved porcini soaking liquid, then simmer for 2 minutes. Stir in the cream with the seasoning and simmer for 1–2 minutes, or until just thickened.

Drain the pasta thoroughly, reserving about 4 tablespoons of the cooking water. Return the pasta to the pan. Pour over the mushroom sauce and toss lightly together, adding the pasta water if the sauce is too thick. Tip into a warmed serving dish or spoon on to individual plates. Garnish with the chopped parsley and serve immediately with grated Parmesan cheese.

Health Rating: 2 points

Chicken & Asparagus with Tagliatelle

Serves 4

Ingredients

275 g/10 oz/2 cups fresh asparagus
50 g/2 oz/½ stick butter
4 spring onions/scallions, trimmed and coarsely chopped
350 g/12 oz boneless, skinless chicken breast fillets, thinly sliced
2 tbsp white vermouth
300 ml/½ pint/1 cup double/heavy cream
2 tbsp freshly chopped chives
400 g/14 oz/4½ cups fresh tagliatelle
50 g/2 oz/½ cup Parmesan or pecorino cheese, grated
snipped chives, to garnish
extra Parmesan cheese (optional), to serve

Using a swivel-bladed vegetable peeler, lightly peel the asparagus stalks, then cook in lightly salted boiling water for 2–3 minutes, or until just tender. Drain and refresh in cold water, then cut into 4 cm/1½ inch pieces and reserve.

Melt the butter in a large frying pan, then add the spring onions/scallions and the chicken and fry for 4 minutes. Add the vermouth and allow to reduce until the liquid has evaporated. Pour in the cream and half the chives. Cook gently for 5–7 minutes, until the sauce has thickened and slightly reduced and the chicken is tender.

Bring a large saucepan of lightly salted water to the boil and cook the tagliatelle for 4–5 minutes, or until *al dente*. Drain and immediately add to the chicken and cream sauce.

Using a pair of spaghetti tongs or kitchen forks, lightly toss the sauce and pasta until it is mixed thoroughly. Add the remaining chives and the Parmesan cheese and toss gently. Garnish with snipped chives and serve immediately, with extra Parmesan cheese, if wanted.

Health Rating: 2 points

Chicken, Gorgonzola & Mushroom Macaroni

Serves 4

Ingredients

450 g/1 lb/4 cups macaroni
75 g/3 oz/¾ stick butter
225 g/8 oz/2½ cups chestnut mushrooms, wiped and sliced
225 g/8 oz/2½ cups baby button mushrooms, wiped and halved
350 g/12 oz/2½ cups cooked chicken, skinned and chopped
2 tsp cornflour/cornstarch
300 ml/½ pint/1¼ cups semi-skimmed/low-fat milk
50 g/2 oz/½ cup Gorgonzola cheese, chopped, plus extra to serve
2 tbsp freshly chopped sage
1 tbsp freshly chopped chives, plus extra chive leaves to garnish
salt and freshly ground black pepper

Bring a large pan of lightly salted water to a rolling boil. Add the macaroni and cook according to the packet instructions, or until *al dente*.

Meanwhile, melt the butter in a large frying pan, add the chestnut and button mushrooms and cook for 5 minutes, or until golden, stirring occasionally. Add the chicken to the pan and cook for 4 minutes, or until heated through thoroughly and slightly golden, stirring occasionally.

Blend the cornflour/cornstarch with a little of the milk in a jug to form a smooth paste, then gradually blend in the remaining milk and pour into the frying pan. Bring to the boil slowly, stirring constantly. Add the cheese and cook for 1 minute, stirring frequently, until melted.

Stir the sage and chives into the frying pan. Season to taste with salt and pepper, then heat through. Drain the macaroni thoroughly and return to the pan. Pour the chicken and mushroom sauce over the macaroni and toss lightly to coat. Tip into a warmed serving dish and serve immediately with extra Gorgonzola cheese.

Health Rating: 1 point

Chicken & Prawn-stacked Ravioli

Serves 4

Ingredients

1 tbsp olive oil
1 onion, peeled and chopped
1 garlic clove, peeled and chopped
450 g/1 lb boned, skinned cooked chicken, cut into large pieces
1 beef tomato, deseeded and chopped
150 ml/¼ pint/⅔ cup dry white wine
150 ml/¼ pint/⅔ cup double/heavy cream
250 g/9 oz peeled cooked prawns/shrimp, thawed if frozen
2 tbsp freshly chopped tarragon, plus sprigs to garnish
salt and freshly ground black pepper
8 sheets fresh lasagne

Heat the olive oil in a large frying pan, add the onion and garlic and cook for 5 minutes, or until softened, stirring occasionally. Add the chicken pieces and fry for 4 minutes, or until heated through, turning occasionally.

Stir in the chopped tomato, wine and cream and bring to the boil. Lower the heat and simmer for about 5 minutes, or until reduced and thickened. Stir in the prawns/shrimp and tarragon. Season to taste with salt and pepper. Heat the sauce through gently.

Meanwhile, bring a large pan of lightly salted water to the boil and add 2 lasagne sheets. Return to the boil and cook for 2 minutes, stirring gently to avoid sticking. Remove from the pan using a slotted spoon and keep warm. Repeat with the remaining sheets.

Cut each sheet of lasagne in half. Place two pieces on each of the warmed plates and divide half of the chicken mixture among them. Top each serving with a second sheet of lasagne and divide the remainder of the chicken mixture among them. Top with a final layer of lasagne. Garnish with tarragon sprigs and serve immediately.

Health Rating: 2 points

Turkey Tetrazzini

Serves 4

Ingredients

280 g/10 oz/3$^{1}/_{4}$ cups green and white tagliatelle
50 g/2 oz/$^{1}/_{2}$ stick butter, 4 slices streaky/fatty bacon, diced
1 onion, peeled and finely chopped
175 g/6 oz/1$^{1}/_{2}$ cups mushrooms, thinly sliced
40 g/1$^{1}/_{2}$ oz/$^{1}/_{3}$ cup plain/all-purpose flour
450 ml/$^{3}/_{4}$ pint/1$^{3}/_{4}$ cups chicken stock
150 ml/$^{1}/_{4}$ pint/$^{1}/_{3}$ cup double/heavy cream
2 tbsp sherry
450 g/1 lb/3 cups cooked turkey meat, cut into bite-sized pieces
1 tbsp freshly chopped parsley, freshly grated nutmeg
salt and freshly ground black pepper
25 g/1 oz/$^{1}/_{4}$ cup grated Parmesan cheese

To garnish:
freshly chopped parsley; grated Parmesan cheese

Preheat the oven to 180°C/350°F/Gas Mark 4. Lightly oil a large ovenproof dish. Bring a large saucepan of lightly salted water to the boil. Add the tagliatelle and cook for 7–9 minutes, or until *al dente*. Drain well and reserve.

In a heavy-based saucepan, heat the butter and add the bacon. Cook for 2–3 minutes, or until crisp and golden. Add the onion and mushrooms and cook for 3–4 minutes, or until the vegetables are tender.

Stir in the flour and cook for 2 minutes. Remove from the heat and slowly stir in the stock. Return to the heat and cook, stirring, until a smooth, thick sauce has formed. Add the tagliatelle, then pour in the cream and sherry. Add the turkey and parsley. Season to taste with the nutmeg and salt and pepper. Toss well to coat.

Turn the mixture into the prepared dish, spreading evenly. Sprinkle the top with the Parmesan cheese and bake in the preheated oven for 30–35 minutes, or until crisp, golden and bubbling. Garnish with chopped parsley and Parmesan cheese and serve straight from the dish.

Health Rating: 1 point

Vegetarian Spaghetti Bolognese

Serves 4

Ingredients

2 tbsp olive oil
1 onion, peeled and finely chopped
1 carrot, peeled and finely chopped
1 celery stalk, trimmed and finely chopped
225 g/8 oz minced Quorn/soy meat substitute
150 ml/$^1/_4$ pt/$^1/_2$ cup red wine
300 ml/$^1/_2$ pt/1$^1/_4$ cup vegetable stock
1 tsp ketchup
4 tbsp tomato puree/paste
350 g/12 oz/4 cups dried spaghetti
4 tbsp half/reduced fat crème fraîche/sour cream
salt and freshly ground black pepper
1 tbsp freshly chopped parsley

Heat the oil in a large saucepan and add the onion, carrot and celery. Cook gently for 10 minutes, adding a little water if necessary, until softened and starting to brown.

Add the minced Quorn/soy meat substitute and cook for a further 2–3 minutes before adding the red wine. Increase the heat and simmer gently until nearly all the wine has evaporated.

Mix together the vegetable stock and ketchup and add about half to the Quorn mixture along with the tomato puree/paste. Cover and simmer gently for about 45 minutes, adding the remaining stock as necessary.

Meanwhile, bring a large pan of salted water to the boil and add the spaghetti. Cook until *al dente*, or according to the packet instructions. Drain well. Remove the sauce from the heat, add the crème fraîche/sour cream and season to taste with salt and pepper. Stir in the parsley and serve immediately with the pasta.

Health Rating: 4 points

Potato Gnocchi with Pesto Sauce

Serves 6

Ingredients

900 g/2 lb floury potatoes
40 g/1½ oz/3 tbsp butter
1 egg, beaten
225 g/8 oz/2 cups plain/all-purpose flour
1 tsp salt
freshly ground black pepper
25 g/1 oz/⅓ cup shaved Parmesan cheese
rocket/arugula salad, to serve

For the pesto sauce:
50 g/2 oz/2 packed cups fresh basil leaves
1 large garlic clove, peeled
2 tbsp pine nuts
125 ml/4 fl oz/½ cup olive oil
40 g/1½ oz/⅓ cup grated Parmesan cheese

Cook the potatoes in their skins in boiling water for 20 minutes, or until tender. Drain and peel. While still warm, push the potatoes through a fine sieve/strainer into a bowl. Stir in the butter, egg, 175 g/6 oz/1½ cups of the flour, the salt and pepper.

Sift the remaining flour on to a board or work surface and add the potato mixture. Gently knead in enough flour until a soft, slightly sticky dough is formed.

With floured hands, break off portions of the dough and roll into 2.5 cm/1 inch thick ropes. Cut into 2 cm/¾ inch lengths. Lightly press each piece against the inner prongs of a fork. Put on a tray covered with a floured dishtowel and chill in the refrigerator for about 30 minutes.

To make the pesto sauce, put the basil, garlic, pine nuts and oil in a food processor and blend until smooth and creamy. Turn into a bowl and stir in the Parmesan cheese. Season to taste.

Cooking in several batches, drop the gnocchi into a saucepan of barely simmering salted water. Cook for 3–4 minutes, or until they float to the surface. Remove with a slotted spoon and keep warm in a covered oiled baking dish in a low oven.

Add the gnocchi to the pesto sauce and toss gently to coat. Serve immediately, scattered with the Parmesan cheese and accompanied by a rocket/arugula salad.

Health Rating: 2 points

Fettucini with Roasted Beetroot & Rocket

Serves 4

Ingredients

350 g/12 oz (about 4) raw baby beetroot, unpeeled
1 garlic clove, peeled and crushed
$^{1}/_{2}$ tsp finely grated orange rind
1 tbsp orange juice
1 tsp lemon juice
2 tbsp walnut oil
salt and freshly ground black pepper
350 g/12 oz dried fettucini
75 g/3 oz/$3^{3}/_{4}$ cups rocket/arugula leaves
125 g/4 oz/1 cup Dolcelatte cheese, cut into small cubes

Preheat the oven to 150°C/300°F/Gas Mark 2, 10 minutes before cooking. Wrap the beetroot individually in kitchen foil and bake for 1–$1^{1}/_{2}$ hours, or until tender. (Test by opening one of the parcels and scraping the skin away from the stem end – it should come off very easily.)

Leave the beetroot until cool enough to handle, then peel and cut each beetroot into six to eight wedges, depending on the size. Mix the garlic, orange rind and juice, lemon juice, walnut oil and salt and pepper together, then drizzle over the beetroot and toss to coat well.

Meanwhile, bring a large saucepan of lightly salted water to the boil. Cook the pasta for 10 minutes, or until *al dente*.

Drain the pasta thoroughly, then add the warm beetroot, rocket/arugula leaves and Dolcelatte cheese. Quickly and gently toss together, then divide between serving bowls and serve immediately before the rocket wilts.

Health Rating: 3 points

Tagliatelle with Broccoli & Sesame

Serves 2

Ingredients

225 g/8 oz/$2^{2}/_{3}$ cup broccoli, cut into florets
125 g/$4^{1}/_{2}$ oz/1 cup baby sweetcorn
175 g/6 oz/$1^{1}/_{2}$ cups dried tagliatelle
$1^{1}/_{2}$ tbsp tahini paste
1 tbsp dark soy sauce
1 tbsp dark muscovado sugar
1 tbsp red wine vinegar
1 tbsp sunflower oil
1 garlic clove, peeled and finely chopped
2.5 cm/1 inch piece fresh root ginger, peeled and shredded
$^{1}/_{2}$ tsp dried chilli flakes
salt and freshly ground black pepper
1 tbsp toasted sesame seeds
radish slices, to garnish

Bring a large saucepan of salted water to the boil and add the broccoli and corn. Return the water to the boil, then remove the vegetables at once using a slotted spoon, reserving the water. Plunge them into cold water and drain well. Dry on absorbent paper towels and reserve.

Return the water to the boil. Add the tagliatelle and cook until *al dente*, or according to the packet instructions. Drain well. Run under cold water until cold, then drain well again.

Place the tahini, soy sauce, sugar and vinegar into a bowl. Mix well, then reserve. Heat the oil in a wok or large frying pan over a high heat and add the garlic, ginger and chilli flakes and stir-fry for about 30 seconds. Add the broccoli and baby corn and continue to stir-fry for about 3 minutes.

Add the tagliatelle to the wok along with the tahini mixture and stir together for a further 1–2 minutes until heated through. Season to taste with salt and pepper. Sprinkle with sesame seeds, garnish with the radish slices and serve immediately.

Health Rating: 4 points

Pasta with Spicy Red Pepper Sauce

Serves 4

Ingredients

2 red peppers
2 tbsp olive oil
1 onion, peeled and chopped
2 garlic cloves, peeled and crushed
4 anchovy fillets (optional)
1 red chilli, deseeded and finely chopped
200 g/7 oz can chopped tomatoes
finely grated rind and juice of ½ lemon
salt and freshly ground black pepper
2–3 tbsp vegetable stock (optional)
400 g/14 oz/5¼ cups dried pasta, such as tagliatelle, linguine or shells

To garnish:
shaved Parmesan cheese
fresh basil leaves

Preheat the grill/broiler. Set the whole peppers on the grill rack about 10 cm/4 inches away from the heat. Turn frequently for 10 minutes, or until the skins are blackened and blistered.

Put the peppers in a plastic container and leave until cool enough to handle. Peel off the skin, then halve the peppers and scrape away the seeds. Chop the pepper flesh roughly and put in a food processor or blender.

Heat the olive oil in a large saucepan and gently fry the onion for 5 minutes. Stir in the garlic, anchovy fillets (if using) and chilli and cook for a further 5 minutes, stirring. Add to the food processor and blend until fairly smooth.

Return the mixture to the saucepan with the tomatoes and stir in the lemon rind and juice. Season to taste with salt and pepper. Add 2–3 tablespoons vegetable stock if the sauce is a little thick. Bring to the boil and bubble for 1–2 minutes.

Meanwhile, bring a large saucepan of lightly salted water to the boil and cook the pasta for 10 minutes, or until *al dente*. Drain thoroughly. Add the sauce and toss well to coat. Tip into a warmed serving dish or on to individual plates. Scatter with shavings of Parmesan cheese and a few basil leaves before serving.

Health Rating: 4 points

Rigatoni with Oven-dried Cherry Tomatoes

Serves 4

Ingredients

350 g/12 oz/3 cups red cherry tomatoes
1 tsp caster/superfine sugar
salt and freshly ground black pepper
2 tbsp olive oil
400 g/14 oz/5¼ cups dried rigatoni
125 g/4½ oz/1 cup frozen peas
2 tbsp mascarpone cheese
1 tbsp freshly chopped mint
1 tbsp freshly chopped parsley
fresh mint sprigs, to garnish

Preheat the oven to 140°C/275°F/Gas Mark 1. Halve the cherry tomatoes and place close together on a nonstick baking tray, cut-side up. Sprinkle lightly with the sugar, then with a little salt and pepper. Bake in the preheated oven for 1¼ hours, or until dry but not beginning to colour. Leave to cool on the baking tray. Put in a bowl, drizzle over the olive oil and toss to coat.

Bring a large saucepan of lightly salted water to the boil and cook the pasta for about 10 minutes, or until *al dente*. Add the frozen peas 2–3 minutes before the end of the cooking time. Drain thoroughly and return the pasta and the peas to the saucepan.

Add the mascarpone to the saucepan. When melted, add the tomatoes, mint, parsley and a little black pepper. Toss gently together, then transfer to a warmed serving dish or individual plates and garnish with fresh mint sprigs. Serve immediately.

Health Rating: 4 points

Pasta Primavera

Serves 4

Ingredients

150 g/5 oz/1 cup French/green beans
150 g/5 oz/1 cup sugar snap peas
40 g/1½ oz/3 tbsp butter
1 tsp olive oil
225 g/8 oz/1 cup baby carrots, scrubbed
2 courgettes/zucchini, trimmed and thinly sliced
175 g/6 oz/¼ cup baby leeks, trimmed and cut into 2.5 cm/1 inch lengths
200 ml/7 fl oz/1 cup double/heavy cream
1 tsp finely grated lemon rind
350 g/12 oz/4 cups dried tagliatelle
25 g/1 oz/¼ cup Parmesan cheese, grated
1 tbsp freshly snipped chives
1 tbsp freshly chopped dill
salt and freshly ground black pepper
fresh dill sprigs, to garnish

Trim and halve the French/green beans. Bring a large saucepan of lightly salted water to the boil and cook the beans for 4–5 minutes, adding the sugar snap after 2 minutes so that both are tender at the same time. Drain the beans and sugar snap peas and briefly rinse under cold running water.

Heat the butter and oil in a large nonstick frying pan. Add the baby carrots and cook for 2 minutes, then stir in the courgettes/zucchini and leeks and cook for 10 minutes, stirring, until the vegetables are almost tender.

Stir the cream and lemon rind into the vegetables and bubble over a gentle heat until the sauce is slightly reduced and the vegetables are cooked.

Meanwhile, bring a large saucepan of lightly salted water to the boil and cook the tagliatelle for 10 minutes, or until *al dente*.

Add the beans, sugar snaps, Parmesan cheese and herbs to the sauce. Stir for 30 seconds, or until the cheese has melted and the vegetables are hot.

Drain the tagliatelle, add the vegetables and sauce. Toss gently to mix. Season to taste with salt and pepper. Spoon into a warmed serving bowl, garnish with a few dill sprigs and serve immediately.

Health Rating: 4 points

Spaghetti with Pesto

Serves 4

Ingredients

200 g/7 oz/1¾ cups freshly grated Parmesan cheese, plus extra to serve
25 g/1 oz/⅓ cup fresh basil leaves, plus extra to garnish
6 tbsp pine nuts
3 large garlic cloves, peeled
200 ml/7 fl oz/¾ cup extra virgin olive oil, plus more if necessary
salt and freshly ground black pepper
400 g/14 oz spaghetti

Health Rating: 2 points

To make the pesto, place the Parmesan cheese in a food processor with the basil leaves, pine nuts and garlic and process until well blended.

With the motor running, gradually pour in the extra virgin olive oil until a thick sauce forms. Add a little more oil if the sauce seems too thick.

Season to taste with salt and pepper. Transfer to a bowl, cover and store in the refrigerator until required.

Bring a large pan of lightly salted water to a rolling boil. Add the spaghetti and cook according to the packet instructions, or until *al dente*. Drain the spaghetti thoroughly and return to the pan.

Stir the pesto into the spaghetti and toss lightly. Heat through gently, then tip the pasta into a warmed serving dish or spoon on to individual plates. Garnish with basil leaves and serve immediately with extra Parmesan cheese.

Four-cheese Tagliatelle

Serves 4

Ingredients

300 ml/½ pint/1¼ cups whipping cream
4 garlic cloves, peeled and lightly bruised
75 g/3 oz/¾ cup fontina cheese, diced
75 g/3 oz/¾ cup Gruyère cheese, grated
75 g/3 oz/¾ cup mozzarella cheese, diced
50 g/2 oz/½ cup Parmesan cheese, grated, plus extra to serve
salt and freshly ground black pepper
275 g/10 oz/3 cups fresh green tagliatelle
1–2 tbsp freshly snipped chives
fresh basil leaves, to garnish

Health Rating: 1 point

Place the whipping cream with the garlic cloves in a medium pan and heat gently until small bubbles begin to form around the edge of the pan. Using a slotted spoon, remove and discard the garlic cloves.

Add all the cheeses to the pan and stir until melted. Season with a little salt and a lot of black pepper. Keep the sauce warm over a low heat, but do not allow to boil.

Meanwhile, bring a large pan of lightly salted water to the boil. Add the tagliatelle, return to the boil and cook for 2–3 minutes, or until *al dente*.

Drain the pasta thoroughly and return to the pan. Pour the sauce over the pasta, add the chives, then toss lightly until well coated. Tip into a warmed serving dish or spoon on to individual plates. Garnish with a few basil leaves and serve immediately with extra Parmesan cheese.

Pumpkin-filled Pasta with Butter & Sage

Serves 6–8

Ingredients

For the pasta dough:

225 g/8 oz/1¾ cups strong plain bread flour, or type '00' pasta flour, plus extra for rolling
1 tsp salt
2 medium/large eggs
1 medium/large egg yolk
1 tbsp extra virgin olive oil

For the filling:

250 g/9 oz/1 cup freshly cooked pumpkin or sweet potato flesh, mashed and cooled
75–125 g/3–4 oz/⅓ cup dried breadcrumbs
125 g/4 oz/1 cup freshly grated Parmesan cheese
1 medium/large egg yolk
½ tsp soft brown sugar
2 tbsp freshly chopped parsley
freshly grated nutmeg
salt and freshly ground black pepper
125 g/4 oz/1 stick plus 1 tbsp butter
2 tbsp freshly shredded sage leaves
50 g/2 oz/½ cup freshly grated Parmesan cheese, to serve

To make the dough, sift the flour and salt into a large bowl, make a well in the centre and add the eggs and yolk, 1 tablespoon oil and 1 teaspoon water. Gradually mix to form a soft but not sticky dough, adding a little more flour or water as necessary. Turn out on to a lightly floured surface and knead for 5 minutes, or until smooth and elastic. Wrap in clingfilm/plastic wrap and leave to rest at room temperature for about 30 minutes.

Mix together the ingredients for the filling in a bowl, seasoning to taste with freshly grated nutmeg, salt and pepper. If the mixture seems too wet, add a few more breadcrumbs to bind.

Cut the pasta dough into quarters. Work with one quarter at a time, covering the remaining quarters with a damp dishtowel. Roll out a quarter very thinly into a strip 10 cm/4 inches wide. Drop spoonfuls of the filling along the strip 6.5 cm/2½ inches apart, in two rows about 5 cm/2 inches apart. Moisten the outside edges and the spaces between the filling with water.

Roll out another strip of pasta and lay it over the filled strip. Press down gently along both edges and between the filled sections. Using a fluted pastry wheel, cut along both long sides, down the centre and between the fillings to form cushions. Transfer the cushions to a lightly floured baking sheet. Continue making cushions and allow to dry for 30 minutes.

Bring a large saucepan of slightly salted water to the boil. Add the pasta cushions and return to the boil. Cook, stirring frequently, for 4–5 minutes, or until *al dente*. Drain carefully.

Heat the butter in a pan, stir in the shredded sage leaves and cook for 30 seconds. Add the pasta cushions, stir gently, then spoon into serving bowls. Sprinkle with the grated Parmesan cheese and serve immediately.

Health Rating: 2 points

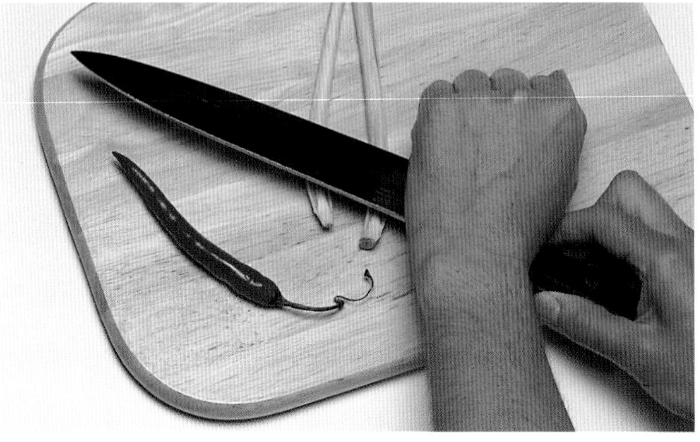

Thai Noodles & Vegetables with Tofu

Serves 4

Ingredients

225 g/8 oz/scant 1 cup firm tofu
2 tbsp soy sauce
rind of 1 lime, grated
2 lemon grass stalks
1 red chilli
1 litre/1¾ pints/1 quart vegetable stock
2 slices fresh root ginger, peeled
2 garlic cloves, peeled
2 fresh coriander/cilantro sprigs
175 g/6 oz dried thread egg noodles
125 g/4 oz/1¼ cup shiitake or button mushrooms, sliced if large
2 carrots, peeled and cut into matchsticks
125 g/4 oz/1 cup mangetout/snow peas
125 g/4 oz/1¼ cups bok choy/pak choi or other Chinese leaf
1 tbsp freshly chopped coriander/cilantro
salt and freshly ground black pepper
coriander/cilantro sprigs, to garnish

Drain the tofu well and cut into cubes. Put into a shallow dish with the soy sauce and lime rind. Stir well to coat and leave to marinate for 30 minutes.

Meanwhile, put lemon grass and chilli on a chopping board and bruise with the side of a large knife, ensuring blade is pointing away from you. Put the vegetable stock in a large saucepan, add the lemon grass, chilli, ginger, garlic and coriander/cilantro. Bring to the boil, cover and simmer gently for 20 minutes.

Strain the stock into a clean pan. Return to the boil and add the noodles, tofu and its marinade and the mushrooms. Simmer gently for 4 minutes. Add the carrots, mangetout/snow peas, bok choy and coriander and simmer for a further 3–4 minutes until the vegetables are just tender. Season to taste with salt and pepper. Garnish with coriander sprigs. Serve immediately.

Health Rating: 5 points

Singapore Noodles

Serves 4

Ingredients

225 g/8 oz thin round egg noodles
3 tbsp groundnut/peanut or vegetable oil
125 g/4½ oz/2 cups field mushrooms, wiped and thinly sliced
2.5 cm/1 inch piece root ginger, peeled and finely chopped
1 red chilli, deseeded and thinly sliced
1 red pepper, deseeded and thinly sliced
2 garlic cloves, peeled and crushed
1 courgette/zucchini, cut in half lengthways and diagonally sliced
4–6 spring onions/scallions, trimmed and thinly sliced
50 g/2 oz/⅓ cup frozen garden peas, thawed
1 tbsp curry paste, 2 tbsp tomato ketchup
salt or soy sauce
125 g/4½ oz/1 cup beansprouts, rinsed and drained

To garnish:
sesame seeds; fresh coriander/cilantro leaves

Bring a large pan of lightly salted water to a rolling boil. Add the noodles and cook according to the packet instructions, or until *al dente*. Drain thoroughly and toss with 1 tablespoon of the oil.

Heat the remaining oil in a wok or large frying pan over a high heat. Add the mushrooms, ginger, chilli and pepper and stir-fry for 2 minutes. Add the garlic, courgette/zucchini, spring onions/scallions and garden peas. Stir lightly.

Push the vegetables to one side and add the curry paste, tomato ketchup and about 125 ml/4 fl oz/½ cup hot water. Season to taste with salt or a few drops of soy sauce and allow to boil vigorously, stirring, until the paste is smooth. Stir the reserved egg noodles and the beansprouts into the vegetable mixture and stir-fry until coated with the paste and thoroughly heated through.

Season with more soy sauce if necessary, then turn into a large warmed serving bowl or spoon on to individual plates. Garnish with sesame seeds and coriander/cilantro leaves and serve immediately.

Health Rating: 5 points

Desserts

Everyone loves dessert! Treat yourself and your family to something sweet. Ranging from the relatively healthy Fruit Salad, to the purely indulgent Mocha Pie, this chapter provides recipes that are the perfect way to finish off a great meal. All are easy to make and will disappear in no time!

Sweet-stewed Dried Fruits

Serves 4

Ingredients

500 g/1 lb 2 oz packet mixed dried fruit salad
450 ml/¾ pint/1¾ cups apple juice
2 tbsp clear honey
2 tbsp brandy
1 lemon
1 orange

To decorate:
half-fat crème fraîche/sour cream
fine strips of pared orange rind

Place the fruits, apple juice, clear honey and brandy in a small saucepan.

Using a small, sharp knife or a zester, carefully remove the zest from the lemon and orange and place in the pan.

Squeeze the juice from the lemon and orange and add to the pan.

Bring the fruit mixture to the boil and simmer for about 1 minute. Remove the pan from the heat and allow the mixture to cool completely.

Transfer the mixture to a large bowl, cover with clingfilm/plastic wrap and chill in the refrigerator overnight to allow the flavours to blend.

Spoon the stewed fruit into four shallow dessert dishes. Decorate with a large spoonful of half-fat crème fraîche/sour cream and a few strips of the pared orange rind and serve.

Health Rating: 5 points

Grape & Almond Layer

Serves 4

Ingredients

300 ml/½ pint/1¼ cups fromage frais/reduced-fat sour cream
300 ml/½ pint/1¼ cups Greek/plain yogurt
3 tbsp icing/confectioners' sugar, sifted
2 tbsp crème de cassis
450 g/1 lb/3 cups red grapes
175 g/6 oz (about 30) Amaretti biscuits/cookies
2 ripe passion fruit

To decorate:
icing/confectioners' sugar
extra grapes (optional)

Mix together the fromage frais/reduced-fat sour cream and yogurt in a bowl. Lightly fold in the sifted icing/confectioners' sugar and crème de cassis with a large metal spoon or rubber spatula until lightly blended.

Using a small knife, remove the seeds from the grapes, if necessary. Rinse lightly and pat dry on absorbent paper towels. Place the deseeded grapes in a bowl and stir in any juice from the grapes from deseeding.

Place the Amaretti biscuits/cookies in a plastic bag and crush roughly with a rolling pin, or use a food processor.

Cut the passion fruit in half, scoop out the seeds with a teaspoon and reserve.

Divide the yogurt mixture between four tall glasses, then layer alternately with grapes, crushed biscuits and most of the passion fruit seeds. Top with the yogurt mixture and the remaining passion fruit seeds. Chill for 1 hour and decorate with extra grapes.

Lightly dust with icing sugar and serve.

Health Rating: 2 points

Fruit Salad

Serves 4

Ingredients

125 g/4½ oz/⅔ cup caster/superfine sugar
3 oranges, 700 g/1½ lb lychees, peeled and stoned
1 small mango; 1 small pineapple
1 papaya; 4 pieces stem ginger in syrup
4 tbsp stem ginger syrup
125 g/4½ oz/¾ cup Cape gooseberries/ground cherries
125 g/4½ oz/1 cup strawberries, hulled
½ tsp almond essence

To decorate:
mint leaves; lime zest

Place the sugar and 300 ml/½ pint/1¼ cups water in a small pan and heat, stirring gently, until the sugar has dissolved. Bring to the boil and simmer for 2 minutes. Once a syrup has formed, remove from the heat and allow to cool.

Using a sharp knife, cut away the skin from the oranges, then slice thickly. Cut each slice in half and place in a serving dish with the syrup and lychees.

Peel the mango, then cut into thick slices around each side of the stone. Discard the stone, cut the slices into bite-sized pieces and add to the syrup. Using a sharp knife again, carefully cut away the skin from the pineapple. Remove the central core using the knife or an apple corer, then cut the pineapple into segments and add to the syrup.

Peel the papaya, then cut in half and remove the seeds. Cut the flesh into chunks, slice the ginger into matchsticks and add with the ginger syrup to the fruit in the syrup. Prepare the Cape gooseberries/ground cherries by removing the thin, papery skins and rinsing lightly.

Halve the strawberries, add to the fruit with the almond essence and chill for 30 minutes.Scatter with mint leaves and lime zest to decorate and serve.

Health Rating: 5 points

Poached Pears

Serves 4

Ingredients

2 small cinnamon sticks
125 g/4 oz/$^2/_3$ cup caster/superfine sugar
300 ml/$^1/_2$ pint/1$^1/_4$ cups red wine
150 ml/$^1/_4$ pint/$^2/_3$ cup water
thinly pared rind and juice of 1 small orange
4 firm pears
orange slices, to decorate
frozen vanilla yogurt or low-fat ice cream, to serve

Place the cinnamon sticks on the work surface and with a rolling pin, slowly roll down the side of the cinnamon stick to bruise. Place in a large heavy-based saucepan.

Add the sugar, wine, water, pared orange rind and juice to the pan and bring slowly to the boil, stirring occasionally, until the sugar is dissolved.

Meanwhile, peel the pears, leaving the stalks on. Cut out the cores from the bottom of the pears and level them so that they stand upright.

Stand the pears in the syrup, cover the pan and simmer for 20 minutes, or until tender.

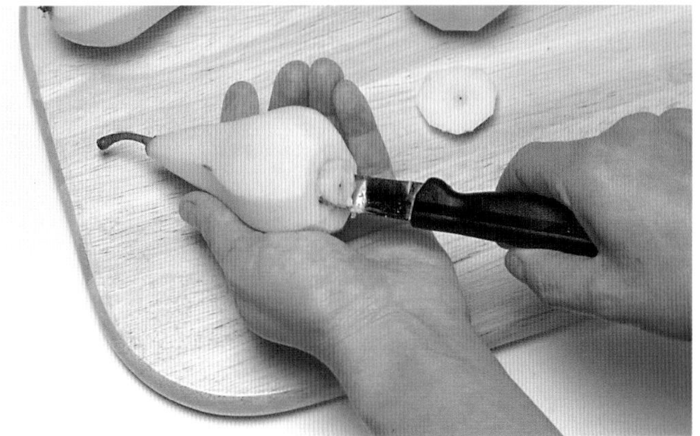

Remove the pan from the heat and leave the pears to cool in the syrup, turning occasionally.

Arrange the pears on serving plates and spoon over the syrup. Decorate with the orange slices and serve with the yogurt or low-fat ice cream and any remaining juices.

Health Rating: 5 points

Stir-fried Bananas & Peaches with Rum Butterscotch Sauce

Serves 4

Ingredients

2 medium-firm bananas, peeled and cut into 2.5 cm/1 inch diagonal slices, 1 tbsp caster/superfine sugar
2 tsp lime juice; 4 firm, ripe peaches or nectarines
1 tbsp sunflower oil

For the sauce:
50 g/2 oz/½ stick unsalted butter
50 g/2 oz/¼ cup soft light brown sugar
125 g/4½ oz/⅔ cup demerara/light brown sugar
300 ml/½ pint/1¼ cups double/heavy cream; 2 tbsp dark rum

Place the bananas in a bowl, sprinkle with the caster/superfine sugar and lime juice and stir until lightly coated. Reserve.

Place the peaches or nectarines in a large bowl and pour over boiling water to cover. Leave for 30 seconds, then plunge them into cold water and peel off their skins. Cut each one into eight thick slices, discarding the stone.

Heat a wok, add the oil and swirl it round the wok to coat the sides. Add the fruit and cook for 3–4 minutes, shaking the wok and gently turning the fruit until lightly browned. Spoon the fruit into a warmed serving bowl and clean the wok with absorbent paper towels.

Add the butter and sugars to the wok and stir continuously over a very low heat until the sugar has dissolved. Remove from the heat and leave to cool for 2–3 minutes.

Stir the cream and rum into the sugar syrup and return to the heat. Bring to the boil and simmer for 2 minutes, stirring continuously, until smooth. Leave for 2–3 minutes to cool slightly, then serve warm with the stir-fried peaches and bananas.

Health Rating: 2 points

Summer Pavlova

Serves 6–8

Ingredients

4 egg whites
225 g/8 oz/1 cup caster/superfine sugar
1 tsp vanilla essence
2 tsp white wine vinegar
1½ tsp cornflour/cornstarch
300 ml/½ pint/1 cup Greek/plain yogurt
2 tbsp honey
225 g/8 oz/2 cups strawberries, hulled
125 g/4½ oz/1 cup raspberries
125 g/4½ oz/1 cup blueberries
4 kiwis, peeled and sliced
icing/confectioners' sugar, to decorate

Preheat the oven to 150°C/300°F/Gas Mark 2. Line a baking tray with a sheet of greaseproof/waxed paper or baking parchment.

Place the egg whites in a clean, grease-free bowl and whisk until very stiff.

Whisk in half the sugar, vanilla essence, vinegar and cornflour/cornstarch and continue whisking until stiff.

Gradually whisk in the remaining sugar, a teaspoonful at a time, until the mixture is very stiff and glossy.

Using a large spoon, arrange the meringue in a circle on the greaseproof paper or baking parchment.

Bake in the preheated oven for 1 hour until crisp and dry. Turn the oven off and leave the meringue in the oven to cool completely. Remove the meringue from the baking sheet and peel away the paper. Mix together the yogurt and honey. Place the pavlova on a serving plate and spoon the yogurt into the centre.

Sprinkle with the strawberries, raspberries, blueberries and kiwis. Dust with the icing/confectioners' sugar and serve.

Health Rating: 2 points

Hazelnut, Chocolate & Chestnut Meringue Torte

Serves 8–10

Ingredients

For the chocolate meringue:

1 medium/large egg white
50 g/2 oz/¼ cup caster/superfine sugar
2 tbsp cocoa powder

For the hazelnut meringue:

75 g/3 oz/½ cup hazelnuts, toasted
2 medium/large egg whites
125 g/4 oz/⅔ cup caster/superfine sugar

For the filling:

300 ml/½ pint/1¼ cups double/heavy cream
250 g/9 oz can sweetened chestnut puree
50 g/2 oz dark/bittersweet chocolate, melted
25 g/1 oz dark/bittersweet chocolate, grated

Preheat the oven to 130°C/250°F/Gas Mark ½. Line three baking sheets with nonstick baking parchment and draw a 20 cm/8 inch circle on each. Beat 1 egg white until stiff peaks form. Add 25 g/1 oz/⅛ cup of the sugar and beat until shiny. Mix the cocoa with the remaining 25 g/1 oz/⅛ cup of sugar, adding 1 tablespoon at a time, beating well after each addition, until all the sugar is added and the mixture is stiff and glossy. Spread on to 1 of the baking sheets within the circle drawn on the underside.

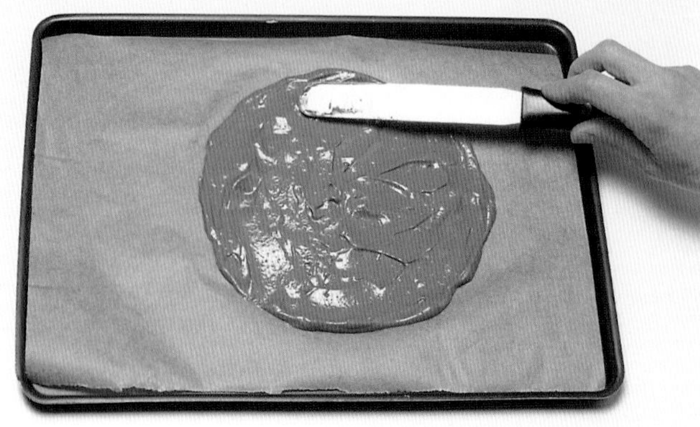

Put the hazelnuts in a food processor and blend until chopped. In a clean bowl, beat the 2 egg whites until stiff. Add 50 g/2 oz/¼ cup of the sugar and beat. Add the remaining sugar about 1 tablespoon at a time, beating after each addition, until all the sugar is added and the mixture is stiff and glossy.

Reserve 2 tablespoons of the nuts, then fold in the remainder and divide between the two remaining baking sheets. Sprinkle one of the hazelnut meringues with the reserved hazelnuts and transfer all the baking sheets to the oven. Bake in the preheated oven for 1½ hours. Turn the oven off and leave in the oven until cold.

Whip the cream until thick. Beat the chestnut puree in another bowl until soft. Add a spoonful of the cream and fold together before adding the remaining cream and melted chocolate and folding together.

Place the plain hazelnut meringue on a serving plate. Top with half the cream and chestnut mixture. Add the chocolate meringue and top with the remaining cream. Add the final meringue. Sprinkle over the grated chocolate and serve.

Health Rating: 1 point

Summer Pudding

Serves 6–8

Ingredients

450 g/1 lb/4 cups redcurrants
125 g/4½ oz/⅔ cup caster/superfine sugar
350 g/12 oz/3 cups strawberries, hulled and halved
125 g/4½ oz/1 cup raspberries
2 tbsp Grand Marnier or Cointreau
8–10 slices white bread, crusts removed
mint sprigs, to decorate
Greek/plain yogurt or low-fat fromage frais/reduced-fat sour cream, to serve

Place the redcurrants, sugar and 1 tablespoon water in a large saucepan. Heat gently until the sugar has just dissolved and the juices have just begun to run. Remove the saucepan from the heat and stir in the strawberries, raspberries and the Grand Marnier or Cointreau.

Line the base and sides of a 1.1 litre/2 pint/1¼ quart pudding basin with two thirds of the bread, making sure that the slices overlap each other slightly.

Spoon the fruit with their juices into the bread-lined pudding basin, then top with the remaining bread slices.

Place a small plate on top of the pudding inside the pudding basin. Ensure the plate fits tightly, then weigh down with a clean can or some weights and chill in the refrigerator overnight.

When ready to serve, remove the weights and plate. Carefully loosen round the sides of the basin with a round-bladed knife. Invert the pudding on to a serving plate, decorate with the mint sprigs and serve with the yogurt or fromage frais/reduced-fat sour cream.

Health Rating: 4 points

Creamy Puddings with Mixed Berry Compote

Serves 6

Ingredients

300 ml/½ pint/1¼ cups half-fat double/heavy cream
250 g/9 oz carton ricotta cheese
50 g/2 oz/¼ cup sugar
125 g/4½ oz white chocolate, broken into pieces
350 g/12 oz/2 cups mixed summer fruits such as strawberries, blueberries and raspberries
2 tbsp Cointreau

Whip the cream until soft peaks form. Fold in the ricotta cheese and half the sugar. Place the chocolate in a bowl set over a saucepan of simmering water. Stir until melted. Remove from the heat and leave to cool, stirring occasionally.

Stir into the cheese mixture until well blended. Spoon the mixture into six individual pudding moulds and level the surface of each pudding with the back of a spoon. Place in the freezer for 4 hours on quick freeze.

Place the fruits and the remaining sugar in a pan and heat gently, stirring occasionally, until the sugar has dissolved and the juices are just beginning to run. Stir in the Cointreau to taste.

Dip the pudding moulds in hot water for 30 seconds and invert on to six serving plates. Spoon the fruit compote over the puddings and serve immediately. Remember to return the freezer to its normal setting.

Health Rating: 2 points

Vanilla & Lemon Panna Cotta with Raspberry Sauce

Serves 6

Ingredients

900 ml/1½ pints/3½ cups double/heavy cream
1 vanilla pod, split
100 g/3½ oz/½ cup sugar
zest of 1 lemon
3 sheets gelatine
5 tbsp milk
450 g/1 lb/3 cups raspberries
3–4 tbsp icing/confectioners' sugar, to taste
1 tbsp lemon juice
extra lemon zest, to decorate

Put the cream, vanilla pod and sugar into a saucepan. Bring to the boil, then simmer for 10 minutes until slightly reduced, stirring to prevent scalding. Remove from the heat, stir in the lemon zest and remove the vanilla pod.

Soak the gelatine in the milk for 5 minutes, or until softened. Squeeze out any excess milk and add to the hot cream. Stir well until dissolved.

Pour the cream mixture into six ramekins or mini pudding moulds and leave in the refrigerator for 4 hours, or until set.

Meanwhile, put 175 g/6 oz/1½ cups of the raspberries in a food processor with the icing/confectioners' sugar and lemon juice. Blend to a puree, then pass the mixture through a sieve. Stir in the remaining raspberries with a metal spoon or rubber spatula and chill in the refrigerator until ready to serve.

To serve, dip each of the moulds into hot water for a few seconds, then turn out on to individual serving plates. Spoon some of the raspberry sauce over and around the panna cotta, decorate with extra lemon zest and serve.

Health Rating: 1 point

Lemon & Apricot Pudding

Serves 4

Ingredients

125 g/4½ oz/scant 1 cup dried apricots
3 tbsp orange juice, warmed
50 g/2 oz/½ stick butter
125 g/4½ oz/⅔ cup caster/superfine sugar
juice and grated rind of 2 lemons
2 eggs, separated
100 g/3½ oz/¾ cup self-raising flour
300 ml/½ pint/1¼ cups milk
custard or fresh cream, to serve

Preheat the oven to 180°C/350°F/Gas Mark 4. Oil a 1.2 litre/2 pint/1¼ quart pie dish.

Soak the apricots in the orange juice for 10–15 minutes, or until most of the juice has been absorbed, then place in the base of the pie dish. Cream the butter and sugar together with the lemon rind until light and fluffy. Beat the egg yolks into the creamed mixture with a spoonful of flour after each addition. Add the remaining flour and beat well until smooth.

Stir the milk and lemon juice into the creamed mixture. Whisk the egg whites in a grease-free mixing bowl until stiff and standing in peaks. Fold into the mixture using a metal spoon or rubber spatula. Pour into the prepared dish and place in a baking tray filled with enough cold water to come halfway up the sides of the dish.

Bake in the preheated oven for about 45 minutes, or until the sponge is firm and golden brown. Remove from the oven. Serve immediately with the custard or fresh cream.

Health Rating: 1 point

Rice Pudding

Serves 4

Ingredients

60 g/2½ oz/⅓ cup pudding rice
50 g/2 oz/¼ cup granulated sugar
410 g/14 oz can light evaporated milk
300 ml/½ pint/1¼ cups semi-skimmed/low-fat milk
pinch freshly grated nutmeg
25 g/1 oz/¼ stick butter
jam/jelly, to decorate

Preheat the oven to 150°C/300°F/Gas Mark 2. Lightly oil a large ovenproof dish. Sprinkle the rice and the sugar into the dish and mix.

Bring the evaporated milk and milk to the boil in a small pan, stirring occasionally. Stir the milks into the rice and mix well until the rice is coated thoroughly.

Sprinkle over the nutmeg, cover with kitchen foil and bake in the preheated oven for 30 minutes.

Remove the pudding from the oven and stir well, breaking up any lumps. Cover with the same kitchen foil. Bake in the preheated oven for a further 30 minutes. Remove from the oven and stir well again.

Dot the pudding with butter and bake for a further 45–60 minutes, until the rice is tender and the skin is browned.

Divide the pudding into four individual serving bowls. Top with a large spoonful of the jam/jelly. Serve immediately.

Health Rating: 2 points

Chocolate Mousse

Serves 6

Ingredients

175 g/6 oz milk/semisweet or dark/bittersweet chocolate
535 g carton/1 lb can ready-made custard
450 ml/¾ pint/2 cups double/heavy cream
12 Cape gooseberries/ground cherries, to decorate
sweet biscuits/cookies, to serve

Break the chocolate into segments and place in a bowl set over a saucepan of simmering water. Leave until melted, stirring occasionally. Remove the bowl in the pan from the heat and allow the melted chocolate to cool slightly.

Place the custard in a bowl and fold the melted chocolate into it using a metal spoon or rubber spatula. Stir well until completely combined.

Pour the cream into a small bowl and whip until the cream forms soft peaks. Using a metal spoon or rubber spatula, fold most of the whipped cream into the chocolate mixture.

Spoon into six tall glasses and carefully top with the remaining cream. Leave the desserts to chill in the refrigerator for at least 1 hour, or preferably overnight.

Peel back the skins from the gooseberries to form petal shapes and use to decorate the chocolate desserts. Serve with sweet biscuits/cookies.

Health Rating: 1 point

Spicy White Chocolate Mousse

Serves 4–6

Ingredients

6 cardamom pods
125 ml/4 fl oz/½ cup milk
3 bay leaves
200 g/7 oz white chocolate
300 ml/½ pint/1¼ cups double/heavy cream
3 medium/large egg whites
1–2 tsp cocoa powder, sifted, for dusting

Tap the cardamom pods lightly so they split. Remove the seeds, then crush lightly in a pestle and mortar. Pour the milk into a small saucepan and add the crushed seeds and the bay leaves. Bring to the boil gently over a medium heat. Remove from the heat, cover and leave in a warm place for at least 30 minutes to infuse.

Break the chocolate into small pieces and place in a heatproof bowl set over a saucepan of gently simmering water. Ensure the water is not touching the base of the bowl. When the chocolate has melted, remove the bowl from the heat and stir until smooth.

Whip the cream until it has slightly thickened and holds its shape but does not form peaks. Reserve.

Whisk the egg whites in a clean, grease-free bowl until stiff a nd standing in soft peaks.

Strain the milk through a sieve/strainer into the cooled, melted chocolate and beat until smooth. Spoon the chocolate mixture into the egg whites, then, using a large metal spoon, fold gently. Add the whipped cream and fold in gently.

Spoon into a large serving dish or individual small cups. Chill in the refrigerator for 3–4 hours. Just before serving, dust with a little sifted cocoa powder.

Health Rating: 1 point

Ricotta Cheesecake with Strawberry Coulis

Serves 6–8

Ingredients

8 digestive biscuits/Graham crackers
100 g/3$^1/_2$ oz mixed/candied peel, chopped
60 g/2$^1/_2$ oz/$^1/_2$ stick butter, melted
150 ml/$^1/_4$ pint/$^2/_3$ cup crème fraîche/sour cream
375 g/13 oz/1 cup ricotta cheese
100 g/3$^1/_2$ oz/$^1/_2$ cup caster/superfine sugar
1 vanilla pod, seeds only
2 large/extra-large eggs
225 g/8 oz/1$^1/_2$ cups strawberries, hulled
2–4 tbsp caster/superfine sugar, to taste
zest and juice of 1 orange

Preheat the oven to 170°C/325°F/Gas Mark 3. Line a 20 cm/8 inch springform tin/pan with baking parchment. Put the biscuits/crackers in a food processor together with the peel. Blend until the biscuits are crushed and the peel is chopped. Add 50 g/2 oz/$^1/_2$ cup of the melted butter and process until mixed. Tip into the tin and spread firmly and evenly over the bottom.

Blend together the crème fraîche/sour cream, ricotta cheese, sugar, vanilla seeds and eggs in a food processor. With the motor running, add the remaining melted butter and blend for a few seconds. Pour the mixture on to the base. Transfer to the preheated oven and cook for about 1 hour, until set and risen round the edges, but slightly wobbly in the centre. Switch off the oven and allow to cool there. Chill in the refrigerator for at least 8 hours, or preferably overnight.

Wash and drain the strawberries. Put into the food processor along with 2 tablespoons of the sugar, the orange zest and juice. Blend until smooth. Add the remaining sugar, to taste. Pass through a sieve/strainer to remove seeds and chill in the refrigerator until needed. Cut the cheesecake into wedges, spoon over some of the strawberry coulis and serve.

Health Rating: 2 points

Raspberry & Almond Tart

Serves 6–8

Ingredients

For the pastry:
225 g/8 oz/2 cups plain/all-purpose flour
pinch salt
125 g/4½ oz/1 stick plus 1 tbsp butter, cut into pieces
50 g/2 oz/¼ cup caster/superfine sugar
grated zest of ½ lemon
1 egg yolk

For the filling:
75 g/3 oz/⅔ stick butter
75 g/3 oz/⅓ cup caster/superfine sugar
75 g/3 oz/¾ cup ground almonds
2 eggs
225 g/8 oz/2 cups raspberries, thawed if frozen
2 tbsp flaked/slivered almonds
icing/confectioners' sugar, for dusting

Preheat the oven to 200°C/400°F/Gas Mark 6, 15 minutes before cooking. Blend the flour, salt and butter in a food processor until the mixture resembles breadcrumbs. Add the sugar and lemon zest and blend again for 1 minute. Mix the egg yolk with 2 tablespoons cold water and add to the mixture. Blend until the mixture starts to come together, adding a little more water if necessary, then tip out on to a lightly floured surface. Knead until smooth, wrap in clingfilm/plastic wrap and chill in the refrigerator for 30 minutes.

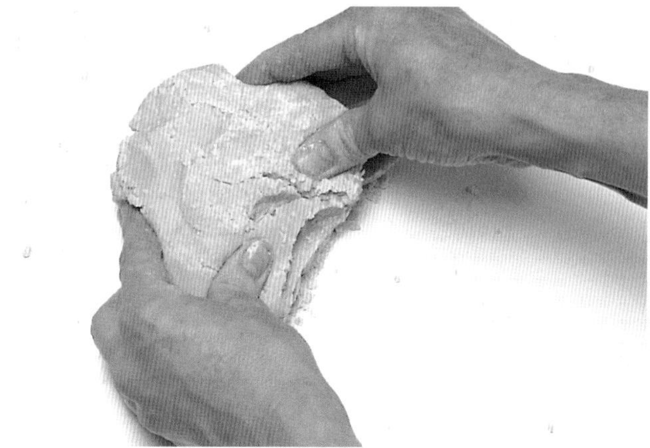

Roll the dough out thinly on a lightly floured surface and use to line a 23 cm/9 inch fluted tart tin/pan. Chill in the refrigerator for 10 minutes. Line the pastry case/shell with greaseproof/ waxed paper and baking beans. Bake for 10 minutes, then remove the paper and beans and return to the oven for a further 10–12 minutes until cooked. Allow to cool slightly, then reduce the oven temperature to 190°C/375°F/Gas Mark 5.

Blend together the butter, sugar, ground almonds and eggs until smooth. Spread the raspberries over the base of the pastry, then cover with the almond mixture. Bake for 15 minutes.

Remove from the oven. Sprinkle with the slivered or flaked almonds and dust generously with icing/confectioners' sugar. Bake for a further 15–20 minutes until firm and golden brown. Leave to cool, then serve.

Health Rating: 2 points

Tiramisu

Serves 4

Ingredients

225 g/8 oz/1 cup mascarpone cheese
25 g/1 oz/¼ cup icing/confectioners' sugar, sifted
150 ml/¼ pint/⅔ cup strong brewed coffee, chilled
300 ml/½ pint/1¼ cups double/heavy cream
3 tbsp coffee liqueur
125 g/4½ oz Savoiardi or sponge fingers/ladyfingers
50 g/2 oz/2 squares dark/bittersweet chocolate, grated or made into small curls
unsweetened cocoa powder, for dusting
assorted summer berries, to serve

Lightly oil and line a 900 g/2 lb loaf tin with a piece of clingfilm/plastic wrap.

Put the mascarpone cheese and icing/confectioners' sugar into a large bowl and, using a rubber spatula, beat until smooth. Stir in 2 tablespoons chilled coffee and mix thoroughly.

Whip the cream with 1 tablespoon of the coffee liqueur until just thickened. Stir a spoonful of the whipped cream into the mascarpone mixture, then fold in the rest. Spoon half of the mascarpone mixture into the prepared loaf tin/pan and smooth the top.

Put the remaining coffee and coffee liqueur into a shallow dish just bigger than the sponge fingers/ladyfingers. Using half of them, dip one side of each sponge finger into the coffee mixture, then arrange on top of the mascarpone mixture in a single layer. Spoon the rest of the mascarpone mixture over the sponge fingers and smooth the top. Dip the remaining sponge fingers in the coffee mixture and arrange on top of the mascarpone mixture. Drizzle with any remaining coffee mixture. Cover with clingfilm and chill in the refrigerator for 4 hours.

Carefully turn the tiramisu out on to a large serving plate. Sprinkle with the grated chocolate or chocolate curls. Dust with cocoa powder, cut into slices and serve with a few summer berries.

Health Rating: 1 point

Steamed Chocolate Chip Pudding

Serves 6

Ingredients

175 g/6 oz/1½ cups self-raising flour
½ tsp baking powder
75 g/3 oz/1¼ cups fresh white breadcrumbs
125 g/4½ oz/1 cup shredded suet
125 g/4½ oz/⅔ cup golden caster/unrefined superfine sugar
2 eggs, lightly beaten
1 tsp vanilla essence
125 g/4½ oz/⅔ cup chocolate chips
150 ml/¼ pint/⅔ cup cold milk
grated chocolate, to decorate

For the chocolate custard:
300 ml/½ pint/1¼ cups milk
1 tbsp cornflour/cornstarch
1 tbsp unsweetened cocoa powder
1 tbsp caster/superfine sugar
½ tsp vanilla essence; 1 egg yolk

Lightly oil a 1.2 litre/2 pint/1¼ quart pudding basin and line the base with a small circle of nonstick baking parchment. Sift the flour and baking powder into a bowl, add the breadcrumbs, suet and sugar and mix well.

Stir in the eggs and vanilla essence with the chocolate chips and mix with sufficient cold milk to form a smooth dropping consistency.

Spoon the mixture into the prepared basin and cover the pudding with a double sheet of baking parchment and then either a double sheet of kitchen foil or a pudding cloth, with a pleat in the centre to allow for expansion. Secure tightly with string.

Place in the top of a steamer, set over a saucepan of simmering water and steam for 1½–2 hours, or until the pudding is cooked and firm to the touch – replenish the water as necessary. Remove and leave to rest for 5 minutes before turning out on to a warmed serving plate.

Meanwhile, make the custard/custard sauce. Blend a little of the milk with the cornflour/cornstarch and cocoa powder to form a paste. Stir in the remaining milk with the sugar and vanilla essence. Pour into a saucepan and bring to the boil, stirring. Whisk in the egg yolk and cook for 1 minute. Decorate the pudding with grated chocolate and serve with the sauce.

Health Rating: 1 point

Mocha Pie

Serves 4–6

Ingredients

1 x 23 cm/9 inch ready-made sweet pastry case/shell

For the filling:

125 g/4½ oz dark/bittersweet chocolate, broken into pieces
175 g/6 oz/1½ sticks unsalted butter
225 g/8 oz/1 cup soft brown sugar
1 tsp vanilla essence
3 tbsp strong black coffee

For the topping:

600 ml/1 pint/2 cups double/heavy cream
50 g/2 oz/½ cup icing/confectioners' sugar
2 tsp vanilla essence
1 tsp instant coffee dissolved in 1 tsp boiling water, cooled
grated dark/bittersweet and white chocolate, to decorate

Place the prepared pastry case/shell on a large serving plate and reserve.

Melt the chocolate in a heatproof bowl set over a saucepan of simmering water. Ensure the water is not touching the base of the bowl. Remove from the heat, stir until smooth and leave to cool.

Cream the butter, soft brown sugar and vanilla essence until light and fluffy, then beat in the cooled chocolate. Add the strong black coffee, pour into the pastry case and chill in the refrigerator for about 30 minutes.

For the topping, whisk the cream until beginning to thicken, then whisk in the sugar and vanilla essence. Continue to whisk until the cream is softly peaking. Spoon just under half of the cream into a separate bowl and fold in the dissolved coffee.

Spread the remaining cream over the filling in the pastry case. Spoon the coffee-flavoured whipped cream evenly over the top, then swirl it decoratively with a palate knife. Sprinkle with grated chocolate and chill in the refrigerator until ready to serve.

Health Rating: 1 point

Chocolate Fudge Sundae

Serves 2

Ingredients

5 g/3 oz dark/bittersweet chocolate, broken into pieces
450ml/¾ pint/1¾ cups double/heavy cream
175g/6 oz/¾ cup golden caster/unrefined superfine sugar
25 g/1 oz/¼ cup plain/all-purpose flour
pinch salt
15 g/½ oz/1 tbsp unsalted butter
1 tsp vanilla essence

For the sundae:
125 g/4½ oz/1 cup raspberries, fresh, or thawed if frozen
4 scoops vanilla ice cream
2 scoops chocolate ice cream
2 tbsp toasted flaked/slivered almonds
2 wafers, to serve

To make the chocolate fudge sauce, place the chocolate and cream in a heavy-based saucepan and heat gently until the chocolate has melted into the cream. Stir until smooth. Mix the sugar with the flour and salt, then stir in sufficient chocolate mixture to make a smooth paste.

Gradually blend the remaining melted chocolate mixture into the paste, then pour into a clean saucepan. Cook over a low heat, stirring frequently, until smooth and thick. Remove from the heat and add the butter and vanilla essence. Stir until smooth, then cool slightly.

To make the sundae, crush the raspberries lightly with a fork and reserve. Spoon a little of the chocolate sauce into the bottom of two sundae glasses. Add a layer of crushed raspberries, then a scoop each of vanilla and chocolate ice cream. Top each one with a scoop of the vanilla ice cream. Pour over the sauce, sprinkle over the almonds and serve with a wafer.

Health Rating: 1 point

White Chocolate Trifle

Serves 6

Ingredients

1 homemade or bought chocolate Swiss/jelly roll, sliced
4 tbsp brandy
2 tbsp Irish cream liqueur
425 g/15 oz can black cherries, drained and pitted, with 3 tbsp of the juice reserved
900 ml/1½ pints/scant 1 quart double/heavy cream
125 g/4 oz white chocolate, broken into pieces
6 medium/large egg yolks
50 g/2 oz/¼ cup caster/superfine sugar
2 tsp cornflour/cornstarch
1 tsp vanilla essence
50 g/2 oz/⅓ cup dark/bittersweet chocolate, grated
50 g/2 oz/⅓ cup milk/semisweet chocolate, grated

Health Rating: 1 point

Place the Swiss/jelly roll slices in the bottom of a trifle dish and pour over the brandy, Irish cream liqueur and a little of the reserved black cherry juice to moisten the Swiss roll. Arrange the black cherries on the top.

Pour 600 ml/1 pint/2½ cups of the cream into a saucepan and add the white chocolate. Heat gently to just below simmering point.

Whisk together the egg yolks, caster/superfine sugar, cornflour/cornstarch and vanilla essence in a small bowl. Gradually whisk the egg mixture into the hot cream, then strain into a clean saucepan and return to the heat.

Cook the custard gently, stirring throughout, until it is thick and coats the back of a spoon. Leave to cool slightly, then pour over the trifle. Leave the trifle to chill in the refrigerator for at least 3–4 hours, or preferably overnight.

Before serving, lightly whip the remaining cream until soft peaks form, then spoon the cream over the set custard. Using the back of a spoon, swirl the cream in a decorative pattern. Sprinkle with grated plain and milk chocolate and serve.

Chocolate Pancakes

Serves 6

Ingredients

For the pancakes/crepes:

75 g/3 oz/⅔ cup plain/all-purpose flour
1 tbsp unsweetened cocoa powder
1 tsp caster/superfine sugar
½ tsp freshly grated nutmeg
2 eggs
175 ml/6 fl oz/¾ cup milk
75 g/3 oz/⅔ stick unsalted butter, melted

For the mango sauce:

1 ripe mango, peeled and diced
50 ml/2 fl oz/¼ cup white wine
2 tbsp golden caster/unrefined superfine sugar
2 tbsp rum

For the filling:

225 g/8 oz dark/bittersweet chocolate
75 ml/3 fl oz/⅓ cup double/heavy cream
3 medium/large eggs, separated
2 tbsp golden caster/unrefined superfine sugar

Preheat the oven to 200°C/400°F/Gas Mark 6, 15 minutes before cooking. To make the pancakes/crepes, sift the flour, cocoa powder, sugar and nutmeg into a bowl and make a well in the centre. Beat the eggs and milk together, then gradually beat into the flour mixture to form a batter. Stir in 50 g/2 oz/¼ cup of the melted butter and leave to stand for 1 hour.

Heat an 18 cm/7 inch nonstick frying pan and brush with a little melted butter. Add about 3 tablespoons of the batter and swirl to cover the base of the pan. Cook over a medium heat for 1–2 minutes, flip over and cook for a further 40 seconds. Repeat with the remaining batter. Stack the pancakes interleaving with greaseproof/waxed paper.

To make the sauce, place the mango, white wine and sugar in a saucepan and bring to the boil over a medium heat, then simmer for 2–3 minutes, stirring constantly. When the mixture has thickened, add the rum. Chill in the refrigerator while making the filling and baking.

For the filling, melt the chocolate and cream in a small heavy-based saucepan over a medium heat. Stir until smooth, then leave to cool. Beat the egg yolks with the sugar for 3–5 minutes, or until the mixture is pale and creamy, then beat in the chocolate mixture.

Beat the egg whites until stiff, then add a little to the chocolate mixture. Stir in the remainder. Spoon a little of the mixture on to a crepe. Fold in half, then fold in half again, forming a triangle. Repeat with the remaining crepes. Brush the crepes with a little melted butter. Bake in the preheated oven for 15–20 minutes, or until the filling is set. Serve hot or cold with the mango sauce.

Health Rating: 2 points

Crunchy Rhubarb Crumble

Serves 4

Ingredients

100 g/3½ oz/1 cup plain/all-purpose flour
50 g/2 oz/½ stick softened butter
50 g/2 oz/⅔ cup rolled oats/oatmeal
50 g/2 oz/¼ cup demerara/light brown sugar
1 tbsp sesame seeds
½ tsp ground cinnamon
450 g/1 lb fresh rhubarb
50 g/2 oz/¼ cup caster/superfine sugar
custard or cream, to serve

Health Rating: 2 points

Preheat the oven to 180°C/350°F/Gas Mark 4. Place the flour in a large bowl and cut the butter into cubes. Add to the flour and rub in with the fingertips until the mixture looks like fine breadcrumbs, or blend for a few seconds in a food processor. Stir in the oats, demerara/light brown sugar, sesame seeds and cinnamon. Mix well and reserve.

Prepare the rhubarb by removing the thick ends of the stalks and cut diagonally into 2.5 cm/1 inch chunks. Wash thoroughly and pat dry with a clean dishtowel. Place the rhubarb in a 1.1 litre/2 pint/1¼ quart pie dish.

Sprinkle the caster/superfine sugar over the rhubarb and top with the reserved crumble/crisp mixture. Level the top of the crumble so that all the fruit is well covered and press down firmly. If liked, sprinkle the top with a little extra caster sugar.

Place on a baking sheet and bake in the preheated oven for 40–50 minutes, or until the fruit is soft and the topping is golden brown. Sprinkle the pudding with some more caster sugar and serve hot with custard or cream.

Queen of Puddings

Serves 4

Ingredients

75 g/3 oz/1¼ cups fresh white breadcrumbs
25 g/1 oz/⅛ cup granulated sugar
450 ml/¾ pt/1¾ cups whole milk
25 g/1 oz/¼ stick butter
grated rind of 1 small lemon
2 medium/large eggs, separated
2 tbsp seedless raspberry jam/jelly
50 g/2 oz/¼ cup caster/superfine sugar

Preheat the oven to 170°C/325°F/Gas Mark 3. Oil a 900 ml/1½ pint/scant 1 quart ovenproof baking dish and reserve.Mix the breadcrumbs and sugar together in a bowl.

Pour the milk into a small saucepan and heat gently with the butter and lemon rind until the butter has melted. Allow the mixture to cool a little, then pour over the breadcrumbs. Stir well and leave to soak for 30 minutes.

Whisk the egg yolks into the cooled breadcrumb mixture and pour into the prepared dish. Place the dish on a baking sheet and bake in the preheated oven for about 30 minutes, or until firm and set. Remove from the oven. Allow to cool slightly, then spread the jam over the pudding.

Whisk the egg whites until stiff and standing in peaks. Gently fold in the caster sugar with a metal spoon or rubber spatula. Pile the meringue over the top of the pudding. Return the dish to the oven for a further 25–30 minutes, or until the meringue is crisp and just slightly coloured. Serve hot or cold.

Health Rating: 1 point

Jam Roly Poly

Serves 4

Ingredients

225 g/8 oz/1¾ cups self-raising flour
¼ tsp salt
125 g/4 oz/1 cup shredded suet
about 150 ml/¼ pint/⅔ cup water
3 tbsp strawberry jam/jelly
1 tbsp milk, to glaze
1 tsp caster/superfine sugar
ready-made jam/jelly sauce, to serve

Preheat the oven to 200°C/400°F/Gas Mark 6. Make the pastry by sifting the flour and salt into a large bowl. Add the suet and mix lightly, then add the water a little at a time and mix to form a soft and pliable dough. (Take care not to make the dough too wet.)

Turn the dough out on to a lightly floured board and knead gently until smooth. Roll the dough out into a 23 cm/9 inch x 28 cm/11 inch rectangle.

Spread the jam over the dough, leaving a border of 1 cm/½ inch all round. Fold the border over the jam and brush the edges with water. Lightly roll the rectangle up from one of the short sides, seal the top edge and press the ends together. (Do not roll the pudding up too tightly.)

Turn the pudding upside down on to a large piece of greaseproof/waxed paper large enough to come halfway up the sides. (If not using nonstick paper, then oil lightly.) Tie the ends of the paper to make a boat-shaped paper case for the pudding to sit in, leaving plenty of room for the roly poly to expand.

Brush the pudding lightly with milk and sprinkle with the sugar. Bake in the preheated oven for 30–40 minutes, or until well risen and golden. Serve immediately with the jam sauce.

Health Rating: 1 point

Golden Castle Pudding

Serves 4–6

Ingredients

125 g/4 oz/1 stick plus 1 tbsp butter
125 g/4 oz/⅔ cup caster/superfine sugar
few drops vanilla essence
2 medium/large eggs, beaten
125 g/4 oz/1 cup self-raising flour
4 tbsp golden/corn syrup
crème fraîche or ready-made custard, to serve

Preheat the oven to 180°C/350°F/Gas Mark 4. Lightly oil four to six individual pudding bowls and place a small circle of lightly oiled greaseproof/waxed paper or baking parchment in the base of each one.

Place the butter and caster/superfine sugar in a large bowl, then beat together until the mixture is pale and creamy. Stir in the vanilla essence and gradually add the beaten eggs, a little at a time. Add a tablespoon of flour after each addition of egg and beat well.

When the mixture is smooth, add the remaining flour and fold in gently. Add a tablespoon of water and mix to form a soft mixture that will drop easily off a spoon.

Spoon enough mixture into each basin to come halfway up, allowing enough space for the puddings to rise. Place on a baking sheet and bake in the preheated oven for about 25 minutes until firm and golden brown.

Allow the puddings to stand for 5 minutes. Discard the paper circle and turn out on to individual serving plates.

Warm the golden syrup in a small saucepan and pour a little over each pudding. Serve hot with the crème fraîche or custard.

Health Rating: 1 point

Baking

Including cakes, cookies and quiches, this chapter makes baking easy and fun. Who can resist the smell of freshly baked bread or the taste of a homemade cake? Get the whole family involved by helping children bake Chocolate Chip Cookies or Shortbread Thumbs. With both sweet and savoury recipes, there is something for everyone.

Stilton, Tomato & Courgette Quiche

Serves 4

Ingredients

For the shortcrust pastry/piecrust:

225 g/8 oz/2 cups plain/all-purpose white flour
pinch salt
50 g/2 oz/4 tbsp white vegetable fat/shortening or lard
50 g/2 oz/½ stick butter or block margarine

For the filling:

25 g/1 oz/2 tbsp butter
1 onion, peeled and finely chopped
1 courgette/zucchini, trimmed and sliced
125 g/4½ oz/1 cup Stilton/blue cheese, crumbled
6 cherry tomatoes, halved
2 large/extra-large eggs, beaten
200 ml/7 fl oz/¾ cups crème fraîche/sour cream
salt and freshly ground black pepper

Sift the flour and salt into a mixing bowl. Cut the fats into small pieces and add to the bowl. Rub the fats into the flour using your fingertips until the mixture resembles fine breadcrumbs. Add 1–2 tablespoons cold water and mix to form a soft, pliable dough. Knead gently on a lightly floured surface until smooth and free from cracks, then wrap and chill for 30 minutes.

Preheat the oven to 190°C/375°F/Gas Mark 5. On a lightly floured surface, roll out the dough and use to line an 18 cm/7 inch lightly oiled flan tin/tart pan, trimming any excess dough with a knife.

Prick the base all over with a fork and bake blind in the preheated oven for 15 minutes. Remove the pastry from the oven and brush with a little of the beaten egg. Return to the oven for a further 5 minutes.

Heat the butter in a frying pan and fry the onion and courgette/zucchini for about 4 minutes until soft and starting to brown. Transfer into the pastry case/tart shell. Sprinkle the Stilton/blue cheese over evenly and top with the halved cherry tomatoes.

Beat together the eggs and crème fraîche/sour cream and season to taste with salt and pepper. Pour into the pastry case and bake in the oven for 35–40 minutes, or until the filling is golden brown and set in the centre. Serve the quiche hot or cold.

Health Rating: 2 points

Beef & Red Wine Pie

Serves 4

Ingredients

700 g/1½ lb stewing beef (chuck or round meat), cubed
4 tbsp seasoned plain/all-purpose flour
2 tbsp sunflower oil
2 onions, peeled and chopped
2 garlic cloves, peeled and crushed
1 tbsp freshly chopped thyme
300 ml/½ pint/1¼ cups red wine
150 ml/¼ pint/⅔ cup beef stock
1–2 tsp Worcestershire sauce
2 tbsp tomato ketchup
2 bay leaves
knob butter
225 g/8 oz/2¼ cups button/white mushrooms
beaten egg or milk, to glaze
parsley sprig, to garnish

For the quick flaky pastry:
125 g/4½ oz/1 stick plus 1 tbsp butter
175 g/6 oz/1½ cups plain/all-purpose flour
pinch salt

Place the butter in the freezer for 30 minutes. Sift the flour and salt into a large bowl. Remove the butter from the freezer and grate using the coarse side of a grater, dipping the butter in the flour every now and again to make it easier to grate.

Mix the butter into the flour using a palette knife, making sure all the butter is thoroughly coated with flour. Add 2 tablespoons cold water and continue to mix, bringing the mixture together. Use your hands to complete the mixing. Add a little more water if needed to leave a clean bowl. Place the dough in a plastic bag and chill in the refrigerator for 30 minutes.

Preheat the oven to 200°C/400°F/Gas Mark 6. Toss the beef cubes in the seasoned flour. Heat the oil in a large heavy-based frying pan. Fry the beef in batches for about 5 minutes until golden brown. Return all of the beef to the pan and add the onions, garlic and thyme. Fry for about 10 minutes, stirring occasionally. If the beef begins to stick, add a little water.

Add the red wine and stock and bring to the boil. Stir in the Worcestershire sauce, tomato ketchup and bay leaves. Cover and simmer on a very low heat for about 1 hour, or until the beef is tender.

Heat the butter and gently fry the mushrooms until golden brown. Add to the stew. Simmer, uncovered, for a further 15 minutes. Remove the bay leaves, spoon the beef into a 1.2 litre/2 pint/1¼ quart pie dish and reserve.

Roll out the dough on a lightly floured surface. Cut out the lid to 5 mm/¼ inch wider than the dish. Brush the rim with the beaten egg and lay the dough lid on top. Press to seal, then knock the edges with the back of the knife. Cut a slit in the lid and brush with the beaten egg or milk to glaze.

Bake the pie in the preheated oven for 30 minutes, or until it turns golden brown. Garnish with the parsley sprig and serve immediately.

Health Rating: 1 point

Three Tomato Pizza

Serves 2–4

Ingredients

For the basic pizza dough:
225 g/8 oz/2 cups strong white/bread flour
½ tsp salt, ¼ tsp quick-acting dried yeast
150 ml/¼ pint/⅔ cup warm water
1 tbsp extra virgin olive oil

For the topping:
3 plum tomatoes; 8 cherry tomatoes
6 sun-dried tomatoes, pinch sea salt
1 tbsp freshly chopped basil
2 tbsp extra virgin olive oil
125 g/4½ oz buffalo mozzarella cheese, sliced
freshly ground black pepper, fresh basil leaves, to garnish

Preheat the oven to 220°C/425°F/Gas Mark 7 and place a baking sheet in the oven to heat up. Sift the flour and salt into a bowl and stir in the yeast. Make a well in the centre and gradually add the water and oil to form a soft dough. Knead the dough on a floured surface for about 5 minutes until smooth and elastic. Place in a lightly oiled bowl and cover with clingfilm/plastic wrap. Leave to rise in a warm place for 1 hour.

Knock the pizza dough with your fist a few times, then divide into four equal pieces. Roll out one quarter of the pizza dough on a lightly floured board to form a 20.5 cm/8 inch round. Roll out the other three pieces into rounds, one at a time. While rolling out any piece of dough, keep the others lightly covered with clingfilm.

Slice the plum tomatoes, halve the cherry tomatoes and chop the sun-dried tomatoes into small pieces. Place a few pieces of each type of tomato on each pizza base, then season to taste with the sea salt. Sprinkle with the chopped basil and drizzle with the olive oil. Place a few slices of mozzarella on each pizza and season with black pepper. Transfer the pizza on to the heated baking/cookie sheet and cook for 15–20 minutes, or until the cheese is golden brown and bubbling. Garnish with the basil leaves and serve immediately.

Health Rating: 2 points

Classic White Loaf

Makes 1 x 900 g/2 lb loaf

Ingredients

700 g/1½ lb/6 cups strong white/bread flour
1 tbsp salt
25 g/1 oz/¼ stick butter, cubed
1 tsp caster/superfine sugar
2 tsp easy-blend dried yeast
150 ml/¼ pint/⅔ cup milk
300 ml/½ pint/1¼ cups warm water
1 tbsp plain/all-purpose flour, to dust

Light wholemeal variation:
450 g/1 lb/4 cups strong wholemeal/whole-wheat flour
225 g/8 oz/2 cups strong white/bread flour
beaten egg, to glaze
1 tbsp kibbled wheat/wheat germ, to finish

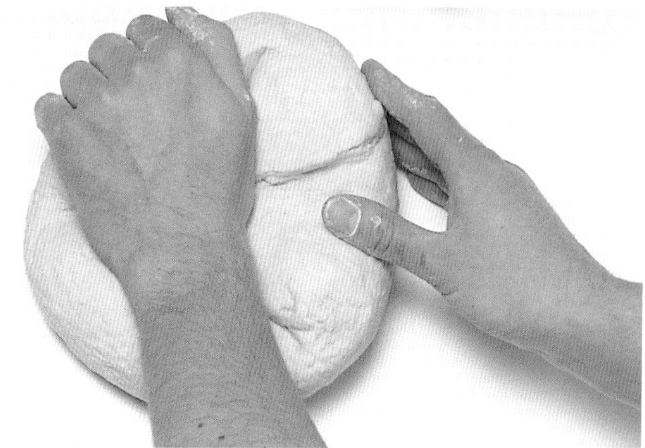

Preheat the oven to 220°C/425°F/Gas Mark 7, 15 minutes before baking. Oil and line the base of a 900 g/2 lb loaf tin/pan with greaseproof/waxed paper. Sift the flour and salt into a large bowl. Rub in the butter, then stir in the sugar and yeast. Make a well in the centre.

Add the milk and the warm water to the dry ingredients. Mix to a soft dough, adding a little more water if needed. Turn out the dough and knead on a lightly floured surface for 10 minutes, or until smooth and elastic.

Place the dough in an oiled bowl, cover with clingfilm/plastic wrap or a clean dishtowel and leave in a warm place to rise for 1 hour, or until doubled in size. Knead again for a minute or two to knock out the air.

Shape the dough into an oblong and place in the prepared tin. Cover with oiled clingfilm and leave to rise for a further 30 minutes, or until the dough reaches the top of the tin.

Dust the top of the loaf with flour or brush with the egg glaze and scatter with kibbled wheat/wheat germ if making the wholemeal version. Bake the loaf on the middle shelf of the preheated oven for 15 minutes.

Turn down the oven to 200°C/400°F/Gas Mark 6. Bake the loaf for a further 20–25 minutes, or until well risen and hollow sounding when tapped underneath. Turn out, cool on a wire rack and serve.

Health Rating: 2 points

(or 3 points for the wholemeal version)

Soft Dinner Rolls

Makes 16

Ingredients

50 g/2 oz/½ stick butter
1 tbsp caster/superfine sugar
225 ml/8 fl oz/1 cup milk
550 g/1¼ lb/5 cups strong white/bread flour
1½ tsp salt
2 tsp easy-blend dried yeast
2 medium/large eggs, beaten

To glaze & finish:
2 tbsp milk
1 tsp sea salt
2 tsp poppy seeds

Preheat the oven to 220°C/425°F/Gas Mark 7, 15 minutes before baking. Gently heat the butter, sugar and milk in a saucepan until the butter has melted and the sugar has dissolved. Cool until tepid. Sift the flour and salt into a bowl, stir in the yeast and make a well in the centre. Reserve 1 tablespoon of the beaten eggs. Add the rest to the dry ingredients with the milk mixture. Mix to form a soft dough.

Knead the dough on a lightly floured surface for 10 minutes until smooth and elastic. Put in an oiled bowl, cover with clingfilm/plastic wrap and leave in a warm place to rise for 1 hour, or until doubled in size. Knead again for a minute or two, then divide into 16 pieces. Shape into balls, braids, coils, cottage buns, or whatever shape you want. Place on two oiled baking sheets, cover with oiled clingfilm and leave to rise for 30 minutes, or until doubled in size.

Mix the reserved beaten egg with the milk and brush over the rolls. Sprinkle some with sea salt, others with poppy seeds and leave some plain. Bake in the preheated oven for about 20 minutes, or until golden and hollow sounding when tapped underneath. Transfer to a wire rack. Cover with a clean dishtowel while cooling to keep the rolls soft, and serve.

Health Rating: 2 points

Chocolate Chip Cookies

Makes about 30

Ingredients

140 g/4½ oz/1¼ sticks butter
50 g/2 oz/¼ cup caster/superfine sugar
60 g/2½ oz/⅓ cup soft dark brown sugar
1 medium/large egg, beaten
½ tsp vanilla essence
125 g/4 oz/½ cup plain/all-purpose flour
½ tsp bicarbonate of soda/baking soda
150 g/5 oz/¾ cup plain or milk chocolate chips

Preheat the oven to 180°C/350°F/Gas Mark 4, 10 minutes before baking. Lightly grease three to four large baking sheets with 1 tablespoon of the butter. Place the remaining butter and both sugars in a food processor and blend until smooth. Add the egg and vanilla essence and blend briefly. Alternatively, cream the butter and sugars together in a bowl, then beat in the egg with the vanilla essence.

If using a food processor, scrape out the mixture with a spatula and place the mixture into a large bowl. Sift the flour and bicarbonate of soda together, then fold into the creamed mixture. When the mixture is blended thoroughly, stir in the chocolate chips.

Drop heaped teaspoons of the mixture on to the prepared baking sheets, spaced well apart, and bake the cookies in the preheated oven for 10–12 minutes, or until lightly golden.

Leave to cool for a few seconds, then, using a spatula, transfer to a wire rack and cool completely. The cookies are best eaten when just cooked, but can be stored in an airtight tin for a few days.

Health Rating: 1 point

Chocolate & Nut Refrigerator Biscuits

Makes 18

Ingredients

165 g/5½ oz/1½ sticks slightly salted butter
150 g/5 oz/¾ cup soft dark brown sugar
2 tbsp granulated sugar
1 medium/large egg, beaten
200 g/7 oz/1½ cups plain/all-purpose flour
½ tsp bicarbonate of soda/baking soda
25 g/1 oz/⅓ cup unsweetened cocoa powder
125 g/4 oz/1 cup pecan nuts, finely chopped

Preheat the oven to 190°C/375°F/Gas Mark 5, 10 minutes before baking. Lightly grease several baking sheets with 1 tablespoon of the butter. Cream the remaining butter and both sugars in a large bowl until light and fluffy, then gradually beat in the egg.

Sift the flour, bicarbonate of soda/baking soda and cocoa powder together, then gradually fold into the creamed mixture together with the chopped pecans. Mix thoroughly until a smooth but stiff dough is formed.

Place the dough on a lightly floured surface or pastry board and roll into sausage shapes about 5 cm/2 inches in diameter. Wrap in clingfilm/plastic wrap and chill in the refrigerator for at least 12 hours, or preferably overnight.

Cut the dough into thin slices and place on the prepared baking sheets. Bake in the preheated oven for 8–10 minutes, or until firm. Remove from the oven and leave to cool slightly. Using a spatula, transfer to a wire rack to cool. Store in an airtight tin.

Health Rating: 1 point

Shortbread Thumbs

Makes 12

Ingredients

100 g/3½ oz/1 cup self-raising flour
125 g/4½ oz/1 stick plus 1 tbsp butter, softened
25 g/1 oz/2 tbsp white vegetable fat/shortening
50 g/2 oz/¼ cup caster/superfine sugar
3 tbsp cornflour/cornstarch, sifted
5 tbsp unsweetened cocoa powder, sifted
100 g/3½ oz/1 cup icing/confectioners' sugar
6 assorted colour glacé/candied cherries, rinsed, dried and halved

Health Rating: 1 point

Preheat the oven to 150°C/300°F/Gas Mark 2, 10 minutes before baking. Oil two baking sheets. Sift the flour into a large bowl, cut 75 g/3 oz/⅔ stick of the butter and the white vegetable fat/shortening into small cubes and add to the flour. Using your fingertips, rub in until the mixture resembles fine breadcrumbs.

Stir in the caster/superfine sugar, sifted cornflour/cornstarch and 4 tablespoons of the cocoa powder. Bring the mixture together with your hands to form a soft and pliable dough. Place on a lightly floured surface and shape into 12 small balls. Place on to the baking sheets at least 5 cm/2 inches apart, then press each one with a clean thumb to make a dent.

Bake in the preheated oven for 20–25 minutes, or until light golden brown. Remove from the oven and leave for 1–2 minutes to cool. Transfer to a wire rack and leave until cold.

Sift the icing/confectioners' sugar and the rest of the cocoa powder into a bowl and add the remaining softened butter. Blend to form a smooth and spreadable icing with 1–2 tablespoons hot water. Spread a little icing over the top of each biscuit and place half a cherry on each. Leave until set before serving.

Chunky Chocolate Muffins

Makes 7

Ingredients

50 g/2 oz dark chocolate, roughly chopped
50 g/2 oz/¼ cup light muscovado/golden brown sugar
25 g/1 oz/¼ stick butter, melted
125 ml/4 fl oz/½ cup milk, at room temperature
½ tsp vanilla essence
1 medium/large egg, lightly beaten
150 g/5 oz/1¼ cups self-raising flour
½ tsp baking powder
pinch salt
75 g/3 oz white chocolate, chopped
2 tsp icing/confectioners' sugar (optional)

Preheat the oven to 200°C/400°F/Gas Mark 6, 15 minutes before baking. Line a muffin or deep bun tray with seven paper muffin cases/baking cups, or else oil the individual compartments well. Place the dark chocolate in a large heatproof bowl set over a saucepan of very hot water. Stir occasionally until melted. Remove the bowl and leave to cool for a few minutes.

Stir the sugar and butter into the melted chocolate, then add the milk, vanilla essence and egg. Sift the flour, baking powder and salt in together. Add the chopped white chocolate.

Using a metal spoon, fold together quickly, taking care not to overmix. Divide the mixture between the paper cases, piling it up in the centre. Bake on the centre shelf of the preheated oven for 20–25 minutes, or until well risen and firm to the touch.

Lightly dust the tops of the muffins with icing/confectioners' sugar as soon as they come out of the oven, if wanted. Leave the muffins in the tray for a few minutes, then transfer to a wire rack. Serve either warm or cold.

Health Rating: 1 point

Chocolate Pecan Traybake

Makes 12

Ingredients

175 g/6 oz/$1\frac{1}{2}$ sticks butter
75 g/3 oz/$\frac{3}{4}$ cup icing/confectioners' sugar, sifted
175 g/6 oz/$1\frac{1}{3}$ cups plain/all-purpose flour
3 tbsp self-raising flour
5 tbsp cocoa powder

For the pecan topping:
75 g/3 oz/$\frac{2}{3}$ stick butter
50 g/2 oz light muscovado sugar
2 tbsp golden/corn syrup
2 tbsp milk
1 tsp vanilla essence
2 medium/large eggs, lightly beaten
125 g/4 oz/$1\frac{1}{4}$ cups pecan halves

Preheat the oven to 180°C/350°F/Gas Mark 4, 10 minutes before baking. Lightly oil and line a 28 x 18 x 2.5 cm/11 x 7 x 1 inch cake tin/pan with nonstick baking parchment. Beat the butter and sugar together until light and fluffy. Sift in the flours and cocoa powder and mix together to form a soft dough.

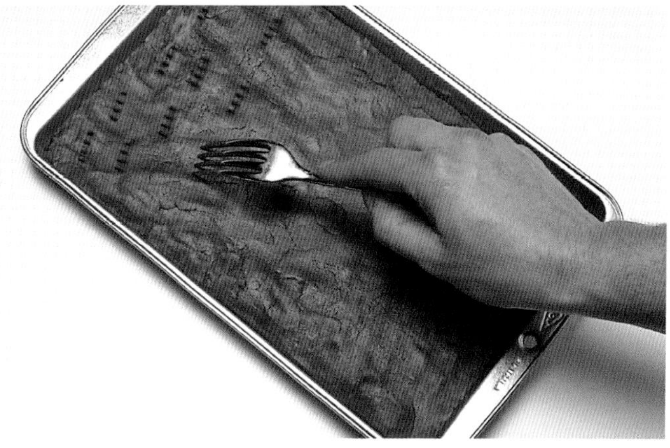

Press the mixture evenly over the base of the prepared tin. Prick all over with a fork, then bake on the shelf above the centre of the preheated oven for 15 minutes.

Put the butter, sugar, golden/corn syrup, milk and vanilla essence in a small saucepan and heat gently until melted. Remove from the heat and leave to cool for a few minutes, then stir in the eggs and pour over the base. Sprinkle with the nuts.

Bake in the preheated oven for 25 minutes, or until dark golden brown but still slightly soft. Leave to cool in the tin. When cool, carefully remove from the tin, then cut into 12 squares and serve. Store in an airtight container.

Health Rating: 1 point

Chocolate Fudge Brownies

Makes 16

Ingredients

125 g/4 oz/1 stick plus 1 tbsp butter
175 g/6 oz dark chocolate, roughly chopped or broken
225 g/8 oz/1 heaping cup caster/superfine sugar
2 tsp vanilla essence
2 eggs, lightly beaten
150 g/5 oz/1 heaping cup plain/all-purpose flour
175 g/6 oz/1½ cups icing/confectioners' sugar
2 tbsp unsweetened cocoa powder
1 tbsp butter

Preheat the oven to 180°C/350°F/Gas Mark 4, 10 minutes before baking. Lightly oil and line a 20.5 cm/8 inch square cake tin/pan with greaseproof/waxed paper or baking parchment.

Slowly melt the butter and chocolate together in a heatproof bowl set over a saucepan of simmering water. Transfer the mixture to a large bowl. Stir in the sugar and vanilla essence, then stir in the eggs. Sift over the flour and fold together well with a metal spoon or rubber spatula. Pour into the prepared tin.

Transfer to the preheated oven and bake for 30 minutes until just set. Remove the cooked mixture from the oven. Leave to cool in the tin before turning it out on to a wire rack.

Sift the icing/confectioners' sugar and cocoa into a small bowl and make a well in the centre. Place the butter in the well, then gradually add about 2 tablespoons hot water. Mix to form a smooth spreadable icing.

Pour the icing over the cooked mixture. Allow the icing to set before cutting into squares. Serve the brownies when they are cold, or store in an airtight container.

Health Rating: 1 point

Oatmeal Raisin Cookies

Makes 24

Ingredients

175 g/6 oz/1½ cups plain/all-purpose flour
150 g/5 oz/2 cups rolled oats/oatmeal
1 tsp ground ginger
½ tsp baking powder
½ tsp bicarbonate of soda/baking soda
125 g/4½ oz/⅔ cup demerara/light brown sugar
50 g/2 oz/⅓ cup raisins
1 medium/large egg, lightly beaten
150 ml/¼ pint/⅔ cup vegetable or sunflower oil
4 tbsp milk

Preheat the oven to 200°C/400°F/Gas Mark 6, 15 minutes before baking. Lightly oil a baking sheet.

Mix together the flour, oats, ground ginger, baking powder, bicarbonate of soda/baking soda, sugar and the raisins in a large bowl.

In another bowl, mix the egg, oil and milk together. Make a well in the centre of the dry ingredients and pour in the egg mixture. Mix together well with either a fork or a wooden spoon to make a soft but not sticky dough.

Place spoonfuls of the dough well apart on the oiled baking sheet and flatten the tops down slightly with the tines of a fork. Transfer to the preheated oven and bake for 10–12 minutes until golden.

Remove from the oven, leave to cool for 2–3 minutes, then transfer the cookies to a wire rack to cool. Serve when cold, or otherwise store in an airtight container.

Health Rating: 2 points

Swiss Roll

Cuts into 8 slices

Ingredients

75 g/3 oz/½ cup self-raising flour
3 large/extra-large eggs
1 tsp vanilla essence
90 g/3½ oz/scant ½ cup caster/superfine sugar
25 g/1 oz/¼ cup hazelnuts, toasted and finely chopped
3 tbsp apricot jam/jelly
300 ml/½ pint/1¼ cups double/heavy cream, lightly whipped

Preheat the oven to 220°C/425°F/Gas Mark 7, 15 minutes before baking. Lightly oil and line the base of a 23 x 33 cm/9 x 13 inch Swiss/jelly roll tin/pan with a single sheet of greaseproof/waxed paper or baking parchment. Sift the flour several times, then reserve on top of the oven to warm a little.

Place a mixing bowl with the eggs, vanilla essence and sugar over a saucepan of hot water, ensuring that the base of the bowl is not touching the water. With the saucepan off the heat, whisk with an electric hand whisk until the egg mixture becomes pale and mousse-like and has increased in volume.

Remove the basin from the saucepan and continue to whisk for a further 2–3 minutes. Sift in the flour and very gently fold in using a metal spoon or rubber spatula, trying not to knock out the air whisked in already. Pour into the prepared tin, tilting to ensure that the mixture is evenly distributed.

Bake in the preheated oven for 10–12 minutes, or until well risen, golden brown and the top springs back when touched lightly with a clean finger.

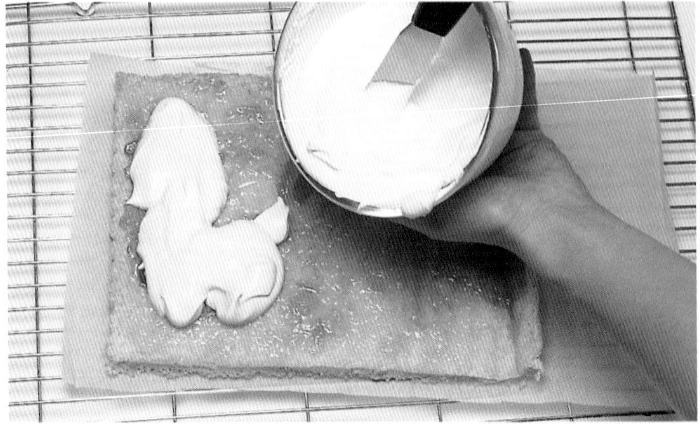

Sprinkle the toasted, chopped hazelnuts over a large sheet of greaseproof paper. When the cake has cooked, turn out on to the hazelnut-covered paper and trim the edges of the cake. Holding an edge of the paper with the short side of the cake nearest you, roll the cake up. When fully cold, carefully unroll and spread with the jam and then the cream. Roll back up and serve. Otherwise, store in the refrigerator and eat within two days.

Health Rating: 1 point

Toffee Apple Cake

Cuts into 6–8 slices

Ingredients

2 small eating apples, peeled
50 g/2 oz/¼ cup soft dark brown sugar
175 g/6 oz/1½ sticks butter or margarine
175 g/6 oz/¾ cup caster/superfine sugar
3 medium/large eggs
175 g/6 oz/1½ cups self-raising flour
150 ml/¼ pint/⅔ cup double/heavy cream
2 tbsp icing/confectioners' sugar
½ tsp vanilla essence
½ tsp ground cinnamon

Health Rating: 2 points

Preheat the oven to 180°C/350°F/Gas Mark 4, 10 minutes before baking. Lightly oil and line the bases of two 20.5 cm/8 inch sandwich tins/layer cake pans with greaseproof/waxed paper or baking parchment. Thinly slice the apples, toss them in the brown sugar and arrange in the prepared tins. Reserve.

Cream together the butter or margarine and caster/superfine sugar until light and fluffy. Beat the eggs together in a small bowl. Gradually beat them into the creamed mixture, beating well between each addition. Sift the flour into the mixture. With a metal spoon or rubber spatula, fold in. Divide the mixture between the two cake tins and level the surface. Bake in the preheated oven for 25–30 minutes until golden and well risen. Leave to cool.

Lightly whip the cream with 1 tablespoon of the icing/ confectioners' sugar and vanilla essence. Sandwich the cakes together with the cream. Mix the remaining icing sugar and ground cinnamon together, sprinkle over the top of the cake and serve.

Banana Cake

Cuts into 8 slices

Ingredients

3 medium-sized ripe bananas
1 tsp lemon juice
150 g/5 oz/$^3/_4$ cup brown sugar
75 g/3 oz/$^2/_3$ stick butter or margarine
250 g/9 oz/2 cups self-raising flour
1 tsp ground cinnamon
3 medium/large eggs
50 g/2 oz/$^1/_3$ cup walnuts, chopped
1 tsp each ground cinnamon and caster/superfine sugar
fresh cream, to serve

Preheat the oven to 190°C/375°F/Gas Mark 5, 10 minutes before baking.

Lightly oil and line the base of an 18 cm/7 inch deep round cake tin/pan with greaseproof/waxed paper or baking parchment.

Mash two of the bananas in a small bowl, sprinkle with the lemon juice and a heaped tablespoon of the brown sugar. Mix together lightly and reserve.

Gently heat the remaining brown sugar and butter or margarine in a small saucepan until the butter has just melted. Pour into a small bowl, then allow to cool slightly. Sift the flour and cinnamon into a large bowl and make a well in the centre.

Beat the eggs into the cooled sugar mixture, pour into the well of flour and mix thoroughly. Gently stir in the mashed banana mixture. Pour half of the mixture into the prepared tin. Thinly slice the remaining banana and arrange over the cake mixture. Sprinkle over the chopped walnuts, then cover with the remaining cake mixture.

Bake in the preheated oven for 50–55 minutes, or until well risen and golden brown. Allow to cool in the tin, turn out and sprinkle with the ground cinnamon and caster/superfine sugar. Serve hot or cold with a jug of fresh cream for pouring.

Health Rating: 2 points

Carrot Cake

Cuts into 8 slices

Ingredients

200 g/7 oz/1½ cups plain/all-purpose flour
½ tsp ground cinnamon
½ tsp freshly grated nutmeg
1 tsp baking powder
1 tsp bicarbonate of soda/baking soda
150 g/5 oz/¾ cup muscovado/golden brown sugar
200 ml/7 fl oz/scant 1 cup vegetable oil
3 medium/large eggs
225 g/8 oz/1¾ cups carrots, peeled and roughly grated
50 g/2 oz/½ cup chopped walnuts

For the icing:
175 g/6 oz/¾ cup cream cheese
finely grated rind of 1 orange
1 tbsp orange juice
1 tsp vanilla essence
125 g/4 oz/1 cup icing/confectioners' sugar

Preheat the oven to 150°C/300°F/Gas Mark 2, 10 minutes before baking. Lightly oil and line the base of a 15 cm/6 inch deep square cake tin/pan with greaseproof/waxed paper or baking parchment.

Sift the flour, spices, baking powder and bicarbonate of soda/baking soda together into a large bowl. Stir in the muscovado/golden brown sugar and mix together.

Lightly whisk the oil and eggs together, then gradually stir into the flour and sugar mixture. Stir well. Add the carrots and walnuts. Mix thoroughly, then pour into the prepared cake tin.

Bake in the preheated oven for 1¼ hours, or until light and springy to the touch and a skewer inserted into the centre of the cake comes out clean. Remove from the oven and allow to cool in the tin for 5 minutes before turning out on to a wire rack. Leave until cold.

To make the icing, beat together the cream cheese, orange rind, orange juice and vanilla essence. Sift the icing/confectioners' sugar and stir into the cream cheese mixture. When cold, discard the lining paper, spread the cream cheese icing over the top and serve cut into squares.

Health Rating: 2 points

Whisked Sponge Cake

Cuts into 6 slices

Ingredients

125 g/4 oz/1 cup plain flour, plus 1 tsp
175 g/6 oz/scant 1 cup caster/superfine sugar, plus 1 tsp
3 medium/large eggs
1 tsp vanilla essence
4 tbsp raspberry jam/jelly
50 g/2 oz (about 25) fresh raspberries, crushed
icing/confectioners' sugar, to dredge

Preheat the oven to 200°C/400°F/Gas Mark 6, 15 minutes before baking. Mix 1 teaspoon of the flour and 1 teaspoon of the sugar together. Lightly oil 2 x 18 cm/7 inch sandwich tins/layer cake pans and dust lightly with the sugar and flour.

Place the eggs in a large heatproof bowl. Add the sugar, then place over a saucepan of gently simmering water, ensuring that the base of the bowl does not touch the hot water. Using an electric whisk, beat the sugar and eggs until they become light and fluffy. (The whisk should leave a trail in the mixture when it is lifted out.)

Remove the bowl from the saucepan of water, add the vanilla essence and continue beating for 2–3 minutes. Sift the flour gently into the egg mixture and, using a metal spoon or rubber spatula, carefully fold in, taking care not to overmix and remove all the air that has been whisked in.

Divide the mixture between the two prepared cake tins. Tap lightly on the work surface to remove any air bubbles. Bake in the preheated oven for 20–25 minutes, or until golden. Test that the cake is ready by gently pressing the centre with a clean finger – it should spring back.

Leave to cool in the tins for 5 minutes, then turn out on to a wire rack. Blend the jam/jelly and the crushed raspberries together. When the cakes are cold, spread over the jam mixture and sandwich together. Dredge the top with icing sugar and serve.

Health Rating: 1 point

Rich Devil's Food Cake

Cuts into 12–16 slices

Ingredients

450 g/1 lb/3½ cups plain/all-purpose flour
1 tbsp bicarbonate of soda/baking soda
½ tsp salt
75 g/3 oz/scant 1 cup cocoa powder
300 ml/½ pint/1¼ cups milk
150 g/5 oz/⅔ cup butter, softened
400 g/14 oz/2 cups soft dark brown sugar
2 tsp vanilla essence
4 large/extra-large eggs

For the chocolate fudge icing:
275 g/10 oz/1⅓ cups caster/superfine sugar
½ tsp salt
125 g/4 oz dark chocolate, chopped
250 ml/8 fl oz/1 cup milk
2 tbsp golden/corn syrup
125 g/4 oz/1 stick plus 1 tbsp butter, diced
2 tsp vanilla essence

Preheat the oven to 180°C/350°F/Gas Mark 4, 10 minutes before baking. Lightly oil and line the bases of 3 x 23 cm/9 inch cake tins/pans with greaseproof/waxed paper or baking parchment. Sift the flour, bicarbonate of soda and salt into a bowl.

Sift the cocoa powder into another bowl and gradually whisk in a little of the milk to form a paste. Continue whisking in the milk until a smooth mixture results.

Beat the butter, sugar and vanilla essence until light and fluffy, then gradually beat in the eggs, beating well after each addition. Stir in the flour and cocoa mixtures alternately in three or four batches.

Divide the mixture evenly among the three tins, smoothing the surfaces evenly. Bake in the preheated oven for 25–35 minutes, until cooked and firm to the touch. Remove, cool and turn out on to a wire rack. Discard the lining paper.

To make the icing, put the sugar, salt and chocolate into a heavy-based saucepan and stir in the milk until blended. Add the golden/corn syrup and butter. Bring the mixture to the boil over a medium-high heat, stirring to help dissolve the sugar. Boil for 1 minute, stirring constantly. Remove from the heat, stir in the vanilla essence and cool. When cool, whisk until thickened and slightly lightened in colour.

Sandwich the three cake layers together with about a third of the icing, placing the third cake layer with the flat side up. Transfer the cake to a serving plate and, using a metal palette knife, spread the remaining icing over the top and sides. Swirl the top to create a decorative effect and serve.

Health Rating: 1 point

Index